CONTEMPORARY SOVIET GOVERNMENT

L. G. CHURCHWARD

Reader in Political Science
University of Melbourne

Fully revised second editi

LONDON

ROUTLEDGE & KEGAN PAUL

First published in 1968
by Routledge & Kegan Paul Limited
Broadway House, 68-74 Carter Lane
London, EC4V 5EL
Reprinted 1971
Fully revised second edition 1975
Printed in Great Britain by
Alden & Mowbray Ltd at the Alden Press, Oxford
© L. G. Churchward 1968, 1975

ISBN 0 7100 8007 7

CONTEMPORARY
SOVIET GOVERNMENT

Contents

	Glossary	xiii
	Preface	xvii
	Preface to the revised edition	xix
	Map	xx–xxi
1	**ELEMENTS OF SOVIET POLITICS**	**1**
	Some difficulties of comparison	1
	Characteristics of Soviet politics	4
	Important issues of Soviet politics	10
	The problem of assessment	14
	Continuity and tradition	17
2	**PRELUDE TO REVOLUTION**	**22**
	The revolutionary tradition	22
	The Decembrists	26
	The Populist Movement	28
	The Russian Social Democratic Labour Party (RSDLP)	30
	Bolsheviks and Mensheviks	32
	The Socialist Revolutionary Party	36
3	**THE BOLSHEVIK REVOLUTION**	**40**
	The 1905 Revolution	40
	The March Revolution	41
	The Provisional Government	42
	The November Revolution	45
	Reasons for the Bolshevik success	50
4	**THE UNFINISHED REVOLUTION**	**53**
	Revolutionary stages	53
	The foundation of the Soviet socialist state	54
	War Communism	57
	The New Economic Policy	58
	Socialist industrialization and collectivization	60
	The consolidation of socialism	63
	The establishment of the new state structure	64
	The war period	64
	Post-war reconstruction	66
	Further development of the socialist system since 1953	67

5 THE DEVELOPMENT OF THE SOVIET STATE
SYSTEM 75

Continuity and change 75
The theory of Soviets 76
The Soviet State 1918–24 78
The establishment of the USSR 79
The 1936 Constitution 80
Amendments to the 1936 Constitution 82
A new Constitution? 85

6 THE THEORY OF THE SOVIET STATE 88

Basis of the theory 88
Stalin's theory 89
Revisions to Stalin's theory 91
Limitations of contemporary theory 96

7 THE ELECTORAL SYSTEM AND THE
ELECTORATE 103

Requirements for free elections 103
Soviet electoral provisions 104
The role of Soviet elections 110
Public opinion 112

8 THE SUPREME SOVIET OF THE USSR 117

Composition 117
Powers and functions 119
Financial powers 121
Legislative powers 124
The committee system 126
Questions 129

9 THE PRESIDIUM AND THE COUNCIL OF
MINISTERS 133

The Presidium of the Supreme Soviet 133
The USSR Council of Ministers 135
Types of legislation 139
Executive and administrative functions 141
The Presidium of the Council of Ministers 141

10 THE ECONOMIC ROLE OF THE SOVIET STATE 145

Extent of state economic activity 145
Characteristics of Soviet economic planning 146
Principles and objectives of planning 147
Machinery of planning 148

	The Economic Plan	150
	Individualism and incentives	151
	Compulsion in the Soviet economic system	153
	Efficiency of Soviet economic planning	154
11	SOVIET FEDERALISM	157
	Meaning	157
	The unified state budget	160
	Assessment of the Soviet budgetary system	163
	The role of Union-Republican government	164
	Conclusions	167
12	SOVIET LOCAL GOVERNMENT	172
	The importance of local government	172
	Structure	173
	Role of local Soviets	179
	Party control of local Soviets	183
	Consequences of Party control	187
13	PARTY AND CLASS	192
	The Communist Party as a working-class party	192
	The 'vanguard' party	195
	The Party and the working class	197
	Soviet trade unions	199
14	THE COMMUNIST PARTY OF THE SOVIET UNION	206
	The theory of Communist Party organization	206
	Inner-party democracy	207
	The record of the CPSU	211
	A return to inner-party democracy?	214
15	PARTY–STATE RELATIONS	223
	Theory	223
	Practice	224
	Press, Radio and Publications	227
	Elections	228
	Soviets	228
	Policy formulation	229
	Executive and administrative functions	232
	The position of the Army	234
	Law Enforcement Agencies	235
16	SOVIET FOREIGN POLICY	238
	The control of foreign policy in the USSR	238
	Formulating agencies	240

Ratifying agencies 245
Agencies of influence on world opinion 246
The role of Marxist Ideology 249
The pursuit of the national interest 252

17 SOVIET DEMOCRACY 257
The Soviet concept of democracy 257
Contemporary theory of Soviet democracy 262
Does Soviet practice conform to the Soviet concept of
    democracy? 267
Soviet democracy is based on socialism? 267
Mass participation 269
Democratic elements in the governmental system 271
Guarantees of individual rights 273
The popular basis of the Communist Party? 274
Conclusions 275

18 THE POST-STALIN ERA 278
The Soviet power struggle 278
Stalinists versus anti-Stalinists 281
A reconstruction of the power struggle since 1953 283
The fall of Khrushchev 286
A perspective on recent changes in the USSR 294
The speed of political change 297
Some significant changes in Soviet domestic policies
    since 1953 298
Conclusion 304

Appendices 308–40
Bibliography 341
Supplementary Bibliography 357
Index 361

Appendices

I   *Marxism–Leninism:* A Recent Soviet Definition.   308

II   *Marxism–Leninism as a Political Weapon:* An Extract from the official *History of the CPSU,* 1960.   311

III   *Rules of the CPSU.* Adopted by the 22nd Congress, October 31, 1961.   315

IV   *On Soviet Economic Development and the Reorganization of Party Guidance of the National Economy:* Excerpts from the Decision of the C.C. of the CPSU, November 23, 1962.   332

V   *On the Unification of Industrial and Rural Oblast and Krai Party Organizations:* Decision of the C.C. of the CPSU, November 16, 1964.   335

VI   *A Soviet Definition of Democracy.*   336

VII   *Text of Certain Articles of the USSR Constitution:* Articles 70, 77 and 78, as amended to December 1973.   338

Tables

1. USSR Industrial Production 1928–37   63
2. USSR Industrial Production 1940–60   67
3. Structure of the Soviet Intelligentsia 1939–59   71
4. Composition of the USSR Supreme Soviet   119
5. Structure of the Council of Ministers, July 1970   136
6. Ministerial Structure within the Territory of the Russian Republic, December 1971   168
7. List of USSR Ministries, December 1971   169
8. Examples of Divided Oblasts, April 1, 1963   175
9. Scheme for Co-ordinating the Work of Volunteer Organizations of the Population of Anastasiev Village Soviet, Krasnodar Krai, RSFSR, 1963   178
10. Percentages of Communist Deputies Returned to Local Soviets in Recent Years   183
11. The Reorganized Party Structure, 1962–64   209
12. Membership of the Leading Organs of the Central Committee of the CPSU between the 23rd and 24th Congresses   220
13. Parallel State and Party Structure, April 1971   226

Tables

1.
2.
3.
4.
5.
6.
7.
8.
9.
10.
11.
12.
13.
14.

Glossary

Aktiv	The leading cadres and most active members of a particular organization or society. The party *aktiv* of the CPSU—the leading party cadres and active workers at all levels right down to the party primary organization.
Apparat	Apparatus, staff. Typically, the apparatus of the CPSU or of the state.
Apparatchik	A member of the apparatus: a Party functionary.
ASSR	Autonomous Soviet Socialist Republic.
AUCCTU	All-Union Central Committee of Trade Unions.
Blat	Pull, influence.
C.C.	Central Committee (of the CPSU).
Comecon (CEMA)	Council of Mutual Economic Assistance. An organization for economic co-operation consisting mainly of East European Communist states. Established January 1949.
Cominform	Communist Information Bureau. Established September 1947, abolished April 1956.
Comintern	Communist International. 1919–43.
CPSU	Communist Party of the Soviet Union (in Russian, KPSS).
Edinonachalie	One-man management.
Goelro	State Commission for Electrification.
Gorispolkom	Executive Committee of a City (Town) Soviet.
Gorkom	City Party Committee.
Gosbank	State Bank.
Gosekonomkomissia	State Economic Commission.

xiii

Gosekonomsovet	State Scientific–Economic Council.
Gosplan	State Planning Committee (Commission).
Gosstroi	State Committee of Construction.
Ispolkom	Executive Committee.
KGB	Committee of State Security.
Kolkhoz	Collective Farm.
Komsomol	YCL. Young Communist League. (Full title—All-Union Leninist Communist League of Youth.)
Krai	Territory. A large, relatively sparsely populated, administrative region.
Kraiispolkom	Executive Committee of a Territorial Soviet.
Kraikom	Territorial Party Committee.
Kulak	Rich peasant.
Mestnichestvo	Localism, regionalism. Pursuit of local interests at the expense of national interests.
MGB	Ministry of State Security.
Mir	See *Obshchina*.
MPA	Main Political Administration.
MTS	Machine Tractor Station.
MVD	Ministry of Internal Affairs.
Narodniki	Populists: a widely-based nineteenth-century revolutionary movement.
NEP	New Economic Policy
NKGB	People's Commissariat of State Security.
NKVD	People's Commissariat of Internal Affairs.
Nomenklatura	Appointment list controlled directly or indirectly by the Party.
Obkom	Province Party Committee.
Oblast	Province, region.
Oblispolkom	Executive Committee of Province Soviet.
Obshchenarodnoe gosudarstvo	State of the whole people. (Official description of the Soviet State since 1961.)
Obshchina	A village community, a commune.
Okrug	Area, district.
Plenum	Full meeting (of the C.C. of the CPSU).

Postanovlenie	Decision.
Raiispolkom	Executive Committee of District Soviet.
Raikom	District Party Committee.
Raion	District; an administrative division of a province, territory, republic, or of a large city.
Rasporyazhenie	Order: a directive of a state executive body.
RSFSR	Russian Soviet Federal Socialist Republic.
RTS	Tractor Repair Station.
Sovetskoe gosudarstvo i pravo	*Soviet State and Law* (abbreviated as *S.G.i.P.* Monthly journal of the Institute of State and Law, Moscow).
Sovety deputatov trudyashchikhsya	*Soviets of Workers' Deputies* (abbreviated as *Sovety*). Monthly government journal issued since July 1957.
Sovkhoz	State Farm.
Sovnarkhoz	Council of National Economy. Established on a regional basis in May 1957.
Sovnarkhoz-USSR.	USSR-Council of National Economy.
Sovnarkom	Council of People's Commissars.
Soyusselkhoztekhnika	All-Union Association for the sale of Agricultural Machinery.
Tolkach	A fixer, pusher. An unofficial agent.
Ukaz	Degree.
USSR	Union of Soviet Socialist Republics.
Vecheka	All-Russian Extraordinary Commission for Combating Counter-Revolution, Sabotage and Speculation.
Vedomosti verkhovnovo Soveta SSSR	Gazette of the USSR Supreme Soviet (issued weekly).
VOKS	USSR Society for Cultural Relations with Foreign Countries.
Voprosy ekonomiki	*Problems of Economics.* Journal of the Institute of Economics.
Voprosy filosofii	*Problems of Philosophy.* Journal of the Institute of Philosophy.

VSNKh (Vesenkha)	Supreme Economic Council.
VTsIK	Central Executive Committee.
Zagotovka	Agricultural deliveries made to the state at a fixed (minimum) price.
Zakon	Statute: a legislative act passed by a Supreme Soviet.
Zakupka	Materials (especially grain) purchased by the state at variable prices.
Zemstvo	Elective district council in pre-revolutionary Russia.

Preface

There are already so many books on Soviet government that the submission of a new one requires an explanation. This is intended to be a textbook with a difference. The difference consists of it being written in a somewhat lop-sided manner in order to redress the balance of existing Western textbooks on Soviet government. It gives particular attention to Soviet political and legal theory. I do this because I believe that the Soviet theory of 'socialist democracy' is more than window dressing and that an understanding of this theory is necessary for a full appraisal of the Soviet political system. I believe that many of the current textbooks on Soviet politics are deficient in their discussion of the theoretical basis of Soviet politics. While most textbooks in use today give some attention to classical Marxism and early Leninism they seldom give much attention to contemporary Soviet political theory. Throughout my book I have sought to discuss the practice of Soviet government against the theory of Soviet government. I believe that it is more important to relate Soviet practice to Soviet theory than it is to criticize both from an alien standpoint of Western liberalism.

This book might be regarded as a Marxist account of Soviet politics but it is intended to be more than this. It represents an attempt at combining a Marxist approach to Soviet politics with the normal methods of Western political science. The framework of the analysis is essentially in the Western tradition but the main line of explanation is Marxist. This comes out in my early historical chapters as well as in my assessment of the nature of the Soviet state and of Soviet politics since the death of Stalin.

The origin of the book was a lecture course first presented to second year political science students at the University of Melbourne in 1959. In preparing a lecture course of upwards of twenty lectures on Soviet government I sought to avoid straight out repetition of material which I felt was treated adequately in existing textbooks. For this reason I avoided detailed discussion of the history of the revolution, the history of the CPSU, the Stalin period, the history of Soviet foreign policy, classical Marxism and early Leninism. I expected students to cover these topics on the basis of existing textbooks and periodical material. Since I wanted to emphasize the contemporary in Soviet politics I was forced to cut down on the historical. This is perhaps strange in one who is by training and inclination an historian. Yet I felt it justified because of the wealth of historical material already available on Soviet politics. I also felt that very often the focus, and therefore the understanding, of contemporary Soviet politics, was damaged by undue reliance on conclusions drawn from earlier historical periods. Because of this the extent and depth of the changes that have occurred in Soviet politics over recent years have been often understated and sometimes quite misrepresented. Finally, after many years of teaching Soviet and American government historically, I have come to the conclusion that this approach can easily be overdone. Certainly with Soviet politics it is rather pointless to expect the undergraduate to remember the various transformations to Soviets since 1917 or the various legislative-executive-administrative agencies of 1918, 1924, 1936 and today. Consequently the historical material in this book has been limited to four topics: the development of the revolutionary movement in tsarist Russia, the 1917 revolutions, the general course of the revolution since 1918, and a bare outline of the development of the Soviet state structure. The longest historical chapter, the chapter on the Unfinished Revolution, is essentially a history of social and economic developments rather than a political history of the period. While some attention is given to the major political decisions of the 1920s, those dealing with industrialization and collectivization, the chapter does not provide a history of either the inner-Party struggles, collectivization, or the early Five-Year Plans.

Readers may wonder at my omission of a chapter on Marxist theory. I wanted to avoid the sort of chapter which covers Marx and Engels and adds a trailer on Lenin and Stalin. In so far as Marxism is covered in the book it is done in this way. In the opening chapter I discuss some of the general problems connected with the role of Marxism in Soviet politics. I have provided an entire chapter on the theory of the Soviet state and introduced a good deal of Marxist political theory into other chapters. I have also included two documents as appendices; a definition of Marxism–Leninism from the 1958 edition of the Soviet *Political Dictionary*, and an extract from the official *History of the CPSU* dealing with the application of Marxist theory by the Party. These extracts illustrate the way in which the present leadership understands Marxism and seeks to apply it.

In writing the book I wanted to provide a corrective to the frequent neglect of governmental institutions and processes (as distinct from party agencies) by Western writers. I believe that these agencies now play a continuous role not only as administrative agencies but as policy-influencing and policy-forming agencies. I hope that my book will serve to place agencies such as local Soviets, Supreme Soviets, and Standing Commissions of Soviets into better focus.

In summary, then, my purpose in writing this book has been to provide both students of Soviet politics and general readers with an up-to-date, medium-length textbook on Soviet government which might be used in conjunction with those already in the field. It is not intended to be a comprehensive textbook. Indeed I do not think that such a book is possible on Soviet government at this juncture.

I would like to express my thanks to the editors of *Soviet Studies* and the *Australian Outlook* for permitting me to reproduce, with some modifications (in Chapters 5 and 12), material which originally appeared in article form. I would also like to thank all those students and colleagues in Australia, Britain, the USA, and the USSR, who directly and indirectly assisted me in preparing this book. In particular I would like to thank Professor W. Macmahon Ball of the University of Melbourne and Dr. T. H. Rigby of the Australian National University, Canberra, for their steady encouragement, advice and friendly criticism.

L. G. CHURCHWARD

University of Melbourne

PREFACE TO THE REVISED EDITION

The revised edition was prepared during 1973. As far as possible the book has been up-dated to December 1973 and minor adjustments have been made to the text of the original edition. The Selected Bibliographies at the end of each chapter have been revised and a Supplementary Bibliography prepared.

L. G. CHURCHWARD

University of Melbourne

B a r e n t s
S e a

Murmansk

Arkhangelsk

RUSSIAN   SOVIET

Tallin
Leningrad
ESTONIA (1,395,000)
Riga
LATVIA (2,419,000)
LITHUANIA
(3,219,000) Vilnius   MOSCOW
BELORUSSIA
(9,171,000)
Kiev
UKRAINE (48,048,000)
MOLDAVIA
(3,695,000) Kishinev

Sverdlovsk

Novosibirsk

Volgograd   **K A Z A K H S T A N**
(13,592,000)

Tashkent   Alma-Ata
GEORGIA   Tbilisi   **UZBEKISTAN**
(4,813,000)   (12,131,000)   Frunze
Baku   **KIRGIZIA** (3,110,000)
Yerevan   **TURKMENIA**
ARMENIA   (2,328,000)   **TADJIKISTAN** (3,149,000)
(2,635,000)   Dushanbe
AZERBAIDJAN   Ashkhabad
(5,375,000)

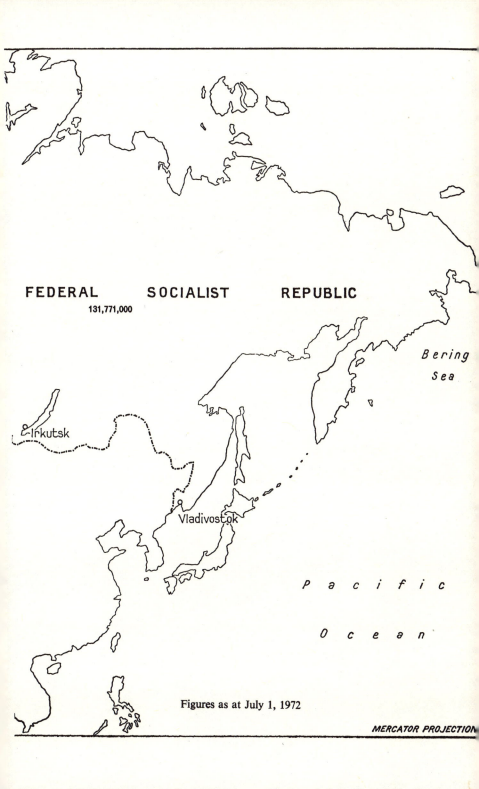

FEDERAL   SOCIALIST   REPUBLIC
131,771,000

Bering
Sea

Irkutsk

Vladivostok

Pacific

Ocean

Figures as at July 1, 1972

MERCATOR PROJECTION

Chapter 1

ELEMENTS OF SOVIET POLITICS

SOME DIFFICULTIES OF COMPARISON

It is not easy to understand the governmental process even in one's own country. The Westerner, seeking to understand the Soviet system, is faced with an unusual range of difficulties. In the first place, he probably has a mental image of Soviet politics which is less accurate than most mental images of foreign political systems. In the second place, he is confronted with a country which he probably has never visited, whose citizens he seldom meets, whose newspapers and literature he is unable to read and whose history and culture are obscure. Thirdly, the political system he is trying to understand is a different kind of political system, not merely a variant of that of his own country.

To say that the Soviet political system is a different kind of political system to that of Britain or Australia is not to say that it is wholly different. All states share certain fundamental characteristics. They are all concerned with political questions such as power and power relationships, with questions of self-preservation and defence, with questions of taxation and financial relationships, with rights and duties, with law and law enforcement. Modern industrial states are invariably bureaucratic, although not uniformly bureaucratic. Whether the state be called parliamentary or totalitarian, capitalist or socialist, it is certain to be bureaucratic because the nature of the problems being handled by modern states makes them bureaucracies. Functions such as police and defence, the administration of social services, the regulation of internal and external trade, transport and communications, banking and credit and so on, require large staffs of administrators with the necessary skill and training to perform them. However, the range of difference between say, the American and the Soviet political systems, is greater than that between any two Western parliamentary states. This is true even if at a formal level certain features of Soviet government—for example, federalism and the existence of a federal upper house—would seem to establish institutional similarities between the Soviet Union and some Western states such as the USA or Australia.

1

Comparative politics always requires the recognition and explanation of differences as well as similarities between political systems. Comparisons are easier to make between variants of a common system, such as between the British, American, Canadian and Australian political systems. Between widely dissimilar political systems such as those of the Soviet Union and the USA some writers deny or ignore similarities altogether. This is particularly so if the writer is using contrasting models or 'ideal types' such as democratic and totalitarian states against which to set his analysis of institutions and events. The reverse tendency, which has recently become more fashionable in the United States, is to forget the basic differences in stressing the similarities. Thus several American writers have sought to interpret the USSR as a modern business corporation writ large.[1] At the time of his death C. Wright Mills was seeking to identify the Soviet counterpart to his American 'power elite'.[2] The danger in this approach is not merely that fundamental distinctions between economic and political systems are blurred but that the specific features of a nation's politics are lost sight of. Thus we may count the Soviet Union as a bureaucracy along with other modern industrial societies but to do this without spelling out the characteristics of bureaucracy as a political type and without examining the peculiarities of Soviet bureaucracy is surely misleading.[3]

The general characteristics of bureaucracy were defined by Max Weber as follows:

1. The principle of fixed and official jurisdictional areas, which are generally ordered by rules, that is, by laws or administrative regulations.
2. The principle of office hierarchy and levels of graded authority resulting in a firmly ordered system of superiority and subordination in which there is a supervision of the lower officers by the higher ones.
3. Bureaucratic management is based on a mass of written documents, files, papers, etc.
4. Office management is largely composed of professionally trained experts.
5. Full involvement of officials in order to complete scheduled tasks, irrespective of normal restricted office hours.
6. The rational application of law in the making of decisions—i.e., the application of general rules.[4]

Soviet bureaucracy includes all of the above characteristics to a greater or lesser degree. But the specific characteristics of Soviet bureaucracy readily stand out if Soviet bureaucracy is placed against this model. What is distinctive about Soviet bureaucracy is not its size, nor its complexity, nor even its centralism. What is distinctive is, first, the extent of its direct control over society and over the economy. Bureaucracies are traditionally conservative or subsidiary agencies of social change. In the Soviet Union the bureaucracy is a main agency of social transformation; it is continually torn between the attraction of routine and the political obligation to direct an entire society into the 'higher' social stage ·of communism. The second specific feature of Soviet bureaucracy is the existence of two parallel duplicating bureaucracies of party and state from the top to the bottom of the political structure. The fact that the party is both in theory and in practice superior to the state immensely complicates the operation of Soviet bureaucracy. Party *apparatchiki* or functionaries are recruited and promoted by somewhat unorthodox 'bureaucratic' procedures, and are frequently interchanged with state officials. This serves to disrupt 'normal' bureaucratic appointments within the state bureaucracy. Again, party decisions follow according to the general party line and this may frequently conflict with the demands of the experts for rational decision-making.

A third distinctive feature of Soviet bureaucracy is job insecurity. Rationality, regularity, and job stability are seemingly less characteristic of Soviet administration than of other bureaucracies. This is not so much because of changes in either the long-range or the short-range goals of the regime, but because of the preoccupation with 'cadres', with getting the right organizational structure to fulfil the urgent tasks of the day and the right man in the right place at the right time. The party operates bureaucratically but it operates without the normal built-in restraints and checks of constitutional bureaucracies. Its power to act unrestrainedly enables the leadership to indulge in frequent institutional and administrative reconstructions. Thus Khrushchev introduced no fewer than five separate reconstructions of rural administration between September 1953 and November 1962. Thus central industrial ministries were removed entirely between 1957 and 1960 only to be restored in 1965.

A fourth specific feature of Soviet bureaucracy is the weakness of autonomous public controls. In a more open capitalist society trusts, state and local governments, parliaments, even labour unions, exert some countervailing power against central government bureaucracy. Instead of these 'natural' restraints on governmental bureaucracy the Soviet Union has sought to develop certain special controlling agencies. Many of these are themselves bureaucratic, as the Procuracy and the Ministry of People's Control. Others, especially at the local level, while not bureaucratic, are not autonomous. They are established and controlled by the lower party organs. Finally, one method of controlling bureaucracy is distinctly anti-bureaucratic. This is the insistence on reducing the number of professional lower office holders by means of the increasing involvement of amateurs (*neshtatny*, i.e. non-staff, or supernumerary) in administrative work in local government.

The above analysis is far from complete, but it does, I hope, indicate the extent to which Soviet bureaucracy and Soviet politics must be examined within themselves. My general purpose in this book will be to bring out the distinctive features of the Soviet system of government. Comparisons will be made where necessary but they will not be sought where they do not exist.

CHARACTERISTICS OF SOVIET POLITICS

What then are the chief distinctive features of the Soviet political system?

The first and perhaps the most distinctive feature of Soviet politics is its socialist basis. Politics, at least in a general way, reflects the underlying social and economic structure. This is universally true as a general proposition. The USSR is a socialist society, in terms of its property relations and its economic system. Consequently much of the substance of politics of capitalist states does not exist in the Soviet Union. Soviet industrial ministries may exert considerable influence within the party command but they do not have the capacity for independent economic decisions on matters of substance. Nor do they wield the political power of the large corporations in a capitalist society. Likewise the limited 'countervailing power' of the big labour unions does not operate in the Soviet Union. Agrarian politics in the sense of farmer and rural business interests operating through pressure groups and political parties or rural parliamentary representatives, do not exist in the Soviet Union. In so far as collective farmers, workers on state farms and other sections of rural society, have separate interests, they must advance them through the single important channel of political influence, the Communist Party. As a socialist society the entire economy is subject to a general economic plan. Economic planning is more direct and more comprehensive than the economic planning of capitalist states. State direction of the economy is more direct and less indirect, and the end of the direction is different; the end being the reconstruction of society into communist society by means of a series of long-range plans.

Not only the economy but the entire society is subject to close control and direction. The usual distinction between the state and society between the political and the non-political world, is much harder to make in the Soviet Union. The long-range objective of establishing communism necessitates the remaking of man, of society, not merely the realization of a more productive and more efficient economic system. The agency for this social reconstruction is the Communist Party. And because the party has functioned without effective opposition since 1918 there has been no limit to the control of the party

4

over social reconstruction other than the limits of circumstances, resources and the resistance of surviving traditional groups (such as the family and the church) and cultural patterns. Until the early thirties different classes continued to exercise important influences both on and through the Communist Party. This limited capacity for semi-independent pressure was removed for the workers and the peasantry between 1928 and 1933. Since then the class antagonism and latent class conflict of worker and peasant has been fairly effectively smothered. It has not however disappeared. One consequence of Bolshevik rule has been to force the pace of Russian industrialization so that today the Soviet Union is the second industrial power in the world. Yet Soviet society is still 'backward' in the sense that a much greater percentage of its population is rural than is the case in Western societies. Even in 1963, 47% of Soviet citizens were rural. This massive rural manpower, although it has limited and strictly controlled avenues of influence on Soviet politics, is nevertheless reflected in the administrative structure of the Soviet state. An extensive governmental network is required to manage the large rural population. At present over 60% of all deputies in local Soviets are in village Soviets. Ever since collectivization the party leadership has considered the *raion* (district) administration to be the 'key link' in the Soviet administrative structure.* This is because the district authorities have usually had the main responsibility in supervising village life and collective farm affairs.

The second characteristic feature of Soviet politics is the political monopoly of the Communist Party. The Communist Party exercises a complete monopoly of political initiative and power. It also maintains an official ideology which is the only operative political ideology. Because of this Soviet society has frequently been considered monolithic or totalitarian. As originally used in the English-speaking world in the 1930s, the term 'totalitarian' meant simply a one-party state. It was commonly applied to Fascist Italy and Nazi Germany, and by some writers to other authoritarian regimes such as Franco Spain and pre-war Japan. It was rarely applied to the Soviet Union before 1947.[5] The general application of the term totalitarian to the Soviet Union is thus a product of the post-war period and was facilitated by the breakdown of the wartime alliance between the Western parliamentary democracies and the USSR and by the development of the Cold War. It was also a product of increased knowledge of the Soviet system and of the development of political sociology in the USA and elsewhere in the Western world. Most of the classical treatments of totalitarianism[6] were written during the decade 1951–60.

* An exception was during the two years November 1962 to November 1964 when the district structure was drastically diminished.

5

Today an increasing number of American political sociologists have begun to criticize the use of the term to describe the contemporary Soviet Union.[7] The reason for this change of mind is not unconnected with the lessening of Cold War tensions. It is, however, more the consequence of the failure of the political sociologists to arrive at a satisfactory and generally accepted definition or model of totalitarianism, and the difficulty of interpreting the rapidly changing Soviet political system against somewhat inflexible models drawn up on the basis of the study of a defunct state (Nazi Germany) and a superseded Soviet regime. Throughout this book I shall refer to the Soviet Union simply as a communist state. This adjective distinguishes it from other states more clearly than any other.

The gradual abandonment of the term totalitarian to describe the contemporary Soviet Union has brought about some modification to the proposition that politics in the full sense of the term does not exist there. For some years now many Western writers have sought to apply group theory to Soviet politics.* But this is difficult to justify. If politics is held to necessitate the open competition for power between rival classes, parties and interest groups, then politics clearly does not exist in the Soviet Union. Factional struggles within the party leadership, struggles between different levels or sections of the party hierarchy, succession struggles, and other forms of power struggle exist. But since these are not given free expression and have restricted organizational basis, they constitute at most a kind of quasi-politics. Differing and potentially conflicting interests do exist in the Soviet Union although we know little about them.

One thing that needs to be emphasized on this matter is the continued resistance and official discouragement of all political competitiveness in the Soviet Union. Competitiveness is not even encouraged at the grass-roots level such as in the nomination of candidates for local Soviets. Despite the claims of Soviet and some Western writers the election nomination system is deliberately contrived to eliminate all competition between candidates because although different collectives advocate candidates they do not as a rule advance candidates for the same electorate.† Nor is 'socialist competition' between brigades, workshops, factories, collective farms or other agencies competitive in the strict sense of the term. Rather, this is a device for fostering the cohesion of Soviet society. Socialist society functions on the basis of mobilizing the individual through the agency of the collective, be it the farm or factory brigade, the classroom, the sector of a research institute or the inhabitants of a group of adjoining apart-

---

* For a discussion of some of these views see Chapter 18.
† See my discussion of Soviet elections in Chapter 7.

ments. From my own observation during an extended stay in the Soviet Union in the first half of 1965 I would say that there is widespread and active participation in many of these officially approved collectives or groups. But this group life is not competitive in the sense of groups seeking to influence political decisions to their own advantage and to the disadvantage of others.

A third characteristic of Soviet politics is its multi-national basis. National groupings play a subordinate role in American politics and a considerable role in a few Western states such as Canada and South Africa but the entire administrative structure of the USSR from the All-Union level down to the intermediate range of local government is deliberately related to nationality groupings. This has been true ever since the first USSR Constitution was established in 1924 even though in certain circumstances particular national groupings have been excluded from the administrative network.[8] At the present time national groupings provide the basis for the division of the USSR into fifteen Union Republics. If the national group is below a certain size or is insufficiently concentrated into a recognizable territory, or has no external (non-Soviet) frontier, then it is ineligible to form a Union Republic but may form an Autonomous Republic within a Union Republic. Smaller national groups are formed into Autonomous Provinces (*oblasts*) and National Areas (*okrugs*). All four levels of national groups are directly represented in the Soviet of Nationalities of the USSR Supreme Soviet. This nationally based administrative structure operates of course only in certain regions of the USSR, chiefly in the Caucasus, transcaucasian, central Asian and northern territories. In 1970, out of every 1,000 citizens in the USSR 534 were Russians, 168 Ukrainians, 37 Belorussians, 38 Uzbeks, 24 Tartars, 22 Kazakhs, and the remaining 177 would come from dozens of smaller national groups. There are twenty national groups besides the Russians and Ukrainians with more than one million members.[9]

In principle Soviet national groups must be both reasonably large and reasonably compact if they are to secure recognition in the administrative structure. In practice, policy varies considerably. Thus the general rule that a national unit is named after the nation that has a majority in that area applies to all the Union Republics with the exception of Kazakhstan and Kirgizia where the Kazakhs and the Kirgiz are minority groups. Similarly in the case of some autonomous republics the 'main' national group is a minority group. Thus in the Tartar ASSR in 1970, 49% of the population were Tartars and 42% Russians, while in the Mari ASSR 44% of the population were Mari and 47% Russian. All the present Union Republics fulfil the requirement of a minimum population of one million, although in the case of Estonia (which had a population of 1·4 millions in 1970) the Estonians number less than a million.

At first sight the administrative map of the USSR seems to coincide fairly closely with the population map. Thus in 1970, 97% of all Georgians in the Soviet Union lived in Georgia, 92% of Estonians lived in Estonia, 87% of Ukrainians lived in the Ukraine and 83% of Russians lived in the Russian Federation. On the other hand under 30% of Tartars lived within the Tartar Autonomous Republic and less than 1% of Jews lived in the Jewish Autonomous Province.[10] Not all national groups are accorded administrative recognition. Thus in 1970 Germans (1,846,000), Poles (1,167,000), Bulgarians (351,000), Koreans (357,000), Greeks (337,000) and many smaller groups had no recognized national territory within the Soviet Union. Russians, and to a lesser extent, Ukrainians, are widely distributed throughout the entire USSR. Thus in 1970 Russians comprised more than 10% of the population of all Union Republics excepting Lithuania, Georgia and Armenia. They formed over 40% of the population of Kazakhstan, almost 30% of that of Kirgizia, over 20% of the population of Latvia and Estonia, and almost 15% of the population of Turkmenia.[11] This spread of Russians throughout the USSR is a legacy of the tsarist period. Well before 1917 there were heavy concentrations of Russian peasants, workers, professionals, administrators and businessmen in non-Russian areas. Rapid industrialization, socialization and sovietization have intensified this process. Whether this process deserves to be called 'colonization' is open to question but it has undoubtedly resulted in curbing nationalism and in considerable social and economic dislocation. This has happened particularly where a crash programme has been carried through such as in Kazakhstan between 1954 and 1960. On the other hand the raising of the cultural and educational standards of formerly backward regions has enabled many non-Russians to migrate to the cities of European Russia.[12]

A fourth characteristic of Soviet politics is the universal application of the principle of 'democratic centralism' to the Soviet governmental and administrative structure. This principle, borrowed from the Communist Party, means that while the structure of the Soviet state is formally federal even in the Western sense it is in practice a unitary system since higher executive bodies may direct, supervise and modify the work of lower bodies. Thus the Executive Committee of a village Soviet is not merely responsible to its village Soviet but is subject to supervision and overruling from the Executive Committee of the District Soviet. This in turn is subject to the same sort of supervision and control from the Executive Committee of the Provincial or Territorial Soviet which in turn is subject to supervision from the Council of Ministers (government) of a Union Republic. Even the Council of Ministers of a Union Republic is subject to supervision from the USSR Council of Ministers. Likewise, a Budget-Finance Department of a District Executive Committee is subject to supervision from the Budget-Finance Department of the Executive Committee of the Province Soviet and so on, right up to the USSR Finance Ministry at the top. The peculiar implications and ramifications of this system will be taken up at a later stage in this book.

A fifth characteristic is that of mass or public participation in the actual process of government. As this concept is understood in the Soviet Union it means much more than the participation of a majority of citizens in the elections as happens in most parliamentary states. The ideal is the participation of millions in the work of administration. It does not involve the encouragement of spontaneous participation in politics but of the steady involvement of an ever-increasing number of citizens in carefully selected social and governmental tasks under the guidance of the Communist Party. While the Soviet system does not ignore professionalism in government it places less stress on it at the lower administrative levels than do most Western states. The extent, quality and value of this 'mass participation' is far from clear. It is an aspect of Soviet politics which has been rather neglected by Western political scientists. It is, however, an aspect in which I have been particularly interested over many years and which I shall discuss in detail later in this book.

The sixth and final feature of the Soviet political system I would like to mention is the strength of revolutionary tradition. This feature marks the Soviet Union off from Britain, Australia, the United States, and in fact from most Western parliamentary states, although not altogether from such countries as Burma, Indonesia and many African and South American states. By stating that revolutionary tradition is an important factor in Soviet politics I do not wish to imply that most of the present population of the Soviet Union had their mental outlook and political attitudes shaped by the actual events of the Bolshevik Revolution. Less than one in ten of the present population is old enough to have any personal recollection of the events of 1917.[13] While the percentage is perhaps greater among the Bolshevik leaders only a very small percentage of these were old enough to participate in the Revolution and the Civil War. However, the revolutionary tradition is kept alive through the press and the radio, through literature and art, through museums, and through the educational system, as well as through the officially organized activities of public holidays such as May Day, November 7 and Soviet Army Day (February 23). Not only official but family tradition keeps the memory of the Civil War alive. The faded photos of relatives who

9

participated in the Civil War still grace the walls of many a Soviet home. Yet it must be recognized that the great historical event for the younger generation was the victory over Nazi Germany or even the death of Stalin rather than the November Revolution.

IMPORTANT ISSUES OF SOVIET POLITICS

The issues of Soviet politics vary from situation to situation and from year to year. The preservation of the regime was the basic issue during the first few years after November 1917, but it has not been a public issue since the early twenties. Pensions reform was an important issue during the first half of 1956 and 1964, but the question is not normally to the forefront of Soviet politics. Educational reform was a major public issue throughout the latter months of 1958. Although in a sense it is a standing issue of Soviet politics it is only occasionally that it occupies the central place in domestic politics. The issues which I raise here seem to me to be perennial issues of Soviet politics, although doubtless the list could be extended.

The first of these perennial issues is defence. Defence is of course an essential issue for almost all modern states. However, geographical factors and historical experience have combined to give this issue peculiar prominence in Soviet politics. The Soviet Union has the longest land frontier of any contemporary state and in many regions it is not clearly demarcated by mountain barriers or seas. The land frontier borders on twelve foreign states. The historical experience of the Russian people over many centuries has been that of invasions of their territory by warlike neighbours—by the Tartars and the Teutonic Knights in the thirteenth century, by the Poles and Lithuanians in the seventeenth century, by the Swedes in the eighteenth century, by the French in the early nineteenth century and by the Japanese, Germans and Turks in the early twentieth century. The historical experience of the Russian people has been even more severe since 1917. Between 1918 and 1921 no fewer than 14 states, including Britain, France, Belgium, Poland, Japan and the USA, were involved in military operations against the Soviet government. The motives for this intervention varied. It was perhaps immediately more concerned with keeping Russia in the war against Germany than with overthrowing the Bolshevik regime. Although the scale of this intervention was not so great it did serve to vindicate the thesis of 'capitalist encirclement'. After 1921 Soviet Russia remained in virtual isolation in a world of unfriendly, and at times, hostile states. Lenin's policy towards the capitalist world was certainly ambivalent. Although on occasions between November 1917 and 1923 he emphasized peaceful economic and diplomatic relations with capitalist countries this was not tied to any notion of continued 'peaceful co-existence' as it was after 1956.

Soviet preoccupation with defence subsided slowly as non-aggression pacts were signed with neighbouring states. This is indicated by the fact that the percentage of the USSR state budget devoted to defence fell from 17·3% in 1923–24 to 3·4% in 1933. The Nazi victory in Germany in 1933 led to a reversal of this trend. The Soviet Union joined the League of Nations in September 1934 and over the next five years Mr. Litvinov, the Soviet foreign affairs commissar, became the leading advocate of 'collective security' measures against the threat of German aggression. The percentage of the Soviet budget devoted to defence rose to 9·1% in 1934 and to 18·7% in 1938. The German–Soviet Non-aggression Pact of August 1939 gave no surety against a German attack and in 1940, 32·9% of the Soviet budget was devoted to defence.

The German attack on June 22, 1941, brought the Soviet Union fully into the war and defence became the overriding issue of Soviet politics until 1945. The experience of the war strengthened the determination of the Soviet government to maintain its defences. In September 1945 a government Commission appointed to investigate war losses reported that 25 million Soviet citizens had been rendered homeless, seven and a half million killed, 1,710 cities and large towns, 70,000 villages, one-third of all collective farms, 31,850 industrial enterprises, 65,000 kilometres of railway track, 40,000 hospitals and medical centres, 84,000 schools and other educational institutes, and 43,000 public libraries had been destroyed.[14] Terrible as this total was it was undoubtedly an underestimate. It was admitted in February 1956[15] that the war had meant a ten-year delay in Soviet economic development. Facts such as these go far towards explaining the determination of the Communist Party to continue the tempo of early industrialization, to replace lost capital as rapidly as possible and to maintain a high level of defence spending. Defence expenditure dropped slowly to reach 20·1% of the budget in 1950. The Korean War involved extensive military assistance to North Korea and to China. The uncertainty of its outcome and the possibility of direct Soviet involvement in the case of United Nations and United States attack on the Chinese mainland, led to an increase in defence expenditure. Soviet defence expenditure formed 23·9% of the budget in 1952, the same percentage as in 1946. Soviet defence expenditure dropped from 18% of the budget in 1956 to 11·9% in 1961.[16] Additional money was voted for defence during 1961 in order—it was claimed—to match increased defence spending in the USA and Western Germany. Defence expenditure represented 16·7% of the 1962 budget. It then began to fall again to reach 12·9% of the 1965 budget. This downward trend was reversed within months following US bombing of North Vietnam and the signing by the Soviet government in March 1965 of an agreement to assist North Vietnam with military equipment. The 1966 budget (passed December 1965) allocated 12·8% of all expenditure to defence while raising the allocation 5% over the previous year. However, continued escalation of the war in Vietnam made it difficult for the Soviet government to stabilize defence expenditure at this level.*

A second important issue of Soviet politics over the years has been industrialization. In the early years the emphasis was on industrial reconstruction but from December 1925 rapid industrialization involving a higher rate of investment in capital than in consumer goods industry has been the rule. In 1953–54[17] and since 1969 consumer goods industry has expanded at the same or a higher rate than capital goods industry. The 9th Five-Year Plan (1971–75) set a target of 44–48% increase in consumer goods compared with 41–45% increase in capital goods. At the present time the emphasis on capital goods is maintained partly in order to lessen the period required for the Soviet Union to overtake the United States in industrial production. It is possible that Soviet citizens accept this priority less willingly today than they did in earlier days when Soviet industry was less developed. Be that as it may, rapid industrialization continues to be a preoccupation of the Soviet government and the Communist leadership.

A third basic issue of Soviet politics is agricultural policy. This is not surprising when it is remembered that even today 40% of the Soviet population is rural. The land hunger of the peasants provided a basis for peasant acquiescence to the Bolshevik Revolution. The initial land settlement (November 1917–February 1918) strengthened peasant proprietorship although it nationalized the land. During the Civil War the government was preoccupied with securing enough food for the army and the urban population. The methods adopted provoked widespread peasant resistance which eventually, in March 1921, forced Lenin to recognize the need for concessions. The essential aim of the New Economic Policy was to restore agricultural production to pre-war levels by means of a series of concessions to the peasants. This aim was largely realized by 1928. Collectivization was accepted by the 15th Party Congress in December 1927 as a pre-condition for the policy of rapid industrialization. However, Stalin accelerated the process. The peasants, especially the

* All figures are official figures. Soviet military expenditure is not fully covered by these figures as some military expenditure is listed under expenditure on the national economy. However, there is no evidence that Soviet budgetary methods have been revised in recent years so that the figures do indicate trends.

richer and middle peasants, resisted enforced collectivization in 1930–31 by various means including killing off their livestock. Soviet agriculture was only beginning to recover from this disaster in the late thirties. Agricultural production dropped off considerably during the war due to losses in the Western regions but a concentration of effort on the part of the government and population resulted in agricultural production surpassing pre-Second World War figures by 1949. But nothing was done to solve the basic weaknesses of the collective farm system and another decline occurred in 1950–51. Since September 1953 the emphasis has again been on agricultural expansion, the methods this time being more varied although not always realistic. Considerable overall expansion of agriculture was achieved between 1953 and 1960. The total crop acreage increased from 157·2 million ha. in 1953 to 204·6 million ha. in 1961.[18] Grain production, according to official figures, increased 61 % between 1953 and 1960. However, the successes of 1953–60 were not sustained. A combination of mismanagement, reduced investment, bad seasons and peasant disinterestedness resulted in a serious decline in production in 1962–63. Thus Brezhnev was forced to admit in March 1965 that while the Seven-Year Plan (1959–65) provided for a 70 % increase in agricultural production, only a 10 % increase had been realized. While agricultural production had increased at an annual rate of 7·6 % over the five years 1955–59 it increased by only 1·9 % per year during 1960–64.[19] It seems certain that agricultural failures played a considerable part in the removal of Khrushchev in October 1964.

The development of new agricultural areas in northern Kazakhstan and southern Siberia in recent years has strengthened the trend towards the development of new industrial regions commenced under the 3rd Five-Year Plan and accentuated by the war losses in the Western regions. Just as in the United States since 1940 the Pacific Coast and lakeside states have developed faster than the national average so in the Soviet Union the Far East, Siberia, Kazakhstan and the Urals, have seen a more rapid development. Between 1939 and 1959 the population of the USSR increased by 9·5 % while that of the Urals region increased by 32%, East Siberia by 34%, Central Asia and Kazakhstan by 38% and the Far East by 70%.[20] Despite extensive effort on the part of the Soviet government these regions remain undeveloped and sparsely populated. Thus Siberia, Kazakhstan, the Far East, the Urals and Central Asia, comprise 78 % of Soviet territory but in 1964 only 29% of the Soviet population lived in these regions.[21]

A fourth important issue of Soviet politics at least since 1949 has been that of the improvement of material living standards. Different methods have been favoured to bring about this improvement. Thus

13

between 1947 and 1953 annual price-cuts resulted in improving the purchasing power of urban wages. In 1956 and again since 1959 the wages of the lowest paid workers have been steadily raised. Housing construction, at least since July 1957, has been an important priority. In 1959–60 the Soviet working week was reduced to forty-one hours (and thirty-six hours in the case of workers in heavy industry). Since 1956 peasant incomes have been considerably improved through policies of tax concessions and higher prices paid by the state for agricultural products.

A fifth and related issue is that of improving social and cultural services. This issue has never been neglected by the Soviet government. Even when wages remained low, housing poor and consumer goods in short supply, the Soviet health and educational services were being steadily expanded. In recent years the emphasis has become somewhat more diversified so that besides health and education, pensions, sport and entertainment, book publishing, public transport and holiday travel and camp facilities have been greatly extended.

The sixth issue of Soviet politics I wish to mention has received much emphasis in recent years, although it had also been emphasized in earlier periods such as the twenties and the late thirties. This is what is called in the Soviet Union 'strengthening Soviet democracy', or to put it less provocatively, improving the efficiency, the reliability and the regularity of Soviet government. Since 1953 a good deal of effort has been directed towards 'strengthening Soviet legality', the improvement of the 'general supervision' functions of the procuracy,[22] the reduction in the size and complexity of the 'apparatus' (the party and state bureaucracy), the curtailment of bureaucratic practices, restricting police control, and strengthening individual rights. The degree of success and the limits of this liberalization will be discussed later in this book.

THE PROBLEM OF ASSESSMENT

Any discussion of the nature of Soviet politics must raise the problem of assessment. How important are the various factors in Soviet government? What is the relative importance of such diverse factors as Marxist ideology, the party leadership, state and party institutions, history and tradition, circumstance and geographical environment? It is perhaps not necessary to discuss all these factors at the outset. However, I feel that it is necessary to say something briefly about the importance of two factors, namely, Marxist ideology and tradition.

The USSR differs from most parliamentary states in that it has an official ideology, Marxism–Leninism.* But to recognize this fact does

* See Appendix I.

14

not tell us very much about how Marxism is used in the Soviet Union. Who determines the content of Marxist theory? Which elements in the theory are constant and which are mutable? Above all, how is Marxism used in the USSR? Does it constitute a sort of dogmatic scholasticism? Is it merely a kind of revolutionary mythology? Is it the application of some sort of system of social engineering?

Soviet Marxism has at different times been all three of the above three things but it has never been wholly the one or the other of these things. The official government patronage of Marxism has produced at least two of the common attributes of a state religion—dogma, and what the Webbs so aptly described as 'the disease of orthodoxy'.[23] Dogmatism has certainly diminished since the criticism of Stalin at the 20th Congress in February 1956, but it is still prevalent. Even in academic circles the practice of quotation-mongering has not been abandoned, and if the Soviet academic or official no longer operates on the basis of the 'lazy Bolshevik' collection of standard quotations on all subjects he is still prone to over-lard his articles and speeches with unnecessary citations from Lenin's *Collected Works*. For several years before October 1964 academics, especially in the social sciences, were apt to take their cue in interpreting some particular problem of Marxism from some speech or aside of the First Secretary.

Marxism as it is used in the Soviet Union has certainly many of the characteristics of a 'revolutionary mythology', especially in respect to the practice of listing the heroes and villains of the revolution. Because of this it is impossible even now to get a fair appraisal in a Soviet publication of the work of Trotsky or Bukharin, even if there has been some revision of the role of Stalin and of the non-Bolshevik parties.

The explanation of Soviet Marxism as some form of social engineering is not entirely devoid of truth. It is probably true to say that the solution of many problems of agriculture and industry and of scientific research generally is not necessarily dependent on the application of a Marxist methodology. Yet it is still a fact that the approach of Soviet experts, especially in the field of the social sciences, is profoundly influenced by their Marxist beliefs. These beliefs influence the problems they concentrate on as well as their approach to solutions. Thus the view that state farms represent a higher (i.e., more socialist) type of agriculture than collective farms is one factor in a complex of factors influencing the Soviet government towards the merging of these two types of farms.[24] The pursuit of the ultimate Marxist objective of communist society has also influenced such recent decisions as educational reorganization (1958), higher living standards, and the extension of the role of various social agencies

15

such as the Volunteer Militia and the Comradely Courts. At this level Soviet Marxism is 'realistic' or 'practical' rather than dogmatic and because of this specific sections of Marxist theory are being revised or extended. The most extreme example of this is probably the revision of Lenin's thesis that wars are inevitable under imperialism. This was first openly challenged at the 20th Congress and within four years the modifications were so extensive as to represent the formation of a new more general theory of international relations than that provided by Lenin's *Imperialism*.[25] However, Soviet revisions to Marxist theory have always operated within certain limits. Thus no revision has involved the repudiation of such Marxist essentials as historical materialism, the primacy of class struggle in politics and the inevitability of the displacement of capitalism by socialism and of the latter's transition to communism.

In analysing the Soviet theory of the state it is essential to consider the official Soviet theory of the state. Although this theory throws light on the functions of Soviet politics it seldoms tallies exactly with the practice. For example, the theory describes the USSR as a socialist democracy, the institutions of which function according to the principles of 'socialist legality'. Such an ideal description is no more accurate as a picture of Soviet government than is the ideal description of any other system of government an accurate description of the actual working of that government. Similarly, constitutional theory vests supreme legislative power in the USSR in the Supreme Soviet. In fact it is exercised more by the Central Committee of the CPSU and by its Politbureau in association with the Presidium of the Supreme Soviet and the Council of Ministers. Proverbial sayings are sometimes more accurate than official theory. Thus over many years the popular admission that '*Blat silnee Sovnarkoma*' (Pull, or Influence is stronger than the government) told one more about the practice of Soviet government than did Art. 30 of the Stalin Constitution.*

The above comments on Soviet ideology do not raise all aspects of its use. It is used by the leadership to legitimize its position and power. It is used to mobilize popular support for party policy. It is thus a chief agency for producing consent, perhaps more important in this regard now than earlier when lagging support could be matched with terror.[26] It also serves to remove the doubts of the leaders and to reinsure them in the pursuit of both short- and long-range objectives. A further problem which might be investigated is the extent to which the ideology reflects the changing structure of Soviet society.

* Art. 30: 'The highest organ of state power in the USSR is the Supreme Soviet of the USSR.'

CONTINUITY AND TRADITION

It is fashionable nowadays to emphasize the Russianness of Bolshevism. This is correct up to a point but it is easily overstated. It is perhaps correct to point out the similarities between the foreign policy objectives of Stalinist and tsarist Russia in relation to access to warm water ports, predominance in the Black Sea and in Eastern Europe. But it is not correct to equate the two foreign policies.[27] Nor is it correct to regard Stalin as a modern slavophil any more than it is correct to regard Lenin as a disciple of Tkachev, Nechayev or Ogarev.[28] The differing material circumstances of nineteenth-century Russia and the differing cultural traditions of Russia exerted a profound effect on Lenin and led him to make drastic modifications to classical Marxism. This is what he called 'the adaptation of Marxism to Russian conditions'.[29] The revolutionary tradition of tsarist Russia certainly influenced Bolshevism—Russian Bolshevism was an integral part of that tradition although a peculiar part of it. Yet to emphasize the similarities and to ignore the differences between Lenin and earlier revolutionaries is to confuse the issue. Moreover, it presents us with a major historical problem in explaining Lenin's success.

There is, however, a continuity in some social institutions and some cultural patterns even across the cataclysm of revolution. The technical backwardness of Russian agriculture, the incomplete industrialization, cultural backwardness, and even the bureaucracy survived the revolution to some extent. Lenin recognized this continuity in March 1923 when he explained Soviet bureaucracy as due to just such tsarist survivals.[30] Not a few sections of the tsarist state structure and many of its officials survived the Bolshevik 'smashing of the bourgeois state'. The use of tsarist officers in the Red Army is well known. Many tsarist taxes were carried on by the Soviet government and the organization of the Finance Commissariat and the structure of the early Soviet budgets can only be understood on the basis of recognizing this continuity.[31]

Some tsarist institutions are incorrectly regarded as precursors of Bolshevik institutions. Thus the *kolkhoz* or collective farm owes next to nothing to the *obshchina* or peasant commune of tsarist Russia.[32] The *obshchina* survived in many regions until as late as 1930 although its functions were reduced and its cohesion lessened by the 1917–18 land reforms. The *kolkhoz* replaced the *obshchina*, it did not grow out of it. It is doubtful if the recollection of the *obshchina* helped the Bolshevik collectivization drive since the *obshchina* was concerned with perpetuating private ownership by means of periodic redistribution of property whereas the object of the collectivization drive

17

was to replace private ownership by collective ownership and collective cultivation. It is perhaps more reasonable to see continuity in a rural institution such as the *skhod* or village meeting. Village meetings have not been entirely displaced by the establishment of Soviets. They have in fact continued and in recent years somewhat revived.[33] The meeting itself and its form of procedure are similar to what they were in pre-revolutionary days, although the range of questions discussed has been considerably extended.

It is sometimes suggested that local Soviets owe something to the *zemstvos*,[34] the local councils which were established in 1864 and following years. However, this is incorrect as the original basis of the local Soviets was vocational rather than territorial and represented classes rather than estates. Moreover, the Soviets appeared as rivals to the *zemstvos* and they held that place during 1917–18 until the elimination of the earlier local councils. Any similarity between their functions and relations with the central government are purely accidental and are not the result of any institutional continuity.[35]

The revival during the war years of patriotism and panslavism[36] is sometimes seen as a direct continuation of outlooks and movements of tsarist Russia. This is true to a degree but to make this point is perhaps less important than to recognize that the socialist element of Soviet patriotism was non-existent in earlier Russian patriotism. The latent strength of patriotism in the Russian outlook made it certain that any sort of Russian government would seek to stimulate it in order to strengthen public morale in wartime.

Certain popular attitudes as well as habits of thinking and behaviour of particular sections of the population may also be traced back to the old regime. For example, ordinary Soviet people still sometimes draw a clear distinction between the government or state (*gosudarstvo*) and the people (*narod*), between 'them' and 'us', in much the same way as Russians did in the nineteenth century.[37] Again, the frequently noted similarities between the behaviour of Soviet and tsarist bureaucrats may owe something to cultural tradition.

While the influence of tradition going back to tsarist Russia should not be ignored it is perhaps proper to emphasize that the influence of traditionalism in Soviet politics today is rather that of the methods and solutions of an earlier period of Soviet industrialization being carried over into the present period. To some extent the struggle between Khrushchev and his supporters on the one hand, and Molotov, Kaganovich, Malenkov and others on the other hand, was such a struggle. Khrushchev sought to label his opponents as 'conservatives'. Younger Soviet citizens would perhaps prefer to link both 1957 factions together as 'traditionalist' or 'conservative'. From their point of view the progressive and humanist politicians are still largely excluded from office by old men who received their training in the Stalin period.

NOTES

[1] For the latest attempt along these lines see Alfred G. Meyer, 1965; cf. D. Granick, 1960.

[2] Cf. C. Wright Mills, 1959.

[3] This to my way of thinking is a weakness in Alfred G. Meyer's recent work, *The Soviet Political System*.

[4] Bureaucracy, Ch. VIII, ed. H. H. Gerth and C. Wright Mills, 1947, pp. 196–8.

[5] Nazi writers occasionally defined the Soviet Union as totalitarian after 1934. Trotsky in 1938 described the USSR as 'totalitarian-bureaucratic'. Hilferding in 1940 described the Soviet Union as having a 'totalitarian state economy, i.e., a system to which the economies of Germany and Italy are drawing closer and closer'. On the other hand books on Soviet government published between 1935 and 1939 by S. and B. Webb, B. W. Maxwell, S. N. Harper, and M. T. Florinsky, made no use of the term totalitarian.

[6] Hannah Arendt, 1951; P. Selznick, 1952; C. J. Friedrich, 1954; C. J. Friedrich, Z. K. Brzezinski, 1956; W. Kornhauser, 1959.

[7] These include Daniel Bell, R. C. Tucker, A. G. Meyer and Merle Fainsod. Daniel Bell, 1961, pp. 315–54; Robert C. Tucker, 1963, Ch. 1; Alfred G. Meyer, 1965, Ch. XXII.

Z. K. Brzezinski on the other hand has contented himself with revising Friedrich's 1956 definition of totalitarianism. Cf. Z. K. Brzezinski, 1962.

[8] For example, four Autonomous Republics were abolished during or at the end of the war—the Crimean ASSR, the Kalmyk ASSR, the Chechen–Ingush ASSR, and the Volga German ASSR. The Chechen–Ingush ASSR, was restored in 1957, the Kalmyk ASSR in 1958.

[9] Based on the Statement of the Central Statistical Administration of the USSR, *Pravda*, April 17, 1971.

[10] Only 14,269 out of 2,268,000 Jews in the Soviet Union in January 1959 were living in the Jewish Oblast. Jews comprised only 8·8% of the population of the Jewish Autonomous Oblast. Jews were only 6·6% of the population in 1970.

[11] The Russian percentage of the total population of the smaller republics in January 1970 was as follows: Kazakhstan 42·8, Latvia 29·8, Kirgizia 29·2, Estonia 24·7, Ukraine 19·4, Turkmenia 14·5, Uzbekistan 12·5, Tadjikistan 11·9, Moldavia 11·6, Belorussia 10·4, Azerbaidjan 10·0, Lithuania 8·6, Georgia 8·5, and Armenia 2·7. *Pravda*, April 17, 1971.

[12] Perhaps the best historical account of this process is that by Richard Pipes, 1954. See also, W. Kolarz, 1952. Of more recent studies, that by J. A. Newth, 'The "Establishment" in Tadjikistan' in *Soviet Studies* Vols. XIV and XV, April, July 1963 is of special interest as an example of what a skilled demographer can ferret out of official Soviet statistics.

[13] At the time of the 1970 census only 11·8% of the people of the USSR were 60 and over. *Pravda*, April 17, 1971.

[14] Figures quoted by V. M. Molotov in a speech at the Paris Peace Conference, August 26, 1946. V. M. Molotov, 1949, pp. 132–3.

[15] N. A. Bulganin, *Report to the 20th Congress of the CPSU*. FLPH., Moscow 1956, p. 16.

[16] Figures up to 1941 are taken from R. W. Davies, 1958. Later figures are from the annual budget reports as published in *Izvestia*.

[17] There is a discrepancy in official Soviet statistics on this question. Using the tables provided in *The USSR Economy: A Statistical Abstract*, English trans. 1957, p. 47, the annual average increase in capital goods industry 1953–54 was 13·5% compared with 13·25% for consumer goods industry. Using the table on p. 46 of the same book the figures are 13·2% and 13·4% respectively.

[18] Naum Jasny, 1965, p. 13.

[19] L. I. Brezhnev, Report to the Central Committee of the CPSU, March 24, 1965. *Pravda*, 27 March, 1965.

[20] Statement of the Central Statistical Board of the USSR. *Izvestia*, 4 February, 1960.

[21] Based on figures given in *Narodnoe khozyaistvo SSSR v 1963g.* Moscow, 1965, p. 12.

[22] Cf. Glen G. Morgan, 'Methods employed by the Soviet Procuracy in Exercising its "General Supervision" Function', *Soviet Studies*, Vol. XII, October 1960, pp. 168–82; and the earlier article by the same author; 'The Procuracy's "General Supervision" Function', *Soviet Studies*, Vol. XI, October 1959, pp. 143–72.

[23] S. and B. Webb, 1937, Ch. XI.

[24] Frank A. Durgin Jr., 'The Growth of Inter-Kolkhoz Co-operation', *Soviet Studies*, Vol. XII, 1960, pp. 183–9.

[25] Cf. L. G. Churchward, 'Soviet Revision of Lenin's *Imperialism*', *Australian Journal of Politics and History*, VIII, May 1962, pp. 57–65.

[26] Western experts vary in their assessment of this aspect of Soviet ideology. Contrast, for example, Z. K. Brzezinski, 1962, with Alfred G. Meyer, 1966.

[27] Cf. Pitirim A. Sorokin, 1944, p. 196: 'Since the middle of the thirties the foreign policy of Stalin has been merely a continuation of the foreign policy pursued by the Czarist régime during the periods of its vigor.'

[28] Cf. Herbert McClosky and John E. Turner, 1960, pp. 32, 42–6. Lenin's indebtedness to Ogarev is overstressed by S. V. Utechin, 1964. pp. 217–18. N. P. Ogarev (1813–70), P. N. Tkachev (1844–86), S. G. Nechayev (1847–82).

[29] Cf. J. Plamenatz, 1954. Alfred G. Meyer, 1957.

[30] V. I. Lenin, 'Better Fewer, but Better'. March 2, 1923, Vol. IX, 1946, pp. 387–401.

[31] Cf. R. W. Davies, 1958, pp. 64–6.

[32] Contrast John Maynard, 1942, pp. 30–3, 285, 298, 312, 448–9. The relationship between the various forms of Soviet collectives and the *obshchina* is discussed at length in Robert G. Wesson, 1963.

[33] Cf. the editorial in *Izvestia*, October 19, 1960, 'The Village Meeting'.

[34] Cf. G. Vernadsky, 1944, pp. 401–2. The comparison made here is in the fields of education and public health.

[35] There is of course some continuity in administrative structures. Thus the modern *oblast* often tallies fairly closely with the *gubernia* of the nineteenth century.

[36] G. Vernadsky, *op. cit.*, pp. 474–5, 478.

[37] For a perceptive essay on this question see, Robert C. Tucker, 1963, Ch. 4, 'The Image of Dual Russia'.

SELECTED BIBLIOGRAPHY

Complete reference to the works cited below will be found in the comprehensive bibliography.

Armstrong, J. A., 1963.
Barghoorn, F. C., 2nd edn., 1972, Chs. 1, 2.
Brzezinski, Z., and Huntington, S. P., 1964, Ch. 1.

Conquest, R., 1960.
Crick, B., 1964, Chs. 1–2.
Dahl, R. A., 1963, Chs. 1–4.
Fainsod, Merle, 1963b.
Hough, Jerry, 1969, Chs. 14–15.
Macridis, R. C., and Ward, R. E., eds., 1963, pp. 438–52.
Male, D. J., 1971, Ch. 1.
Meyer, A. G., 1966.
Plamenatz, J., 1954.
Reshetar, John S. Jr., 1971, Chs. 1–2.
Schlesinger, R., 1947, pp. 169–76.
Scott, D. J. R., 4th edn., 1969, Ch. 1.
Tucker, Robert C., 2nd edn., 1972, Ch. 6.
Ulam, A. B., 1960, Ch. 5.

Chapter 2

PRELUDE TO REVOLUTION

THE REVOLUTIONARY TRADITION

Looking at Russian history over the three hundred years prior to the 1917 Revolution one might be tempted to draw the conclusion that insurrection and revolution were traditional Russian methods of politics. From Stenka Razin's Cossack rebellion and the *streltsi* revolt in the seventeenth century through the Pugachev uprising in the late eighteenth century to the whole range of revolutionary movements of the nineteenth century, the history of tsarist Russia seems studded with revolutionary movements.

If the revolutionary tradition of Russia was particularly strong and entrenched in 1917 it was certainly not due to some special facet of the Russian national character. It is not in the Russian soul but in the social and political structure of tsarist Russia that the key to this revolutionary tradition is to be found. The nineteenth-century Russian state was noted for its social and political backwardness. Serfdom remained the basis of Russian agriculture generations and centuries after its abolition in western Europe. The large landed estates depended entirely on serf labour and the landowner's wealth was measured not by the production of his lands but by the number of his serfs. The Crimean War and increased peasant unrest stimulated the reform movement and eventually persuaded Alexander II to abolish serfdom in 1861. Yet even after the Edict of Emancipation Russian agriculture remained very backward and semi-feudal. Only a minority of Russian landlords succeeded in developing anything approaching scientific capitalist agriculture. The majority became absentee landowners or continued personally to exploit the peasantry who still owed many forms of service to their former owners. The contrast between these two approaches to the problem is vividly illustrated by the farming experience of three of the leading characters in Tolstoy's *Anna Karenina*. Vronsky belonged to the minority of scientific capitalist farmers—'he tried to carry on his husbandry as if it were a factory'. His whole estate smacked of business efficiency with its reliance on machinery and hired labour, its new farm buildings and

22

home with English and French furnishings, its English park and gardens, its hospital and dispensary. Levin, although also interested in 'scientific agriculture' was hopelessly entangled in feudal survivals and his efforts at producing labour efficiency through combining variants of the *otrabotki* system* with wage labour was doomed to inevitable failure, as he himself admitted in his franker moments. Levin's brother-in-law, Oblonsky, followed a third course. Although a landowner he abandoned all effort at living on his agricultural income. He became a salaried government official and later an administrative official in a private finance company.

Even more with the peasants than with the landlords only a minority were capable of developing as capitalist farmers. As a result of the Emancipation the peasantry secured small family holdings which averaged less than what they had cultivated as serfs. The landlords secured more than half of the land previously cultivated by the serfs, including the pick of the pasture land, meadow land and arable land. At the end of the nineteenth century the landlords and their families, comprising one-fivehundredth of the population owned 27 per cent of the land. The average landlord holding was 333 times that of the average peasant holding.[1] The majority of peasants became indebted to the landlords (either directly or indirectly through the state) being liable for a solid annual rental for the land received from the landlord at Emancipation. This rental was paid either in money or in labour. Various traditional dues and labour services, although formally abolished by the Emancipation Edict, were in many cases continued. The family holdings of the peasantry were not as a rule consolidated. They were subjected to the control of the village community (the *mir* or *obshchina*) and were periodically redistributed as a series of widely scattered strips. It was not until 1870 that peasants were allowed to give up their allotments. Until the Stolypin reforms of the early twentieth century the process by which a peasant could contract out of the *mir* and consolidate his holding remained difficult, requiring a two-thirds vote of the village meeting and even then giving not an individual title but a household title. Under this system the proportion of poor peasants steadily increased and many were forced into a semi-proletarian status, becoming hired agricultural labourers to the landlords and rich peasants, or moving into the factories for employment yet keeping their peasant status. While the majority of peasants were becoming worse off the more enterprising and fortunate minority (the *kulaks* or rich peasants) were steadily improving their status and wealth by means of consolidating their holdings and by acquiring or renting extra land. Lenin's analysis of

* A system which involved the peasant in cultivating the landlord's land with his own implements, partly for payment in money and partly in kind.

23

Russian agriculture at the end of the nineteenth century showed that 30% of Russian peasants were horseless and that another 30% possessed one horse only. The top 12% of the peasants owned 31% of the peasant land, the bottom 81% owned 35% of the land.[2] Although about three million peasants broke away from the *mir* and established themselves as individual farmers between 1906 and 1915, even in 1917 only about one-fifth of peasant holdings were consolidated.[3]

Russian industry remained relatively backward until late in the nineteenth century. Up to 1861 many industries were operated on serf labour. The emancipation of the serfs and the steady depression of peasant agriculture produced an adequate supply of wage labour and industry developed more rapidly from then on. Deficiencies in local sources of capital were increasingly met by foreign capital investment. By 1900 it was estimated that more than 1,000 million roubles of foreign capital was invested in Russian industry, chiefly in transport, mining, oil, banking and textiles.[4] It was this concentration of British, French, German, Belgian and American capital in tsarist Russia which led Lenin to describe Russia as an imperialist state which was itself a semi-colony. Although Russia was still a relatively undeveloped industrial country in 1914 it was advancing very rapidly. After 1890 Russian industry expanded more rapidly than that of Western Europe. Although the modern industrial proletariat numbered only about 3½ millions in 1914 it was unusually concentrated. Thus in 1910, 53·5% of Russian industrial workers were employed in factories and enterprises employing 500 or more, whereas only 33% of United States industrial workers were so employed.[5] The common observation of Western scholars that the Russian Revolution disproved Marx because it took place in the least industrialized of the major countries of Europe must be qualified by the fact that in 1914 the Russian proletariat was more concentrated than that of Britain, USA, or Germany. However, the industrial proletariat formed only a small minority of the total population. Lenin claimed that if the 'rural proletariat' and the 'semi-proletarians' were added to the industrial proletariat there was a proletarian majority in Russia even in 1900. While this was an ingenious modification of Marx, Lenin certainly exaggerated the extent of the proletarianization of the Russian peasantry.[6]

The political system of tsarist Russia may be characterized as one of unrestrained despotism frequently degenerating into brutal repression and martial law. No representative institutions of any sort existed until 1864 and these (the *zemstvos*) were organized on an estate basis in order to ensure the continued domination of the landlord class. At the national level the first approximation to a parliament was not established until the revolution of 1905 and its original representation and powers were so curtailed in 1907 that it ceased to bear any real resemblance to a modern parliament. As it operated between 1907 and 1917 the Duma was no more representative of the nation than was the Estates General of pre-revolutionary France. The political history of nineteenth-century Russia is traditionally regarded as one of alternating phases of reform and reaction. It would be more accurate to consider it as a series of 'holding operations' in which the Tsars sought to retain their absolutism undiluted and landlords sought to retain their social and political domination. Liberal periods stemmed partly from the intermittent liberal convictions of individual Tsars such as Alexander I and Alexander II, as well as from the fear of popular revolt. The methods used by the tsarist government to control the political situation in Russia are so well known as to require little elaboration here. In addition to a rigorous but somewhat inefficient censorship on all publications a continued police offensive was operated against radical opinions and organizations. Because of this reform groups inevitably became revolutionary and all opposition political groups had to withstand the regular decimation of arrest, imprisonment, exile and even execution of their leaders and most active supporters. Following the assassination of Alexander II in 1881 by members of the *Narodnaya Volya* (People's Will) group all important cities and towns were placed under a modified martial law which enabled arrests without warrant or trial, administrative exile and rigid control on the movement of individuals from place to place. To the directly coercive power of the state as exercised through police, secret police, army, courts and censorship, we must add the use made by the state of such traditional agencies as the church and the *mir* for regulating and controlling the activities of the peasants. Members of non-Russian nations such as Ukrainians, Poles, Tartars, Georgians, Armenians, Kazakhs, Uzbeks and others, suffered a double oppression. Hence the frequency with which Russian revolutionary movements throughout the nineteenth century sought allies within national liberation movements operating inside the Russian Empire.[7]

Thus in order to explain the revolutionary tradition of tsarist Russia it is not necessary to go beyond the facts of Russian life. It was a direct outcome of the social and cultural backwardness of Russia and especially of the anachronistic and repressive political system.

Lenin divided the nineteenth-century Russian revolutionary movement into three periods, an aristocratic period (1825–61), an intellectual (or bourgeois-democratic) period (1861–95), and a proletarian period (from 1895 onwards).[8] This classification has no more than general accuracy. Intellectuals provided the essential leadership at all stages. The bourgeoisie or middle class was weakly represented in the revolutionary movement at all stages. Revolutionary organizations based on the working class go back at least to the early 1870s.[9]

It is not my purpose to give a summary of the development of the Russian revolutionary movement between 1815 and 1917. This would require more space than I can afford. It would also introduce unnecessary detail about individuals and organizations. It will be sufficient to deal with three movements which represented three major approaches to revolution and, to a certain degree, three phases in the Russian revolutionary movement. These three movements were the Decembrists, the Populists and the modern revolutionary parties, Socialists and Socialist Revolutionary.

THE DECEMBRISTS

The Decembrists took their name from the revolt which took place in the Senate Square, St. Petersburg, on December 14, 1825. Decembrist organizations began during the Napoleonic Wars when Russian officers—inspired by the patriotism of the ordinary Russian people and by the ideals of the French Revolution—began to form secret societies for the reform of Russian society and Russian government. The first of these, 'The Union of Salvation', was founded as early as 1816. This was succeeded by 'The Union of Welfare' in 1818. While the former had only thirty or so members the latter numbered hundreds and existed on a regional basis. It also had the distinction of an 'inner' and an 'outer' organization, membership of the former being confined to zealous revolutionaries. The members of these revolutionary circles were almost entirely drawn from the gentry whose members used their military positions to extend their influence. Political programmes varied somewhat from group to group and from individual to individual. 'The Russian Truth', drafted in 1824 by Pestel, the leader of the Southern Society, included demands for the abolition of serfdom, the replacement of autocracy by a democratic republic and the curtailment of landlordism. It advocated the creation of a national land fund based on the confiscation of the monastic lands and the surplus land of the landowners. From this fund land grants were to be made available to all willing to till the land. The constitution of the proposed democratic republic was clearly inspired by the French Directory of 1795. It provided for a Central Assembly of five hundred based on manhood suffrage, a Supreme Synod of one hundred and twenty Elders, and a Sovereign Council of five elected for a five-year term. Other Decembrists, however, favoured less radical social and political reform seeking a solution through a constitutional monarchy. Unfortunately for the

Decembrists their plans to revolt were known to the government well in advance of the date decided on. The revolt was quickly and mercilessly suppressed. The Decembrist circles were smashed, one hundred and twenty-six persons exiled to Siberia, and others imprisoned or sentenced to exile in less remote parts. Five of the leaders, including Pestel, were hanged.[10] The youthful Pushkin escaped sharing in this punishment of the Decembrists only because he had been earlier exiled from the capital.

The Russian revolutionary movement for the generation after the suppression of the Decembrist revolt was characterized by the increasing incidence of peasant revolts and by the increasing influence of writers and students. Peasant revolts varied from refusals to pay taxes or to render military service to open attacks on the landlords. They were mainly local and disconnected but in a few cases extended over several provinces and developed into an elementary political movement. There were two hundred and eighty recorded peasant revolts in the first quarter of the nineteenth century, seven hundred and twenty-eight in the second quarter. European revolutions and wars seemed to occasion peasant revolts in Russia. This occurred in the case of the 1830 and 1848 Revolutions and also during the Crimean War and the Russo-Japanese War. There were one hundred and seven peasant revolts recorded in 1848 alone.[11] The peasant revolts of 1854–55 had such an impact that the ruling class recognized the impossibility of retaining serfdom. Rumours of emancipation stimulated many further peasant revolts in the years 1856–60.[12]

The influence of writers and poets in the Russian revolutionary movement was characteristic of the nineteenth century as a whole but it was especially characteristic of the period from 1830 onwards. Pushkin and some of his contemporary writers were involved in the Decembrist movement and later writers developed under the stimulus of its heroic failure. Herzen, Belinsky, Turgenev, Goncharov, Chernyshevsky and many other leading writers were actively involved in revolutionary agitation. Dostoevsky, Saltykov-Shedrin and Chernyshevsky were all directly influenced by the revolutionary Pretrashevtsy in the 1840s. Nekrasov was actively associated for a time with the Populist movement. This prominence of literary figures in the Russian revolutionary movement was partly the result of the fact that more open political writing and agitation were proscribed. Hence literary journals such as Herzen's *Kolokol* (The Bell) or Nekrasov's *Sovremennik* (The Contemporary)[13] played a much more important part in political struggle than is usually the case with literary journals. Literary articles often provided the basic literature for political agitation. Thus Belinsky's 'Letter to Gogol' (July, 1847) which contained a sharp exposure of tsarist absolutism and of the

Orthodox Church was one of the main documents used by the Petrashevtsy. Chernyshevsky's *What is to be done?* (1863), although a novel in form was hardly less influential than Lenin's pamphlet of the same name (1902) as an inspirer of revolutionary action. Venturi says of this book that it 'moulded a whole generation of Populist students and revolutionaries'.[14]

After the failure of the 1848 Revolution in Western Europe Russian progressives such as Herzen, Chernyshevsky and Dobrolyubov abandoned their belief in liberalism and parliamentary reforms and turned to theories of peasant revolution. They began an active campaign for the emancipation of the serfs and for the development of Russian society towards agrarian socialism rather than capitalism. This change represented not so much the conversion of westerners to the ideals of the Slavophils as the recognition that English and French liberalism had little to offer as a solution to the peculiar conditions of Russia. They correctly recognized that the abolition of serfdom and peasant emancipation were preconditions of progress in Russia.

Underground student groups and student demonstrations played an important role in the revolutionary movement in these years. In 1857 and following years students at Moscow, St. Petersburg, Kiev, Kazan and other centres were frequently involved in clashes with government authorities, in some cases with the active support of their professors. Manifestoes such as *To the Young Generation* (1861),[15] served to rally considerable numbers of young intellectuals behind the older revolutionary writers. Students were actively involved in all revolutionary movements from the early *Zemlya i Volya* (Land and Liberty) groups of the early sixties through the various Populist organizations to the Social Revolutionary and Socialist groups at the end of the century.

THE POPULIST MOVEMENT

The *Narodniki* or Russian populists took their name from the Russian word *narod* meaning 'people'. The name is an apt one since although the populist movement included many diverse elements its most typical concern was that of activizing the Russian population against tsarism. The movement was orientated towards the people. The term 'movement' is used deliberately as the Narodnik influence was much wider than that of the political parties it spawned. It was a literary influence and a general cultural trend as well as a specifically political movement and few Russian intellectuals who reached maturity between the years 1861 and 1905 escaped its influence.

Because of the universality of its influence Russian populism is difficult to pin down. The political attitudes of the populists, as distinct from their political programmes, included a distrust of liberalism and parliamentary democracy, a belief in the possibility of an autonomous development of socialism in Russia through the preservation of the village community (the *obshchina*) and the avoidance of capitalism. The object of 'going to the people' was primarily designed to broaden the popular resistance to tsarist autocracy. It was not necessarily based on any veneration of the Russian peasant, although this was often present. Since nine-tenths of Russians were rural and since the majority of them were peasants, it was natural that any political movement seeking to secure a popular basis should be concerned with activizing the peasantry. At times, as with the Chaikovskists in 1872–73 Russian populists concentrated on organizing the urban workers. Yet even here the concentration was sometimes not on urban workers as developing industrial proletariat but on urban workers as peasants temporarily employed in the cities who were better educated than their fellow villagers and therefore more easy to influence. It was expected that they would soon return to their villages taking the message of populism back with them.[16]

Populism, like earlier movements based essentially on the intellectuals, favoured the 'study group' form of organization. Groups of students, writers, teachers and others formed clandestinely for the organization of libraries of prohibited books, the compilation of books of political extracts, publication of popular pamphlets and political education. These groups soon extended to include workers and peasants. In the early years of the movement the groups were locally organized and only loosely linked. This was true even with the first *Zemlya i Volya* groups which were organized during the early 1860s. Although these groups were soon shattered by arrests and exile new groups replaced them, with new leaders but with a similar orientation and purpose. In 1876 a new *Zemlya i Volya* organization was formed. Unlike the earlier organization of the same name this was more disciplined and more centralized and was in fact a political party in the modern sense. The influence of this second *Zemlya i Volya* was wider than the first. In addition to a central group of about 25 there were fixed centres in several provincial towns. From these centres teachers, students, doctors and *zemstvo* officials and other intellectuals moved out to influence the peasantry in the surrounding countryside. The organization reached a new stage in October 1878 with the appearance of the journal *Zemlya i Volya*. This was printed abroad but was widely distributed inside Russia. However, even at the time when this journal was launched, the organization was showing signs of internal strain. In reaction to increased police persecution and to the failure of the policy of arousing the peasants a large

29

section of its members increasingly favoured terrorism as a political method. In 1879 this group organized within the *Zemyla i Volya* a tightly disciplined terrorist group called the *Narodnaya Volya* (People's Will). The non-terrorists, including the later socialist, G. V. Plekhanov, separated themselves off from the *Narodnaya Volya* and formed the *Cherny Peredel* (Black Redistribution).* Whereas the former group concentrated its activities increasingly towards the assassination of the Tsar, the latter group continued the older emphasis on influencing workers and peasants and in popularizing its programme of immediate reforms. The division between the terrorist and non-terrorist wings of the populist movement was largely confined to differences over political strategy. Both groups favoured the same sort of political programme. This involved demanding the election of a Constituent Assembly based on universal suffrage, regional self-administration on the basis of the autonomy of the *mir*, land nationalization and the distribution of the landed estates to the peasantry, workers' control of factories, freedom of conscience, speech, press, meeting, association and electoral agitation.[17]

The assassination of Alexander II on March 1, 1881, led to a quick and savage retaliation. Hundreds of Narodniks were arrested; several were executed, the remainder being sentenced to long terms of imprisonment and exile. Police control was strengthened, especially in the larger towns. Populist political organization did not recover from this attack although the Narodnik influence survived, especially in the later Socialist Revolutionary Party. Many of the early Russian Marxists, including Plekhanov and Lenin, were influenced by populism and the early Marxist groups, despite their repudiation of populism, absorbed much of its tradition and some of its programme. The fact that Marxist writers such as Plekhanov, Martov and Lenin were forced to devote a good deal of their time and energy as late as 1900[18] in exposing the 'errors' of populism is a tribute to the strength of the populist tradition in Russia.

THE RUSSIAN SOCIAL DEMOCRATIC LABOUR PARTY

The Populists were the first to introduce Marx to Russia and they were the first to base political groups on the working class.[19] The first specifically Russian Marxist group, 'The Emancipation of Labour' group, was formed by Plekhanov in Geneva in 1883. Marxist groups appeared in Russia in 1884 and in following years and became more numerous during the 1890s. Lenin, Krupskaya and other future Bolsheviks were actively engaged in this work at St.

---

* They took their name from their central objective of dividing up the landed estates among the peasantry.

Petersburg during 1893–95. These developments were not entirely separate and internal and external groups collaborated to form the Russian Social Democratic Labour Party. The first programme was drafted at Geneva in 1884 but the formal organization was not established until the First Congress of the Party in 1898 and the full organization was not really established until the celebrated 2nd Congress in 1903.

The first Russian Marxists were mainly intellectuals although the groups operating within Russia soon gained working-class recruits and began to organize workers' strikes and other protests. The Russian Marxists were very orthodox Marxists at the outset. Their orthodoxy was shown in their arguments with the Narodniks. These arguments turned around three main problems. The first of these was the possibility of Russia avoiding capitalism. The Narodniks had sought to justify their own thesis on the basis of Marx. Marx himself was somewhat undecided on the possibility of Russia avoiding capitalism although he clearly believed that it had developed rapidly in that direction since 1861. Before his death in 1895 Engels had become more than ever convinced that the primitive peasant commune of Russia was doomed to extinction.[20] In contrast with Marx and Engels' hesitation on this matter the early Russian Marxists argued unequivocally that Russia was following the same path of economic and social development as Western Europe. Lenin's *The Development of Capitalism in Russia* (1899)[21] provides a good example of how the early Marxists argued this question out. Using official tsarist statistics Lenin showed conclusively that much of Russian industry was already geared to the large-scale market, that the legal equality of the peasants within the *mir* was already a myth since class-differentiation was already well advanced in rural Russia, and that the industrial proletariat was being increasingly swollen by the influx of displaced peasants.

The second basic difference between the Marxists and the populists was in their understanding of the class basis of the revolution. While the populists stressed the peasantry the Marxists stressed the industrial working class as the class which was historically destined to establish socialism. The third point of difference arose out of the different evaluations of the historical process made by the populists and the Marxists. The Marxists stressed social and class factors in their explanation of history and this led them to reject such political methods as terrorism. Whereas sections of the Narodniks considered the assassination of the Tsar as the essential step necessary to bring about popular revolt the Marxists invariably rejected this view. Plekhanov's writings, especially his works *On the Development of the Monist View of History* (1895) and *On the Role of the Individual in*

31

History (1898), exerted a considerable influence in developing support for Marxism. It is an ironical commentary on the tsarist censorship that for a time it permitted the circulation of Marxist works in competition with Populist works as it considered them less dangerous because less applicable to Russian conditions.

BOLSHEVIKS AND MENSHEVIKS

The division between Bolshevik (Majority) and Menshevik (Minority)* wings of the Russian Social Democratic Party first developed at the 2nd Congress in 1903. Although this division was not complete for many years afterwards separate organizations were in fact maintained from 1903 onwards. This happened despite the decision of the Congress to appoint a representative editorial board to the party paper *Iskra*.

Accounts of the relations between the two wings of the Russian Social Democratic Party between 1903 and 1917 can be found in many standard texts,[22] so it is quite unnecessary for me to discuss the matter here. However, it is necessary to say something on the question of the differences between these two groups.

The differences between the Bolsheviks and the Mensheviks related chiefly to objectives and to organization and methods of work. Both parties claimed to be Marxist parties and both sought socialism but believed that socialism was not possible as an immediate programme. The immediate programme of both groups was the carrying through of what was known as the 'bourgeois revolution'. This involved the overthrow of the tsarist state and its replacement by a democratic republic, land reform, legislation to guarantee workers' conditions (such as a statutory eight-hour day), the establishment of freedom of speech, press, assembly and organization, and similar democratic measures. Lenin formulated the proposal on the programme which was submitted to the 1903 Congress and it was carried almost unanimously, only one delegate voting against it. This programme remained the programme of both wings until 1917.

At the outset there was no difference on how the two factions viewed the sequence and inter-relation between the two revolutions, the bourgeois revolution and the eventual socialist revolution. Differences on this question arose only during the 1905 Revolution. This revolution, which was characterized by spontaneous working-class, peasant and middle-class revolutionary actions, demonstrated the revolutionary potentialities of the peasantry and also the unreliability of the middle class. This point was recognized by Lenin in his

* In fact the Bolsheviks were the minority group until shortly before the November Revolution.

pamphlet *The Two Tactics of Social-Democracy in the Democratic Revolution* (July, 1905). In this pamphlet Lenin argued the following propositions:

(a) The proletariat must take the lead in initiating and carrying through the bourgeois revolution. It was quite inadequate for them to play second fiddle to the bourgeoisie and await the maturing of capitalism before playing a decisive role in politics. This arose because of the fact that the Russian bourgeoisie was weak and indecisive in its political actions and already feared to push the bourgeois revolution to completion since it found the tsarist state an indispensable ally against the workers.

(b) The proletariat would only succeed in carrying through the bourgeois revolution if they allied themselves with the peasantry. The peasantry included many semi-proletarian elements as well as semi-bourgeois elements. This gave rise to unstable political activity, but unlike the bourgeoisie the peasantry was interested in destroying one important form of private property, namely the landed estates. This made it a more determined enemy of tsarism and a natural ally of the revolutionary workers.

(c) The political form of this worker–peasant alliance would inevitably be that of a dictatorship for an armed uprising and the arming of the masses was a necessary step for the overthrow of tsarism.

The essence of Lenin's position at this time is contained in the sentence:

We cannot jump out of the bourgeois-democratic boundaries of the Russian revolution, but we can enormously extend those boundaries, and within those boundaries we can and must fight for the interests of the proletariat, for its immediate needs and for the prerequisites for training its forces for the complete victory that is to come.[23]

Thus in 1905 Lenin did not go as far as Trotsky did in his *Our Revolution* (published 1906). Even in September 1905 Lenin went only so far as talk of 'the uninterrupted revolution' whereas Trotsky used the phrase 'the permanent revolution' to cover his view that it was no longer possible to argue that the bourgeois revolution could be kept separate from the socialist revolution in Russia, and that the very attempt on the part of the proletariat to complete the bourgeois revolution would involve it in initiating the socialist revolution.[24] Lenin's revision of orthodox Marxist theory on this point was incomplete in 1905 but his 1905 analysis was to provide the basis in 1917 for his *Letters from Afar* and his *April Theses* in which he argued for the quick development of the bourgeois revolution into the socialist revolution. This view was eventually accepted by the Bolshevik Party at its 7th Party Conference in May 1917 and its acceptance paved the way for the admission of Trotsky and his small group of supporters into the Bolshevik Party some months later. On the other hand the Mensheviks right up to the November Revolution remained firmly attached to the original Marxist perspective of the two revolutions being separated by a long gap in time and of the proletariat playing merely a subordinate role in the bourgeois revolution.

If the difference between the Bolsheviks and Mensheviks on programme and revolutionary perspective became only partly clear in 1905 and only fully clear in 1917 the difference over organization and methods of work was clear even in 1903. Lenin's views on organization were contained in his pamphlet *What is to be done?* published in 1902 in advance of the 2nd Congress. His critics came to the Congress well prepared to counter these views and in fact succeeded in carrying a majority of the delegates behind their counter-proposals on party organization. The sharpness of this division is not clear from a reading of the two formulations on the party which provoked the split. Lenin's draft of paragraph 1 read:

A Party member is one who accepts the program and who supports the Party both financially and by personal participation in one of the Party's organizations.

Martov's draft proposed that:

A Party member is one who accepts the program, supports the Party financially and renders it regular personal assistance under the direction of one of its organizations.[25]

The broad difference here was between a party of activists and a larger and more loosely knit party. This difference is easily grasped but the finer points of Lenin's conception of a revolutionary party are even now often misunderstood by his critics. It is therefore necessary to emphasize the following points. Firstly, Lenin believed that the workers could set the pace for the Russian Revolution only if they became more class conscious, i.e. more convinced as a class of their historical role in the revolution. Class consciousness developed only slowly and only so far spontaneously. Therefore one of the essential tasks of the Party was to stimulate and enlarge the class consciousness of the workers, to link the immediate economic struggles of the workers to the larger struggle for socialism.[26] The Mensheviks on the other hand with a narrower perspective on the possibilities of the immediate future always concentrated on legal methods, on 'parliamentary' and trade union organization and on awaiting events rather than on seeking to determine them—a position frequently covered by the word 'spontaneity'.

Secondly, Lenin did not advocate a party of intellectuals which was to lead the working class from outside its ranks. What he argued for was a party of revolutionary socialists. Revolutionary socialism or Marxism he regarded as a world outlook which required something more than ordinary working-class experience to produce it. Hence the need for socialist intellectuals in the working-class movement.[27] But these intellectuals were to become proletarian in outlook and, as most of the members of the party were expected to be actively engaged in leading working-class struggles and in developing the class consciousness of the workers, the party would be truly proletarian.* Such is clear from a careful reading of *What is to be done?* and of other early works such as 'The Reorganization of the Party' which Lenin wrote in November 1905. In this latter work Lenin wrote that:

The relations between the functions of the intellectual and of the proletariat (workers) in the Social-Democratic labour movement can perhaps be fairly precisely expressed by the following general formula: the intelligentsia can very well solve problems of 'principle', draw up good schemes, reason very well about the need for doing certain things . . . but the workers act; they transform drab theory into vital life.[28]

Thirdly, Lenin did not exclude legal activity, work in trade unions, in elections, in the Duma, etc. On the contrary he encouraged it and utilized it to its fullest extent. However, he never considered that such activities could of themselves bring about socialism and therefore he insisted on the use of illegal organizations and methods, especially in periods of repression such as the years following 1907. Lenin had no illusions about the possibility of the peaceful reform of tsarism.

Fourthly, Lenin advocated a small, tightly knit party of professional revolutionaries. Many factors influenced Lenin's preference for such a party; the influence of the Russian revolutionary tradition, the exigencies of the political situation in Russia, and his psychological make-up and political style.† Lenin was above all an impatient and an ambitious revolutionary who always sought to establish his individual leadership of the revolutionary movement. This was easier to do within a small revolutionary party than within a larger, more popular party. However, right from its inception Bolshevik organization distinguished between the full-time revolutionaries and the ordinary members who worked in the workshops, in factories, in the

* In fact the majority of the Social-Democrat leaders, Bolshevik and Menshevik alike, were bourgeois intellectuals. See the interesting study by R. S. Lane, 'Social and Organisational Differences between Bolsheviks and Mensheviks, 1903–1907.' Univ. of Birmingham, Centre for Russian and East European Studies. Series RC/C, No. 1, 1964.

† For an interpretation of the rise of Bolshevism which emphasizes Lenin's personality structure see, Stanley W. Page, *Lenin and World Revolution*, N.Y. Univ. Press, 1959.

railways, in agriculture and in various professional occupations. Moreover, when circumstances permitted the Bolshevik Party sought mass recruitment. This happened in 1905–6[29] and again in 1917. Bolshevik membership increased tenfold—from 23,000 to 240,000— between March and November 1917.[30] But at all stages Lenin argued for a minority party in the sense that he felt that the Party must act as the vanguard of the working class and must never lose its identity in the larger whole.

Fifthly, Lenin's preference for a centrally organized Party in which the lower leaders were selected by the centre rather than democratically elected from below was originally determined by his recognition of the impossibility of open socialist organization in tsarist Russia. This preference was strengthened by his study of earlier revolutionary organizations but was determined by the nature of the political environment in which the Party operated rather than by earlier models or by any authoritarian element in Marxism. The original model survived the overthrow of tsarism because after the November Revolution the Bolsheviks were faced with the task of directing the development of socialism against the opposition or the apathy of the majority of the Russian people.

THE SOCIALIST REVOLUTIONARY PARTY

The most influential Russian revolutionary party before 1917 and the most popular in 1917 was the Socialist Revolutionary Party. It was stronger than the Mensheviks or Bolsheviks in March 1917 and even in November 1917 it enjoyed more support than the Bolshevik Party. The broad support for this party arose chiefly from the fact that it was peasant-based, although like all other revolutionary parties its leaders came chiefly from the intellectuals. It was generally regarded as the direct successor to the earlier populist parties and this fact brought it much support. Like the Narodniks before them the Socialist Revolutionaries concentrated their efforts towards organizing the peasants and they continued to use acts of terror against individual officials as a weapon against tsarism.

The Socialist Revolutionary Party was established amid the peasant revolts of 1902. Its members played a leading part in the peasant uprisings of 1905 and also in the Soviets. The programme of the Socialist Revolutionary Party adopted at the 1st Congress of the Party in 1905 contained a programme for liberal democracy and an agrarian programme which proposed the distribution of the landed estates among the peasantry, but which endorsed private property and capitalism in general. Like the Social Democrats the Socialist Revolutionaries split almost at birth into two wings, a moderate wing

36

known as Popular Socialists and a radical, extremist wing, the Maxi-malists. The former based themselves on the acceptance of the re-forms promised in the October Manifesto.[31] The latter demanded the realization of the full programme of the Party adopted earlier in the year, i.e. land nationalization, the confiscation of landed estates and the distribution of the land to the peasantry. This division was on the basis of tactics and minimum programme rather than on organiza-tion and the two factions remained linked rather more closely than did the two factions of the Social Democratic Party over the years between 1905 and 1917. During this period the Party was generally dominated by the more moderate and bourgeois elements and it was at times difficult to distinguish its policies from those of the Cadet (Constitutional Democrat) Party. It took the Revolutions of 1917 to clarify the situation and it was only in December 1917 that the left Socialist Revolutionaries separated completely from the right Socialist Revolutionaries. This division within the ranks of the Socialist Revolutionaries enabled the Bolsheviks to broaden the basis of their government which from the end of November 1917 until February 1918 operated as a coalition government of Bolsheviks and left Socialist Revolutionaries.

NOTES

[1] A. M. Pankratova, ed., 1948, Part III, p. 28.

[2] Cf. Christopher Hill, 1947, pp. 84–5.

[3] Consolidation of peasant holdings was uneven throughout Russia ranging from 1·7% in the north-east to 8·3% in the Moscow region to 29·2% in New Russia. John Maynard, 1942, p. 60. Cf. Male, D. J. 1971, Ch. 1.

[4] A. M. Pankratova. ed., 1948, Part III, p. 15.

[5] Merle Fainsod, 1954, p. 25.

[6] Lenin estimated that in 1897 63·7 million out of 125·6 million people in Russia were proletarians and semi-proletarians. See *The Development of Capitalism in Russia*, FLPH, Moscow, 1956, p. 554.

[7] Cf. F. Venturi, 1960, pp. 123–4, 265, 271 *et seq.*, 287–8, 317.

[8] Cf. M. G. Sedov, 1959, p.3.

[9] F. Venturi, *op. cit.*, Chs. 18 and 19.

[10] V. A. Federov, 1957.

[11] *Ibid.*, pp. 21–2.

[12] F. Venturi, *op cit.*, p. 205 *et seq.*

[13] *Kolokol* (The Bell) a weekly newspaper was started by Herzen in London in July 1857. Although prohibited in Russia it was smuggled in in vast numbers and was widely read even by tsarist officials. It was perhaps the strongest radical force in Russia until 1861. The paper continued publication until the late 1860s, from London and after 1864 from Geneva, but it was a declining influence after 1861. A second short-lived *Kolokol* was issued between April and May 1870, the year of Herzen's death.

Sovremennik (The Contemporary) was perhaps the most influential Russian review of the century. It was started by Pushkin in 1836 and continued by his friend Professor Pletnev after his death in 1837. In 1846 the poet Nekrasov took over the paper. During his control of the paper (1846–66) Belinsky, Turgenev, Tolstoy, Saltykov-Shchredin, Chernyshevsky and Dobrolyubov and other progressive writers published many articles, stories and sketches in the journal. Between 1856 and 1866 when the journal was suppressed and its editor Chernyshevsky imprisoned, it was dominated by the extreme left of the Russian revolutionary intellectuals.

[14] F. Venturi, *op. cit.*, pp. 178–9.

[15] Ibid., pp. 227–8, 246–7.

[16] F. Venturi, *op. cit.*, Ch. 18.

[17] F. Venturi, *op. cit.*, pp. 677–8. See also S. V. Utechin, 1964, Ch. 7.

[18] e.g. Plekhanov's works *Socialism and the Political Struggle* (1883), *Our Differences* (1885), *On the Development of the Monistic View of History* (1895), *On the Materialist Conception of History* (1897), and *On the Role of the Individual in History* (1898); and Lenin's *What the 'Friends of the People' are* (1894), and *The Development of Capitalism in Russia* (1899).

[19] Workers' groups were organized by the Chaikovskists in St. Petersburg in 1872–73. Both the Workers' Union of South Russia (Kiev) 1879 and the Northern Union of Russian Workers, 1879, were organized by Populists.

[20] Cf. F. Engels to N. F. Danielson, October 17, 1893.

'For me . . . the present capitalistic phase of development in Russia appears to be an unavoidable consequence of the historical conditions as created by the Crimean war, the way in which the change of 1861 in agrarian conditions was accomplished, and the political stagnation in Europe generally.' Karl Marx and Frederick Engels, *Selected Correspondence*. FLPH, Moscow, 1956, p. 545. See also Letters 157, 220, 224, 225, 233 and 239.

[21] V. I. Lenin, 1956.

[22] Useful accounts may be found in the following:

Merle Fainsod, 1954. Ch. 2; Herbert McClosky and John E. Turner, 1960, Ch. 3; E. H. Carr, 1950, Vol. I, Chs. 1–3; L. Schapiro, 1960, Part I.

[23] 'Two Tactics of Social Democracy', *Selected Works*, 1946, Vol. 3, p. 77. Cf. p. 102:

'While absolutely recognising the bourgeois character of the revolution, which cannot *immediately* go beyond the bounds of a merely democratic revolution, our slogan *pushes forward* this particular revolution and strives to mould it into forms most advantageous to the proletariat; consequently, it strives for the utmost utilisation of the democratic revolution for a most successful further struggle of the proletariat for socialism.'

[24] Cf. I. Deutscher, 1954, Ch. VI; B. D. Wolfe, 1956, pp. 289–94.

[25] Merle Fainsod, 1954, p. 41.

[26] Cf. this statement from 'Two Tactics of Social-Democracy'; 'The proletariat seeks its salvation not by avoiding the class struggle, but by developing it, by extending its scope, its own class consciousness, organisation and determination. The Social-Democrat who debases the tasks of the political struggle becomes transformed from a tribune of the people into a trade union secretary. The Social-Democrat who debases the proletarian tasks in a democratic bourgeois revolution becomes transformed from a leader of the people's revolution into a mere leader of a free labour union.' *Selected Works*, 1946, Vol. 3, p. 121.

[27] Cf. this statement from *What is to be done ?*:

'We said that *there could not yet be* Social-Democratic consciousness among the workers. This consciousness could only be brought to them from without. The history of all countries shows that the working class, exclusively by its own effort, is able to develop only trade union consciousness, i.e. it may itself realise the necessity for combining in unions, for fighting against the employers and for striving to compel the government to pass necessary labour legislation, etc. The theory of socialism, however, grew out of the philosophic, historical and economic theories that were elaborated by the educated representatives of the propertied classes, the intellectuals. According to their social status, the founders of modern scientific socialism, Marx and Engels, themselves belonged to the bourgeois intelligentsia. Similarly, in Russia, the theoretical doctrine of Social-Democracy arose quite independently of the spontaneous growth of the labour movement; it arose as a natural and inevitable outcome of the development of ideas among the revolutionary socialist intelligentsia.' *Selected Works*, 1944, Vol. 2, p. 53.

This is clearly intended as an historical explanation of the relation between Marxism and trade unionism and not as a prescription for the class composition of a revolutionary socialist party once established.

[28] *Selected Works*, 1946, Vol. 3, pp. 465–6.

[29] Cf. M. Lyadov, 1956, especially pp. 84–92.

[30] Contrast E. H. Carr's view in *The Bolshevik Revolution*, Vol. VI, Ch. 19, that the mass party really dates from the Lenin enrolment in 1924.

[31] This Manifesto, issued by the Tsar in October 1905, promised to guarantee basic civil and political rights, to introduce a democratic franchise, and required all laws to have the consent of the Duma.

SELECTED BIBLIOGRAPHY

Carr, E. H., 1950–64, Vol. 1, Chs. 1–3.
Deutscher, Isaac, 1954, Ch. 6.
Fainsod, Merle, 1963a, Chs. 1–2.
Lane, David, 1970, Chs. 1–2.
Male, D. J., 1971, Ch. 1.
Meyer, A. G., 1957, Ch. 6.
Perrie, Maureen, 1972.
Schapiro, L., 1960, Part I.

Chapter 3

THE BOLSHEVIK REVOLUTION

The Soviet state was established in the fire of revolution in November 1917. Although this happened over fifty years ago it is not possible to understand the modern Soviet state without first considering the November Revolution, and in order to understand the November Revolution it is first necessary to understand something of the earlier revolutions of 1905 and March 1917.

THE 1905 REVOLUTION

The 1905 Revolution was a revolution against the repression and incompetency of tsarist absolutism. It was a genuinely popular revolution—a series of separate but associated demonstrations and revolts involving the peasantry, the working class and the middle class. It was spontaneous rather than deliberately planned and consequently lacked cohesion and clear direction. The peasant revolts of 1905 were widespread but sporadic and arose mainly out of the land hunger of the peasantry. The workers' strikes and demonstrations of 1905, although they came increasingly under the influence of Social Democratic groups (both Menshevik and Bolshevik), were essentially spontaneous. The middle-class opposition to the regime was based partly on its absolutism and lack of political liberty and parliamentary institutions, partly on its incompetence as evidenced by its failure to prevent peasant disorders, workers' strikes or military defeats. The October Manifesto served to divide the Russian liberals, as some groups such as the Constitutional Democrats (Cadets) regarded these concessions as altogether inadequate. This division of forces as between the various separate class struggles on the one hand, and the division over political tactics of both liberals and Socialist Revolutionaries on the other, made it easy for the tsarist regime to weather the storm of 1905–6. Both the Petersburg and Moscow Soviets had been suppressed by December 1905, and although the Duma remained, its powers were drastically reduced in 1907.

THE MARCH REVOLUTION

The revolutionary outbreaks of 1905 were occasioned by the military defeats in the Russo-Japanese War. The outbreak of the First World War in August 1914 brought temporary support for the regime but in the long run the strains of war and defeat worsened the position of the Russian people and intensified their revolutionary struggles. The middle classes did not oppose the war but they resented the military defeats which they felt resulted from the incompetency of the tsarist government and from its corrupt and pro-German advisers. The Duma had no say in the conduct of affairs and hence could not serve as an agency for peaceful replacement of the administration. The peasantry suffered directly through the war as the majority of the 15 million Russians mobilized in 1915 were peasants. Casualties were heavy and morale was low so that desertions increased to reach a peak of one and a half million in 1916. Besides the misery and the hardship of the front the fear that land distribution would be carried out in their absence led many peasant soldiers to desert and vote against the war with their feet. The peasants also resented the fact that agricultural prices were pegged during the war while the prices of industrial goods rose rapidly. This 'scissors' movement in prices led to the withholding of grain from the market and resulted in severe food rationing for the urban population. The industrial workers suffered a worsening of living standards throughout the war caused by the decline in the purchasing power of their wages, rationing and unemployment.

Despite severe repression workers' strikes and protests became more common during 1916 and early 1917 and they became more political in character. Thus on January 22, 1917, the anniversary of 'bloody Sunday,'* huge anti-war demonstrations were held in Petrograd, Moscow, Baku and other cities. Although these demonstrations were suppressed the suppression was temporary only. Further anti-war demonstrations were touched off by the opening of the new session of the Duma in Petersburg on February 27. In March further reductions in the bread ration (from 1 lb. to ¾ lb. per day) caused fresh demonstrations. On this occasion the troops sided with the demonstrators and refused to fire on them. By March 9, an estimated 200,000 workers were on strike in the capital, by March 10 a situation approaching a general strike prevailed. On March 12 the demonstration passed into an open uprising and the Petrograd Soviet of Workers' and Soldiers' Deputies was established.

* An incident in the 1905 Revolution when a peaceful workers' demonstration in the capital was fired on by tsarist troops with great loss of life.

The Duma had not been able to keep control of this developing revolutionary situation. It had warned the Tsar of the seriousness of the situation and in return it had been dissolved. It refused to accept dissolution and on March 14 it established a provisional Government. The Tsar returned to the capital on the following day and accepting the advice of the Duma, abdicated. The provisional government established on March 14 was dominated by the Cadets and was under the Chairmanship of the liberal landlord, Prince Lvov, although it included one Socialist Revolutionary member Kerensky as Minister of Justice. The provisional government immediately declared its intention of organizing elections for a Constituent Assembly, an objective which conformed with the programme of all the revolutionary parties as well as that of the liberals.

The events briefly described above constituted the March (or February) Revolution. This was a liberal-democratic or bourgeois revolution which ended tsarist absolutism and brought to power a temporary government of middle-class politicians. At the outset the Cadets were the dominant group in the government but from May onwards Socialist representation increased and from July 21 it was under the Chairmanship of the right wing Socialist Revolutionary, Kerensky. Although the provisional government was essentially a middle-class government established by a bourgeois revolution, the working class was responsible for the situation which produced it and for its chief victories, including its defence against early attempts at counter-revolution.

THE PROVISIONAL GOVERNMENT

In the eight months between March and November 1917 Russia was nominally under the control of the provisional government. Although established by the March Revolution this government could claim a quasi-legal authority since it was responsible to the Duma, an institution which had been established by the Tsar in 1905 and to which the Tsar had abdicated on March 15, 1917. It also secured early recognition from the Allies. For a time it enjoyed the support of the majority of the Russian people. Actually, as Lenin pointed out in his *April Theses*, Russia was under a dual government, the provisional government (based on the bourgeoisie and the liberal landlords) and the Soviets (based on the workers and peasants). Since the demands of the classes on which these two authorities were based were essentially different and conflicting, the first wanting to continue the war, the second wanting peace and land, the two authorities were almost certain to come into conflict. However, while the Soviets were dominated by the Socialist Revolutionaries and the Mensheviks, it

42

was not likely that there would be any attempt to replace the provisional government. This was so because the leaders of these two parties participated in the provisional government and accepted it as the legal government. At most they regarded the Soviets as supervisory agencies through which pressure could be brought to bear on the more conservative elements in the provisional government to ensure that they lived up to their promises. They expected they would build up sufficient support during this period to enable them to form the constitutional government which would follow the Constituent Assembly. They did not oppose the war since they now regarded it as a defensive war to defend the democratic republic from destruction.

At the outset the provisional government secured some sort of sanction from the Petrograd Soviet. On March 14 a joint decree was issued by the provisional government and the Petrograd Soviet. This decree established a number of common principles including the declaration of a general amnesty for political prisoners, freedom of the press, speech, religion and association; freedom for trade unions and the recognition of the right to strike; the summoning of a Constituent Assembly and the establishment of universal suffrage; formation of a people's militia to replace the tsarist police and the authorization for the revolutionary army units to remain in the capital. However, on the very same day, the Petrograd Soviet issued independently of the provisional government its Order No. 1. This order clearly involved a direct challenge to the authority of the provisional government. It provided that each military detachment should elect a Soldiers' Committee and that each military detachment should obey the Soviet in political matters. It further provided that orders of the Military Commission of the State Duma were to be obeyed only if they did not contradict orders of the Soviet, and that all weapons were to be under the control of Soldiers' Committees and were not to be delivered to the officers.[1]

This latent antagonism between the provisional government and the Soviets first developed into open conflict over the issue of the war. The provisional government wanted to continue the war, and, under pressure from the Allies they agreed to the opening up of a new offensive. Thus Milyukov the Foreign Affairs Minister issued a statement to the Allied representatives on March 18 in which he promised that Russia would 'fight by their side against the common enemy until the end'.[2] The policy of the Soviet at this time was shown by its proclamation of March 27 calling on the common people everywhere to make 'a concerted and decisive action in favour of peace'. However the Mensheviks and Socialist Revolutionaries and even some of the Bolsheviks were not consistently anti-war. Bolshevik policy as formulated by Lenin in October 1914[3] was based on the belief that the war was an imperialist struggle for the redivision of the world and therefore was of no direct interest to the workers. However, the policy of 'turning the imperialist war into a civil war' seemed to some Bolsheviks inapplicable after March 1917 as they accepted the view that the war was being fought to defend the democratic revolution. It was not until after Lenin's return and the April Party Conference that Bolshevik policy became consistently anti-war.

The clarification of Bolshevik policy on the war, the steady increase in Bolshevik strength and influence in the Soviets combined with the failure of the new military offensive produced more vigorous opposition to the war by the workers. The 1917 May Day celebrations were specifically directed against the war. The demonstrations were so clearly in opposition to government policy that Milyukov felt it necessary to send a telegram to the Allies pledging Russia to 'continue the war until decisive victory is achieved'.[4] News of this message produced a powerful protest in the form of a huge anti-war march on May 3. The provisional government only extricated itself from the situation by dropping Milyukov and Guchkov (the War Minister) from the government and by appointing Kerensky as Minister of War.

The second major problem of the provisional government was that of improving the food situation. But the food situation could not be improved without the support of the peasantry and the peasantry's support of the provisional government was conditional on the latter carrying out a major land reform. The provisional government, which represented middle class and liberal landlord interests mainly, had no desire to end landlordism and consequently it stalled as long as it could. It began to collect evidence on the matter but took no decisive action. In fact the general opinion in the provisional government was that land reform would have to be postponed until after the Constituent Assembly had met. The government established a state monopoly in grain in April but it was unable to enforce deliveries and by August only 10% of the grain required for feeding the armies and the cities had reached the government stores. Peasant insurrections occurred in many provinces from July onwards and peasants acted directly to overthrow the landlords and to confiscate their property. The insurrections reached a new peak in September–October and further reduced the food supply in the towns. In the capital the daily bread ration was reduced from 1½ lb. to 1 lb., then to ¾ lb., ½ lb. and eventually to ¼ lb.[5]

With growing disorder and peasant insurrection in the countryside and with increasing misery and opposition in the cities, the provisional government was clearly losing its popular basis. A mistimed workers' insurrection in Petrograd in mid-July had enabled the government to arrest many of the Bolshevik leaders and to restrict the Soviet for a time. However, Kerensky proved incapable of extricating the government from the contradictory pressures exerted by peasants, workers, army officers and the Allies. In August he conceded to the request of the Allies and appointed the reactionary tsarist General Kornilov as Commander-in-Chief. Kornilov then attempted to suppress the Soviets. Martial law was established in the cities and early in September Kornilov moved the 3rd Mounted Corps against Petrograd. Kerensky, after some hesitation, accepted the aid of the Petrograd Soviet and its Red Guards. The Soviet organized the defence of the city and despatched representatives to meet the advancing troops. These were persuaded not to attack the city but to arrest their officers and throw in their lot with the workers.

The failure of the Kornilov conspiracy meant the survival of the provisional government but it brought it no credit and it continued to lose support. In contrast, the prestige of the Petrograd Soviet increased as a result of its successful defence of the revolution. From early September it was dominated by the Bolsheviks and under their leadership it began to strengthen its military units in case either the provisional government or counter-revolutionary generals should challenge its position. Kerensky's position was weakened by the lack of reliable military units in the capital. In November 1917 when he sought to use troops against the Bolsheviks and the Soviet he acted altogether too slowly and too indecisively.

THE NOVEMBER REVOLUTION

Since the November (or October*) Revolution was carried through under the direction of the Bolsheviks we must retrace our steps and begin again with the March Revolution.

In March 1917 the Bolsheviks were a small party of 23,000, predominantly working class in membership.[6] Most of its leaders were in exile in Western Europe or in Siberia. No member of the Bolshevik Central Committee was on the scene at Petrograd until March 26, when Stalin and Kamenev arrived. Under these conditions the Bolsheviks were less influential in the Soviets than either the Mensheviks or the Socialist Revolutionaries, although they controlled a significant minority of delegates in both the Petrograd and Moscow Soviets.

Between March and mid-April the Bolsheviks for the most part adhered to their pre-1914 programme. This was based on the demand for the overthrow of the tsarist monarchy, the calling of a

---

* The old Russian calendar was 13 days behind that of the rest of the world. Thus the March Revolution commenced in February (O.S.) and the November Revolution in October (O.S.).

Constituent Assembly for the drafting of a constitution for a democratic republic, universal suffrage, proportional representation, the secret ballot, freedom of speech, press and assembly. Like the programme of the other revolutionary parties the Bolshevik programme gave no special recognition to Soviets. The more conservative Bolsheviks led by Kamenev sought to re-unite with the Mensheviks and support the provisional government. Stalin, who had taken over the editorship of *Pravda* from the end of March, was somewhat uncertain of the situation but he did seem to realize that the old programme was not fully applicable and that the Bolsheviks should seek to build up the Soviets.[7]

This was the situation when Lenin returned and presented his *April Theses*.[8] In these theses Lenin emphasized the need to continue opposition to the war, even though it was now the provisional government and not the tsarist government which was leading the armies. He argued that the present situation was transitional as it represented a situation of dual power in which the provisional government was being challenged by the Soviets. He advised no support for the provisional government since it represented the middle classes and was opposed to the interests of the workers and peasants. The Bolsheviks should not aim at establishing a parliamentary republic but a republic of Soviets of Workers', Peasants' and Soldiers' Deputies. He further advocated the confiscation of the landed estates and land nationalization. This demand for a radical revision of party policy, first made on April 17, was not finally accepted by the Party until the Party Conference held at the end of April. By then the party membership had grown to 76,000 and the party was already beginning to challenge Menshevik and Socialist Revolutionary domination of the Soviets. On the basis of Lenin's theses the April Conference adopted the slogan 'All power to the Soviets'. However, this was adopted as a short range rather than as an immediate objective. It was not accepted as an immediate objective as the Bolsheviks were still only in a minority in the Soviets. Bolshevik strength was developing but mainly in the cities. Thus the Bolsheviks could secure three-quarters of the delegates to a Conference of Factory Committees held at Petrograd on June 12 but only 13% of the delegates to the First All-Russian Congress of Soviets (representing City Soviets, some Provincial Soviets and Army Soviets), which opened on June 16.[9]

The Bolsheviks suffered a temporary setback as a result of the failure of the July Insurrection. This is still sometimes regarded as an attempted Bolshevik seizure of power. However, there is little or no evidence to support this interpretation.[10] It was in fact a spontaneous demonstration which was inspired by Bolshevik policy and slogans but was not organized or led by the Bolsheviks. The Bolsheviks considered that any attempt to overthrow the provisional government was premature so they endeavoured to blunt the objective of the demonstration and to divert it into peaceful channels. However, the government acted quickly to isolate the insurrection. Troops broke up the demonstrations and cut off the workers' suburbs. The workers' organizations survived this suppression in a weakened form. Kerensky used his opportunity and launched a full-scale attack on the Bolsheviks who were accused of being traitors and German agents. Many leading Bolsheviks and their supporters were arrested and imprisoned. Others, including Lenin, went into hiding. The party had only a quasi-legal existence for several weeks following the July Insurrection. However, the revival occurred even before the Kornilov conspiracy in September. By the 7th Party Congress in August 1917 a membership of 240,000 was claimed, almost ten times that of March.

In a later analysis of the July Insurrection Trotsky wrote that:

The real mistake of our Party in July . . . was only this . . . that the Party still considered possible a peaceful development on the part of the Soviets. In reality the Mensheviks and the Socialist Revolutionaries had always tangled and bound themselves up by compromises with the bourgeoisie and the bourgeoisie had become so counter-revolutionary that there was no longer any use of talking about a peaceful development.[11]

If this was Trotsky's view at the time it coincided with Lenin's, as Lenin also drew the immediate conclusion that a peaceful development of the revolution was no longer possible.[12] However, it is incorrect to date the decision to organize an insurrection from as early as this. The revival of Bolshevik strength after August, the securing of a Bolshevik majority in the Petrograd Soviet in September and a near majority in the Moscow Soviet early in October led Lenin to revert to the policy of peaceful development. Although during the last week of September Lenin had argued that an uprising was necessary both in Petrograd and in Moscow if the revolution was to be saved from its internal and external enemies he had not attempted to plan the details of this uprising.[13] As late as October 9–10 Lenin wrote:

One does not know whether the Soviets can go further than the leaders of the Socialist Revolutionaries and Mensheviks and thus secure a peaceful development of the revolution, or whether they will continue to mark time, and thus render a proletarian uprising inevitable.
That one does not know.
It is our business to help in every possible way to secure a 'last' chance for a peaceful development of the revolution. We can help to bring this

about by expounding our programme, by explaining its general national character and its absolute harmony with the interests and demands of the absolute majority of the population.[14]

This programme was based on the following proposals: the complete exclusion of the bourgeoisie from the government (this involved the replacement of the provisional government); all power to the Soviets; peace; the confiscation of the landed estates, without compensation, and the land to the toilers; workers' control of industry; the suppression of bourgeois counter-revolutionary papers; and the peaceful development of the revolution towards socialism. Although this programme seemed to envisage no place for a Constituent Assembly there was no open repudiation of the demand for calling the Constituent Assembly.[15] To have made this repudiation specific at this stage would have lost some support for the Bolsheviks and would have accentuated divisions within the Central Committee.

Lenin's October 9–10 letter represented his last attachment to the course of a peaceful development of the revolution. Its timing was undoubtedly influenced by the current negotiations between the Bolsheviks, Mensheviks and Socialist Revolutionaries for a Democratic Conference, a kind of pre-conference to the Constituent Assembly. Lenin did not approve of this specific project but he still retained a small hope for a peaceful revolution. But by October 12 Lenin had reached a new appraisal of the situation. On that date he finally came to the conclusion that a 'revolutionary crisis' had matured and that the time was ripe for the overthrow of the provisional government by force and the seizure of power by the Soviets.

Why did Lenin come to the conclusion that the Bolsheviks must seize power? Although some highly fanciful reasons have been advanced to explain this[16] the reasons were fairly fully stated by Lenin himself. In his article 'The Crisis has Matured' (October 12, 1917) Lenin analysed the domestic and international situation and concluded that a modification of Bolshevik strategy was necessary. Various events such as troop mutinies in Germany and increased working-class opposition to the war in Western Europe led him to conclude that Europe was 'on the eve of a world-wide revolution'. He felt that the crucial point of the revolution had occurred in Russia. This was indicated by the developing peasant revolt in the provinces and by growing working-class militancy and increasing support for the Bolsheviks in the cities. Under these circumstances Lenin argued that if the Bolsheviks refused to take power they would be betraying both the Russian and the international revolution.

Once he took this decision in mid-October Lenin did not look back to earlier tactics. However, he still had to convince the Bolshevik leadership to accept his views. This was not easy since he was still in hiding in Finland. He threatened to resign if the Central Committee refused to organize the insurrection. The resignation was rejected but the Central Committee still avoided a decision. Lenin returned secretly to Russia on October 22 and the Central Committee by a 10–2 vote approved of his policy on October 23. Six days later an enlarged Central Committee endorsed this decision. The next day Kamenev and Zinoviev, who had opposed the decision at both meetings of the Central Committee, revealed it to Maxim Gorky, then the editor of an independent socialist paper *Novaya zhizn* (New Life). Gorky immediately publicized the Bolshevik plans for insurrection. Despite this Kerensky took a whole week to act and it was not until November 6 that he moved troops up to seize the Bolshevik press. The *Pravda* office was defended by a detachment of Red Guards, forces controlled by the Military Revolutionary Committee of the Petrograd Soviet. Following the successful defence of the *Pravda* office the Red Guards put the Bolshevik plans into execution and in the next twenty-four hours seized control of railway stations, post and telegraph offices, the State Bank and other key buildings. The only real resistance was provided by a group of military cadets and women auxiliaries occupying the Winter Palace and this was cut short by the shelling of the palace by the cruiser *Aurora*. By the time the Second All-Russian Congress of Soviets opened on November 7, the revolutionary forces were in full control of the capital. The revolution, at least in Petrograd, was almost bloodless. As the Bolsheviks had 51% of the delegates at the second Congress of Soviets there was no fear of the Congress refusing to endorse the revolution. In actual fact the Left Socialist Revolutionaries also supported the seizure of power and it was a very small minority of Menshevik and Right Socialist Revolutionary delegates who refused to approve of the dismissal of the provisional government and walked out of the Congress in protest. The Congress then declared the provisional government deposed and assumed power in its stead. It proposed immediate peace, the transfer of the landed estates to the peasantry, workers' control of industry, the early summoning of the Constituent Assembly, and guaranteed to all nations in Russia the right of self-determination.[17] The Congress immediately replaced the provisional government by another, the Council of People's Commissars, with Lenin as Chairman, Trotsky in charge of Foreign Affairs and Stalin of Nationalities. At the outset this government was entirely Bolshevik in complexion but before the end of November it was broadened to include some Left Socialist Revolutionaries.

REASONS FOR THE BOLSHEVIK SUCCESS

The Bolshevik Revolution succeeded because the Bolshevik leadership was more resolute than that of its opponents. Lenin's personal contribution to this success can hardly be exaggerated since without Lenin the Bolsheviks might well have missed the chance to seize power*. Lenin's timing was superb, for he selected the time at which the Bolshevik uprising had the maximum chance of success and when no effective outside intervention was possible.

An essential element in a 'revolutionary situation' for Lenin was the disintegration of the ruling class and its state structure.[18] This was clearly the situation in 1917. The tsarist government had been overthrown and the tsarist state structure disintegrated rapidly under the provisional government. Yet the provisional government neither fully eliminated the old state structure nor established a new one. The army in November was mostly far from the scene and in any case too uncertain in its loyalties to make it a ready weapon for the provisional government. Consequently Kerensky lacked the military force to use against the Bolsheviks.

The Bolsheviks had emerged as the main working-class party by early October and by the end of the month as a party with considerable peasant backing. While the Bolsheviks did not ever simply adopt the agrarian programme of the Socialist Revolutionaries[19] the similarity between their two programmes after April 1917 was very close and sections of the peasantry gradually shifted their allegiance to the Bolshevik policy.

The November Revolution was planned in an immediate sense but it was very different from the revolution the Bolsheviks had expected in earlier years. It was very different from the classical proletarian revolution which Marx and Engels had predicted. It was in fact a combination of two revolutions, a majority peasant revolution against the feudal–capitalist land system, and a minority working-class revolution. In its land programme and its immediate political programme the November Revolution was the completion of the bourgeois revolution initiated by the March events. It went beyond the limits of a bourgeois revolution when it replaced the provisional government by Soviet power and on that basis prepared for a rapid transition to socialism. Lenin realized the opportunity of combining these two separate revolutions into one revolutionary movement directed against the provisional government. But the decision to take the risk of insurrection was deeply influenced by his belief that a pro-

* Some historians dispute that either Lenin or Trotsky directed the seizure of power. Cf. Robert V. Daniels, 1964, pp. 78–82.

letarian revolution was imminent in Western Europe. Had he foreseen the failure of the latter it is by no means certain that he would have insisted on the urgency of the former.

NOTES

[1] G. Vernadsky, 1944, pp. 236–7.

[2] *Ibid.*, p. 241.

[3] 'The War and Russian Social-Democracy', October 1914. Lenin, *Selected Works*, 1944, Vol. 5, pp. 123–30.

[4] A. M. Pankratova, ed., 1948, Part III, p. 58.

[5] John Reed, 1935, p. 11.

[6] E. H. Carr, 1950, Vol. I, p. 205.

[7] Cf. Stalin's *Pravda* article, March 27(14), 1917, in which he urged that 'The revolutionary Social-Democrats must work to consolidate these Soviets, form them everywhere, and link them together under a Central Soviet of Workers' and Soldiers' Deputies as the organ of the revolutionary power of the people.' J. Stalin, *Works*, 1953, Vol. 3, p. 7.

[8] The *April Theses* were presented by Lenin on April 17, the day after his arrival in Petrograd, first to a meeting of Bolsheviks and then to a joint meeting of Bolsheviks and Mensheviks. These theses were published on April 20 as 'The Tasks of the Proletariat in the Present Revolution' (*Selected Works*, 1946, Vol. 6, pp. 21–26). A fuller and more careful statement of the theses was published April 23 as *The Tasks of the Proletariat in Our Revolution*.

[9] A. M. Pankratova, ed., 1948, Part III, p. 160.

[10] Cf. E. H. Carr, 1950, Vol. I, pp. 90–1; S. W. Page, 1959, pp. 51–4; L. Schapiro, 1960, pp. 166–7.

[11] L. D. Trotsky, 1932–33, Vol. 2, p. 79.

[12] Cf. Lenin 'On Slogans' (July 1917) in which he stated that the slogan 'All power to the Soviets', 'was a slogan for a peaceful development of the revolution, which was possible between March 12, and July 17, and which was, of course, most desirable, but which now is absolutely impossible.' *Selected Works*, 1946, Vol. 6, p. 168.

Cf. V. I. Nemtsova, 1957, pp. 37–8; S. W. Page, 1959, pp. 55–6.

[13] See in particular the two letters to the Central Committee, 'The Bolsheviks must assume Power', September 25–27, and 'Marxism and Insurrection', September 26–27, 1917. *Selected Works*, 1946, Vol. 6, pp. 213–23.

[14] *Selected Works*, 1946, Vol. 6, p. 241.

[15] Cf. *Selected Works*, 1946, Vol. 6, p. 241.

[16] Thus S. W. Page in *Lenin and the World Revolution*, 1959, p. 68, argues that, the key factor in Lenin's decision to seize power was his fear that the Germans would capture Petrograd and thus prevent him from exercising control over the revolution in Europe. This pseudo-psychological interpretation of Lenin's actions misses the mark as at no stage in 1917 did Lenin evince any belief in his ability to command the international proletarian revolution. Moreover, the threat to Petrograd was most serious early in September after the German capture of Riga (September 3), and yet Lenin did not fully abandon the strategy of peaceful development of the revolution until October 12. Lenin's references to Petrograd in the context of the insurrection are to be found in 'Marxism and Insurrection' (September 26–27), *Selected Works*, Vol. 6, pp. 221–2.

[17] Declaration to the Workers, Soldiers and Peasants. Printed in full in John Reed, 1935, pp. 109–10.

[18] Cf. Lenin's statement, April 27, 1920:

'In these circumstances we must not only ask ourselves whether the vanguard of the revolutionary class has been convinced, but also whether the historically effective forces of *all* classes—positively of all classes in the given society without exception—are aligned in such a way that the decisive battle has fully matured, in such a way that (1) all the class forces hostile to us have become sufficiently confused, are sufficiently at loggerheads with each other, have sufficiently weakened themselves in a struggle beyond their strength; that (2) all the vacillating, wavering, unstable, intermediate elements—the petty-bourgeoisie and the petty-bourgeois democrats as distinct from the bourgeoisie—have sufficiently disgraced themselves before the people, and have sufficiently disgraced themselves through their practical bankruptcy; and that (3) among the proletariat a mass mood in favour of supporting the most determined, unreservedly bold, revolutionary action against the bourgeoisie has arisen and begins to grow powerfully. Then indeed, revolution is ripe; then indeed, if we have correctly gauged all the conditions indicated above, briefly outlined above, if we have chosen the moment rightly, our victory is assured.' 'Left-Wing Communism, an infantile disorder', *Selected Works*, Vol. 10, pp. 137–8.

[19] Cf. Bertram D. Wolfe, 1956, p. 365;

'In mid-1917 it would be charged against him that he, suddenly "stole" the land programme of the Social Revolutionary Party; but those who made the changes were too short of memory. The programme on which the Social Revolutionaries claimed exclusive copyright was one of the related alternatives which he kept in mind from 1906 onward.'

Lenin's agrarian programme of April 1917 provided for confiscation of all landed estates and land nationalization, the land to be in charge of the local Peasants' Soviets. A provision of this programme was for the creation of model farms on the estates of the former landowners. This latter provision was not emphasized in October but it was implemented in the February 1918 land decree in the provision of various forms of collectives.

SELECTED BIBLIOGRAPHY

Carr, E. H., 1950–64, Vol. 1, Ch. 4.
Carr, E. H., 1969, Ch. 1.
Daniels, R. V., 1964, Ch. 4.
Fainsod, Merle, 1963a, Ch. 3.
Hill, C., 1947.
Kochan, L., 1966, Parts 2 and 3.
Page, S. W., 1959.
Ponomarev, B. N., ed., 1960, Ch. 7.
Rabinovitch, A., 1968.
Rigby, T. H., 1969, Ch. 1.
Saul, N. E., 1973.
Wolfe, B. D., 1969, Part 1, Ch. 1; Part 2.

Chapter 4

THE UNFINISHED REVOLUTION

REVOLUTIONARY STAGES

Revolution for the Marxist means more than the overthrow of the capitalist state. It involves the reconstruction of society on a socialist basis and the eventual transformation of socialism into communism. In this sense the revolution initiated by the Bolsheviks in November 1917 is still in progress. Even if the claim that the Soviet Union represents a society which is moving in the direction of communism be rejected it is still necessary to recognize that the Bolshevik revolution is a developing one. All writers agree that the revolution has passed through various phases and that the strategy and tactics of the Bolsheviks, if not their objectives, have changed. Furthermore, each phase has its own special economic and political structure, although unity and continuity throughout is provided by the Communist Party monopoly of leadership.

Although it is easy to recognize that the Bolshevik revolution has not stood still it is not easy to decide on how many stages it has passed through. The number of periods accepted depends on the criteria adopted for determining periodization; whether it is economic, social or political. Stalin recognized two phases in the development of the Soviet state up to 1936, the first from 1917 to the early 1930s he described as the period of 'the elimination of the exploiting classes'; the second phase he defined as 'the period from the elimination of the capitalist elements in town and country to the complete victory of the socialist economic system and the adoption of the new Constitution,'[1] i.e. roughly from 1931 to 1936. Such a classification was clearly based mainly on socio-economic factors, although it did not neglect political factors such as the balance of class forces and the political form of the state. In recent years Soviet writers have reopened this question and a wide disagreement exists between various writers on this matter. Until 1961 most Soviet writers accepted the elementary division of Soviet history into two main phases, although they quarrelled among themselves as to whether the dividing year between the two phases should be placed in 1931, 1933 or 1936. They also differed in how they subdivided these two main periods in the development of the Soviet state.[2] Since the 22nd Congress Soviet

53

writers have tended to recognize three periods in the development of the Soviet state. The third period, dating from 1956 or 1959, is regarded as marking the final victory of socialism within the Soviet Union and the commencement of full-scale Communist construction. In this stage the Soviet state has become 'the state of the whole people'.* Clearly the periodization of Soviet history depends largely on which factors are emphasized, especially on the relative weight given to basic economic factors on the one hand and to 'superstructural' factors (such as state structure, politics, law, etc.) on the other.

My own periodization, which is detailed in the following pages, is based mainly on changes in the economic basis. Political and other superstructural factors are used to assist in marking off smaller periods within the basic phases in the development of Soviet socialism. I would suggest that the following main phases and lesser periods can be conveniently recognized.

Phase 1: The Transition from Capitalism to Socialism

(1) The November Revolution and the foundation of the Socialist State. November 1917–July 1918.
(2) War Communism. July 1918–March 1921.
(3) The New Economic Policy. March 1921–1928.
(4) Socialist industrialization and collectivization of agriculture. 1929–36.

Phase 2: The Consolidation of Socialism

(1) The establishment of a new state structure. 1937–40.
(2) The War Period. 1940–September 1945.
(3) Post-war Reconstruction. 1945–52.
(4) Further development of the socialist system. 1953 onwards.

THE FOUNDATION OF THE SOVIET SOCIALIST STATE

The period from November 1917 to July 1918 was in a sense the 'honeymoon period' of the revolution. The Bolshevik revolution had succeeded on the basis of the growing militancy of workers and peasants. The successful overthrow of the provisional government strengthened popular backing for the Bolsheviks. This was clearly reflected in the broadening of the government at the end of November to include representatives of the Left Socialist Revolutionaries. Although this coalition was fractured in February–March 1918, largely through disagreements over the Brest-Litovsk Treaty, the coalition was not entirely shattered. Until July 1918 the Left Socialist Revo-

* Cf. F. Burlatsky, 1965, Ch. III.

54

lutionaries were represented in the Central Executive Committee (TsIK) to which the Council of People's Commissars (*Sovnarkom*) was responsible in between meetings of the larger All-Russian Congress of Soviets.

In January 1918 the Constituent Assembly finally met. The elections had been held in November 1917, during the first days of the Bolshevik revolution. The Bolsheviks received almost 25% of the vote (9,562,358) and 175 seats. This was much more than the Mensheviks and the Cadets secured but much less than the Socialist Revolutionaries. The latter secured 17,450,837 votes and 410 out of 707 seats, an absolute majority. However the Bolsheviks had no intention of surrendering power. They first excluded the Cadets. Then they attempted to get the Constituent Assembly to endorse the November Revolution. Although some Left Socialist Revolutionaries supported the Bolsheviks they failed to get a majority. Following this reverse the Bolsheviks and their allies withdrew from the Assembly. A few hours later red guards dispersed the Assembly. Lenin justified this action on the grounds that the elections did not accurately reflect the rural vote because the decisive split in the Socialist Revolutionary Party had taken place after the elections. He also claimed, more pertinently, that the Bolsheviks had clearly secured the largest vote of any party in all the main cities, including Petrograd and Moscow.* And for the Bolsheviks the support of the industrial proletariat meant more than the absence of a popular majority.

The dismissal of the Constituent Assembly marked the end of Russian liberalism for the Assembly was never reconvened and was quickly forgotten. The Assembly could hardly have had any other fate in 1918 for even if the Bolsheviks had been able to get it to endorse their revolution it would have had no future since it represented a redundant institution so far as the proletarian revolution was concerned.[3] If it ever had a chance of success it was during the provisional government and not after the Bolshevik revolution.

The chief concern of the Bolsheviks in this first period of the revolution was to retain power. This involved them in trying to consolidate support for the government, in destroying the remnants of the tsarist state, in building up new defensive organs for the revolutionary state, and in winning support for both the immediate programme and for the future policy of socialism. Although Lenin in his address to the Second Congress of Soviets on November 7 had declared that 'We shall now proceed to construct the socialist order,'[4] this could not be immediately realized. Actually, most of the first decrees of the Soviet government, as Trotsky later conceded,[5] were 'more

* In Petrograd the Bolsheviks secured 424,027 votes out of 942,333; in Moscow, 366,148 out of 764,763.

propaganda than actually administrative measures'. They were meant to secure the support of the masses in Russia and the sympathy of workers and oppressed nations throughout the world. In so far as they had any other value it was only that they expressed a goal, an objective that would be striven for when circumstances became favourable. Thus measures such as the Proclamation to the Peoples and Governments of all the Belligerent Nations (November 8, 1917) or the Decree establishing the eight-hour day and giving workers insurance at full wages for any length of time (November 12, 1917) could not possibly be implemented by the Soviet government.

Other decrees were often merely a legislative recognition of some action which had already been carried out by the masses. Thus the first decree on land (November 8, 1917) declared that private ownership of landed estates was ended but recognized peasant proprietorship. This merely recognized the situation at the time. Later, in February 1918, all land was declared nationalized, although it was left for the most part in the hands of the peasants. However, the seeds of future policy were discernible in the decision to set up *kolkhozy* (collective farms) on some former estates.

Many of the early decrees were passed to record the sweeping away of the structure of the old regime which the Provisional Government had not basically changed. Thus a decree of November 23, 1917, ended the old division of the population into estates and abolished titles. A decree of December 5, 1917, abolished the old courts and replaced them by the People's Courts. Similarly the tsarist police was replaced by the People's Militia, and early in December 1917 the *Cheka* (All-Russian Commission to Combat Counter Revolution and Sabotage) grew into the place vacated by the abolition of the *Okrana*. The Red Army was established on the basis of the decree of January 28, 1918.[6]

The economic policy of the government during this early period is sometimes taken as evidence of Lenin's syndicalist leaning at this period.[7] It would be more correct to regard it as a series of expedients, prompted by the necessity of meeting somehow or other a whole series of emergencies and influenced to a considerable degree by non-Leninist groups, including syndicalist trade unionists and Socialist Revolutionaries.[8] While ideology exerted a major influence on policy the ideology was more diversified and less unified than it became in later years. Many of the economic measures of this period were obviously emergency measures. Such measures as the state grain monopoly (May 1918), surplus appropriation of agricultural products, and the Workers and Peasants Inspectorate were limited to the first few years of the regime. Some measures, however, were more permanent, including the state monopoly of foreign trade, banking, large-scale industry, and the elements of economic planning developed even in these early years through such agencies as *Goelro* (State Commission for Electrification).

WAR COMMUNISM: JULY 1918–MARCH 1921

Although some of the special agencies and policies of War Communism date from before July 1918 it is convenient to date the period from then as it marks the elimination of the Socialist Revolutionaries from the government and the establishment of the Bolshevik monopoly of political power. The period was characterized by the tightening up of Bolshevik control through the extension of the Red Army, *Cheka*, and the reliance on revolutionary agencies such as the Workers and Peasants Inspectorate. Civil war and wars of intervention resulted in a considerable loss of territory and in uncertain control over many other regions. The war and the accompanying administrative disorganization resulted in a steady decline in both agricultural and industrial production in this period. By 1921 industrial production was only 31 %[9] of that of 1913 while coal production had sunk to 7 million tons in 1920. This industrial decline weakened the class basis of the revolution. Although more peasants joined the Party during this period the industrial working class dwindled. Many workers reverted to peasants, others were killed in the war, while others were absorbed into the growing administrative structure of the new state. By 1921 the industrial working class of Russia was only half that of 1913.[10]

During the first three or four years of the revolution almost every policy decision of the Party was preceded by a policy conflict both within and without the Party. This resulted from a number of factors. Firstly, the Bolshevik Party had no clearly worked-out plan for building socialism. Secondly, the circumstances in which the Bolshevik Party operated were exceedingly difficult and more difficult than had been expected before the seizure of power. This forced many modifications to policy, many postponements and compromises, and not all Party members were as flexible as Lenin. Thirdly, many members of the Bolshevik Party, and many of their supporters, were not fully in accord with Lenin's policies, and these non-Leninist views sometimes prevailed. The Bolsheviks did not have a monopoly of political power until July 1918 and for some years after this date remnants of rival revolutionary parties and policies constituted a challenge to the Bolshevik Party. The main opposition after 1918 came from organized factions within the Bolshevik Party, from Left-Communists, Workers' Opposition, and many smaller groups. Lenin's views on these opposition programmes are clear from

Left-Wing Communism: an infantile disorder (April 1920) and from other of his writings over this period. Trotsky, while not siding with any of the main opposition groups of this period, was often arguing a different policy to Lenin. This he did on the Brest-Litovsk Treaty in February–March 1918, on trade unions and on early industrial policy. The 10th Party Congress in March 1921 sought to prevent this internal disunity in the future by outlawing factions. The adoption of this decision was followed by the first major purge which resulted in almost one-fifth of the membership being expelled. Many supporters of the Left-Communists and Workers' Opposition as well as other critics of the new NEP line were excluded on this occasion. It is perhaps worth noting that all those who were to suffer in later years from the operation of this ban on factions, including Trotsky and Bukharin, gave it strong support in 1921.

THE NEW ECONOMIC POLICY: MARCH 1921-28

The New Economic Policy was introduced because of the economic exhaustion of the country and because of the growing opposition to the regime from both peasants and workers. This opposition reached a peak in March 1921 with the revolt of the naval garrison at Kronstadt, formerly a Bolshevik stronghold. The revolt and its suppression merely underlined the fact that the policy of War Communism could not be continued indefinitely. The initial policy change agreed to at the 10th Party Congress in March 1921 was to replace the method of surplus appropriation of grain by a tax in kind. Any grain produced above the tax could be freely consumed or marketed by the peasant. This policy change was quickly followed by other concessions to private industry, trade and agriculture, the general purpose of which was to stimulate economic recovery. Many old Bolsheviks found it difficult to accept such a retreat and a widespread purge followed the 10th Congress. However, the actual retreat was by no means complete. The Bolsheviks retained state power and in the following years regained a good deal of the support they had lost during the period of the Civil War. Although the urban 'nepmen' (the private traders and industrialists) recovered to some extent their economic position, they were denied the vote and consequently exerted only an indirect influence on politics. The peasants also had a diluted voting power throughout the entire period of the NEP and although complaints were frequently made about kulak domination of the Village Soviets they had very little direct power above the level of district government. Furthermore, the key economic positions such as banking, heavy industry, foreign trade, and transport remained state monopolies.

Some writers[11] maintain that the NEP period was a period of uncertain direction of policy, a period of doubt and vacillation. It is however easy to exaggerate the uncertainty of Bolshevik policy in this period. As early as the 11th Party Congress in March 1922 Lenin called for a halt to the retreat and demanded the development of co-operatives and state and collective farms as a means of checking the growth of capitalism in the countryside.[12] Lenin didn't abandon his pursuit of socialism although he did concede that it would take longer to develop in Russia than he had initially believed. Thus in one of his last articles, 'Better Fewer, but Better' (March 2, 1923) he emphasized the cultural backwardness of Russia and the necessity of overcoming it:

In order to rebuild our state apparatus we must at all costs set ourselves the task, first, of learning, second, of learning, and third, of learning, and then of testing what we have learnt so that it shall not remain a dead letter or a fashionable phrase. . . .[13]

He concluded by admitting that:

We too, lack sufficient civilisation to enable us to pass directly to Socialism, although we have the political requisites for this.[14]

In line with this emphasis the Bolshevik government concentrated in this period on elementary tasks such as the elimination of illiteracy. Literacy increased from 32% of the Russian population in 1920 to about 60% in 1928.[15]

Although Lenin and the Communist Party clearly accepted the NEP as nothing more than a temporary strategic retreat in 1921-22, the way out of this retreat was not at all clear, especially after Lenin's death (January 1924). Broadly speaking, only two courses were open for the economic development of Russia in this period. The first course represented the continuation of the policy of concessions to the kulaks. On the basis of further concessions agricultural production might increase so that the surplus could be exported to pay for the import of capital goods. The danger of this course was that it depended on the further development of capitalism in the countryside and on further class differentiation within the peasantry. This cut across the Communist policy of relying on the workers and poorer peasants and in any case the kulaks were not likely to prove steady supporters of the regime. As a solution to industrialization it seemed too slow as the kulaks demanded more industrial goods in return for grain sold and this meant that imports of capital equipment would need to be reduced in order to allow for increased consumer goods. Quite apart from this impact on imports, kulak demand would cause a concentration on the production of consumer goods by Russian industry and thus slow down the process of investment in capital goods industry. The political difficulties of this course were so obvious that none of the Party leaders fully supported it, although in 1924 Rykov and Kamenev and in 1928–29 Bukharin and others inclined towards this solution.

The second course favoured the proportional taxation of the peasantry to provide the funds for industrial expansion. The difficulty of this approach was the certainty that the kulaks would begin to restrict production if they were taxed too heavily. Sooner or later this policy would necessitate the reorganization of agriculture because quick industrialization could not be achieved without large-scale restriction of peasant consumption to provide funds for investment in capital goods industry and this involved some form of socialized agriculture because without it the process would be unmanageable and the proletarianization of the peasantry too slow. By 1927 this had become the majority policy for the solution of Russia's economic development.

SOCIALIST INDUSTRIALIZATION AND COLLECTIVIZATION OF AGRICULTURE, 1929–36

The basic policy decisions relating to industrialization and collectivization were not, as is sometimes held, taken in 1928–29, several years after they had been advocated by Trotsky. The basic decisions were taken in the middle of the NEP period in 1925–27.[16] The first of these basic policy decisions related to the priority of investment in capital goods industry in order to secure a more rapid development of capital goods industry than of consumer goods industry. This also involved the acceptance of the priority of the development of large-scale as against small-scale industry. Such a decision meant a reversal of the trends of 1922–25. In August 1925 the *Gosplan* (State Planning Commission) produced the 'Control Figures for the National Economy 1925–26', under which large-scale industry was to be developed at almost double the rate of small-scale industry and heavy or capital goods industry was to be developed more rapidly than other sections of industry. These proposals were accepted by the 14th Party Congress in December 1925.[17] This priority for capital goods industry operated from 1926 until the late 1960s. Although it was briefly and cautiously challenged by Malenkov in 1953–54 it was not finally abandoned until 1970.[18]

The second basic policy decision, that relating to the collectivization of agriculture, was in a sense predetermined. Lenin had pointed out that, 'As long as we live in a small peasant country there is a surer economic basis in Russia for capitalism than communism.'[19] The 11th Party Congress in March 1922 had decided to foster the

60

development of collective and state farms. In actual fact, however, they declined during the NEP period so that in 1927 state and collective farms supplied only 2% of agricultural products and 7% of market produce.[20] Clearly, a new assessment of the situation and a new policy was needed if the decline in collective agriculture was to be stopped. The decision favouring rapid industrialization which was taken in December 1925 necessitated a complementary decision on collectivization, but it was not taken immediately. That it was not taken immediately was partly because of the difficulty of openly challenging the established policy, because of the risks involved and because the inner-Party struggle prevented a fully rational consideration of the problem. Yet even more than these political factors the economic situation did not warrant the reversal of the New Economic Policy earlier than the end of 1927, nor was economic planning so advanced as to render it possible. 1927 was the first year in which the physical volume of industrial production exceeded 1913. The physical volume of industrial production reached 113% of the 1913 figure in 1927 and 132% by 1928.[21]

Agricultural recovery was fairly complete by 1927, production of grain as well as stock figures being well above 1916 figures.[22] The preliminary planning for the first Five-Year Plan was done in late 1927 so that to delay further the decision to collectivize meant to risk the failure of the first general plan for economic development. Finally, a considerable proportion of the grain supplied to the Red Army in 1924–28 came from the kulaks and this was considered a political risk which ought to be eliminated.[23] The decision to collectivize therefore accompanied the adoption of the general outlines of the first Five-Year Plan by the 15th Party Congress in December 1927.[24] However, the December 1927 decision merely favoured the rapid development of collective farms and the first Five-Year Plan set a modest target of 20% collectivization. The decision to accelerate the rate of collectivization (which of course grossly distorted the economic plan) was taken by Stalin late in 1929. The exact reasons for this decision are somewhat obscure and are still in dispute.* By January 20, 1930, 21·6% of peasant households were in collective farms. The figure had been raised to 55·6% by March 1, 1930. The following day, March 2, *Pravda* published Stalin's famous article 'Dizzy with Success'. This resulted in some temporary de-collectivization but not before the crash programme of forced collectivization had done the peasantry, Soviet agriculture and the Party incalculable harm.

Besides industrial and agricultural recovery another precondition

* For recent views on collectivization see Nicholas Spulber, 1964; Robert G. Wesson, 1963, Ch. 10; Alec Nove, 1964, pp. 17–66. See also the discussion in *Soviet Studies* January and April 1965, January 1966.

of the decision to fully implement the policies of rapid industrialization and collectivization was the existence of an adequate planning machinery and of a general economic plan. General economic plans had been advocated by Krasin in 1920 and by Trotsky in 1923, but until the end of the twenties the planning agencies (including both Gosplan and the Central Statistical Administration) were too inexpert to attempt the job of a general economic plan. Although some of the professional economists such as Strumilin favoured going beyond partial control of particular sectors of the economy to the production of a general plan, it was only in August 1925 that the first annual control figures for the national economy were produced and only in December 1927 that the first draft of a general Five-Year Plan was prepared and presented to the 15th Party Congress. After a fierce debate in which the right-wing put up alternative proposals in the form of a less ambitious two-year plan based mainly on agricultural development the Congress adopted the 'optimum' plan. The plan was officially launched on October 1, 1928, although it was not formally adopted by the Congress of Soviets until May 1929.[25]

The decisions favouring rapid industrialization were not taken simply because the Bolsheviks were determined to industrialize as industrialization was a precondition for the development of socialism. A rapidly expanding heavy industry was regarded as essential for the adequate defence of the revolution. This was fully accepted long before the Nazi Revolution in Germany, although that event gave it greater prominence in the objectives of Communist economic planning. Thus Stalin in his speech to a Conference of Industrial Managers, February 4, 1931, made this objective fully clear:

It is sometimes asked whether it is not possible to slow down the tempo somewhat, to put a check on the movement. No, comrades, it is not possible! On the contrary we must increase it as much as is within our powers and possibilities. This is dictated to us by our obligations to the workers and peasants of the USSR. It is dictated to us by our obligations to the working class of the whole world.

To slacken the tempo would mean falling behind. And those who fall behind get beaten. No, we refuse to be beaten! One feature of the history of old Russia was the continual beatings she suffered because of her backwardness. She was beaten by Mongol khans. She was beaten by the Turkish beys. She was beaten by the Swedish feudal lords. She was beaten by the Polish and Lithuanian gentry. She was beaten by the British and French capitalists. She was beaten by the Japanese barons. All beat her—because of her backwardness, political backwardness, industrial backwardness, agricultural backwardness. They beat her because to do so was profitable and could be done with impunity.

We are fifty to a hundred years behind the advanced countries. We must make good this distance in ten years. Either we do it or we shall go under.[26]

It was in fact ten years and a hundred and thirty-seven days from the day of that speech that the Germans launched their attack on the Soviet Union. That the Soviet Union did not go under was largely due to the forced industrialization of the previous decade.

THE CONSOLIDATION OF SOCIALISM

By the end of the second Five-Year Plan the USSR was, broadly speaking, socialist in the Marxist sense. That is to say the USSR was already by 1936-37 a society in which the main means of production and exchange were publicly owned and operated, in which exploiting classes had ceased to exist, in which political power was based on the working class and exercised by a socialist party, the Communist Party, and where the economy was operated on the basis of a general economic plan. In 1937 semi-socialist and socialist agriculture (collective and state farms) accounted for 98·5% of the value of agricultural production sold to the state. In 1924 it accounted for only 1·5%. Socialist and co-operative industry accounted for 99·8% of the value of all industrial production in 1937 compared with 76·3% in 1924.[27] The propertied classes of landlords, big and small bourgeoisie and kulaks had comprised 16·3% of the Russian population in 1913 but by 1937 they had been eliminated as classes. On the other hand workers and employees who had comprised 17% of the population in 1913 represented 36·2% of the population in 1937 while 57·9% of the population of the entire country belonged to collective farms.[28] By 1937 the second Five-Year Plan was nearing completion and the planning machinery, while not invariably efficient, had clearly demonstrated its capacity to direct the economic development of the country on the basis of the official economic plan.* This economic advance was most clearly recorded in heavy industry and power, as is shown from the accompanying table.

USSR Industrial Production: 1928-37

	1928	1937
Pig iron	3·3 million tons	14·5 million tons
Steel	4·3 ,, ,,	17·7 ,, ,,
Coal	35·5 ,, ,,	128·0 ,, ,,
Oil	11·6 ,, ,,	28·5 ,, ,,
Electrical power	5·0 milliard kWh.	36·2 milliard kWh.

(Source: *The USSR Economy: A Statistical Abstract.* USSR Council of Ministers, 1957, pp. 48, 55-8.)

* On the other hand many Western economists argue that the industrial advance of the early thirties owed little to economic planning. See in particular the comments by Herbert J. Ellison and J. L. H. Keep on the views of R. Schlesinger. *Soviet Studies*, January 1965, pp. 326-9; April, pp. 467-70.

THE ESTABLISHMENT OF THE NEW STATE STRUCTURE

The achievement of socialism in the economic and social structure is clearly recorded in Chapter 1 of the USSR Constitution adopted in 1936. The basic principles of economic planning are stated in Art. 11 of the Constitution and the powers and scope of the central government are set out in later articles. The new Constitution established universal suffrage and thus removed the restrictions on suffrage which had operated since 1918. It replaced the indirectly elected Congress of Soviets by a directly elected Supreme Soviet. It recognized a new structure of lower Soviets and a different relationship between the various levels of Soviets. It included a new and much more elaborate formulation of the basic rights of citizens.

The years 1937–39 were taken up with implementing the new constitution and with establishing its institutions. Thus the first elections to the USSR Supreme Soviet were held in December 1937, the first session of the Supreme Soviet was held in January 1938 and the first government under the new constitution appointed. The first elections to local Soviets under the new constitution were held in December 1939.

In another sense, however, the years 1937–39 represented a failure to implement the provisions of the new constitution, especially the sections dealing with the basic rights of citizens. For these were the years of the Great Purge which saw an increase in the police power and widespread use of arbitrary arrest and punishment of suspect citizens. Not only the Old Bolsheviks but a large percentage of Stalin's loyal supporters in the party were destroyed by the purge. Khrushchev testified in 1956 that more than 70% of the members of the Central Committee elected by the 17th Party Congress early in 1934 had disappeared by the time the next Congress assembled in March 1939. Indeed, after the Old Bolsheviks, the purge fell heaviest on the higher- and middle-level party cadres and government administrators. Altogether several millions of people were arrested, tried in camera and sentenced to exile, forced labour, or death during the Great Purge of 1936–38. In these years, and for many years afterwards, terror formed an integral element in the Soviet political system.

THE WAR PERIOD

Most Soviet writers recognize the Great Patriotic War as a definite period in the development of the Soviet system, dating the period from June 22, 1941, to September 2, 1945; i.e. from the German attack on the USSR to the unconditional surrender of Japan. However, from the political point of view it would be more accurate to date this period from the middle of 1940 to September 1945. The third Five-Year Plan was changed in mid-stream in 1940 to provide for a more rapid development of defence. Defence expenditure rose from 18·7% of the Soviet budget in 1938 to 32·6% in 1940. October 1940 saw the introduction of many wartime measures including the tightening up of labour discipline, the establishment of special trade and factory schools for the training of labour reserves, the extension of the working day from 7 to 8 hours and the extension of overtime, and the introduction of fees in the top three forms of the secondary school and in the university. On May 7, 1941, Stalin's leadership of the Soviet State received formal recognition when he became Chairman of the Council of People's Commissars, a position he held until his death twelve years later. The German attack was followed within days by the establishment of the State Defence Committee. This body, initially of five but later extended to eight persons, under the chairmanship of Stalin, acted as a sort of 'war cabinet' of the Soviet government during the years of the war.[29]

The impact of the war on the Soviet economy was soon felt in the dropping off of consumer production and the switch to war production. So successful was this move that the Soviet Union was able to supply the bulk of its war material,[30] despite heavy losses in the more industrialized western regions.

The precise importance of American, British and Canadian supplies to the Soviet war effort is impossible to establish. Since 1945 Russians have tended to underestimate it while some Western writers have exaggerated it. A. Rothstein (*A History of the U.S.S.R.*, 1950) accepts the Soviet official evaluation. Warren B. Walsh (*Russia and the Soviet Union*, 1958) scales this down but even so estimates that roughly four-fifths of the material used by the Red Army was Soviet made. However, he argues that qualitatively Western aid was more significant because it included materials and equipment which the Soviets lacked or had in inadequate quantities.

Although agricultural production also dropped off, especially in the western regions of the country, the Soviet also supplied the bulk of its food requirements during the war years, despite a severe civilian rationing which operated until 1947.

The war losses of the Soviet both in physical and in human terms were tremendous. Bulganin, in addressing the 20th Congress of the CPSU in February 1956 estimated that the war had retarded the Soviet Union by ten to eleven years in the realization of its basic economic objective of overhauling the West in *per capita* production.[31] Agriculture and industry suffered equally. One consequence of the war on Soviet agriculture was the weakening of the collective farm system. Although the system was not destroyed even in areas of German occupation the collective agriculture suffered at the expense of private peasant agriculture so that between 1942 and 1947 many collective farms had little more than a formal existence.

On the positive side, the war and consequent losses in the European parts of the USSR accentuated the agricultural and industrial development of the Urals, Siberia and the Far East. During the war four hundred and fifty-five major industrial enterprises were removed from the western regions to the Urals. They were not shifted back at the end of the war.[32] Similarly, the withdrawals of skilled men into the forces accelerated the entrance of women into agriculture, industry, government and administration, and into the professions. At the end of the war over 70 % of collective farm chairmen were women and although the percentage of women has dropped back in this and many other occupations it is still much higher than it was before the war. Today, women not only supply the majority of teachers and doctors but almost half of those with a completed tertiary education working in the USSR are women.

POST-WAR RECONSTRUCTION

The period of post-war reconstruction which all belligerent countries went through after the last war, was peculiarly trying and protracted in the USSR. This was mainly because of the amount of the war losses. These were estimated in September 1945 at 679,000 million roubles, or more than twice the 1945 State Budget.[33] However, the strain of post-war reconstruction was increased by the fact that the Party leadership set very high targets for this reconstruction drive. The objective was not merely to regain pre-war peaks of industrial and agricultural production. The objective was to surpass pre-war levels of production as quickly as possible and to reach a far higher level of production in order to reduce the gap between the levels of industrial production in the USSR and the capitalist world as soon as possible. Stalin, in speaking to his electorate on February 9, 1946,[34] suggested the following targets for industrial production over the next fifteen years;

Pig iron	50 million tons	
Steel	60	,, ,,
Coal	500	,, ,,
Oil	60	,, ,,

Such targets could only be met by continuing the higher rate of investment in capital goods industry, by continuing the wartime labour conditions (both the longer working day, overtime and strict discipline) into the post-war period, by the rapid increase in the size of the labour force, and by the rationalization and technical re-equipment of Soviet industry.

The realization was quicker and greater than the demand made in 1946. This is shown by the fact that the Soviet succeeded in abolishing food rationing in 1947 and by 1949 agricultural production was above pre-war figures. By June 1949 it was claimed that the average daily gross output of Soviet industry was 41% higher than in 1940. As for Stalin's targets, the extent to which they were realized is clear from the following table.

USSR: Industrial Production 1940–60

	1940	1950	1960
Pig iron	14·9 million tons	19·2 million tons	46·8 million tons
Steel	18·3 ,, ,,	27·3 ,, ,,	65·3 ,, ,,
Coal	165·9 ,, ,,	261·1 ,, ,,	513·0 ,, ,,
Oil	31·1 ,, ,,	37·9 ,, ,,	148·0 ,, ,,
Electricity	48·3 milliard kWh.	91·2 milliard kWh.	292·0 milliard kWh.

(Source: 1940 and 1950 figures from *The USSR Economy: A Statistical Abstract*. Lawrence & Wishart, 1957, p. 55.
1960 figures are from the Statement of the Central Statistical Administration, *Izvestia*, January 26, 1961.)

By 1950 Soviet capital goods industry was producing at 105% above 1940, while consumer goods industry was merely 23% above 1940.[35]

The post-war industrial expansion resulted in the development of many new industrial ministries. The total number of ministries (all-Union and Union-Republican) rose from 18 in 1936 to 59 in 1947, an increase mainly caused by the creation of new industrial ministries. Amalgamations reduced the number in 1949 but they stood at 51 in 1952.

FURTHER DEVELOPMENT OF THE SOCIALIST SYSTEM SINCE 1953

Since this matter will be treated in detail later in the book only a few general points need to be made at this stage. Firstly, agricultural development, which had been relatively neglected in the earlier years of industrialization, has secured more emphasis since the September 1953 plenum of the Central Committee of the CPSU. At first the main emphasis was on the crash programme of ploughing up marginal land in northern Kazakhstan and southern Siberia. Over 100 million acres of 'virgin land' was ploughed up between 1954 and 1960. While this expansion was going on a good deal of agricultural land in the Ukraine and central Russia passed out of cultivation. More recently fallowing and crop rotation, necessary to check soil erosion and to preserve fertility, have reduced the acreage of sown land in

Kazakhstan and Siberia. One consequence of the virgin lands campaign was the creation of over 400 new state farms. As early as 1958 it was claimed that 40% of the grain supplied to the state came from state farms, a much higher percentage than in the immediate postwar years.[36] The virgin lands campaign involved a vast increase in capital investment in agriculture. It was, however, insufficient and was reduced after 1958. Since the fall of Khrushchev (October 1964) several increases have been made to state investments in agriculture. The 8th Five-Year Plan adopted by the 23rd Party Congress in 1966 provided for a 25% increase in agricultural production over the previous five years and a state investment of 41,000 million roubles. Since 1963–64 agricultural policy has become steadier and less spectacular. The targets have become more moderate and the means more varied.

Secondly, industrial development has continued, although at a lower annual rate of expansion than in the early decades. The higher rate of expansion of capital than of consumer goods industry was continued until 1969. Only twice before that, in 1953–54 and in 1965 (when capital goods industry expanded by 8·7% and consumer goods industry by 8·5%)[37] did the rates of expansion become almost equal. The 9th Five-Year Plan, introduced early in 1971, provided for an expansion of the output of capital goods industry of 41–45% as against a 44–48% increase for consumer goods industry. According to one Western estimate,[38] Soviet industrial growth over the decade 1950–59 represented an increase of 136·6%. Soviet industry, especially since the middle of 1955 has stressed technical advance and automation, and many government agencies operate at all levels to promote this development. The industrial decentralization of 1957, which involved the dismantling of the centralized industrial ministries and the transfer of most of industry to the control of regional economic councils (sovnarkhozy) was expected to improve the rate of industrial growth. However it seems to have contributed substantially to the lowering of the rate of industrial growth. In 1965 the regional economic councils were abolished and the industrial ministries restored.

A third thing to notice about the USSR over recent years is that its economic strength and maturity is clearly reflected in its foreign aid programme. Since 1955 the Soviet Union has emerged as a lending nation which has offered large sums at low interest for the economic development of underdeveloped countries.[39] At the same time she has increased her assistance to allied socialist states in Eastern Europe and to China,* Mongolia and North Korea in Asia. The

---

* Assistance to China has been largely withdrawn since 1961.

greater confidence in Soviet foreign policy since 1955 is a reflection of its industrial maturity and especially of its technical ability to out-build its rivals in modern weapons. It is shown in the confident challenge made in 1957 that the USSR would quickly overtake the USA in *per capita* output in basic agricultural commodities and industrial products. The USSR overtook the USA in *per capita* production of butter in 1959 and in total production of milk, although not in *per capita* production. However, in 1959 Soviet meat production was only 42% that of the USA so that she still has considerable leeway to make up if her agricultural production is to match that of the USA. Khrushchev, speaking at Bhilai in India, in February 1960[40] confidently predicted that the USSR would overtake the USA in *per capita* production of main industrial products by 1970 or 1972. Although this claim was not realized there is no gainsaying the fact that the Soviet Union is rapidly overhauling the USA in the output of basic industries. A recent West German estimate was that the production of basic industries in the USSR represented 20·5% of USA production in 1950 and 41·4% of USA production in 1959.[41]

A fourth point to make is that the Soviet leaders since early 1959 have been claiming that the USSR is on the eve of the transition to communism.[42] It is argued that the economic maturing of the socialist economic system has provided the basis for achieving the material and technical foundation for Communist society. This is so because a pre-condition of communism is a plenitude of material consumer goods and this can be secured today. It was not possible simultaneously to drive for the rapid increase in capital goods and in consumer goods in earlier plans. In fact the Seven-Year Plan (1959–65) was the first economic plan to give strong emphasis to both objectives. The raising of communism as an early objective has stimulated a revival of discussion on the present and future role of the state. Although some writers have suggested its early withering the official line is one favouring its slow transformation from a coercive political agency into a non-coercive agency of social self-administration.[43]

Perhaps the best measure of the social changes and economic development of the Soviet Union since the Revolution is that provided by the last three censuses (1939, 1959 and 1970). Manual and office workers, who comprised 17% of the population in 1913 formed 52·5% in 1939, 68·3% in 1959 and 78·4% in 1970. Collective farmers who comprised 44·9% of the population in 1939 constituted only 31·4% in 1959 and 21·5% in 1970. Individual peasants and artisans constituted 66·7% of the population in 1913, 74·9% in 1928, 2·6% in 1939, 0·3% in 1959[44] and only 0·03% in 1970.[45]

The increasing urbanization of Soviet society is also reflected in the steady rise in the number of cities. In January 1970 there were 10 cities in the USSR with above one million inhabitants, 23 cities with between 500,000 and a million inhabitants and 188 cities with a population of between 100,000 and 500,000. In 1970,[46] 56% of the population was living in urban areas.[47]

A further indication of the rising cultural level of the Soviet population is provided by the growth of the Soviet intelligentsia. According to the census figures published on this matter the total number of persons who earned their living by mental labour rose from 11,791,800 in 1939 to 18,609,700 in 1959.* This represented 18·7% of the working population in 1959. Over this twenty-year period the number of Soviet engineers increased by 237%, draftsmen and surveyors by 186%, laboratory workers by 179%, technicians by 87%, doctors by 166%, academics by 184% and secondary school teachers by 68%. On the other hand the figures for the expansion of agricultural scientists and workers in trade and distribution clearly reflect the relative retardation of these branches of the Soviet economy in this period. Agricultural scientists (agronomists and zootechnicians) increased by only 58% over these twenty years, while workers in trade, catering, purchasing, supplying and selling agencies, increased by only 39%. Likewise the number of qualified lawyers of all sorts increased by only 26% while the number of top level public servants actually fell by 12%.† The crucial importance attached to developing health and education is shown by the fact that 9·9% of all persons employed in the Soviet Union in 1959 worked in these professions, compared with 5·9% in 1939.[48] The present composition of the Soviet intelligentsia into broad classes is shown in the accompanying table. The figures in this table are as revealing in their own way as those which show that the basic emphasis in employment in the Soviet Union today is still in agriculture, construction, industry and transport.[49] Fifty years after the November Revolution the civilian workforce of the USSR was divided fairly evenly between primary, secondary and tertiary sectors. Primary production (agriculture, fishing and forestry) claimed 29% of the workforce, secondary industry (including construction) 36%, and tertiary industry 35%.[50]

* The overall figure of 20·7 millions of persons 'occupied chiefly in mental labour' is given in the 1959 census figures (and 24·1 million in January 1964) but the occupational breakdown in the census covers only 18·6 millions. Possibly students have been included in the larger figure.

† Comparisons between the structure of the Soviet intelligentsia and the intelligentsia of Western states have rarely been published. An interesting comparison between the British and the Soviet workforce was made by Alec Nove some years ago. It has now been reprinted in *Was Stalin Really Necessary?* 1964, pp. 260–85.

Structure of the Soviet Intelligentsia*: 1939–59
Numbers in 1000s.

	1939	1959	1959 as %age of 1939
1. Heads of state depts., social organizations and their structural divisions	445·2	392·1	88
2. Chiefs of industrial enterprises and of their main divisions	757·0	955·2	126
3. Engineers and technicians	1,656·5	4,205·9	254
4. Agricultural scientists, veterinaries and forestry experts	294·9	477·2	162
5. Medical workers	679·6	1,702·5	251
6. Teachers and academics	1,553·1	2,835·6	183
7. Workers in literature and the press	58·0	104·1	179
8. Cultural workers	285·0	462·3	162
9. Art workers	143·3	190·6	133
10. Judiciary and Procuracy staffs	62·4	78·7	126
11. Communications workers	265·4	476·4	180
12. Workers in trade, public catering, purchasing, supplying, selling	1,626·1	2,268·2	139
13. Planning, accounting, and control personnel	3,102·0	3,501·9	113
14. Business correspondence personnel	484·4	535·9	110
15. Workers in municipal enterprises and repair services	202·5	277·1	137
16. Agents and forwarding agents	176·4	146·0	83
TOTAL	11,791·8	18,609·7	

* Intelligentsia here represented persons gainfully employed in intellectual labour and therefore students are excluded. (Source: Based on a section of the Statement of the Central Statistical Board of the USSR, published in *Voprosy ekonomiki*, January 1961, pp. 65–6.)

NOTES

[1] Report to the 18th Congress of the CPSU(B.), March 10, 1939. J. V. Stalin, 1945, pp. 636–7.

[2] L. G. Churchward, 'Contemporary Soviet Theory of the Soviet State', *Soviet Studies*, Vol. XII, No. 4, April 1961, pp. 404–19.

[3] Cf. V. I. Lenin in 'The Proletarian Revolution and the renegade Kautsky', *Selected Works*, 1946, Vol. 7, espec. pp. 152–60.

[4] Quoted in M. Fainsod, 1954, p. 84.

[5] L. D. Trotsky, 1932–3. Vol. 3, pp. 316–43 for Trotsky's review of the first decrees of The Soviet Government.

[6] M. Fainsod, *op. cit.*, p. 391.

[7] Cf. James Burnham, 1945, p. 178 *et seq.*

[8] S. V. Utechin in 'Bolsheviks and their Allies after 1917: The Ideological Pattern', *Soviet Studies*, Vol. X, October 1958, No. 2, pp. 113–35, identifies nine other important trends besides Leninism.

[9] *The USSR Economy: A Statistical Abstract*. USSR Council of Ministers Central Statistical Administration, 1957, p. 45.

[10] E. H. Carr, Vol. II, 1952, pp. 193–4.

[11] Cf. John Maynard, 1942, Book I, p. 149.

'The epoch of the New Economic Policy was therefore an epoch of doubt, vacillation, experiment, contradiction: of groping towards an uncertain goal: and also an epoch of material restoration, purchased by a partial surrender to the old Mammon. Seven years of deterioration were to be followed by seven years of recovery, before a leader could find courage to declare that the path of socialism was found, and to follow it, undeterred by the groans of those over whose bodies it passed.'

[12] Political Report of the C.C. to the 11th Congress of the R.C.P.(B.), March 27, 1922. *Selected Works*, Vol. 9, 1946, pp. 324–69.

[13] *Selected Works*, Vol. 9, p. 388.

[14] *Ibid.*, p. 400.

[15] The 1926 census showed 56·6% of the population aged 9–49 years literate. *Izvestia*, February 4, 1960.

[16] It is of course true that Stalin's collectivization policy of 1928–30 differed greatly from the 1927 decision. Cf. H. J. Ellison, 'The Decision to Collectivise Agriculture', *American Slavic & East European Review*, XX, April 1961, pp. 189–202.

[17] The most useful short account in English for the policy divisions at the 14th Congress is that by E. H. Carr in *Socialism in One Country 1924–1926* (Part Two), Vol. 6 of *A History of Soviet Russia*, 1959, Ch. 17.

[18] It was not openly challenged by Malenkov during 1953–55. Cf. his speech to the Supreme Soviet 8 August, 1953—G. M. Malenkov, 1953.

Malenkov, like Khrushchev in 1961, merely urged a faster rate for the expansion of consumer goods industry. Cf. N. S. Khrushchev, Speech to the Plenum of the C.C. of the CPSU, January 17, 1961. *Izvestia*, January 21, 1961.

[19] Quoted by Stalin in 'The Results of the First Five-Year Plan', January 7, 1933. *Problems of Leninism*, 1945, p. 399. The quotation is from Lenin's Report to the 8th Congress of Soviets, December 22, 1922. *Selected Works*, Vol. 8, pp. 247–78.

[20] J. Stalin, Report to the 15th Congress of the CPSU(B.), *Works*, Vol. 10, 1954, p. 314.

[21] *The USSR Economy: A Statistical Abstract*, 1957, p. 45.

[22] *Ibid.* Based on the table on p. 118, the number of cattle in 1928 was 111% that of 1916, pigs 112%, and sheep and goats 117%.

[23] Cf. Stalin, 'The Results of the First Five-Year Plan', January 7, 1933. *Problems of Leninism*, 1945, pp. 390–426.

[24] Cf. *A History of the Communist Party of the Soviet Union* (Bolsheviks). Authorized by the C.C. of the CPSU(B.), 1938. Current Book Distributors, Sydney, 1942, Ch. 10.

[25] The full details of the first Five-Year Plan were adopted by the 16th Party Conference in April 1929, and by the 5th All-Union Congress of Soviets in May 1929.

[26] J. Stalin, *Works*. 1955, Vol. 13, pp. 40–1.

[27] A. I. Kossoi, 1957, pp. 83–4.

[28] *The USSR Economy: A Statistical Abstract*, 1957, p. 19.

[29] As originally constituted this Committee consisted of Stalin, Molotov, Voroshilov, Malenkov and Beria. Later Kaganovich, Voznesensky and Mikoyan were added, and Bulganin replaced Voroshilov.

[30] A. Rothstein, 1950, pp. 323–4. Official Soviet statistics perhaps understate the contribution of American aid, especially in planes and transport.

[31] N. A. Bulganin, Report on Directives of the 20th Congress of the CPSU for the Sixth Five-Year Plan for the development of the USSR, 1956–1960. FLPH, Moscow, 1956, p. 16.

[32] V. M. Kosmennikov, 1958, p. 56.

[33] V. M. Molotov, 1949, p. 133.

[34] J. V. Stalin, Speech delivered at an Election Rally in Stalin Electoral Area. Moscow, February 9, 1946. Information Bulletin, Embassy of the USSR., Washington, D.C. March 1946, p. 14.

[35] Based on the table in *The USSR Economy: A Statistical Abstract*, 1957, p. 46.

[36] *Izvestia*, November 6, 1958.

[37] Based on figures given in *The USSR Economy: A Statistical Abstract*, 1957, pp. 46–7.

[38] F. Seton, 'Soviet Progress in Western Perspective', *Soviet Studies*, XII, October 1960, pp. 126–44. Statistics taken from p. 137.

[39] According to the *New York Times* (International Edition) October 23, 1960 Communist aid (mainly Soviet) to 15 neutral countries in Asia, the Middle East and Africa since 1955 amounted to $2,835 million. In 1962 the Soviet Union was rendering economic aid to 28 developing countries and building about 600 industrial enterprises and workshops, irrigation installations, railways, roads, ports, etc. Among these enterprises were 34 iron and steel and non-ferrous metal works, 12 collieries and ore mines, 20 chemical factories and oil refineries and over 45 engineering and metal-working plants. R. A. Ulyanovsky, 1965, p. 176.

[40] *Izvestia*, February 16, 1960.

[41] The estimate of the German Institute of Economic Research. Reported in Rolf Krengel: 'Soviet, American and West German Basic Industries: A Comparison'; *Soviet Studies*, XII, October 1960, pp. 113–25. Figures are for volume of gross production, p. 121.

[42] Cf. the speech by M. A. Suslov to the 21st Congress of the CPSU, January 30, 1959, in which he stated that; 'Socialism in our country has achieved such a degree of maturity, advantages have resulted of such magnitude and on such a scale that now the immediate task of our society has become the building of Communism.' *Izvestia*, January 31, 1959.

[43] F. Burlatsky, 1965, Chs. 4–6.

[44] Statement of the USSR Central Statistical Administration, published in *Voprosy ekonomiki*, No 1, 1961. Earlier figures from *The USSR Economy: A Statistical Abstract*, London, 1957.

[45] Figures for 1970 census are given in *Nar. kh. SSSR v 1969g.*, p. 30.

[46] Statistics on cities are taken from *O predvaritelnykh vsesoyuznoi perepisi naselenia 1970 godu*, Moscow, 1970, pp. 11–15.

[47] Statement of the USSR Central Statistical Administration, *Pravda*, April 17, 1971.

[48] Statement of the USSR Central Statistical Administration. *Voprosy ekonomiki*, No 1, 1961. Also published in booklet form as *Chislennost, sostav i r azmeshchenie naselenia SSSR*, Gosstatizdat, Moscow, 1961.

[49] Thus, in 1959, 38·8% of those engaged in material production were workers in construction, industry, transport and communications; 32·0% were collective farmers; and 6·7% were employed in state farms or other agricultural enterprises. Statement of the USSR Central Statistical Administration, *Voprosy ekonomiki*, No 1, 1961.

[50] *Nar. kh. SSSR v 1969g.*, p. 527.

SELECTED BIBLIOGRAPHY

Carr, E. H., 1969, Chs. 6–7.
Daniels R. V., 1964, Ch. 4.
Ellison, H. J., 1961.
Hutchings, R., 1971.
Lewin, M., 1968.
Macridis, R. C., and Ward, R. E., eds., 1963, pp. 453–72.
Meyer, A. G., 1960, Chs. 6, 8, 10.
Nove, A., 1964, Ch. 9, pp. 150–71.
Pethybridge, R. W., 1966.
Schlesinger, R., *Science & Society*, 1962.

Chapter 5

THE DEVELOPMENT
OF THE SOVIET STATE SYSTEM

CONTINUITY AND CHANGE

A characteristic of the Soviet State system since its inception has been its extreme structural fluidity. This fact is recorded in the separate constitutions of 1918, 1924 and 1936, as well as in the many amendments since 1936. This situation might be compared with other revolutions such as the Puritan Revolution in England which saw extreme variety in constitutional experiment over the years 1649–60, or with the French Revolution which produced new constitutions in 1791, 1793, 1795 and 1801. However, in the Soviet case there has been more continuity throughout these changes, the continuity being provided by the fact that the basic unit of government since November 1917 has been the Soviet, and the Communist Party has served as the continuing directing force throughout the entire period.

The official explanation of the changes in the Soviet Constitution since 1918 is that, 'In Soviet Constitutions we have the formal record and legal confirmation of socialist conquests won in the separate stages of the historical development of the Soviet State.'[1] The first constitutions of 1918–20 were adopted during the Civil War period when only the first steps towards the socialist reconstruction of society had been undertaken. The 1924 USSR Constitution was introduced after the Civil War and during the NEP period. It recorded the re-establishment of control by the central government over the outlying non-Russian regions. The Stalin Constitution of 1936 came after collectivization and towards the end of the second Five-Year Plan. It was thus held to confirm the victory of socialism in the USSR. The frequent amendments to the 1936 Constitution reflected either changes in the general circumstances confronting the Soviet government (e.g., War or Post-War Reconstruction), or the changing material basis of Soviet society. Thus over the four years 1957–60, 25 out of 152 articles of the Soviet Constitution (or 16% of the Constitution) were subjected to amendment, deletion or replacement.

THE THEORY OF SOVIETS

The basic governmental unit of the Soviet system is the Soviet. The Russian word *soviet* means council. The original Soviets were established by workers and peasants during the 1905 Revolution. These first Soviets were simply local Councils of workers' or peasants' delegates. They were 'spontaneous' creations of the masses and owed little or nothing to the conscious policy of any of the revolutionary parties. During the 1905 Revolution Lenin recognized the Soviets as important proletarian agencies to be used in the overthrow of the tsarist system. However, these first Soviets had all been suppressed by the beginning of 1906 and the experience left little obvious impression on either Bolshevik or Menshevik political theory.

In March 1917 the workers of Petrograd re-established their Soviet. The action was quickly copied by workers in other cities, by peasants and by revolutionary soldiers and sailors. Within a month of the outbreak of the March Revolution several hundreds of Soviets had been established. They remained essentially local organizations but moved towards a loose federation with the convening of the First All-Russian Congress of Soviets in June 1917. It was this rapid development of the Soviets which forced Lenin in his *Letters from Afar* and in the *April Theses* to re-evaluate the role of the Soviets in the proletarian revolution. By April 1917 Lenin had come to the conclusion that the Soviets must be made the main popular agency for the overthrow of the provisional government and the special form for the establishment of the dictatorship of the proletariat. This view became Bolshevik policy from the end of April 1917. The opening of the 2nd All-Russian Congress of Soviets coincided with the Bolshevik seizure of power in November and the revolutionary government established in the form of the Central Executive Committee (VTsIK) and the Council of People's Commissars (*Sovnarkom*) was directly based on the intricate structure of lower Soviets represented in the Congress of Soviets.

Bolshevik theory on Soviets was mainly formulated by Lenin during the years 1917–18. The dismissal of the Constituent Assembly in January 1918 increased the criticism by overseas socialist parties of the Bolshevik regime. Lenin in works such as *The Proletarian Revolution and the Renegade Kautsky* (November 1918) was forced to defend Bolshevik actions and in the process he argued strongly for the superiority of the Soviet over the parliamentary system of government. Stalin's *Foundations of Leninism* (April 1924) merely summarized Lenin's views on Soviets. Although minor modifications to this theory have been made since 1924 the basic theory as formulated over the years 1917–24 still stands.

The Communist theory of Soviets might be stated briefly as follows. First, the socialist revolution could be carried through only on the basis of the 'dictatorship of the proletariat'. The dictatorship of the proletariat Lenin defined in *The State and Revolution* as, 'the domination of the proletariat over the bourgeoisie, untrammelled by law and based on violence and enjoying the sympathy and support of the toiling and exploited masses'. Secondly, inasmuch as parliaments were considered 'bourgeois agencies' and Soviets 'proletarian agencies', the latter were to be made the basis of government during the dictatorship of the proletariat. Thus Stalin, in the *Foundations of Leninism*, argued that:

The Soviet power is a new form of state organization different in principle from the old bourgeois-democratic and parliamentary form—a new type of state, adapted, not to the task of exploiting and oppressing the masses, but to the task of completely emancipating them from all oppression and exploitation, to the tasks facing the dictatorship of the proletariat.
The republic of Soviets is thus the political form, so long sought and finally found, within the framework of which the economic emancipation of the proletariat and the complete victory of socialism is to be established.[2]

Finally, since the Soviets were considered to be based on the masses, the workers and peasants who constituted four-fifths of the population of Russia, they were regarded as being more democratic than any parliamentary regime, which notwithstanding liberal forms remained the agency of minority rule. Thus we are presented with the apparent paradox that the dictatorship of the proletariat is claimed to be the most democratic state in existence. Thus Lenin in *The Proletarian Revolution and the Renegade Kautsky* wrote that:

In Russia the bureaucratic apparatus has been completely smashed up, razed to the ground; the old judges have all been expelled, the bourgeois parliament has been dispersed—and *far more accessible* representation has been given to the workers and peasants; *their* Soviets have replaced the bureaucrats, or *their* Soviets now control the bureaucrats, and *their* Soviets now elect the judges. This fact alone is enough to cause all the oppressed classes to recognise the Soviet government, i.e., the present form of the dictatorship of the proletariat, as being a million times more democratic than the most democratic bourgeois republic.[3]

When this claim was made the Bolshevik Party already dominated the Soviet structure—Bolshevik delegates represented 61% of all delegates at the 3rd All-Russian Congress of Soviets in January 1918 and almost 97% of all delegates at the 6th All-Russian Congress of Soviets in November 1918.[4] Long before Stalin repeated this claim in April 1924,[5] the Soviet state bureaucracy had established considerable immunity from Soviet control. But the claim remained

77

unmodified—the Soviets were intrinsically democratic because they were agencies of the proletarian and peasant masses.

THE SOVIET STATE 1918-24

The first Russian Soviet Constitution was not adopted until July 1918, at the 5th All-Russian Congress of Soviets, more than eight months after the establishment of Soviet Russia. This constitution became the model for other Soviet Republics. Under this constitution the highest agency was the All-Russian Congress of Soviets. This was to be elected by Town Soviets on the basis of one deputy for every 25,000 workers and by Regional Congresses of rural Soviets on the basis of one deputy for each 125,000 inhabitants.[6] Thus two characteristic features of Soviet constitutions up to 1936, weighted representation of the proletariat and indirect elections, were established. The former device was defended on the ground that the proletariat was the leading class in the revolution, although numerically weaker than the peasantry. The latter practice was defended by Lenin in 1918 in these words:

The indirect elections to the non-local Soviets make it easier to hold Congresses of Soviets, they make the *entire* apparatus less costly, more flexible, more accessible to the workers and peasants at a time when life is seething and it is necessary to be able quickly to recall a deputy or to elect him to the general Congress of Soviets.[7]

The All-Russian Congress of Soviets held supreme state power but legislative and executive powers were shared by the Central Executive Committee (VTsIK), its Presidium and the Council of People's Commissars. Since the Central Executive Committee met only four times a year effective power was in the hands of the two smaller bodies. Although the Central Executive Committee was supposed to exercise legislative power when the Congress was not in session, the administrative agency *Sovnarkom* also acted as legislature, although its legislation consisted of decisions and orders and not of decrees or statutes.

The 1918 Constitution thus records a clear stage in the development of the complexity of the Soviet state structure. Although the system was still flexible in its provision for indirect elections, recall of deputies and unevenly spaced elections, it had become largely formalized. The original Soviets were local agencies but the term Soviet under the 1918 Constitution referred to a whole range of agencies. Thus there were local Soviets, Congresses of Soviets, and the government itself, the Council of People's Commissars, was also a Soviet. The complexity is increased with later constitutions. Because of this I shall for the remainder of this book translate the Russian word *sovet* by Soviet only when the institution is an elected representative agency. In other cases where the agency is one exercising delegated powers and is not an elected agency I shall use the English word council.

THE ESTABLISHMENT OF THE USSR

Although the Soviet form of political organization developed rapidly during 1918 and 1919 in most parts of the old Russian Empire there was no organic link formed between Russia and other Soviet Republics until after the Civil War during 1922–23. The Declaration of the Rights of the Peoples of Russia of November 15, 1917,[8] declared the equality of the peoples of Russia and their right to self-determination. On this basis the Ukrainian, Belorussian, Georgian and Armenian Soviet Republics were established during 1918–19 and recognized as independent. However, the experience of invasion by Germans and others soon brought about alliances between the various Soviet Republics. Thus the Ukrainian government in February 1919 issued a summons to all Soviet Republics to form 'a close defensive union against attempts of every sort to overthrow the worker-peasant authority established at the price of such heavy sacrifice'.[9] A military union was established between Russia and the Ukraine late in 1919 and with Azerbaidjan, Georgia and Armenia in 1920–21.

By the end of 1922 the desirability of forming a closer union of Soviet states had become clear. Although the immediate threat of foreign intervention had ended the danger was latent. The NEP required closer co-operation between the Soviet states in the economic sphere as well as in the spheres of defence and foreign policy. The Communist Party already existed as a centralized political organization throughout the entire Soviet territories. Under these circumstances the Party launched a unification campaign during 1922 and in October 1922 adopted a series of theses on unification. The First All-Union Congress of Soviets met at the end of December 1922 and established the USSR government, although the Constitution was not formally adopted until the 2nd All-Union Congress in January 1924.

This process of unification was far from peaceful. The main agencies throughout were the Communist Party and the Red Army. Thus the independent Georgian Menshevik government was overthrown in February 1921 by a combination of an uprising of local Bolsheviks and an invasion by the Red Army. Divisions occurred within the Central Committee between Stalin who favoured a unitary state with merely 'cultural autonomy' for national minorities, and Lenin who insisted on a multi-national federal state in which the constituent states would have the right of withdrawal from the federation.

Many Communist leaders in the transcaucasian states resisted the process of unification and were consequently purged. Late in 1922 the transcaucasian states of Georgia, Armenia and Azerbaidjan were forced into a Transcaucasian Federation which joined the USSR in 1923 as a single state. In this way Georgian nationalism was smothered, at least for the time being.

The structure of government established in 1924 was very similar to that of the earlier Russian Constitution. The highest Soviet body was the Congress of Soviets of the USSR. The Congress elected a bicameral Central Executive Committee which elected a Presidium and a Council of People's Commissars.

THE 1936 CONSTITUTION

By 1935 the USSR was well advanced in its second Five-Year Plan. Collectivization of agriculture had been virtually completed. The kulaks no longer existed as a class and the NEP private trading economy had almost disappeared. In February 1935 the Central Committee of the Communist Party directed that Molotov should recommend to the next Congress of Soviets of the USSR the formation of a new constitution which would acknowledge these changes. This decision was duly taken by the 7th Congress later in the same month. The Congress appointed a Constitutional Commission of 31 persons with Stalin as Chairman. In June 1936 the Commission published its draft of the new constitution. This was widely discussed in the USSR both in party and in public meetings and in the press. It was later claimed that 51·5 million people or 55% of the adult population participated in this public discussion.[10] This process of public debate produced 154,000 suggestions and amendments. Eventually forty-three of these were adopted. Most of the amendments adopted were verbal changes but they included a few of some importance, such as the direct election of the Soviet of Nationalities instead of the indirect election as suggested in the draft constitution. The new (Stalin) Constitution was adopted by the 8th Congress of Soviets of the USSR in December 1936 and the first elections under the new Constitution were held a year later in December 1937.

The main changes introduced by the 1936 Constitution were as follows. Firstly, universal suffrage replaced a system of restricted suffrage in which certain groups such as members of the former ruling class, priests, etc., were disfranchised. The principle of one man one vote was adopted and the earlier system of weighting the votes of workers was abolished. The secret ballot was also adopted.

Secondly, direct elections replaced the earlier system of indirect elections. Henceforth all Soviets from local Soviets right up to the

USSR Supreme Soviet were to be directly elected on the basis of single member electorates. This applied also in the Soviet of Nationalities. Thus at present each Union Republic is divided into 32 equal electoral districts for the Soviet of Nationalities, each Autonomous Republic into 11 equal electorates, and each Autonomous Province into 5 electorates. Each National Area returns one member to the Soviet of Nationalities.

Thirdly, a bi-cameral Supreme Soviet replaced the old Congress of Soviets of the USSR. Both chambers were to be directly elected on the basis of single member electorates. Both chambers were to be approximately equal in size and they were to have equal powers in all respects. The old Central Executive Committee was abolished but the Presidium and the Council of People's Commissars were to be retained. Both bodies were to be appointed by the Supreme Soviet.

Fourthly, the Constitution included an elaborate and expanded statement of democratic rights.* An entire chapter of the Constitution, Chapter 10, consisting of sixteen Articles, was taken up with democratic rights and duties. The Constitution guaranteed the right to work, the right to rest, the right to material security in old age and sickness, the right to education, equal rights to women, equal rights to all citizens, freedom of conscience, freedom of speech, press, assembly and meetings, processions and demonstrations, the right to political organization, the inviolability of the person, the inviolability of homes and correspondence and the right of asylum to foreign citizens. The obligations included the obligation to observe the Constitution and laws, the obligation to safeguard socialist property and the obligation to military service. Apart from the obvious emphasis on social rights rather than on conventional civil and legal rights, this section of the Constitution was interesting because it ostensibly provided concrete guarantees for each right. Thus the original Art. 121 was worded:

Art. 121. Citizens of the USSR have the right to education. This right is ensured by universal compulsory elementary education, free of charge, including higher education, by the system of state stipends for the overwhelming majority of students in higher schools, instruction in schools in the native language, and organization of free industrial, technical and agronomic education for the toilers at the factories, state farms, machine tractor stations and collective farms.

Finally, the 1936 Constitution differed from the earlier 1924 Constitution in that it contained an open recognition of the special role of the Communist Party in the government of the Soviet Union. This was covered by two articles, Art. 126 and Art. 141:

* See pp. 273–4 below for a brief discussion of the operation of this chapter of the Constitution.

Art. 126. In conformity with the interests of the working people, and in order to develop the organizational initiative and political activity of the masses of the people, citizens of the USSR are guaranteed the right to unite in public organizations, trade unions, co-operative societies, youth organizations, sport and defence organizations, cultural, technical and scientific societies; and the most active and politically conscious citizens in the ranks of the working class and other sections of the working people unite in the Communist Party of the Soviet Union (Bolsheviks), which is the vanguard of the working people in their struggle to strengthen and develop the socialist system and is the leading core of all organizations of the working people, both public and state.

Art. 141. The right to nominate candidates is secured to public organizations and societies of the working people: Communist Party organizations, trade unions, co-operatives, youth organizations, and cultural societies.

The new Soviet Constitution seemed to embody certain elements of parliamentary democracy—universal suffrage, direct elections, equal electoral districts, guarantees to individual rights, etc. Many writers in the West hailed it as a proof that the Soviet Union was moving towards a parliamentary system, which was a comforting thought to those who supported an alliance between the Western parliamentary states and the USSR against the Axis. Western writers up to the present have continued to suggest that an important reason for the introduction of the Constitution was the determination of the Soviet government to woo liberal opinion abroad and thus maximize the chances of its new foreign policy of collective security being adopted.[11] However, there is little evidence from Soviet sources to support such an interpretation. Stalin's Report on the Draft Constitution[12] emphasized that the new Constitution was introduced in order to make the political system consistent with the existing social and economic system, the chief features of which were summarized in the first chapter of the Constitution. The international significance of the new Constitution which he stressed was not that it represented any sort of *rapprochement* with liberal democracy but that it would stimulate the workers in other countries to follow the Soviet example.[13] The 1936 Constitution in fact meant no change in the traditional Soviet system of Communist Party government. On the contrary this was now openly acknowledged in the Constitution. If it represented any claim to greater democracy it was the claim to greater Soviet democracy and not to liberal democracy.[14]

AMENDMENTS TO THE 1936 CONSTITUTION

The Soviet Constitution is perhaps the most easily amended written constitution in the world. Art. 146 provided that the Constitution may be amended only by decision of the Supreme Soviet adopted by a majority of not less than two-thirds of the votes in each of its chambers. Since Communists have comprised more than two-thirds of the total number of deputies in each chamber since 1938 the necessary vote is not difficult to obtain. In fact many amendments are carried in the form of decrees of the Presidium and are already operative before they are ratified by vote of the Supreme Soviet. It is therefore not surprising to learn that in the first twenty years of its existence the USSR Supreme Soviet approved constitutional amendments at no fewer than twenty-three out of thirty-one sessions.[15] The majority of these amendments were concerned with the state structure (Chapter 2) or with the organs of state administration (Chapter 5). Until February 1957 the USSR Constitution not only enumerated the Union Republics (the constituent states) but also the Autonomous Republics, the Territories, Provinces and Autonomous Provinces, within the various Union Republics. Thus any changes in the internal boundaries due to the amalgamation of existing units, the creation of new units or the elevation of Autonomous Provinces to the higher status of Autonomous Republic required a constitutional amendment. The natural fluidity of the system was strengthened during the war years by the inclusion of new territories and the creation of new Union Republics. Thus in August 1940 the Constitution was amended to admit the 4 new Union Republics of Moldavia Latvia, Lithuania and Estonia. The new Republic of Moldavia was formed by the amalgamation of the Moldavian ASSR (formerly included in the Ukraine) with the territories of Bessarabia and northern Bukovina gained from Rumania.[16] When the Constitution was adopted in 1936 there were 11 Union Republics. By the end of 1940 there were 16 but since the absorption of the Karelo–Finnish Republic into the RSFSR as an Autonomous Republic in February 1956 there have been 15 Union Republics; the Russian Soviet Federative Socialist Republic; Ukraine, Belorussia and Moldavia; the 3 Baltic Republics (Latvia, Lithuania and Estonia); the 3 trans-Caucasian Republics (Georgia, Azerbaidjan and Armenia); and the 5 Central Asian Republics (Kazakhstan, Uzbekistan, Kirgizia, Tadjikistan and Turkmenia). There are at present (1973) 20 ASSRs of which 16 are in the RSFSR, 2 in Georgia, 1 in Uzbekistan and 1 in Azerbaidjan. There are 8 Autonomous Provinces, 5 in the RSFSR, and 1 each in Georgia, Azerbaidjan and Tadjikistan. There are 10 National Areas, all within the RSFSR. Since all administrative units based on the nationality principle excepting National Areas are still recorded in the Constitution we may expect more constitutional amendments to cover future re-groupings. However, since the transfer of the power of defining internal administrative divisions to the Union Republics (February 1957) these amendments are likely to be less frequent. Thus over the twenty-two years from 1936–57 the number of *oblasts* (provinces) increased from 34 to 121 and each addition required a constitutional amendment. From March 1957 to January 1964 the number of oblasts fell from 121 to 104 while the number of *krais* (territories) rose from 6 to 9* but none of these changes required constitutional amendments.

The exact size of the Supreme Soviet is not stated in the Constitution. However, Article 35 establishes the representation in the Soviet of Nationalities. The original draft of this article provided for each Union-Republic to have 10 representatives, each Autonomous Republic 5, each Autonomous Province 2 and each National Area 1. This was changed to provide enlarged representation of these units on the basis of 25† for each Union Republic, 11 for each ASSR, 5 for each Autonomous Province and 1 for each National Area.

Changes in the distribution of functions as between central and republican governments since 1944 have involved a number of changes to the Constitution, chiefly to Articles 14, 60, 77 and 78. Articles 77 and 78 have also been affected by the periodical re-groupings of Ministries which has occurred every few years since 1937. Thus the February 1944 extension to the Union Republics of the right to conduct their own foreign relations, to control their armies and defence, resulted in the addition of two new articles, Articles 14a and 14b. The transfer of several Ministries from an All-Union to a Union-Republican basis in May 1956 involved the amendment of Articles 77 and 78. The reorganization of industry in May 1957 and the establishment of the *sovnarkhozy* (Regional Economic Councils) involved further amendments to the same articles. Over the twenty years 1938–57 Article 77 was amended at 18 sessions of the Supreme Soviet, while Article 78 was amended at 15 sessions.[17] In the three years 1958–60 Article 77 was amended at two sessions of the Supreme Soviet and Article 78 at three sessions. The thoroughgoing reorganization of Soviet industry approved by the Supreme Soviet on May 10, 1957, necessitated amendments not merely to Articles 77 and 78 but to Articles 14, 60, 68, 69, 70, 82 and 83, and the addition of a new article, Article 88a.[18] Further changes consequent on the May 1957 law resulted in further amendments to articles 70, 77 and 78, and the insertion of a new article, Article 88b.[19] The restoration of industrial ministries resulted in new texts for Articles 70, 77 and 78, in October 1965. A change in nomenclature adopted in March 1946—the adoption of the name Council of Ministers in place of Council of People's Commissars—resulted in amendments to more than a score of articles.

* Reduced to 7 in November 1964.
† Changed to 32 in March 1966.

Chapter 10, which deals with the Fundamental Rights and Duties of Citizens, has seen less frequent alteration. In fact, only three articles in this Chapter, Article 119, 121 and 122, have been amended. The extension of the normal working day from 7 to 8 hours and the adoption of a 7-day working week in June 1940 meant that for a number of years the constitutional-guarantee of a 7-hour day was disregarded. Article 119 was amended in February 1947 to provide a working day of 8 hours. In May 1960,[20] Article 119 was again amended to record the reduction of the working day to 7 hours and to 6 hours for those with arduous work conditions.

In October 1940 the government introduced fees for the higher grades (8–10) of secondary schools and also for universities. Although this involved a departure from the constitutional guarantee of free education at all levels (Article 121), the Constitution was not amended until February 1947. The reorganization of the education system in December 1958[21] which provided for the extension of compulsory primary education from 7 to 8 years and for a variety of ways of completing secondary education, was accompanied by amendments to Article 121. As amended in December 1958 Article 121 then read:

Art. 121. Citizens of the USSR have the right to education. This right is ensured by universal, compulsory, eight-year education; by the wide development of secondary general polytechnical education, by professional-technical education, by secondary specialist and higher education on the basis of the connection of training with life and production; by the all-round development of evening and correspondence courses, all types of schools being conducted in the native language, by organization in the factories, state farms and collective farms of free vocational, technical and agronomic training for workers.

Article 122 was amended in February 1947 to take account of the recently adopted system of state aid to mothers of large families and to unmarried mothers.[22]

A NEW CONSTITUTION?

The need to bring the Soviet Constitution up to date was stressed by Khrushchev in his report to the 21st Congress in January 1959.[23] Khrushchev pointed out that the existing Constitution had been drafted over twenty years ago when the socialist economy was much less developed and when socialism existed only in the one country. Since the 21st Congress various articles have appeared in the Soviet press suggesting specific alterations to the text of the Soviet Constitution. Several writers have emphasized the need to amend articles in Chapter 1. As this chapter now stands it makes no allowance for new forms of property relations, such as inter-kolkhoz and state-kolkhoz enterprises.[24] It has also been suggested that the Constitution would be improved by the inclusion of a clear statement of the aim and purpose of the socialist state—i.e. the building of a communist society, and also of the means of realizing such an objective.[25] The Constitution should also take recognition of the fact that the USSR is building communism not in isolation but in alliance with other socialist countries. Recent changes in the basic rights of citizens, the rapid development of agencies of self-administration, etc., also seem to warrant changes in the Constitution.

In April 1962 the USSR Supreme Soviet elected a Constitutional Commission of ninety-seven persons under the Chairmanship of N.S. Khrushchev to prepare a new constitution. For two years very little was said in public about the work of this Commission. Despite some rumours that the draft Constitution would be brought down late in 1963 nothing materialized. A meeting of the Constitutional Commission held on July 16, 1964 at the conclusion of a session of the USSR Supreme Soviet was reported in *Izvestia* and other Soviet papers. This meeting heard reports from Khrushchev as well as from the Chairmen of a number of sub-commissions, including reports by Brezhnev, Kosygin and Mikoyan. Unfortunately the newspaper report did not give a clear indication of the substance of any of these reports. In view of the subsequent confirmation of the existence of differences within the leadership it seems reasonable to suppose that these differences affected the work of the Commission and prevented it from reaching agreement on a draft of the new Constitution. In due course the Supreme Soviet when it met in December 1964 replaced Khrushchev by Brezhnev as Chairman of the Constitutional Commission.

On the occasion of the 50th anniversary of the formation of the USSR in December 1972 it was announced that the draft text of the new Constitution would be presented to the next Party Congress, due to meet early in 1976.[26]

NOTES

[1] A. Y. Vyshinsky, 1948, p. 87.

[2] J. Stalin, 1945, pp. 47–8.

[3] V. I. Lenin, *Selected Works*, Vol. 7, 1946, p. 136.

[4] *Ibid.*, p. 160 and FN, p. 194.

[5] J. Stalin, *op. cit.*, p. 48.

[6] The full text of the Constitution is printed in *Source Book on European Governments*, Van Nostrand, N.Y., 1937, Part V, pp. 67–87.

[7] V. I. Lenin, *Selected Works*, Vol. 7, p. 135.

[8] The text is printed in Van Nostrand, *op. cit.*, Part V, pp. 60–2.

[9] A. Y. Vyshinsky, *op. cit.*, p. 243. The fullest and best account of this process available in English is that in E. H. Carr, Volume I, Chs. 10–14.

[10] *Voprosy sovetskovo gosudarstva i prava 1917–1957*, Akad. Nauk SSSR, Moscow 1957, p. 195.

[11] For example, Herbert McClosky and John E. Turner, 1960, p. 292; L. Schapiro, 1960, pp. 407–8; K. Zilliacus, 1949, p. 64.

[12] J. Stalin, *op cit.*, pp. 540–68.

[13] J. Stalin, *op. cit.*, p. 567.

[14] *Ibid.*, pp. 550–1. Cf. also R. Schlesinger, 1945, pp. 219–20.

[15] *Voprosy sovetskovo gosudarstvennovo prava*, Akad. Nauk SSSR, Moscow 1959, p. 107.

[16] *Voprosy sovetskovo gosudarstva i prava 1917–1957*, Akad. Nauk SSSR, Moscow, 1957, pp. 201–2.

[17] *Voprosy sovetskovo gosudarstvennovo prava*. Akad. Nauk SSSR, Moscow, 1959, p. 127.

[18] These amendments were all carried in May 1957.

[19] Added December 1960.

[20] In May 1960 the Supreme Soviet passed a law which provided for the transition of all workers to a seven- or six-hour working day during 1960. *Izvestia*, May 8, 1960.

[21] Law on the Strengthening of the Connection of Schools with Life and on the Further Development of Public Education in the USSR. *Izvestia*, December 25, 1958.

[22] Decree of the Presidium of the USSR Supreme Soviet, July 8, 1944.

[23] N. S. Khrushchev, Control Figures for the Economic Development of the U.S.S.R. for 1959–1965, January 27, 1959, FLPH, Moscow, 1959, pp. 146–7; 'Comrades, now that our country has entered a new and momentous stage in its development, the time is ripe for introducing certain amendments and addenda to the Constitution of the U.S.S.R. More than twenty years have elapsed since its adoption, years crowded with events of epochal significance. Socialism has emerged from the framework of one country to become a powerful world system. Important changes have taken place in the political and economic life of the Soviet Union. The building of communist society has become the immediate and practical goal of the Party and the people. All these sweeping changes in the life of the country and in the international situation should find expression and legislative embodiment in the Constitution of the Soviet Union, the Fundamental Law of the state.'

[24] For example V. Kotok and D. Gaidukov, 'A New Stage in the Development of the Soviet State and Constitution of the U.S.S.R.', *Sovety*, No 8, 1959, pp. 21–6.

[25] *Ibid.*, p. 25.

[26] Speech by L. I. Brezhnev at the joint meeting of the Central Committee of the CPSU and the Supreme Soviets of the USSR and the RSFSR, December 21, 1972. *Pravda*, December 22, 1972.

SELECTED BIBLIOGRAPHY

Denisov and Kirichenko, 1960, Chs. 7, 11.
Fainsod, M., 1963a, Ch. 11.
Pipes, R., 1968, rev. edn.
Schlesinger, R., 1945, pp. 219–32.
Stalin, J. V., 1945, pp. 540–68.

Chapter 6

THE THEORY OF THE SOVIET STATE

BASIS OF THE THEORY

Soviet explanations about the nature of the Soviet state are founded on the Marxist theory of the state. The original Marxist theory of the state contained three essential propositions. In the first place the state was regarded as an agency for the mediation of class conflicts in the name of society though not necessarily in the interests of society as a whole. Thus Engels wrote in 1884 that 'the state arose from the need to keep class antagonisms in check'.[1] Secondly, the state was regarded as an agency or machine for the oppression of one class by another. Engels stated that 'the state arose in the thick of the fight between classes', and that it was 'normally the state of the most powerful, economically ruling class'.[2] The relationship between these two propositions was not always stated with consistency. Engels, in *The Origin of the Family, Private Property and the State* (1884) conceded that in 'exceptional periods', when the warring classes were nearly equal in forces, the state might act as an 'apparent mediator' and acquire 'for a moment a certain independence in relation to both'. This, he said, applied to the absolute monarchy of the seventeenth and eighteenth centuries which balanced the nobility against the bourgeoisie, and to the Bonapartist Empires which balanced the bourgeoisie against the proletariat. However, the state was more often seen as an agency of the ruling economic class. Thus Engels wrote in 1892 that 'the state was an official representative of society as a whole: the gathering of it together into a visible embodiment. But it was this only in so far as it was the state of that class which itself represented, for the time being, society as a whole; in ancient times the state of the slave-owning citizens, in the middle ages the feudal lords; in our time, the bourgeoisie.'[3] Lenin, in *The State and Revolution* (completed in September 1917) ignored this qualification and regarded the state as purely 'an organ of class rule, an organ for the oppression of one class by another'.[4] On this point both Stalin and his heirs have followed Lenin. Thus the 1958 edition of the *Soviet*

Political Dictionary defines the state simply as 'the political organization of society, the organ of the dictatorship of the economically dominant class'.[5]

The third of the essential Marxist propositions about the state is that it is regarded as a temporary phenomenon. Since it arose with the emergence of class divisions in society it will disappear with the final abolition of classes. The state, as an agency of oppression, will eventually wither away, although various non-coercive social organizations will remain. A crucial question here is that of when does the withering away process begin. This was a purely speculative question for Marx and Engels but it clearly had some direct political significance to Lenin and the Bolshevik Party after the November Revolution. On the eve of this revolution (in *The State and Revolution*) Lenin conceded that the withering away of the state would be 'a rather lengthy process' and that it would not be completed until the higher stage of socialist society, communism, had been achieved. Here he followed Marx and Engels. At the same time Lenin in September 1917 clearly underestimated the complexity of the proletarian state structure. Thus he wrote that:

The exploiters were naturally unable to suppress the people without a very complex machine for performing this task but *the people* can suppress the exploiters even with a very simple 'machine', almost without a 'machine', without a special apparatus, by the simple *organisation* of the armed masses....[6]

This view was rapidly modified by Lenin when confronted with the necessity of organizing a complex proletarian state to defend and extend the revolution. This positive role of the proletarian state during the transition from capitalism to socialism and eventual communism was given even greater stress by Stalin.

STALIN'S THEORY

The fullest statement of Stalin's theory of the Soviet state is contained in his report to the 18th Congress of the CPSU in March 1939.[7] This statement was undoubtedly provoked not merely by speculation within the party on the question of the withering away of the state (prompted by the 1936 announcement that socialism had been achieved), but by a recognition of the need to provide some rationalization for the obvious increase in the coercive role of the Soviet state during the period of the purges.

Stalin accepted Engels' forecast that the state would wither away under socialism, when there was no longer any class to be held in subjection, but he held that Engels had not considered the possibility

89

of socialism being established in one country ahead of others. Since the Soviet socialist state existed within a circle of capitalist states the Soviet state could not be expected to wither away. The prime reason for the continuation of the state under socialism was the need to defend the achievements of socialism from foreign attack. In fact, the state would remain even under communism 'unless the danger of foreign military attack has disappeared'.

However, while the state remained under socialism and would perhaps remain under communism, the form of the state was changing and would continue to change in line with the development of Soviet society and with changes in the international situation. Stalin considered that the Soviet state had passed through two main phases in its development since 1917. The first phase he defined as 'the period from the October Revolution to the elimination of the exploiting classes', i.e. apparently to 1931. The second phase he defined as 'the period from the elimination of the capitalist elements in town and country to the complete victory of the socialist economic system and the adoption of the new Constitution',[8] i.e. from 1931 to 1936–38. The main functions of the Soviet state in the first phase were stated to be three, the suppression of the overthrown classes within the country, the defence of the country from foreign attack, and the beginning of the work of economic organization and cultural education. However, the third function was poorly developed in this period. The principal tasks of the Soviet state in the second phase were said to be four; the establishment of the socialist economic system all over the country and the elimination of the last remnants of the capitalist system; the protection of socialist property largely replaced the earlier function of class suppression; the function of defending the country from external attack was fully maintained; and finally, the function of economic organization and cultural education remained and became fully developed. Stalin considered that this final function had become the main internal function of the Soviet state since he declared that:

Now the main task of the state inside the country is the work of peaceful economic organization and cultural education. As for our army, punitive organs and intelligence service, their edge is no longer turned to the inside of the country but to the outside against external enemies.[9]

Stalin's theory of the Soviet state as expounded in the years 1933–39 was not seriously challenged inside the Soviet Union in his lifetime. The inflexibility of Stalin's thinking in his closing years is reflected in his re-affirmation in 1950 of his 1939 explanation of the survival of the Soviet state being conditioned by the capitalist encirclement of the USSR.[10] The concepts of 'socialism in one country' and 'capitalist encirclement', which were clearly inexact descriptions of post-war international relations, were never explicitly revised by Stalin, although in a sense the Zhdanov Report on the International Situation (September 1947)[11] and Stalin's *Economic Problems of Socialism in the U.S.S.R.* (1952) provided the basis for the further revaluation of situation and theory which was carried out at the 20th Congress in 1956. It was an appreciation of such facts as that 'the socialist sixth' had become 'the socialist third', that socialism had expanded beyond a single country into an alliance of socialist states, that imperialism was on the retreat in the Colonial World, which enabled the leadership at the 20th Congress to introduce certain modifications into Stalinist ideology. Perhaps because of this the revisions which were made at this Congress were in the fields of international relations and revolutionary strategy rather than directly on the theory of the state.[12]

REVISIONS TO STALIN'S THEORY

Criticism of Stalin's theory of the state was not initiated by the 20th Congress although it was undoubtedly stimulated by it. The criticism has also gained something from the limited revival of empirical studies in the sphere of government as such studies have served to bring out some of the more obvious deficiencies of Stalin's over-schematic picture of the Soviet state. The theory is being currently re-examined at three points: the class basis of the Soviet state, the periodization of the Soviet state and its functions in the various stages of development; and the role of the socialist state in the transition to communism. The limits of this theoretical revision will become clear as we summarize the main arguments of recent years on each of these questions.

The question of the class basis of Soviet society has not been directly re-examined but it has been partially discussed in at least two contexts. The first of these was an extended discussion among Soviet philosophers in the journal *Voprosy filosofii* mainly over the years 1955–56.[13] The controversy was conducted in highly philosophical, almost metaphysical terms, but some at least of the writers[14] argued, in contrast to Stalin, that there were elements of antagonistic contradiction (i.e. of class struggle) still operating in Soviet society. However no Soviet writer has openly admitted, as has Mao Tse-tung,[15] the possibility of contradictions operating between government and people under socialism because it is universally asserted that both the Communist Party and the Soviet state represent the interests of the whole of Soviet society.[16] By the same token the existence of a peasant class (*kolkhozniki*) separate from the working class does not warrant the existence of a separate agrarian party. The second context in which the class basis of Soviet society has been referred to is in the development of the 1956 criticism of Stalin's thesis that the class struggle must necessarily become more intense with the further development of socialism.[17] Academics following in the wake of official criticism have insisted on some revaluation of the past and future functions of the Soviet state.

Direct discussion of the development and functions of the Soviet state reached its peak in 1958–59. One of the first writers to grapple with this problem was M. I. Piskotin whose article, *Concerning the Question of the Functions of the Soviet State in the Present Period*, appeared in the journal *Sovetskoe gosudarstvo i pravo* in January 1958. Piskotin argued that Stalin's 1939 statement on the basic functions of the Soviet state required a more detailed formulation based not merely on the nature of the Soviet state but on the actual functions of the existing state at its various administrative levels. The same critical approach was taken by other writers. The result was not one but a whole series of revisions to Stalin's periodization of the Soviet state. All Soviet writers continued to operate within the framework of two stages in the development of the Soviet state but there was no longer any agreement on the dividing line between the two periods or on the recognizable stages within each period.[18]

The problem of the functions and the development of the Soviet state was one of the subjects reported on at the Conference of the Social Sciences Section of the USSR Academy of Sciences in Moscow, June 23–26, 1958. The main report on the subject was given by R. S. Romashkin,[19] then Director of the Law Institute of the Academy of Sciences. Romashkin's concern was with the two main phases of its development rather than with periodization within these phases, and with the functions of the Soviet state during the transition to communism. He criticized Stalin for underestimating the importance of the economic-organizational and the cultural-educational functions of the Soviet state during its first phase and for his omission of the function of the defence of socialist legality and individual citizen rights in both phases. He also considered that Stalin's formulations on the foreign policy function of the Soviet state in both phases were incomplete, since in the first phase it was concerned with maintaining the peaceful coexistence of socialism and capitalism as well as with the defence of the USSR, while in the second phase it was concerned with strengthening the friendship and fraternal co-operation between countries of the socialist camp and with improving relations with capitalist states. Other speakers at this Conference expressed rather different views on the problem, thus underlining the fact that there is no longer any clearly defined official line on these matters. The particular criticisms made of Stalin's theory in this controversy clearly reflect the stimulus of doctrinal corrections begun at the 20th Congress. However, they equally reflect the recognition of elements in the objective situation which Stalin's formulations ignored.

The role of the state in the transition to communism was merely a matter for speculation in 1936. The problem had become more urgent since the official pronouncements made prior to and during the 21st Congress that the Soviet Union was on the eve of transition to communism. Unlike the debate on the question of the functions of the Soviet state this discussion has been initiated and wholly inspired by official Communist Party statements. A further factor has been criticism of the Soviet state and of Soviet bureaucracy by Yugoslav socialists.[20]

The main reports at the 21st Congress in January 1959, especially those by Khrushchev and Suslov,[21] emphasized the view that there was no 'impenetrable barrier', 'no wall separating these two stages (socialism and communism) of social development', and that the transition to communism in the future would proceed at an accelerated tempo.

On the question of the withering away of the state it was argued that this implied 'the development of the socialist state into communist self-administration (*samoupravlenie*), for under communism too there would remain certain public functions similar to those now performed by the state, but their nature and the methods by which they will be exercised will differ from those obtaining in the present stage'.[22] Khrushchev argued that this transfer of functions from state to social organizations was already happening and he gave as examples the handling of health and other social services in the cities by the trade unions and the transfer of the control of physical culture and sports from a State Committee to a Voluntary Sports Organization, a proposal which was carried into effect in April 1959. Other indications of the growth of social control were the Comradely Courts and the Volunteer Militia. However, such developments did not imply a weakening of the role of the socialist state in the building of communism but rather its strengthening since it would broaden popular participation in the government. The state would continue to be necessary because of its defence role[23] and because of its economic role. Even under communism some social organizations would be necessary, although it was impossible to say in advance what these would be.

These official utterances of the Communist Party leaders have been repeated and detailed in countless articles and pamphlets.[24] The essential claim is that the Soviet state is developing in a contradictory fashion, simultaneously reducing some functions and enlarging others.[25] Functions which are alleged to be currently declining are those of police control and certain administrative functions such as the control of public health, sport and physical culture. Developing functions—apart from defence—are those defined by Stalin as economic—organizational and cultural-educational. The former is expanding because the transition to communism is held to be not a cautious gradual process but one of accelerated development in industry and agriculture, requiring strong state direction. The latter function is increasing not merely because of the need to struggle more and more strongly against capitalist survivals in the communal psychology but because of the need for educating people to the requirements of communist society.[26]

The following statement from a recent Soviet pamphlet is a good example of the dialectical view of the present and future of the Soviet state:

The state of socialist society, with the greater and greater development of socialist democracy, gradually transfers functions of administration to different democratic institutions. It follows that the withering away of the socialist state should be understood as the transfer of separate state functions to different social organizations and the transformation of the state as a social and political organ into social communist self-administration. This of necessity is a prolonged process and cannot be completed as a result of the victory of communism in one country or even in a group of countries. However, the tendency is such that the very strengthening and development of the functions of the socialist state leads to the transformation step by step of different state functions into functions of social self-administration.[27]

This concept of 'social self-administration' received even greater emphasis at the 22nd Congress of the CPSU in October 1961. The new programme of the CPSU established the objective of achieving the material basis for communist society by 1980. The Soviet state has finally ceased to be described as a dictatorship of the proletariat and is now held to be a 'public state' (obshchenarodnoe gosudarstvo) which Khrushchev defined as 'a new stage in the development of the socialist state, an important landmark on the road to transforming socialist statehood into communist self-administration'.[28]

Two special problems which have come up in the discussion on the eventual withering away of the socialist state are the fate of the party and of local Soviets. The transfer of additional functions from central to local Soviets was mentioned by Khrushchev in January 1959 (Report to the 21st Congress) as part of the process of transforming state agencies into social organizations. The apparent contradiction between this claim and the fact that local Soviets are obviously a part of the state structure is resolved only when it is remembered that local Soviets are not merely state agencies but are simultaneously agencies of mass participation and public control.[29] As such they are expected to survive the establishment of communism and the withering away of the state. But the Soviets which survive under communism will eventually cease to be agencies of state power and will serve merely as social agencies.[30]

As with the Soviet state it is considered necessary for the role of the Communist Party to be strengthened rather than reduced during the transition to communism. The need for party leadership will increase as various administrative functions are progressively transferred from state to social organizations. It is sometimes freely admitted that continued party control is necessary to prevent the development of anti-social tendencies such as 'localism' or 'departmentalism'.[31] The 22nd Congress emphasized the increased responsibility of the party not only in regard to the above tasks but as the leading agency in the difficult task of educating the entire Soviet people to communist consciousness.[32] The party is to survive the establishment of communist society but its methods and forms of work and its internal structure will change. Thus we find that recent prescriptions on the process of the withering away of the state frequently omit any mention of the ultimate fate of the party. The recent Academy of Sciences textbook on the *Foundations of Marxist Philosophy* covers the problem in these terms:

The withering away of the state involves: (1) the disappearance of the need for coercion by the state and its agencies; (2) the transformation of the economic-organizational and cultural-educational functions from state to social organizations; (3) the involvement of all citizens in social administrative matters and the necessary transformation in the organs of political power. When all traces of class division in society have been transformed, when communism has become victorious throughout the entire world, the need for the state will no longer arise. Society will no longer need special detachments of armed people in order to maintain order and discipline. And then, as Engels expressed it, it will be possible to relegate the state machine to the museum of history along with the spinning wheel and the bronze axe.[33]

If any mention is made of the eventual withering away of the party it is as something which can only happen in the remote future. Thus D. I. Chesnokov has recently stated that:

The party will occupy the leading position for a long time under communist society. Even in the early stages of the victory of communism on a world scale the party as the embodiment of all that is most progressive and original will need to exist. The people will need many years, decades of life under communism while all the new mechanism of social organization is sorted out and coordinated, till at length the conditions will be created for the withering away of the party. This process will be long and protracted. It will be realized as all members of society reach the level of consciousness and organizational experience of party members. Gradually the difference between communists and non-party persons will disappear. The party will turn into a universal organization coinciding with the organizations of self-administration.[34]

Thus the party will wither away only many years after communism is victorious all over the world. Eventually, when communism has matured neither state nor party will remain although there will be a complex of social organizations which will be formed by the merging and absorption of now separate organizations like Soviets, trade unions, co-operatives and the party.

LIMITATIONS OF CONTEMPORARY THEORY

The above summary of recent Soviet theory on the state makes it clear that the general Stalinist revisions of the classical Marxist theory have been preserved. Criticism has been at a secondary level on such aspects as the date at which the Soviet state might be said to have entered the second or socialist stage of its development, or the precise functions of the Soviet state in the first two phases of its development. General propositions such as the class basis of the state, the fundamental differences between socialist and capitalist states,[35] the survival of the state and the party even under communism have been retained. Revision of these general propositions has consisted essentially of a restatement with additional detail. This revision may be said to reflect changes in the objective situation in which the Soviet Union has operated—for example, the contrast between the capitalist encirclement of 1933–39 and the socialist camp of the post-1949 world—and the subjective evaluation of these changes in the Soviet Union itself.[36]

The usefulness of even this modified Marxist theory for the interpretation of Soviet politics is open to question. Most Western critics would regard it as irrelevant if not deliberately misleading. However, it is worth emphasizing that Soviet Marxism does provide a general theory against which many if not all of the recent changes in the Soviet state system can be examined and assessed. Thus the reduction in the size and complexity of the Soviet administrative apparatus,[37] or the increase in the powers and to some extent in the performance of local Soviets[38] since 1954* do indicate a modification and, at certain levels, a reduction of state functions, although not necessarily a withering away of the state. I have already referred to the claims

* See Chapter 12 below.

which Soviet writers make about the significance of social organizations replacing state organizations. This is not a new development (trade union control of social insurance dates back to 1933) but it has been enormously extended since 1957. The decision to extend trade union powers taken by the December 1957 plenum of the Central Committee of the CPSU was quickly implemented and the new legislation extended the functions of factory, works and local trade union committees and of trade unionists in the supervision of industrial production, plan fulfilment, technical development, workers' safety, social insurance and welfare. Most Western critics would regard this as merely additional evidence that Soviet trade unions are state agencies. But does the performance of functions which are generally regarded in capitalist democracies as 'governmental functions' necessarily transform Soviet trade unions into state agencies? While the achievements here are perhaps less substantial than Soviet writers claim the trend is clearly towards extending the semi-governmental and public activities of trade unions. The explanation for this might be chiefly that it assists the realization of cheaper public administration. But this objective in itself finds its rationale only within the context of the general Soviet theory of the state.* The same might be said of the increasing role of trade unions in judicial matters. Besides serving as appeal tribunals for labour disputes trade union committees supervise the Comradely Courts established within the factories and industrial plants.

If we turn to the rapid development of public (or social) organizations in local government we find a similar problem. Public organizations such as Volunteer Militia Squads, Comradely Courts, Volunteer Fire Brigades, Parents' Committees in Schools and Kindergartens, Library Councils, Street and Flat Committees, Women's Councils, etc., obviously enable a considerable reduction in the size of the paid local civil service. This saving is extended by the increasing use of non-staff (unpaid) officials and inspectors working under the control of the Executive Committees of local Soviets. But can the concerted efforts of the Party in this direction over the past two decades be wholly explained in terms of savings in the cost of local government? A full explanation seems to require some reference to the underlying ideology.

The peculiar importance that these changes have for Soviet writers[39] cannot be understood without recognizing that the Soviet theory of the state seems to require just such a remodelling and transformation of controlling agencies as a first step in the realizing of the ultimate objective of the withering away of the state.

Soviet theory also provides a basis for the partial explanation of

* See my discussion of this problem in Chapter 17 below.

recent modifications in Soviet foreign policy. It is obvious that there has been a qualitative change in the nature of Soviet foreign policy, a change which might be categorized as the extension of a policy aimed at national defence into one aimed at the defence and mutual development of a system of socialist states. It is a recognition of this change that has produced the modification of Stalin's formulation of the external function of the Soviet state as being exclusively that of national defence.[40]

It should also be noted that Soviet scholars are quite ready to recognize the existence of evidence which seems to contradict the official view that the size and complexity of the administrative structure is being steadily reduced. Many writers have pointed to such inconsistencies or contradictions as the increase in the size of Gosplan staffs since 1957 and the increase in the size of regional bureaucracy occasioned by the establishment of the *sovnarkhozy* (regional economic councils).[41] Occasionally a writer will challenge the official conclusions about the relevancy of a particular change to the objective of building communism. Thus A. V. Mitskevich challenged the official interpretation of the use of social agencies (such as Comradely Courts and Volunteer Militia) to handle petty crime and disorder as indicative of the gradual transformation of the coercive apparatus of the state into control by social organizations by declaring that, 'Such a practice leads only to unnecessary parallelism in the work of the social and state organs of order. It doesn't lead to the promotion of habits of self-administration, but only leads to the replacement of one coercive apparatus by another'.[42]

The changes which have occurred in the Soviet state structure since 1953 undoubtedly represent a conscious attempt on the part of the Soviet leadership to adjust the political superstructure to the changing material and cultural basis of Soviet society but it is an open question as to whether or not they represent any basic transformation of the state as such. Even if the leadership is deliberately striving to transform the state and eventually to ensure its withering away this in itself is no guarantee that this objective is any nearer today than it was in Stalin's day. It is worth recalling that the Khrushchevian decentralization and regionalization of the administrative-economic apparatus had a precedent in the 1920s and that these earlier parallels were sometimes accompanied by theoretical argument about the transformation of the state.[43]

I have already indicated the limited value of the Soviet theory of the state for the empirical study of that state. It is also necessary to recognize that the theory, at least as it is currently handled in the USSR, does not provide a key to the analysis of many other features of the Soviet political system. For example, both Lenin and Trotsky made an attempt at a Marxist analysis of Soviet bureaucracy.[44] Whereas Lenin and Trotsky sought the causes of Soviet bureaucracy in historical, cultural and class terms, the explanation provided by the present leadership is almost entirely in terms of individual short-comings. This is even more so in the contemporary analysis of such problems as the rise of Stalin and Stalinism, the internal function of the police and the coercive power of the state over the greater period of its existence. For these, the explanation is again essentially in terms of individuals rather than institutions or society. Thus the starting point for Khrushchev's criticism of Stalin at the secret session of the 20th Congress was the shortcomings of Stalin's personality as analysed by Lenin in the suppressed testament of 1922–23,[45] and of the personality weaknesses of the countless 'little Stalins' who had contributed to Stalin's despotism.

NOTES

[1] F. Engels, 1942, p. 124.

[2] Ibid., p. 124.

[3] F. Engels, 1932, pp. 75–6.

[4] V. I. Lenin, 'The State and Revolution', Selected Works, London, 1946, Vol. 7, p. 9.

[5] Politichesky slovar, 2nd edition, ed. B. N. Ponomarev, Moscow, 1958, p. 136.

[6] V. I. Lenin, op. cit., pp. 82–3.

[7] J. Stalin, Problems of Leninism, 1945, pp. 631–8. This can be compared with earlier and later formulations, e.g., Report to the Joint Plenum of the C.C. and the C.C.C., CPSU(B.), January 1933 (Works, Moscow 1955, Vol. 13, pp. 211 ff.). On the Draft Constitution of the USSR, November 25, 1936 (Problems of Leninism, pp. 540–68), and Concerning Marxism and Linguistics, 1950. Soviet News Booklet, London, 1950, pp. 36–7.

[8] J. Stalin, Problems of Leninism, pp. 636–7.

[9] Ibid., p. 637. Contrast Stalin's statement in January 1933; 'The abolition of classes is not achieved by the extinction of the class struggle, but by its intensification. The state will wither away not as a result of the weakening of the state power, but as a result of strengthening it to its utmost, which is necessary for finally crushing the remnants of the dying classes and for organising defence against the capitalist encirclement, which is far from being done away with as yet, and will not soon be done away with.' Report to the Joint Plenum of the C.C. and the C.C.C. of the CPSU(B.), January 1933 (Works, Vol. 13, p. 215).

[10] 'Soviet Marxists, on the basis of studying the present-day world situation, came to the conclusion that in the conditions of capitalist encirclement, when the socialist revolution has been victorious only in one country, and capitalism reigns in all other countries, the land of victorious socialism should not weaken, but in every way strengthen its state, state organs, intelligence organs, and army, if that land does not want to be crushed by the capitalist encirclement.' Reply to comrade A. Kholopov in Concerning Marxism and Linguistics, p. 36.

[11] A. Zhdanov, 1947. Speech delivered at the Conference of Communist Parties held in Poland, September 1947.

[12] Cf. N. S. Khrushchev Report of the Central Committee of the CPSU to the 20th Congress, 14 February, 1956. Moscow, FLPH., pp. 38–46. The questions dealt with by Khrushchev in this section of his report were the peaceful coexistence

99

of capitalism and socialism, the possibility of preventing war in the present period, and forms of transition to socialism in different countries. The latter question, which might perhaps have invited a review of Stalin's theory of the state in fact avoided it as working class control (the dictatorship of the proletariat) was made a condition for any peaceful transition to socialism.

[13] The discussion began by the evaluation of a book by V. Kozlovski, *Antagonisticheskie i neantagonisticheskie protivorechiya*, Moscow, 1954.

[14] Cf. the article by L. N. Kogan and I. D. Glazunov in *Voprosy filosofii*, 1955, No. 6.

[15] 'On the Correct Handling of Contradictions among the People', February 27, 1957. English trans. in Supplement to *People's China*, No. 13, July 1, 1957.

[16] Cf. F. Burlatsky, *Kommunist*, No. 13, September 1961, pp. 37–48; and N. G. Aleksandrov, 1961.

[17] For this thesis see, *inter alia*, J. Stalin, Report to the Joint Plenum of the C.C. and the C.C.C. of the CPSU(B.) January 1933, *Works*, Vol. 13, pp. 161–219. On recent official criticism of this thesis see the Resolution of the C.C. of the CPSU, June 30, 1956, *Pravda*, July 2, 1956; and L. F. Ilichev, Report to Conference on Ideological Work, December, 1961, *Izvestia*, December 28, 1961.

[18] For details on this discussion see my article 'Contemporary Soviet theory of the Soviet State', in *Soviet Studies*, Vol. XII, April 1961, No. 4, pp. 404–19. The two stages were replaced by three stages after the 22nd Congress, October 1961.

[19] *Voprosy stroitelstva kommunizma v SSSR*, Moscow, 1959, pp. 105–28.

[20] Cf. N. S. Khrushchev, Control Figures for the further development of the USSR for 1959–1965, *Izvestia*, January 28, 1959; D. I. Chesnokov, *Voprosy filosofii*, 1958, No. 7, pp. 30–47; A. I. Lepeshkin, 1958, *et al*.

[21] N. S. Khrushchev, Speech printed in *Izvestia*, January 28, 1959, and Suslov's speech in *Izvestia*, January 31, 1959.

[22] *Izvestia*, January 28, 1959.

[23] Cf. P. S. Romashkin. 'The state must be retained under communism if the imperialist camp survives until then; it will be necessary for the military defence of communist society against imperialism. But the main functions of the state under communism will be external ones.' *S.G.i.P.*, 1958, No. 10, p. 17.

[24] See my article in *Soviet Studies*, Vol. XII, April 1961, No. 4, pp. 412–13 for details on this point.

[25] Cf. 'Clearly the withering away of the state is a complex and contradictory process. Its dialectic is such that one function of the state is completely transformed or disappears while another is retained or even strengthened.' *Osnovy Marksizma-Leninizma*, Moscow, 1959, p. 722.

'. . . it is impossible to contrapose the task of strengthening the socialist state with the perspective of its withering away; they are two sides of the one medal.' *Osnovy marksistkoi filosofii*, Moscow, 1959, p. 535.

[26] Cf. V. Nikolaev, *Rol Sovetskovo gosudarstva v periode razvernutovo stroitelstva kommunizma*, Moscow, 1959; and P. S. Romashkin, *S.G.i.P.*, 1960, No. 2, pp. 17–30.

[27] I. A. Khlyabich, 1960, p. 30.

[28] Report on the Draft Programme of the CPSU, October 18, 1961. *Izvestia*, October 19, 1961, p. 6. of A. P. Kositsyn in *S.G.i.P.*, No. 3, 1962, pp. 21–33. Kanet, R. E., 1968; Shendrik, M. P., 1970; and Belykh, A. K., 1972.

[29] D. I. Chesnokov, 1960, p. 39; and F. Kalinychev and V. Vasilev in *Sovety deputatov trudyashchikhsya*, 1960, No. 9, pp. 34–41; and F. I. Kalinychev, 1961, pp. 29–67.

[30] See also *Programma Kommunisticheskoi Partii Sovetskovo Soyuza*, Moscow,

1961, Part II, pp. 102–6; and N. S. Khrushchev Report to the 22nd Congress of the CPSU on the Programme of the CPSU, October 18, 1961, Part IV, Section 2. *Izvestia*, October 19, 1961.

[31] *Osnovy Marksizma-Leninizma*, p. 724.

[32] Cf. *Programma Kommunisticheskoi Partii Sovetskovo Soyuza*. Moscow, 1961, Part II, Section V, and N. S. Khrushchev, Report to the 22nd Congress on the Programme, Part IV, Section 4.

[33] *Osnovy marksistkoi filosofii*, pp. 535–6. The same vagueness about the eventual fate of the party is present in Khrushchev's reports to the 21st and 22nd Congresses.

[34] D. I. Chesnokov, *op. cit.*, pp. 25–6.

[35] Cf. the statement by A. L. Lepeshkin, 1958, p. 22;

'J. V. Stalin was absolutely correct in formulating that the functions of economic-organizational and cultural-educational work were inherent only in socialist states. No exploiting states possess these functions.'

Cf. N. G. Aleksandrov, 1961, p. 7;

'A public state, which appears as the organ representing the interests and will of the entire people, can only exist in a society where there are no antagonistic classes, where the social, moral and political unity of society has been established.'

[36] N. S. Khrushchev's admission in his report to the 21st Congress in January 1959 that 'the socialist countries will enter the higher phase of communist society more or less simultaneously . . .', represented a tacit revision of Stalin's 1939 claim that Communism in one country was possible which was made more explicit by the Programme adopted by the 22nd Congress in October 1961. *Vide, Programma Kommunisticheskoi Partii Sovetskovo Soyuza*, Moscow, 1961, Part II, Section VI, pp. 132–5.

[37] Soviet statistics are far from adequate on this point. Perhaps the clearest guide to the general trend is provided by the fact that budget expenditure on administration has been falling absolutely each year since 1954, and that it fell on a percentage basis from $3 \cdot 9\%$ of the total expenditure in 1940 to $1 \cdot 2\%$ in 1966.

[38] Over the years 1957–59 more than forty regulations extending the powers and scope of local Soviets were issued by the Supreme Soviets of the Union Republics. Cf. Yu. A. Tikhomirov; *S.G.i.P.*, 1960, No. 1, pp. 76–88.

[39] Cf. D. A. Gaidukov and N. G. Starovoitov, eds., 1965, Ch. VII; V. I. Razin; ed., 1965.

[40] Cf. A. I. Lepeshkin, *op. cit.*, 1957; and R. S. Romashkin, *op. cit.*, 1956.

[41] For example, A. Kozlov, in *Izvestia*, April 9, 1959, claimed that the Ukrainian Gosplan apparatus was six times as large as it was in 1955. M. Savalev, in *Sovety*, 1960, No. 1, p. 15, claimed that there were 85,000 employed directly by the apparatus of the *sovnarkhozy* and in the administration of subsidiary organizations.

[42] *S.G.i.P.*, 1959, No. 9, pp. 24–33.

[43] Cf. E. H. Carr, Vol. 6, (*Socialism in One Country 1924–1926*. Part Two), 1959, pp. 294, 303, 365–72.

[44] See for example, V. I. Lenin; 'Better Fewer, but Better', March 1923, and L. D. Trotsky; 'The New Course', 1923. Trotsky continued his attempt to explain Soviet bureaucracy in Marxist terms in *The Revolution Betrayed*, 1936, and in later works.

[45] This is true of the later criticism. See for example, The Resolution of the Central Committee of the CPSU, June 30, 1956. *Pravda* July 2, 1956; and the various criticisms made by Khrushchev, Mikoyan and others of both Stalin and the Stalinist 'anti-Party group' (Molotov, Malenkov, Kaganovich, etc.), at the 22nd Party Congress in October 1961.

SELECTED BIBLIOGRAPHY

Brinkley, G. A., 1961.
Brinkley, G. A., 1973.
Glezerman and Ukraintsev, 1958.
Kanet, R. E., 1968.
Lenin, V. I., 1943–46, Vol. 7, pp. 1–112.
Lenin, V.I., 1950.
Marcuse, H., 1961, Ch. 5.
Stalin, J. V., 1945, pp. 631–38.
Trotsky, L. D., 1937, Ch. 5.

Chapter 7

THE ELECTORAL SYSTEM AND THE ELECTORATE

REQUIREMENTS FOR FREE ELECTIONS

Many Western writers[1] tend to equate the Soviet electoral process with that of Fascist Italy or Nazi Germany. In a one-party state it is said elections are necessarily managed; they act as a plebiscite designed to secure a near to unanimous endorsement of government policy rather than to provide the opportunity for the election of an alternative government. Whatever their real function, as elections they are mere window-dressing. Such an evaluation is inaccurate, especially in its confusion of the role of elections in the Soviet Union with elections in a fascist state. For the one system places a premium on elections while the other ignored or despised them.

The requirements of free elections as understood in the West may be stated as follows:

(a) universal suffrage;

(b) frequent and regular elections, although there is no agreement on exactly how frequent they should be;

(c) equal voting rights for all electors and proportional representation or, if single member electorates are preferred, electorates which are reasonably equal in population;

(d) direct elections;

(e) secret ballot;

(f) no restrictions on the choice of candidates;

(g) convenient polling arrangements so that voters are not inconvenienced by the requirements to register or to vote;

(h) a ballot that allows an exercise of choice and preference;

(i) the right to choose a policy which is not that of the government;

(j) equal access to publicity by all candidates and parties.

Most electoral systems in operation in parliamentary states today fall considerably short of the standard recorded above. Thus there is no universal suffrage throughout the United States, secrecy of voting

103

is frequently breached and polling arrangements are notoriously disadvantageous to workers and poorer persons generally in many American states. Both in America and Australia federal and state electorates are often unequal while in France the electoral law is designed and operated to deflate the considerable electoral support for the Communist Party. In the Federal Republic of Germany the Communist Party is illegal and is therefore unable openly to contest elections. But how far does the Soviet Union fulfil the requirements for free elections?

SOVIET ELECTORAL PROVISIONS

The Soviet Constitution and electoral law establish the right to vote for all persons of eighteen years or more irrespective of sex, class, race or creed. The age qualification for candidates for election is 18 for local Soviets, 21 for Republican Soviets and 23 for the USSR Supreme Soviet. The only exceptions to the right to vote and to nominate are insane persons and persons convicted by a court of law whose sentences include deprivation of electoral rights.[2] Voting is not formally compulsory but in practice it is difficult to avoid the obligation.

Elections are certainly frequent. The USSR Supreme Soviet and republican Supreme Soviets are elected at four-yearly intervals, local Soviets at two-yearly intervals. In this way an election occurs in three out of every four years. Thus local Soviet elections occurred in March 1969, in June 1970 a new USSR Supreme Soviet was elected while in June 1971 there were elections to the Supreme Soviets of the Union Republics, Autonomous Republics and to local Soviets. There were no elections in 1972.

Electoral districts for all Soviets are single member electorates. This means that the electorates vary in size from electorates of several millions in the case of Russian electorates for the Soviet of Nationalities to electorates of 100 in the case of many village Soviets. Electorates for the Soviet of the Union have approximately 300,000 inhabitants and the list of electorates is revised two months before each election. Electoral districts for the Soviet of Nationalities are also single member electorates. Each Union Republic is divided into 32 equal electorates; each Autonomous Republic into 11; each Autonomous Province (oblast) into 5; while each National Area (okrug) forms a single electorate. All Soviets are directly elected, which means that a voter in an election when republican Soviets as well as local Soviets are being elected will vote simultaneously for candidates in two or three levels of local Soviets and also for his Republican Supreme Soviet.

The electoral law provides for screened polling booths to ensure secrecy. The supervision of the actual balloting is done not by paid electoral officials but by amateurs, by members of the electoral commission for the electorate concerned. The electoral commissions are responsible for counting the vote and for sending in the returns.

When we come to consider whether or not the Soviet electoral system allows for the free choice of candidates it is obvious that two restrictions operate. In the first place, no independent candidates are possible since each candidate must be proposed by a section of the Communist Party or by some recognized social organization,[3] such as a trade union, factory or farm collective, Komsomol or cultural society. Secondly, only one party—the Communist Party—can nominate. Other restrictions operate in actual practice. Thus the Communist Party, while it does not make all the nominations, certainly screens them. At the lower levels this is often done through tight control over the nomination (pre-selection) meeting.[4] At the level of the Supreme Soviet, where electorates are 300,000 for the Soviet of the Union and sometimes much larger for the Soviet of Nationalities, it is done more by the control which the Communist Party exercises over the various nominating organizations having the right to nominate candidates within the individual electorate. If this screening is occasionally inadequate it is still possible for the electoral commissions, in which party control is unquestioned, to refuse to register the candidature of an 'undesirable' candidate and to ensure that only one candidate remains in each electorate when the ballot papers are finally printed. This power of the electoral commissions to exclude candidates is occasionally mentioned by Soviet writers and is generally emphasized by Western political scientists.[5] However, my own on-the-spot investigation of the 1965 local Soviet elections* convinced me that it is not a normal function of the electoral commission. The electoral commissions do not normally exclude candidates for the simple reason that—at least in elections to local Soviets—there is normally only one candidate nominated. Many collectives secure a right to nominate regularly to particular electorates. Under these circumstances any competition—and this is rare —is between candidates coming from the same nominating collective. The claims of rival candidates are sorted out within the collective. By the time the formal nomination meeting of the electors takes place (a fortnight to a month before the election) there is almost always only one candidate.

* I spent three months in the USSR as the guest of the USSR Academy of Sciences from February 9, 1965, investigating the Soviet electoral system and various aspects of local government. A report of my findings appeared in *Soviet Studies*, April 1966.

On the matter of convenient polling arrangements the Soviet system scores well. The electoral law requires that the polling day must be fixed and announced two months in advance, that it must be a non-working day, and that the hours of polling be from 6 a.m. to 10 p.m.* Voters' lists are prepared for each election by the Executive Committees of local Soviets† and they must be published thirty days in advance of the election. Complaints against the non-inclusion or incorrect inclusion of names must be made to the Executive Committee of the Soviet concerned, with the right of appeal to the Courts if no satisfaction is obtained. Persons turning up to vote who find that their name is not on the list may cast a vote if they produce a certificate of the right to vote and identification papers.[6] As well as covering persons who have been overlooked, this provision covers both those who have changed their address to another electorate since the voters' list‡ was completed and those who are absent from their electorate on the polling day. This peculiar method of providing for absentee votes gave rise to the curious anomaly that on several occasions Stalin was returned by a majority of more than 100 per cent.[7]

The supervision of the elections and the counting of votes is done by the electoral commissions. These election commissions are appointed by the Presidiums of the Supreme Soviets and by the Executive Committees of local Soviets and are formed of representatives of the agencies and groups having the right to nominate candidates for the election.[8] They range in size from 3–5 members in the case of electoral commissions in precincts with less than 300 inhabitants to 27 members in the case of the Central Electoral Commission. Candidates for deputy cannot be members of the electoral commission in the area in which they are nominated. In all more than nine million persons are involved in serving on electoral commissions during a Soviet election. Soviet writers acclaim this as a proof of the popular control of Soviet elections. It is difficult to attest the accuracy of this claim at all levels. In the case of the main electoral commissions at least, the members would seem to be genuinely the nominees of the social or political organization they represent. Thus the Chairman of the 1962 Central Electoral Commission, V. V. Grishin, was appointed by the All-Union Council of Soviet Trade Unions of which he was the Chairman. Since he was also a member of the Presidium of the Central Committee of the CPSU it is quite certain that his

* Until March 1966 voting closed at midnight.

† In fact the actual preparation of the voters' lists is done by the Electoral Commissions on behalf of the Executive Committee of the appropriate Soviet.

‡ In the cities voters' lists are prepared on the basis of a ward (*uchastok*). Each ward will include several electorates for City District Soviet and several wards will comprise an electorate for the City Soviet. This makes the lists manageable at about 2,000–2,500 voters on each, in Moscow and Leningrad.

appointment to the Electoral Commission was approved if not initiated by this body. Similarly, the Central Committee of the Komsomol nominated its first secretary, S. P. Pavlov; the Moscow Party Committee its second secretary, N. G. Egorychev, while L. M. Leonov was appointed to represent the union of Soviet Writers and M. V. Keldysh the USSR Academy of Sciences.[9] Despite the certainty of the results of Soviet elections the nominating agencies are represented by observers who attend the vote counting by electoral commissions.

A basic shortcoming of the Soviet ballot is that it does not in fact allow the exercise of choice and preference by the voter. The electoral law and the standard ballot form provide for this since they require the listing of all candidates (by surname, patronymic and christian name), and also of the agencies which nominated them. The voter is instructed to 'Leave uncrossed out the name of the candidate you are voting for'. However, the exhaustive pre-selection system which is operated in all electorates, reduces the field to one official 'Communist and non-Party candidate' in each electorate. This means that the voter has either to vote for the official candidate, in which case his paper is merely folded and dropped, unmarked, into the ballot box; or to vote against the official candidate by crossing his name out. To act in the second way is to run the gauntlet of public opinion since any marking of the ballot paper can only be for the purpose of voting against the official candidate or for writing in a comment on the ballot paper. In any case the choice is a strictly limited one between voting for (and acquiescing to) or against a candidate. The individual voter cannot at the election exercise a choice between candidates, nor can he even write in the name of any candidate he may prefer. Only if sufficient voters vote against the candidate so as to cause him to be defeated will a fresh election with a fresh official candidate occur and provide the voter with a limited if belated alternative. The fact that such defeats do occur even in a limited number of electorates is significant for it clearly establishes the possibility of rejecting the official candidate. However, the mechanics of the ballot make it very difficult to operate in the larger electorates. Thus in the 1957 local Soviet elections candidates failed to secure a majority in 169 electorates, all of them at the level of the Village, Settlement or District Soviets. In the 1961 local Soviet elections candidates failed to secure majorities in 249 electorates to Village, Settlement, Town and District Soviets.* I know of no case where candidates have failed to be elected in city, provincial or territorial Soviets, much less in the Supreme Soviets of the Union Republics or in the USSR Supreme Soviet.

* 208 candidates failed to secure majorities in March 1965. In the June 1973 local Soviet elections only 80 candidates failed to secure election.

Why then does the Soviet Union practise such a restricted ballot? This question was easier to answer in the Stalin era than it is today. The rationale for the present system was recently stated by the Soviet jurist N. G. Starovoitov in these words:

It is well known that neither the Soviet Constitution nor the Electoral Regulations exclude the right of nominating and registering several candidates for the same electorate. However, because of the actual composition of the social organizations and workers' societies, they nominate and put forward to the precinct electoral commission as a rule only one candidate, but if they have nominated two or more candidates (and this has in fact happened in past elections) then the other candidates have withdrawn their candidatures in favour of one candidate.[10]

That Soviet writers are so sensitive to criticism on this score is an indication of their lack of conviction on the justification of the system as well as perhaps some latent public demand for its revision. The answer to this problem would seem to be the fear that the Soviet leadership has of getting something less than unanimous support from a freer ballot. Official statements sometimes give guarded recognition of this fact. Thus the official government newspaper *Izvestia* in an editorial February 16, 1958, wrote that:

In agreeing on a general candidate the participants in the precinct pre-selection meeting proceed from the fact that the nomination of several candidates for the electoral division would result in the opposing of one candidate to another, thus breaking up the bloc of Communist and non-Party candidates. And the Soviet people are certainly interested in retaining and strengthening this unity, as in it is to be found the source of the strength of our society, the basis of all the successes of the Soviet people in the building of communism.

The Soviet system requires the mobilization of the entire population behind the policy of the party. Because of this a Soviet election does not and cannot permit the electorate to have the choice of supporting an alternative policy to that of the government. While the system does not require that all candidates should be party members they must all be party supporters. Even to allow for the free choice between candidates of one mind would undoubtedly encourage the latent divisions in Soviet society. The system as it operates maximizes and perhaps seriously distorts public support for the government. Nevertheless the 99% plus of the electorate which votes for (or does not vote against) the official candidate is hailed as clear proof of the unity of Soviet society. As a recent writer puts it:

The dazzling victory of the Party and non-Party bloc in Soviet elections is a clear expression of the monolithic cohesion of the Soviet people, of its faith, love and devotion to the Communist Party and to the Soviet

Government, to its wholehearted readiness to march behind the Party along the road to communism.[11]

Soviet theory holds that a party is part of a class and that the only justification for the existence of several parties is where several classes exist. In the Soviet Union it is claimed that there are no antagonistic classes but only two friendly classes, workers and peasants, and a social stratum, the intelligentsia.[12] This would seem to warrant the existence of a peasant (or agrarian) party as well as the Communist Party. Yet theory and fact do not recognize this possibility. In theory the present Communist Party is held to represent the whole of Soviet society, workers, peasants and intellectuals. In fact there has been no peasant party since the disappearance of the Socialist Revolutionary Party during the Civil War. It is sheer idealism to expect the Soviet leadership to permit the revival of independent political organization after more than fifty years of monopoly of political power. It is indeed doubtful if any section of the Soviet population, peasantry or other, sees any use in an alternative political party. But they may well expect some relaxation of party supervision and control of the pre-selection process and indeed there is some evidence of this occurring on a limited degree in elections to Village and District Soviets.[13]

The Soviet electoral law provides that organizations which nominate candidates shall be guaranteed the right to campaign without interference for their candidates, at meetings, in the press, and by other means in accordance with Art. 125 of the USSR Constitution.[14] In fact, since most of the public campaigning is done after the pre-selection of the candidates, there can be no competition in this process. At this stage the campaigning is mostly designed to illustrate party policy and to establish—by selective coverage—the fact that 'the best sons and daughters of the people are elected to the Soviets'.

One final element in the Soviet electoral system requires comment, and that is the right of recall of deputies. This was emphasized by Lenin in 1918 as one of the superiorities of the Soviet system over the parliamentary system. The practice, however, largely disappeared with the reform of the electoral system in 1936 and it has only recently been revived. A case occurred in 1957 when a deputy to the Latvian Supreme Soviet was recalled because of drunkenness and unsatisfactory performance of his duty.[15] He was recalled not by a majority of the electorate which he represented but by the workers and employees of the Machine Tractor Station which had originally nominated him. This is a good illustration of the fact that the Soviet electoral system, although formally based on territorial electorates, retains vestiges of the earlier functional representation.[16] The right of recall of deputies was legalized by a Law of the USSR Supreme Soviet in October 1959[17] and by the Supreme Soviets of the Union Republics in following months. This legislation provides for the recall of a deputy by a vote of a majority of electors in his district for failure to fulfil the voters' requests or because of action unbecoming to the position of a deputy. The initiative in the recall process belongs to all social organizations having the right to nominate candidates. The actual recall decision is made by majority vote by show of hands at an electoral meeting representing all nominating agencies and groups and general meetings of workers. The deputy and all nominating groups are guaranteed freedom of propaganda for or against the recall. No figures are available for the number of deputies recalled since the passage of this legislation but several cases involving the recall of deputies to local Soviets have been quoted in Soviet sources and the recall of a deputy to the Belorussian Supreme Soviet was reported early in 1961. In this case the recall was initiated by the members of the collective farm of which the deputy was chairman. The recall was voted for at an electoral meeting in which 12,066 of the 12,080 who participated voted for the recall while 10 abstained and only 4 voted against the recall.[18] That recall is increasingly used is indicated by the fact that 446 deputies of local Soviets were recalled during 1963.[19]

The only possible conclusion from this analysis is that the Soviet system, while it contains many admirable features and provisions for ensuring a widespread vote on a democratic basis, is not democratic if an essential element of a democratic election is that it allows the choice of another government. However, it can claim to be democratic within the context of the Soviet theory of democracy. It is also probable that it is moving, within the limits of the system, towards more democratic practices. The emphasis in recent years on such things as Soviet legality, the need for widespread participation in the pre-selection of candidates, on the obligation of deputies to make regular reports to their electors,[20] as well as the limited revival of the practice of recall of deputies, are indications of this trend.

THE ROLE OF SOVIET ELECTIONS

At this point it is perhaps necessary to ask the question of what exactly is the role of Soviet elections? No simple answer to this question is possible. Soviet elections serve as a mechanism for the election (or selection) of deputies, although not to change the government. Since upwards of two million deputies are elected every second year this is no small function. Secondly, they are designed to educate the electorate, designed to serve as 'a school for the education of millions of Soviet citizens'. This was acknowledged in the editorial in *Izvestia*, March 25, 1961, which declared that:

Elections to the organs of state power for us are not considered only as nominations of candidates and voting for them. The political content of the election campaign is much wider. On each occasion the work of preparing for and carrying out elections is linked with the present tasks of communist construction, with the perspective of the further development of the economy and culture of the country, with the practical fulfilment of the policy of our party and the Soviet government, with improving the operation of our state apparatus.

In contrast with fascist states elections in the Soviet Union are characterized by an intensive campaigning in which deputies, candidates, party members and hundreds of thousands of 'activists' take part. The object of this campaign—apart from ensuring widespread interest and participation by the electorate in order to produce the requisite number of suitable candidates—is to present the record of the party and the government over the term of the retiring Soviet (i.e. 2–4 years) and to encourage questions and discussion about immediate and future plans. Election meetings are not confined to those concerned with the nomination of candidates but continue on a wide scale right up to the election itself. These meetings include meetings of electors at which deputies 'report back', 'question and answer' evenings in workers' and village clubs, as well as the more intimate personal canvassing by the agitators on a door to door basis and through the innumerable 'agitation centres'. Soviet newspapers over the two months preceding and the fortnight following elections carry an enormous amount of election material ranging from editorial statements, statements issued by the Communist Party and by leading candidates, to news items on candidates' records and how the campaign is proceeding at various centres. Local, trade union and provincial papers as well as the national dailies are involved. The Soviet periodical press, including the less political journals such as *Ogonyek* and *Krokodil* contains a good deal of election comment, some of it fairly critical. Radio, television and posters are extensively used. It is certain that as the more ambitious plans for the building of Communist society are put into force the public educational or morale-boosting function of Soviet elections will be intensified.

Thirdly, and linked to the above function, Soviet elections are designed to demonstrate the unity of Soviet society and the support of the entire Soviet people for the Communist Party and the government. Elections are officially regarded as 'powerful means for rallying the Soviet people and for strengthening the Soviet state'.

Fourthly, Soviet elections serve the purpose of allowing deputies to report back to their electorates and to allow local demands to be formulated. These demands are formulated into a list and become mandates (*nakazy*) on the fulfilment of which deputies are obliged to

111

report regularly to their electors.[21] The elections thus serve to ensure that deputies are fully aware of public opinion on local issues. They also enable the Soviet leadership to sound out the reaction of the public to the targets of the current economic plan, a process which may result in modifications to the details of the plan.

PUBLIC OPINION

In conclusion, it is necessary to say something about the role of public opinion in the Soviet Union. The first thing to notice here is that public opinion is far from negligible as a factor in politics. This is true even though public opinion cannot change the political complexion of the government or modify the long-range plans of the party. However, it is doubtful if the average MP of the Australian Parliament is so effectively linked to the views of his electors as is his Soviet counterpart. The Soviet deputy continues in his occupation and does not become a professional parliamentarian. He is subject to recall at any time during his term. He is required to report back regularly to his electorate and to render an account of his activities. Deputies are expected to be available at any time to take up grievances and for this purpose most local Soviets maintain a Deputies' room in which the deputy receives requests and answers questions at regular times each week. Around the deputy is gathered a group of citizens who assist in agitational work and in working on various Standing Commissions and Committees. This group is known as the *aktiv*. In this way many besides deputies are involved in the actual process of government and administration. Thus the local Soviets elected in June 1971 appointed 326,243 Standing Commissions to which 1,749,029 deputies and 2·4 million non-deputies were elected.[22] This involvement of ordinary citizens in the actual work of government enlists not merely their physical power but their criticism and suggestion.

One of the difficulties in assessing the Soviet system is to measure the effectiveness of public criticism. For some years now private oral opinion has been virtually unrestricted and hence it covers the whole range of government policy and sometimes challenges the very foundations of the Soviet system. Written public criticism is more restricted and does not extend to open criticism of the Soviet socialist system or to criticism of basic Communist policy. However, its scope is probably wider than most Western critics are prepared to concede and it is steadily widening. It now covers not merely criticism of minor and intermediate officials but criticism of bureaucracy at all levels. It extends to the criticism of the details of government policy and often results in its modification. Such modifications occurred as a result of the public and Supreme Soviet discussions on the Pensions Law in 1956, on the industrial reorganization in March–May 1957, on the agricultural reorganization in 1958, and on the educational reform in 1958–59.

The chief avenues for public criticism are the daily press,[23] the trade union press, factory bulletins and wall newspapers, journals, literature and the theatre. At present the main types of critical literature are the editorial (often stimulated by letters and reports from special correspondents), the letter to the editor, the contributed article, the satirical sketch (or *feuilleton*) and the cartoon.

The range of issues covered by criticism in the Soviet press is certainly wide but it is mainly concerned with breaches of Soviet legality, with cases of *blat* (pull, or influence), with bureaucracy in local Soviets, with administrative inefficiency, with waste, failure to fulfil plans, and with improper interference of Communist Party officials in Soviet administration. The range might be illustrated by taking *Izvestia* over a typical fortnight (May 1–14, 1958). The paper over this period, exclusive of editorials, and articles and letters of commendation, contained critical items on these issues:

(i) Cases of deputies transferring from their region and yet retaining their positions in local Soviets and even being excused their duties as deputy (May 7).

(ii) The slow transport of railway trucks containing mineral fertilizer and the harmful effects this has on farming activities (May 7).

(iii) The inadequacy of market gardening in the Moscow *oblast* (May 7).

(iv) The inadequacy of the supplies of clothing and footwear in the Yaroslav *oblast* and the steps being taken to overcome this (May 8).

(v) Evidence of work avoidance in Ashkhabad (Turkmenia) (May 8).

(vi) Insufficiency of the powers of local Soviets in face of the tasks facing them. Criticism of the USSR Ministry of Finance (May 11).

The average Soviet citizen is perhaps no worse informed on international affairs than his American or Australian counterpart; it is probable that he is better informed on local and national domestic political issues. It is equally certain however that the restrictions which still operate on the free purchase of foreign newspapers, journals and books,* place unnecessary difficulties in the way of many

* The availability of short-range radios overcomes this restriction to some extent. Many Soviet citizens listen in regularly to the B.B.C. and to the Voice of America.

Soviet citizens seeking a different picture of the external world than that presented through Soviet sources. The Soviet specialist on the other hand is increasingly well-informed on overseas developments in his own field. This goes for the economists, historians, and other social scientists as well as for the physical scientists, as a reading of Soviet academic journals will soon demonstrate. Moreover, the increasing number of tourists (both in groups and individuals) passing through the main Soviet cities in recent years as well as the increasing travel of Soviet citizens abroad, has tended to destroy the fostered isolationism of the Stalin era. What still remains of this isolationism is more the outcome of the general preoccupation with the material and cultural advance of Soviet society than of any official policy.

Some of the most effective criticism is recorded during the 'open season' of the major public discussions. These discussions are officially stimulated and are partly designed to promote public enthusiasm for official policies. The machinery for the discussion consists of many thousands of public meetings, combined with articles and letters to the newspapers. The scale of such public debates is astounding. Thus the debate on the reorganization of the Machine Tractor Stations (mainly between February 28 and March 25, 1958) involved 576,879 public meetings at which almost 50 million people attended and over 3 million spoke. During the debate the newspapers and journals received 126,000 articles and letters of which, it was claimed 82% were published.[24] The public discussion on the Seven Year Plan was even wider. This discussion was initiated by the Central Committee of the CPSU issuing draft control figures (on November 12, 1958), for the development of the economy over the next seven years. This was followed by a public debate which concluded with the opening of the 21st Congress of the CPSU on January 27, 1959. It was claimed that 968,000 public meetings had been held to discuss the plan and that over 70 million people were involved. Over $4\frac{1}{2}$ million persons participated in the discussions at meetings while over 300,000 written contributions were received by the Soviet press.[25] At the same time as this discussion was going on there was a parallel debate on the reorganization of Soviet education. It was claimed that 9 million Communists and 82 million non-Party persons participated in the public discussion on the new draft programme of the CPSU (July 30–October 14, 1961).[26]

A less dramatic but more frequent and perhaps more effective means of enlisting public support for party policy and expert criticism of its detail is the Conference. Conferences are organized on a vocational or a vocational-regional basis and may involve engineers, agricultural scientists and other agricultural specialists, teachers, writers, architects, doctors and medical workers, historians, economists, etc.

114

Twenty major Conferences were held over the four years 1953–56 involving 30,000 participants.[27] There were 25,000 key persons involved in the zonal agricultural Conferences over the two months following the January 1961 plenum of the Central Committee of the CPSU.[28] The 22nd Congress (October 1961) was followed not merely by delegates reporting back to meetings of party members but by a whole series of zonal conferences lasting over several weeks. Conferences of experts have become even more frequent since the fall of Khrushchev but public nation-wide debates have been fewer.[29]

NOTES

[1] e.g. Merle Fainsod, 1954, pp. 322–4; H. McClosky and J. E. Turner, 1960, pp. 324–32.

[2] The power of the courts to deprive certain criminals of voting rights is stated in the USSR Constitution, Art. 135, and was endorsed in the 'Law Concerning the removal of the Individual's voting rights by Courts', passed by the USSR Supreme Soviet, December 25, 1958. *Izvestia*, December 26, 1958, p. 3.

[3] Art. 141 of the USSR Constitution guarantees the right to nominate candidates to, 'Communist Party organizations, trade unions, co-operatives, youth and cultural societies'. The Regulations repeat this (in Art. 57) and add (Art. 58), 'The right to nominate candidates is exercised by the central bodies of the public organizations and societies of the working people and their republican, territorial, provincial, *uyezd* and district bodies, as well as by general meetings of workers and other employees in enterprises, of servicemen in army units, general meetings of peasants in the collective farms, villages and *volosts*, and of workers and other employees of state farms.'

[4] Confirmation of this is occasionally provided by the Soviet press. For an analysis of some of these in the March 1957 elections to local Soviets, see my article in *Soviet Studies*, Vol. IX, July 1957, No. 1, pp. 87–9.

[5] Cf. George Barr Carson, Jr., 1955, p. 71. Many Western writers make this claim although there is little evidence to support it.

[6] Art. 82. Regulations on Elections to the Supreme Soviet of the USSR, January 9, 1950. *Sbornik zakonov SSSR i ukazov prezidiuma verkhovnovo Soveta SSSR. 1938–1958*. Moscow, 1959, pp. 89–103.

[7] Thus in the 1950 elections to the Moscow City Soviet Stalin received a vote of 152% in his electorate. G. B. Carson, Jr., *op. cit.*, p. 84.

[8] Regulations on Elections to the Supreme Soviet of the USSR, January 9, 1950, Ch. V.

[9] *Izvestia*, January 6 and 13, 1962.

[10] N. G. Starovoitov, 1961, p. 88.

[11] Yu. K. Filonovich, 1958, p. 36.

[12] Cf. J. Stalin, 'On the Draft Constitution of the USSR' (November, 1936), in *Problems of Leninism*, pp. 556–7.

[13] Cf. my article in *Soviet Studies*, Vol. IX, July 1957, No. 1, pp. 87–9.

[14] Regulations on Elections to the Supreme Soviet of the USSR, January 9, 1950, Art. 70.

[15] Yu. K. Filonovich, *op. cit.*, p. 18.

[16] Thus army units serving outside the USSR were given separate representation within the USSR Supreme Soviet (cf. the old soldiers' deputies). Soviet deputies when reporting back to their electorates often report back to the nominating group rather than to the electorate as a whole. Thus a peasant deputy may report

back to a general meeting of collective farmers or a worker deputy to his factory or workshop. Recently, some Soviet writers have urged modifications to the Soviet electoral system so as to increase these elements. Thus F. Burlatsky in *Kommunist*, No 13, September 1961, pp. 37–48, suggested the reversion to the practice of formally electing deputies by collectives in large factories and plants. This he claimed, would allow for a more democratic election of candidates and for more direct links of the deputies with their electors.

[17] See *Sovetskaya Rossia*, October 31, 1959.

[18] P. F. Mazhutova in *Sovety deputatov trudyashchikhsya v period razvernutovo stroitelstva kommunizma*, Moscow, 1961, pp. 307–24. The same source gives examples of the recall of deputies of local Soviets. See also, *Sovety deputatov trudyashchikhsya*, No 1, 1962, pp. 52–5, and No 2, 1962, p. 5. The latter article states that between October 1959 and the end of 1961, 5 deputies to the USSR Supreme Soviet, 28 deputies to Supreme Soviets of Union Republics and over 100 deputies to local Soviets had been recalled.

[19] *Sovety dep. trud.*, No 10, 1964, pp. 93–4. In 1972, on the other hand, 718 deputies to local Soviets were recalled. *Ibid.*, No 5, 1973, pp. 74–7.

[20] 80% of all deputies of local Soviets reported back to electors in 1959 and 90% in 1960. *Izvestia*, March 6, 1961. In 1972, 98·9% of all deputies to local Soviets reported back to electors and 78·7% reported back twice or more. *Sovety*, No 5, 1973, pp. 74–7.

[21] Cf. G. F. Ryabchuk, 1958. The demands of course relate to local issues only such as housing, streets, sewerage, water supply, parks, school equipment, shopping facilities, transport, cultural facilities. They are only accepted as 'mandates' if they have been examined by the electoral meeting and found to be reasonable. V. K. Vasenin, 1965.

[22] *Sovety*, No 6, 1972, pp. 84–8.

[23] In 1968 there were 8,754 central, republican, regional, city and district newspapers with a circulation of 126 million. *Kommunist*, No 4, 1970, p. 70.

[24] A summary of this discussion is to be found in *Soviet Studies*, X, July 1958, pp. 84–97.

[25] *Sovetskaya Rossia*, January 28, 1959.

[26] *Izvestia*, October 15, 1961.

[27] Ya N. Umansky, 1959, p. 242.

[28] *Izvestia*, March 26, 1961.

[29] The fullest Soviet discussion of this aspect of the Soviet system to be published in the USSR in recent years is that by V. F. Kotok, 1964.

SELECTED BIBLIOGRAPHY

Black, C. E., 1958.
Carson, G. B., 1955.
Churchward, L. G., 1957.
Churchward, L. G., 1966.
Churchward, L. G., 1973, Chs. 6, 7.
Denisov and Kirichenko, 1960, Ch. 11.
Hazard, J. N., 1968, 4th edn., pp. 49–57.
Schlesinger, R., 1957.
Scott, D. J. R., 1969, 4th edn., pp. 89–99.

Chapter 8

THE SUPREME SOVIET OF THE USSR

COMPOSITION

The Supreme Soviet of the USSR is often referred to, even in the Soviet Union itself, as the Soviet Parliament. This is inaccurate except in a purely formal sense. The Supreme Soviet is not and never has been the main legislative body in the Soviet Union. On the other hand it is not merely a kind of collective 'rubber stamp' for the automatic registration of decisions arrived at elsewhere.

The USSR Supreme Soviet is elected every four years, usually in June. It is a bi-cameral body, each chamber having identical powers. The Constitution requires that sessions must be held at least twice a year. Since the normal session lasts only two to four days this means that the Supreme Soviet is not normally in session. Its busiest year since the death of Stalin was in 1957 when it met four times (in February, May, November and December) and sat for fourteen days in all. In 1958 the USSR Supreme Soviet met twice (in March and December), each session lasting four days. Although the shortness of the sessions of the USSR Supreme Soviet is occasionally criticized in the Soviet Union there is as yet no trend towards lengthening them. Thus the 5th USSR Supreme Soviet (1958–62) met seven times over the four years of its existence, twenty-five days in all. The 6th USSR Supreme Soviet (1962–66) met eight times, twenty-two days in all.

Although the constitutional requirement for at least two sessions a year has generally been met in recent years,[1] sessions are not at all regular. The nearest to regular is the late year session (normally in December) at which the state budget and the economic plan are passed.

Many provisions of the Constitution relating to the Supreme Soviet have never operated. Thus Art. 46 provides that extraordinary sessions of the Supreme Soviet may be convened 'on the demand of one of the Union Republics'. In fact, all sessions to date have been convened by the Presidium of the Supreme Soviet. The Constitution (in Art. 47) provides for a double dissolution in the event of a continued deadlock between the two chambers which cannot be settled by means of a conciliation commission. But no deadlock has ever occurred nor could it ever occur within the Soviet system. Art. 148 of the USSR Constitution requires a two-thirds majority vote in both chambers in cases of constitutional amendment. This is meaningless as all amendments are carried unanimously.

The USSR Constitution establishes only the basis for representation in the Soviet of the Union and the Soviet of Nationalities but does not fix the size of either chamber in exact figures. The natural increase in population, the inclusion of new Union Republics, and the enlargement of their representation (in 1966) has tended to keep both chambers steadily enlarging. The 5th USSR Supreme Soviet, elected in March 1958, consisted of 1,378 deputies, 738 in the Soviet of the Union and 640 in the Soviet of Nationalities. Seven deputies in each chamber were returned by army constituencies, although the Constitution makes no provision for this. The 6th USSR Supreme Soviet (elected in March 1962) consisted of 1,443 deputies, elected from 784 electorates in the Soviet of the Union, 645 electorates in the Soviet of Nationalities, plus 7 army electorates in each chamber. The 7th USSR Supreme Soviet (elected in June 1966) consisted of 1,517 deputies, 750 elected by the Soviet of Nationalities and 767 by the Soviet of the Union. Although the army constituencies were abolished before the election of this Supreme Soviet, the increase in the number of representatives in the Soviet of Nationalities coming from each Union Republic (32 instead of 25) brought about a substantial increase in the size of the Soviet of Nationalities. Despite an increase in the number of electors the number of seats for the Soviet of the Union fell. This could only have been brought about by a reconstruction of electorates. The USSR Supreme Soviet has grown from a body of 1,143 deputies in December 1937 to 1,517 today.

The Supreme Soviet is regarded by Soviet writers as being representative of all sections of Soviet society. In fact the most significant thing about it is the preponderance of Communists. Communists (including candidate members) have comprised between 72% and 76% of the deputies of the last four USSR Supreme Soviets. They comprised 72·2% of deputies elected to the 8th USSR Supreme Soviet June 1970.[2] Soviet authorities emphasize the large representation of industrial workers and collective farmers in the Supreme Soviet. These two classes comprised 46% of the deputies elected in June 1966 (industrial workers 26·6%, collective farmers 19·4%). However, almost half of the deputies are drawn from white collar workers and intelligentsia, and the largest single representation (34·1% in 1966) comes from the apparatus—party, state, trade union and *komsomol*. Slightly more than one in four of all deputies are women,[3] while more than three-quarters are holders of government orders and medals.[4] This latter fact is regarded as a vindication of the claim that 'the best sons and daughters of the people' are elected as deputies. It might equally be held to establish the fact that the position of deputy to the USSR Supreme Soviet is honorific, reserved as a reward for good service to the regime. More than half of all deputies (51·4% in 1966) have received a tertiary (complete or unfinished) education. The majority of deputies (58·5% in 1966) will be over forty, a minority under forty.

Composition of the USSR Supreme Soviet

Supreme Soviet	Total number of Deputies	Soviet of Union	Soviet of Nats.	Men	Women	Party Memb.	Non-Party
1st, 1937–46	1143	569	574	954	189	870	273
2nd, 1946–50	1339	682	657	1062	277	1085	254
3rd, 1950–54	1316	678	638	1036	280	1099	217
4th, 1954–58	1347	708	639	999	348	1050	297
5th, 1958–62	1384	738	646	1015	369	1052	332
6th, 1962–66*	1443	791	652	1053	390	1094	349
7th, 1966–70†	1517	767	750	1092	425	1141	376
8th, 1970–74†	1517	767	750	1054	463	1096	421

* Figures for the 6th USSR Supreme Soviet are taken from *Izvestia*, April 25, 1962.

† Figures for the 7th USSR Supreme Soviet are taken from *Pravda*, August 4, 1966. Figures for the 8th USSR Supreme Soviet, *Pravda*, July 15, 1970.

This table is based on that given in M. G. Kirichenko, *Verkhovny Sovet SSSR*, Moscow, 1962, p. 75.

POWERS AND FUNCTIONS

Article 30 of the USSR Constitution describes the Supreme Soviet as 'the highest organ of state power in the USSR', while Art. 32 states that, 'the legislative power of the USSR is exercised exclusively by the Supreme Soviet of the USSR'. In fact effective legislative power is exercised by the Presidium. The Presidium, however, is accountable to the Supreme Soviet and, apart from the war years, the accounting has been regularly performed. The Constitution also entrusts the Supreme Soviet with the appointment of the Council of Ministers (Art. 70). This is done in the case of a new Supreme Soviet at its first session but resignations and replacements are done by the

Presidium if they happen while the Supreme Soviet is not in session (Art. 49 (g)).

We have already seen that the Supreme Soviet is the highest organ of state power and the supreme legislative body in the USSR. Yet the answer to the question, 'What does the Supreme Soviet do?' is to be found neither in the Constitution nor in the textbooks of Soviet jurists but only in the empirical study of the institution. On this practical basis we can say that the Supreme Soviet fulfils the following functions in the contemporary Soviet state system:

(*a*) It appoints the Presidium and the Council of Ministers.

(*b*) It ratifies decrees (*ukazy*) of the Presidium of the Supreme Soviet, including replacements to and changes in the structure of the Council of Ministers.

(*c*) It passes the State Budget and the State Economic Plan.

(*d*) It passes a limited number of important laws.

(*e*) It maintains an active committee system.

(*f*) It provides an agency for asking questions of the government.

These six functions are discussed at some length below.

The function of appointing the Presidium and the Council of Ministers normally occurs only once in four years, at the first session of a newly elected Supreme Soviet. The size of both these appointed bodies is determined in the Constitution (in Arts. 48 and 70). The personnel is never debated in the Supreme Soviet as a whole although there is some evidence of the personnel of the non-ex-officio members of the Presidium being discussed by the Council of Elders, the senior deputies.[5] The personnel of the Council of Ministers is never debated by the Supreme Soviet as a whole. Thus in March 1958 Voroshilov, the then Chairman of the Presidium, proposed on behalf of the Central Committee of the CPSU that N. S. Khrushchev should be appointed as Chairman of the Council of Ministers. This was approved unanimously. At the close of the same session Khrushchev announced the composition of his Ministry which was also ratified without debate.

The normal procedure in the case of ratifying decrees and appointments of the Presidium is for the Secretary of the Presidium to present a report to the Supreme Soviet on the work of the Presidium since the last regular session of the Supreme Soviet. These reports are quite brief and merely summarize the main decrees passed and the main appointments made. Texts of the decrees are not included in these reports but they are known to the deputies and have been examined by the Legislative Proposals Commissions. No debate ever occurs on these reports. The Presidium's report is voted on as a

120

whole and is invariably adopted unanimously. Despite this, the procedure is not lightly regarded and is meticulously observed. While it does not allow for the exercise of the degree of supervision that is required by the conventions of responsible government it is not intended to do this but merely to ensure the accountability of the Presidium to the Supreme Soviet and this it certainly achieves. It should be noted that some acts of the Presidium—those not involving any change to existing statutory law—do not require Supreme Soviet confirmation.[6] The accountability is thus designed merely to protect the Supreme Soviet's position as the ultimate legislative authority.

FINANCIAL POWERS

Under the present Budget Law (adopted October 1959) the USSR State Budget is adopted by the Supreme Soviet towards the end of the year preceding the year covered by the budget. Thus the 1960 budget was adopted in October 1959, the 1961 budget in December 1960 and the 1962 budget in December 1961. The budget contains a statement of estimates for income and expenditure for the USSR as a whole and for each Union Republic. It also contains estimates for the USSR (although not for the Union Republics) of the amount to be raised from various sources of revenue and the amounts to be spent in the main fields of expenditure (i.e., national economy, defence, social services and administration). As well as approving the estimates for the following year the Supreme Soviet is asked to approve the fulfilment of the budget for the previous year. Thus in December 1961 the USSR Supreme Soviet passed two financial laws, the one confirming the 1960 budget, the other approving the 1962 budget.[7] The economic plan and budget presented in December 1963 covered two years, 1964–65. However, the Supreme Soviet approved a new increased plan and budget for 1965 when it met in December 1964 after the fall of Khrushchev.

Budget debates are usually linked to a debate on the economic plan. This occurred in October 1959 and in December 1960 and in subsequent years. When this happens the two reports will be given to a joint sitting of the two Chambers. The Chambers will then meet separately to hear co-reports from the Budget Commission and, in the case of the Soviet of Nationalities, from the Economic Commission.* The debate which follows in each chamber will range freely over the budget and the economic plan and will involve rather more deputies than if it is a straight budget debate. Thus 80 deputies (exclusive of *rapporteurs*) participated in the combined plan-budget debate in October 1959, 64 in December 1960, 58 in December 1961 and

* Replaced by the Planning-Budget Commission, August 1966.

43 in December 1964. On the other hand only 35 deputies took part in the straight budget debate in December 1958. A combined budget-plan debate[8] will last between two and three days.

Although budget debates vary in detail they fall into a fairly standard pattern. Therefore it is not unfair to examine a single debate, that of December 1961. At 11 a.m. on December 6, 1961, after brief separate meetings, a joint meeting of the chambers of the Supreme Soviet was held in the great hall of the Kremlin. Reports were made by V. N. Novikov, deputy Chairman of the USSR Council of Ministers and Chairman of the USSR Gosplan, on the Economic Plan and by V. F. Garbuzov, USSR Minister of Finance, on the USSR State Budget for 1962 and the fulfilment of the 1960 Budget. After a brief interval the two chambers reassembled separately. In each case the debate was opened by reports from the chairmen of the relevant Standing Commissions (from the Budget Commissions and, in the case of the Soviet of Nationalities, from the Economic Commission). The debate 'from the floor' then commenced and lasted the remainder of that day, all the following day and until midday on the third day. The debates were followed by a joint sitting at which Novikov and Garbuzov replied to the discussion. The vote was then taken and carried unanimously. *Rapporteurs* apart, 58 deputies spoke in the debate, 30 in the Soviet of the Union and 28 in the Soviet of Nationalities.[9]

The main reports consisted of an optimistic survey of recent achievements and future prospects. The co-reports made by the chairmen of the Standing Commissions were rather more critical and contained various proposals for the modification of the government proposals, especially in the case of the Budget Commission reports. Thus in the 1961 debate the Budget Commissions accepted the government decision to increase defence expenditure (by 13% as compared with 1961). They contained recommendations for more uniform application of the policy of economies in public administration, suggestions that the finances of the new agricultural organization (*soyuzselkhoztekhnika*) should be more closely controlled by Gosplan, Gosbank and the Finance Ministries. They reported on requests received from Councils of Ministers of the Union Republics for supplementary finance and recommended increases of expenditure amounting to 88,420,000 roubles, including 20 millions for capital investment. The latter recommendation was also made by the Economic Commission of the Soviet of Nationalities.[10]

Deputies who spoke in the debate ranged from completely uncritical adulation of party and government policy to sharp criticism of failures in detail. The criticism was usually limited to the failures of central governmental agencies and Ministries over a limited area such as a city, an Autonomous Republic or even a Union Republic. Many speakers urged additional finance to enable plans for education, hospital services, transport, sewerage, flood control, housing, capital development, and so on, to be carried out. Thus a deputy from the Kirgiz Republic in the Soviet of Nationalities requested an increase of 12 million roubles in the marketing fund for cloth.[11] A deputy from Tashkent stated that 'the collective of the Tashkent Textile workers has directed me to raise these questions in the session of the USSR Supreme Soviet and to request that the appropriation for housing construction, and also for the construction of public buildings, schools and kindergartens, should be increased.'[12] A deputy from Turkmenia[13] requested alterations to the national economic plan and budget relating to his republic and asked for increased allocations for repairs and equipment for health and educational establishments. A deputy of the North Ossetian ASSR complained that the production plans of several enterprises in his republic had been changed three times during the last year but that the costs of such changes had to be met by the republican budget. This had meant additional expenditure of 2·2 million roubles. Because of this he had no compunction in asking the Ministry of Finance to increase the allocation for flood control in the urban areas of his republic by half a million roubles![14] A Moldavian deputy requested additional allocations for the construction of rural schools and also 1·5 million roubles for the purchases of visual aids, appliances and equipment, and climaxed this by adding, 'We have various other difficulties.' These included the complaint that not a single theatre had been built in the capital, Kishinev, since 1945; that six theatres shared two quite inadequate buildings; and that the local chemicals industry was so starved for capital that it never fulfilled its plan.[15]

The 'concluding words' speeches by the Ministers usually involve the acceptance of the main recommendations of the Standing Commissions. Individual requests however are acknowledged but as a rule no definite promises are made. At most the deputy will be assured that his proposals will be looked into and if found practicable, will be included in next year's plan. Occasionally local requests meet with a sharp rebuke. Thus deputy Orlov who requested in the December 1961 debate that 100% of the profit of local industry in Kamchatka should go to local Soviets for the development of local industry was told incisively that the percentage of profits of local industry to go to local budgets in Kamchatka in 1962 was 83% whereas the USSR average was only 17%, and that this ought to be enough even for Kamchatka![16]

Thus the budget-economic plan debates serve as an occasion for detailed criticism of government policy but not for a general debate on that policy. The minority of speakers who discuss general and international issues merely endorse official policy.

LEGISLATIVE POWERS

In assessing the legislative record of the Supreme Soviet it must be remembered that although the Constitution gives the legislative power exclusively to the Supreme Soviet it also gives the power of delegated legislation to the Presidium and the Council of Ministers (Arts. 49 and 66). As far as the power of initiating legislation goes it is possessed by the following bodies:

(a) each of the chambers of the USSR Supreme Soviet;

(b) the Presidium of the Supreme Soviet of the USSR;

(c) The Council of Ministers of the USSR Supreme Soviet;

(d) Commissions of both chambers of the Supreme Soviet of the USSR;

(e) Deputies of the Supreme Soviet, either individually or in groups;

(f) The Supreme Court of the USSR,[17] the Procurator-General, the AUCCTU, and the Supreme Soviets of Union Republics.

As far as actual legislative power goes the Presidium, the Council of Ministers and individual Ministries exercise aspects of this power although only the USSR Supreme Soviet has complete legislative power including the power of constitutional amendment. A good deal of what would pass as parliamentary legislation in Britain or Australia is passed as decrees and decisions of the Presidium of the USSR Supreme Soviet and as decisions and orders of the Council of Ministers. However, since 1956 many important measures have been brought before the Supreme Soviet, often draft bills have been published and publicly discussed. Yet there is little evidence to suggest that either the Supreme Soviet itself or its Legislative Proposals Commissions take the initiative in legislation. They act on the initiative taken elsewhere, usually in the Politbureau of the Central Committee of the CPSU.

Important legislation passed by the Supreme Soviet since 1956 includes the following statutes:

(i) The *Pensions Law* (July 1956). This was adopted after a debate in which twenty-four deputies in each chamber spoke. Various amendments recommended by the Legislative Proposals Commissions and by individual deputies were adopted. These included the extension of the age range of pensions and an increase in the allocation for pensions of almost 4% on the amount proposed by the government.[18]

(ii) On May 10, 1957, the law concerning the further improvement of the organizations of direction of industry and construction, was adopted by the Supreme Soviet. The main proposals of this law were contained in the theses of the Central Committee of the CPSU published on March 30, 1957. An extensive public debate lasting five and a half weeks occurred before Khrushchev made his report to the Supreme Soviet on May 7. Thirty deputies took part in the Supreme Soviet debate.[19]

(iii) The March 1958 'Law on the further development of the Collective Farm System and the Reorganization of the Machine Tractor Stations' followed a report by Khrushchev to the Central Committee (published March 1, 1958) and an extensive public discussion over four weeks. Forty-three deputies spoke in the Supreme Soviet debate.[20]

(iv) The Education Act adopted by the Supreme Soviet in December 1958 followed a public debate over several months and a Supreme Soviet debate in which thirty-six deputies (eighteen from each chamber) participated.[21]

(v) The laws reforming the Criminal Code and the Judicial System, nine in all, were debated and adopted by the Supreme Soviet in December 1958. The drafts of the new codes were prepared by the Legislative Proposals Commissions of the Supreme Soviet and were extensively discussed, especially in legal circles. Only seven deputies took part in the limited debate in the Supreme Soviet.[22]

(vi) The Supreme Soviet in October 1959 passed a new Law on the Budgetary Powers of the USSR and the Union Republics and a Law on the Method of Recall of Deputies of the USSR Supreme Soviet. Both laws were introduced by the Legislative Proposals Commissions. The debates on these measures were conducted in joint meetings of the two chambers and were of limited duration, only five deputies speaking on the former and six on the latter.[23]

(vii) In January 1960 the Supreme Soviet passed a Law on the Reduction of the Armed Forces of the USSR by 1·2 millions in one year. This was passed without any special debate following a report by Khrushchev which dealt mainly with international affairs and which was followed by a debate in which thirty-three deputies spoke.[24]

(viii) In December 1961 the USSR Supreme Soviet passed the Basic Civil Code of the USSR and the Union Republics, and the Basic Code of Civil Procedure. Only four deputies spoke in the limited debate on these measures conducted at a joint sitting of both chambers.[25]

(ix) In July 1964 the Supreme Soviet passed two important statutes the first granting pensions to collective farmers, the second substantially increasing the salaries of workers in certain services such as public health, education, house services, trade and public catering. Twenty-one deputies spoke in the debates on these proposals in the Soviet of the Union and twenty-three spoke in the Soviet of Nationalities.

(x) In October 1965, following the decisions taken in the Central Committee of the CPSU in the previous month, the government proposed the reorganization of the planning and industrial administrative structure. This important statute, which cancelled the May 1957 reform was followed by a limited debate in which thirty-six deputies (eighteen in each chamber) participated.

The increasing legislative activity of the USSR Supreme Soviet is shown by the fact that whereas the 2nd USSR Supreme Soviet (1946–50) passed 9 statutes (*zakony*), exclusive of laws ratifying decrees, and the 3rd USSR Supreme Soviet (1950–54) passed 10, the 4th USSR Supreme Soviet passed 24 and the 5th USSR Supreme Soviet (1958–62) passed 27.[26]

Besides passing a small number of important laws the Supreme Soviet frequently passes laws amending the Constitution. Thus laws amending various articles of the Constitution have been passed at sessions in February, May and December 1957, in December 1958, October 1959, May and December 1960, December 1961, April and December 1962, December 1963 and 1964, October and December 1965, August 1966, June 1968, July and December 1969 and September 1972.

All amendments have been passed without debate and in fact the legislation has merely served as formal ratification of amendments already carried into effect by the Presidium.

THE COMMITTEE SYSTEM

The Committee System of the USSR Supreme Soviet is considerably developed, much more so than that of the Australian Parliament although much less than that of the United States Congress or even of the British Parliament. Until 1966 each chamber operated the following Standing Commissions:

> Credentials (21 members in each),
> Budget (39 members in each),
> Foreign Affairs (23 members in each),
> Legislative Proposals (31 members in each).

The Soviet of Nationalities also operated over the years 1957–66 an Economic Commission (31 members). Following criticisms of the inadequacy of these commissions at the 23rd Party Congress in April 1966 the system was reorganized by the Supreme Soviet in August 1966. In addition to the Credentials Commission (31 members in each) each chamber then had nine Standing Commissions—Planning-Budget; Industry, Transport and Communications; Construction and Industrial Building Materials; Agriculture; Health and Social Security; Education, Science and Culture; Trade and Everyday Services; Legislative Proposals; and Foreign Affairs. By 1970 two further Standing Commissions, those on Youth Matters and the Defence of Nature, had been added and some of the earlier Commissions had been enlarged. The proportion of deputies serving on Standing Commissions rose from 15% in the 6th Supreme Soviet to 49% in the 7th to 60·7% in the 8th Supreme Soviet in 1970.

Until recently very little was known about the work of the Standing Commissions. However, over the past few years a good deal of detailed information has been published in the Soviet Union.[27] Unfortunately this work is not widely known in the West. The Standing Commissions operate mainly through sub-commissions of ten to twelve members which consider the details of legislation relating to specific departments and agencies. The only case quoted of legislation actually being initiated by the Legislative Proposals Commissions was the constitutional amendment passed by the USSR Supreme Soviet in February 1957 under which questions of regional and territorial administrative structure were transferred from USSR control to the control of the Union Republics.[28] Most of the work of the Legislative Proposals Commissions would seem to consist of surveying and drafting legislation proposed by the Presidium, the Council of Ministers, individual departments, the Supreme Court or the Procuracy, and here the main work is performed by the sub-commissions.[29] Out of twenty-seven statutes passed by the 5th USSR Supreme Soviet (1958–62) fourteen were prepared by the Standing Commissions.[30]

The Credentials Commissions perform largely routine functions. The Chairmen of these Commissions present fairly full reports on the composition of their chambers after each general election, and twice a year present brief reports on by-elections which have occurred since the previous session.

The Planning-Budget Commissions examine the draft (departmental) budget two to three months before the Supreme Soviet session at which the budget is to be presented. Following this report given by the Finance Minister the draft budget is examined in detail by various sub-commissions, each one headed by a member of the Planning-Budget Commission but including representatives of Gosplan, Gosbank, Ministries and various economic departments.

The budgets of the Union Republics are examined by members of the Planning-Budget Commissions working in collaboration with representatives of the Union Republics (nominated by the Union Republican Councils of Ministers). These investigations form the basis of the modifications to the budget which are presented by the Planning-Budget Commissions during the budget-plan debate. The consolidation of formerly separate Budget and Economic Commissions in August 1966 was clearly intended to facilitate the simultaneous review of the draft budget and the annual economic plan.

The Standing Commissions on Foreign Affairs examine material on foreign affairs, examine and make recommendations on draft treaties, give answers to questions raised by deputies, draft resolutions on foreign affairs, and participate in inter-parliamentary exchanges. International parliamentary exchanges are of growing importance. Thus during the 4th USSR Supreme Soviet (1954–58) thirty countries sent parliamentary delegations to the USSR while the Supreme Soviet sent delegations to twenty-three foreign countries. Soviet participation in Inter-Parliamentary Union Conferences is also handled by the Standing Commissions on Foreign Affairs. An indication of the growing importance of these Foreign Affairs Commissions is provided by the fact that they are normally under the chairmanship of a leading Communist. Thus the Chairman of the Soviet of Nationalities Commission on Foreign Affairs during the 5th Supreme Soviet was N. A. Mukhitdinov, who during this period was a member of the Central Committee and for a time a member of the Secretariat and the Presidium of the Central Committee of the CPSU. Mukhitdinov led the 'parliamentary delegation' to India in March 1959. The Chairman of the Foreign Affairs Commission of the Soviet of Nationalities appointed in August 1966 was M. A. Suslov a member of the Politbureau and the Secretariat of the Central Committee of the CPSU. The Chairman of the Foreign Affairs Commission of the Soviet of the Union appointed in August 1966 was B. N. Ponomarev, a member of the Secretariat of the C. C. of the CPSU.

The Economic Commission of the Soviet of Nationalities which operated between February 1957 and August 1966 proved itself a useful agency for the scrutiny of draft economic plans and for suggesting revisions to meet the desires of national minorities and non-Russian regions of the USSR. It was responsible for several amendments to the Seven-Year Plan (1959–65) and to annual plans submitted between 1958 and 1965. Much of the detailed work of this Commission was done through its four sub-commissions covering Industrial Construction, Transport and Communications; Agriculture and Purchasing; Health and Housing Construction; and, Trade and Income. Between 1960 and 1965 the Economic Commission worked in close co-operation with the two Budget Commissions. Only in October 1959 was a disagreement reported, when the Budget Commission recommended a lowering of capital investment by 126·2 million roubles (old style) while the Economic Commission recommended an increase of 440 million roubles.[31] This rare disharmony in the Soviet system was resolved by the adoption of the recommendations of the Economic Commission. The reorganization of August 1966 made it possible for the work of review and criticism of both economic plan and budget to be handled by one commission in each chamber. The functions of the earlier Economic Commission have been absorbed by the Planning-Budget Commissions. The Standing Commissions include deputies from all walks of life and from all parts and national groups of the country. However, since the work of the Commissions places a premium on education and knowledge rank-and-file workers and collective farmers are somewhat under-represented while professionals (especially party and state officials) are overrepresented. Persons with a complete tertiary education represented 48·4% of all deputies to the 8th Supreme Soviet but 58·5% of members of the Standing Commissions.

QUESTIONS

The final function of the USSR Supreme Soviet is to allow deputies to ask questions of the government or of individual Ministers. Over recent years groups of deputies have several times asked questions on foreign affairs. Whether 'arranged' or not, these questions permit the Foreign Minister to make a statement on foreign policy and allow a limited discussion on foreign affairs. Thus during the December 1958 session one group of deputies asked for information on the Western Powers' attitude to Soviet proposals on Berlin, while another group asked for information on the progress of negotiations on the ending of nuclear weapons tests. Both questions were answered some days later by the Foreign Affairs Minister, Gromyko, in a report to a joint session. Five deputies spoke in the limited debate which followed.[32]

The Supreme Soviet does not provide anything equivalent to the 'question time' of a British Parliament. However, despite the fact that deputies seldom ask questions publicly during a session it is certain that they spend a good deal of time during sessions or on other visits to Moscow taking up local problems with the Ministry or Department concerned. Deputies of the Supreme Soviet, like deputies of lower Soviets, are now required by law to make regular reports back to their electorate and are expected to maintain regular contacts with their electors. The fact that the majority of them spend most of their time in their electorates and not in Moscow facilitates this contact. However, while the Soviet system of 'amateur parliamentarians' does facilitate contact between the deputy and the collective which nominated him (usually his workplace) it makes it difficult for him to establish close relations with the rest of his very large electorate. Because of this a deputy recently urged that deputies of the USSR Supreme Soviet should receive one to four days a month of paid time off from work in order to enable proper relations with electors to be maintained.[33]

The conclusions I would draw from this analysis of the contemporary Supreme Soviet are as follows. Firstly, the Supreme Soviet is not the main legislative body of the USSR but its role as a law-making as distinct from a law-ratifying agency is certainly increasing. Secondly, the Supreme Soviet does not afford the possibility of extensive debate on domestic and foreign policy. The sessions are too short, the debates too restricted and too few deputies participate in the debates for this to happen. In December 1958 less than 8% of deputies spoke, exclusive of reports. In October 1959, a record for debate, there were 8 reports and co-reports, 6 speeches in reply and 99 speeches in the debate; slightly over 8% of deputies. In December 1960, 71 deputies spoke, exclusive of reports, barely 6% of the total number of deputies.

Thirdly, the Supreme Soviet does allow for a limited discussion of government policy and it does play an important secondary role in legislation. In addition to its regular debate of the two most important legislative measures of the year, the Budget and the State Economic Plan, it discusses at least some of the more important legislative enactments. The customary Western evaluation of the USSR Supreme Soviet serving merely as an automatic rubber stamp for legislation prepared in the inner circles of the Communist Party is not fully accurate. Nor does the Communist Party monopoly necessarily mean that all legislation is rushed through the Supreme Soviet without allowing time for its consideration. It is perhaps worth remembering that the amendments to the Commonwealth Crimes Act (Australia) 1960 were introduced by the government in September, rushed through Parliament after a two-day debate at the second-reading stage, and passed under the guillotine before the end of the same year, whereas the USSR Basic Criminal Code took six months to pass the Supreme Soviet and more than two years to go through the Union Republics.[34]

Finally, in assessing the legislative role of the USSR Supreme Soviet, the work of the Standing Commissions as well as the sessions of the Soviet itself must be borne in mind. If only 5–8% of deputies participate in the discussions on policy in the Supreme Soviet one out of every two deputies (one out of six in the 6th USSR Supreme Soviet)[35] participate in the work of the Standing Commissions, and a bigger percentage is involved in committee work if the various temporary committees are included.

NOTES

[1] Although there was only one session in 1959 and in 1961 it must be remembered that the Supreme Soviet year then ran from March to March.

[2] Based on the two reports of the Credentials Commissions as reported in *Pravda*, July 15, 1970.

[3] Women comprised 26·5% of the USSR Supreme Soviet elected March 1958, 27·1% of that elected March 1966, and 27·0% of that elected June 1966, 30·5% of that elected in June 1970.

[4] 87% of deputies elected March 1958 held orders and medals. Cf. 76·6% of deputies elected March 1962 and 76·6% of deputies elected June 1966.

[5] Ya. N. Umansky, 1959, p. 274. 'During the period of work of sessions of the Supreme Soviet each Chamber chooses a Council of Elders from the deputies groups of the various republics, territories and provinces. This auxiliary organ possesses neither administrative nor legislative powers. The Council of Elders may propose for the consideration of the USSR Supreme Soviet proposals relating to the agenda of the session, the candidature of organs chosen by the USSR Supreme Soviet, and so on.'

[6] *Ibid.*, pp. 284–7.

[7] *Izvestia*, December 7 and 9, 1961.

[8] While the Constitution does not require that either the Budget or the State Economic Plan should be submitted to the Supreme Soviet the present practice is for the Budget and the Annual State Economic Plan to be submitted. Thus the annual economic plan has been discussed and approved by the Supreme Soviet in February 1957, December 1957, October 1959, December 1960, December 1961, December 1961, December 1962.

[9] Based on the reports of the session contained in *Izvestia* December 7–10, 1961.

[10] *Izvestia*, December 8, 1961.

[11] T. Kulatov, *Izvestia*, December 8, 1961.

[12] N. A. Ignatov in the Soviet of Nationalities, *Izvestia*, December 9, 1961.

[13] A. A. Annaliev, in the Soviet of Nationalities, *Izvestia*, December 9, 1961.

[14] B. D. Zangrev, in the Soviet of Nationalities, *Izvestia*, December 9, 1961.

[15] A. P. Lupan in the Soviet of the Union, *Izvestia*, December 9, 1961.

[16] Concluding words of V. F. Garbuzov in *Izvestia*, December 9, 1961.

[17] Ya. N. Umansky, *op. cit.*, p. 266. Cf. M. G. Kirichenko: *Verkhovny Sovet SSSR*, 1962, pp. 45–8.

[18] *Pravda*, July 11–16, 1956.

[19] *Izvestia*, May 8–11, 1957.

[20] *Izvestia*, March 28–April 1, 1958.

[21] *Izvestia*, December 24–25, 1958.

[22] *Izvestia*, December 26, 1958.

[23] *Izvestia*, October 28–31, 1959.

[24] *Izvestia*, January 15–16, 1960.

[25] *Izvestia*, December 7–10, 1961.

[26] *S.G.i.P.*, No. 3, 1962, p. 3. Important statutes passed by the USSR Supreme Soviet since 1966 include the following:

Statute on Universal Military Training, October 1967;
Basic Law on Marriage and the Family, June 1968;
Basic Agrarian Law, December 1968;
Statute on Corrective Labour, July 1969;
Basic Law on Health Services, December 1969;
Basic Labour Code of the USSR and the Union Republics, July 1970;
Basic Water Regulations of the USSR and the Union Republics, December 1970;
Statute on Deputies of Soviets, September 1971;
Basic Code of the USSR and the Union Republics on Education. July 1973.

[27] For example, P. P. Lobanov in *S.G.i.P.* No. 3, 1958, pp. 15–31; Ya. N. Umansky, *op. cit.*, pp. 274–80; A. Denisov and M. Kirichenko, 1960, pp. 224–8; S. G. Novikov, *Postoyanny komissii verkhovnovo Soveta SSSR*, Moscow, 1962. The report by N. V. Podgorny to the Supreme Soviet, August 2, 1966, also contained an appraisal of the commission system. *Pravda*, August 3, 1966. The fullest Soviet account of the work of the Standing Commissions of the Supreme Soviet to appear to date is that by Kutafin, O. E., 1971.

[28] P. P. Lobanov, *S.G.i.P.*, No. 3, 1958.

[29] More than forty statutes, decisions and other acts adopted by the 5th USSR Supreme Soviet (1958–62) were drafted and formally proposed by the various Standing Commissions. M. G. Kirichenko, 1962, p. 41.

[30] Kh. Makhnenko in *S.G.i.P.*, No. 8, 1964, pp. 56–66.

[31] The Budget Commission reports were made by M. A. Yasnov in the Soviet of Nationalities and I. S. Senin in the Soviet of the Union. The Economic Commission report was made by O. I. Ivashchenko. *Izvestia*, October 28, 1959.

[32] *Izvestia*, December 26, 1958.

[33] V. Markina, 'To the Replacement!', *Sovety*, No. 5, 1966, pp. 24–8.

[34] Cf. R. Schlesinger, in *Soviet Studies*, X, pp. 295 ff., and XII, April 1961, pp. 456–64.

[35] This of course represents a much lower involvement of deputies of the Supreme Soviet in the Standing Commissions than is the case with the local Soviets. This fact, and other shortcomings in the work of the Standing Commissions, was recently sharply criticized by Kh. Makhnenko in 'The Greater Role and Improvement of the Activities of the Standing Commissions of the Supreme Soviets in drafting Bills', in *S.G.i.P.* No. 8, 1964, pp. 56–66. The reconstruction of the Commission system in 1966 was designed to improve this situation.

SELECTED BIBLIOGRAPHY

Braham, R. L., 1965, pp. 310–29.
Chkhikvadze, V. M., ed., 1972, pp. 95–124.
Denisov and Kirichenko, 1960, Ch. 6.
Little, D. R., 1972.
McClosky and Turner, 1960, pp. 332–49.
Scott, D. J. R., 4th edn. 1969, pp. 99–110.

Chapter 9

THE PRESIDIUM AND
THE COUNCIL OF MINISTERS

THE PRESIDIUM OF THE SUPREME SOVIET

The two higher bodies of the Soviet state system are sometimes confused. The Presidium is even now sometimes referred to in the West as the 'government'. This is inaccurate. Formally, the term 'government' in the USSR is identified with the USSR Council of Ministers. In reality the term government might more accurately be applied to the Politbureau of the Central Committee of the CPSU. This underlying fact even intrudes itself into the formality of Soviet political reportage, as for instance when the newspapers enumerate the personnel of the Party Politbureau as occupying the 'government box' in a session of the USSR Supreme Soviet.

The Presidium of the USSR Supreme Soviet is a body without even a remote parallel in the British parliamentary system. It is the modern equivalent and the direct descendant of the earlier Central Executive Committee (TsIK). However, while the earlier body was large and unwieldy the present body is a relatively small body of thirty-seven members.* Its composition is set out in Art. 48 and consists of a President, fifteen Vice-Presidents (one from each Union Republic), a Secretary, and twenty ordinary members. It is elected at a joint sitting of both chambers of the Supreme Soviet and is accountable to the Supreme Soviet.

The Presidium is best described as a combination of a standing committee of the legislature and a collective presidency. In its former capacity its powers include the issuing of decrees, the issuing of decisions based on laws of the USSR already in operation, annulling decisions and orders of the USSR Council of Ministers and of the Councils of Ministers of the Union Republics which do not conform to law, and the ratification and denunciation of international treaties. In its presidential role it performs a large number of formal and

* Prior to August 1966, thirty-three members.

133

ceremonial functions such as convening sessions of the Supreme Soviet, dissolving the Supreme Soviet, ordering elections and appointing the Central Election Commission. It appoints and relieves Ministers of the USSR (when the Supreme Soviet is not in session), awards decorations and honours (as decided upon by the government), exercises the right of pardon, and receives foreign statesmen and diplomats.

The Presidium has at one time or other exercised most of its formal functions but it is mainly before the people through its handling of the following:

(a) Issuing *decrees* and *decisions;*
(b) Making appointments to the USSR Council of Ministers;
(c) Conferring awards and honours;
(d) Holding receptions to foreign statesmen and diplomats.

Very little information is available on the organization of the Presidium. We do not even know how often it meets or even if it always meets as a whole. Although both decrees (*ukazy*) and decisions (*postanovlenia*) are required to be arrived at collectively they are invariably issued under the signatures of the President and the Secretary and without any accompanying information as to when or how the decision was arrived at. Many ceremonial functions, such as for example, the receiving of letters of credence and recall of foreign ambassadors and diplomatic representatives are handled by the President or Vice-Presidents on behalf of the Presidium. Similarly the President will sometimes represent the Soviet state in foreign countries.

The accountability of the Presidium to the Supreme Soviet is regularly performed even if it is largely routinized. The powers of the Presidium, especially in the fields of legislation, are far from formal. This is recognized by most Soviet writers. Thus Denisov and Kirichenko state that:

Final decisions on some of the most important questions within the jurisdiction of the higher state organs of the USSR can be passed only by the Supreme Soviet of the USSR, since the settlement of these questions either necessitates the introduction of certain amendments into the Constitution of the USSR, or affects the composition of the state organs which, according to the Constitution are formed by the Supreme Soviet of the USSR, or concerns legislation of all-Union importance. Taking into account, however, that in the rather long intervals between sessions of the Supreme Soviet certain questions relating to the jurisdiction of the Supreme Soviet of the USSR may in some cases require urgent settlement and that the convocation of extraordinary sessions of the Supreme Soviet for this purpose is inexpedient, the Presidium of the

Supreme Soviet is empowered to decide such questions independently, subject to subsequent confirmation by the Supreme Soviet of the USSR.[1]

The powers of the Presidium are considerably extended during wartime when it is responsible for ordering mobilization and proclaiming martial law in various regions. During the Second World War (1940–45) the Presidium carried through several constitutional amendments which were not formally approved by the Supreme Soviet until February 1947. Some decrees of the Presidium do not require subsequent approval by the Supreme Soviet. These consist of decrees relating to questions which are within the exclusive jurisdiction of the Presidium. These include such matters as interpreting the laws of the USSR in operation, annulling decisions and orders of the Councils of Ministers of the USSR and of the Union Republics, issuing awards and honours, instituting military titles, ratifying and annulling international treaties, etc. Powers enumerated in Art. 49 and not also exercised by the USSR Supreme Soviet are exercised exclusively by the Presidium. Decrees of the former sort are classified by Soviet jurists as 'normative', while the latter are regarded as 'non-normative'.[2]

Besides decrees the Presidium sometimes issues decisions (*postanovlenia*), often relating to the work of the Executive Committees of Provincial Soviets. Both decrees and decisions of the Presidium become operative ten days after publication in *Izvestia* or *Vedomosti verkhovnovo Soveta SSSR*.

The relative importance of the position of the President is difficult to determine with precision. It is difficult to determine precisely the importance of the President. Until recently the post of President seemed to be inferior to that of Chairman of the Council of Ministers. Since the 24th Congress (April 1971) Podgorny has apparently been ranked ahead of Kosygin in the Party leadership. This would seem to indicate a re-evaluation of the importance of the position, an upgrading which is partly a consequence of the increased role of the Presidium in the work of supervising Soviets and especially Standing Commissions of Soviets.

THE USSR COUNCIL OF MINISTERS

The USSR Council of Ministers is sometimes described as the Soviet 'cabinet' although this is inaccurate. It may fairly accurately be described as the government of the USSR.

The composition of the Council of Ministers is detailed in Art. 70 of the Constitution with the consequence that every change in the structure of the body requires a constitutional amendment. Over the past few years it has been a body of upwards of fifty members. Thus

The Structure of the July 1970 Council of Ministers

(1) *Chairman:*	A. N. Kosygin	
First Vice-Chairmen (2):	K. T. Mazurov	
	D. S. Polyansky	
Vice-Chairmen (9):	N. K. Baibakov	(Chairman of *Gosplan*)
	V. E. Dymshits	(Chairman of State Committee on Material-Technical Supplies)
	M. T. Efremov	
	V. A. Kirillin	(Chairman of State Committee on Science and Technology)
	M. A. Lesechko	
	V. N. Novikov	
	I. T. Novikov	(Chairman of State Committee on Construction)
	L. V. Smirnov	
	N. A. Tikhonov	

	 12
(2) *Ministers* (not included in 1)	 57
(3) *Chairmen of State Committees and other control agencies*	 11
(4) *Chairmen of Councils of Ministers of Union Republics* (ex officio)	 15
	TOTAL 95

the Council of Ministers elected in April 1962 consisted of seventy-one members, that elected in August 1966 consisted of eighty-four and that elected in July 1970 consisted of ninety-five members.[3]

The exact size of the USSR Council of Ministers cannot be determined from the text of Art. 70 of the Constitution. This is because central Ministries and departments change more rapidly than the text of the Constitution and because extra persons are sometimes included. Thus the Council of Ministers appointed in April 1962 included six representatives of *Gosplan* but the Constitution accorded that right only to the Chairman of Gosplan.

The size of the Council of Ministers suggests that much of its work must be handled by inner bodies. This has probably always been the case although there is some evidence to suggest that full meetings of the Council of Ministers are more frequent today than they were in Stalin's day. Legally, it is not necessary for all regulations of the

Council of Ministers to be taken collectively.[4]

The Council of Ministers is elected by the Supreme Soviet at the first session following an election. Replacements are appointed by the Presidium, subject to ratification by the Supreme Soviet. The practice under Stalin was for Stalin as Chairman of the retiring as well as the incoming Council of Ministers to recommend the composition of the Council to the Supreme Soviet which invariably ratified this unanimously. In March 1953 on the death of Stalin, a joint meeting of the Presidium of the Supreme Soviet, the Council of Ministers and the Central Committee of the CPSU, was convened and this extraordinary body, with no constitutional position, recommended Malenkov as Chairman of the Council of Ministers. This recommendation was carried by a special session of the Supreme Soviet on March 15, 1953. Malenkov's resignation was also somewhat unorthodox. This was made in February 1955 by way of a letter to the Supreme Soviet.[5] This undoubtedly followed criticism of Malenkov's administration and a decision to remove him taken at the January 1955 plenum of the Central Committee. Malenkov's resignation was accepted unanimously. Khrushchev then proposed on behalf of the Central Committee that Bulganin should be appointed as Chairman. This was also carried without debate. The only reshuffle in the government which occurred at this time was the promotion of Zhukov to head the Defence Ministry vacated by Bulganin's promotion to the Chairmanship. This change was not announced until February 28, after the Supreme Soviet had concluded its session.

Bulganin's replacement in March 1958 also involved an element of novelty which, as future events showed, sprang from divisions within the Presidium of the Central Committee. Although Bulganin was present at the Supreme Soviet session he did not announce his own retirement. This was done by Voroshilov, the President of the Presidium, who also proposed Khrushchev as the candidate of the Central Committee. Khrushchev was then elected unanimously. Membership of the new Council of Ministers (which included Bulganin as Chairman of *Gosbank*) was announced some days later and was adopted unanimously. April 1962 saw a reversion to the procedure followed in the Stalin period. N. V. Podgorny, a member of the Party Presidium, recommended on behalf of a number of deputies (including those from Moscow, Leningrad, Gorki and Sverdlovsk) that the Supreme Soviet approve the activities of the retiring government and entrust comrade Khrushchev to make recommendations on the composition of the new Council of Ministers. Khrushchev did this on the following day and the list of 71 persons as decided on by the Central Committee was accepted without discussion.

Khrushchev's resignation in October 1964 clearly followed a

majority decision of the Central Committee, or perhaps, of an enlarged Presidium of the Central Committee. The official announcement, printed in *Pravda* on October 16, merely stated:

On 14 October this year there took place a meeting of the plenum of the Central Committee of the CPSU.

The plenum of the C.C. of the CPSU met the request of comrade N. S. Khrushchev to be relieved of his duties as First Secretary of the C.C. of the CPSU, as a member of the Presidium of the C.C. of the CPSU, and as Chairman of the USSR Council of Ministers because of advancing age and continued worsening of health.

The plenum of the C.C. of the CPSU chose L. I. Brezhnev First Secretary of the C.C. of the CPSU.

While the statement did not acknowledge that the Party Presidium had chosen Kosygin to succeed Khrushchev as Chairman of the Council of Ministers there can be no doubt that it had. The same issue of *Pravda* reported that the Presidium of the USSR Supreme Soviet had met on October 15 under the chairmanship of Mikoyan and accepted Khrushchev's resignation from the Premiership for the reasons stated above. The Presidium then unanimously decided to appoint A. N. Kosygin, formerly First Deputy Chairman, to the vacant post of Chairman of the Council of Ministers. These decisions were unanimously endorsed by the Supreme Soviet itself in December 1964.

In August 1966 A. N. Kosygin announced the retirement of the government to the newly elected 7th USSR Supreme Soviet. Kosygin was immediately re-elected Chairman and asked to report later in the session on the composition of the new government. The following day, Kosygin proposed the composition of the new Council of Ministers as 'approved by the C.C. of the CPSU'. The Supreme Soviet unanimously endorsed the list. In July 1970 Brezhnev, on behalf of the Central Committee of the CPSU and the Councils of Elders of both Chambers proposed that Kosygin should again be appointed to head the government.

The above outline makes it clear that the Central Committee of the CPSU (or rather its inner organs, the Politbureau and the Secretariat) is the sole agency for selecting the Soviet Premier. It is also probable that the Politbureau has a decisive voice in filling the more important posts in the Council, including the Vice-Chairmanships. However, two qualifications to this need to be remembered. Firstly, the Chairman of the Council of Ministers exercises a major say within the party decision-making body and may well seek to use his position to promote his own supporters. Secondly, the fact that most members of the Council of Ministers are administrators rather than policy-makers means that there is always a certain degree of continuity in the persons holding such Ministries as Foreign Affairs, Defence, Health and Finance. Thus A. G. Zverev was Finance Minister from 1946 until his replacement by V. F. Garbuzov in 1960. He was Commissar of Finance from 1938 to 1946. V. M. Molotov was Commissar, then Minister for Foreign Affairs, from May 1939 to March 1949, and again from March 1953 to June 1956.

TYPES OF LEGISLATION

The Constitution defines the Council of Ministers as 'the highest executive and administrative organ of the state power of the USSR' (Art. 64). But the Council of Ministers also has wide legislative powers, although legally these are confined to 'delegated legislation'. Thus Art. 56 authorizes the Council of Ministers 'to issue decisions and orders, on the basis of and in pursuance of the laws in operation. . . .' In fact, these decisions and orders are no less effective than decrees of the Presidium or statutes of the Supreme Soviet. Most important legislative acts are issued jointly in the name of a state agency and the Central Committee of the CPSU. Sometimes, sections of the same legislation come through partly as decisions (authorized by the Council of Ministers and the Central Committee of the CPSU), and partly as decrees (issued by the Presidium of the Supreme Soviet. This was the case with the legislation relating to the tightening of controls over private livestock in August 1956, the section of this legislation relating to inhabitants of villages being covered by a decision, that relating to the inhabitants of towns by a decree.[6]

Similarly, the decision of the Central Committee on agriculture March 26, 1965, was followed by a spate of legislation issued during the following month. All this legislation acknowledged the earlier decision of the Central Committee as its basis. Seven main pieces of legislation were issued April 10–20; one decree of the Presidium of the USSR Supreme Soviet, three decisions of the USSR Council of Ministers, and three joint decisions of the C.C. of the CPSU and the USSR Council of Ministers.

Many decisions of the Council of Ministers are issued without any joint authorization by the Central Committee of the CPSU. Thus in April 1958 the Council of Ministers issued a decision relating to the increase of the production of furniture and for improving its quality during the years 1958–1960.[7] In some cases these decisions, while not specifically authorized by the Central Committee, openly acknowledge decisions of that body as their basis. Thus in June 1958 the Council of Ministers issued a decision to abolish compulsory deliveries and payment in kind for the work performed by Machine

Tractor Stations, and to abolish the *zagotovka* system in favour of a simple *zakupka* system in payment of agricultural products delivered to the state. This decision referred to the decision along these lines taken by the Central Committee of the CPSU in June 1958.[8]

At this point it is perhaps necessary to attempt a precise statement of the exact differences between the various legislative acts referred to in this chapter. Although Soviet jurists do not agree on all the finer points of the problem[9] the following would seem to be the essence of the distinctions:

(*a*) *zakony* or statutes may be passed only by the USSR Supreme Soviet or, within the limits of their powers, by the Supreme Soviets of the Union Republics or the Autonomous Republics.

(*b*) *ukazy* or decrees are the exclusive right of the Presidium of the USSR Supreme Soviet (and within their sphere of competency, of the Presidiums of Republican Soviets). Decrees generally cover a broader field than decisions and are generally based on the USSR Constitution. Decrees issued by the Presidium on the basis of the constitutional powers of the Supreme Soviet or supplementing or changing statutory law require the approval of the Supreme Soviet at its next session. These are the so-called *normative decrees*. Decrees based on the exclusive powers of the Presidium and which do not involve amendment to existing statutory law do not require approval by the Supreme Soviet. These are the so-called *non-normative decrees*.

(*c*) *postanovlenia* or decisions may be issued by the Supreme Soviet and the Presidium of the Supreme Soviet as well as by the Council of Ministers. They may also be issued by lower Soviets and Executive Committees of local Soviets. Decisions, whether taken by the USSR Council of Ministers or by a subordinate agency must be taken collectively.

(*d*) *rasporyazhenia* or orders may be issued by any of the executive bodies of the USSR state system including Executive Committees of local Soviets. However, the scope of orders issued by lesser executive agencies is restricted. Orders, like decisions of the Council of Ministers, are administrative acts which must be based on existing all-Union legislation (either on a statute or on a decree). Orders are usually more specific and limited in scope than decisions. Unlike decisions, orders may be taken individually and issued on the authority of one of the deputy chairmen of the Council of Ministers.

However, the distinction between the legislative fields of the Supreme Soviet, its Presidium and Council of Ministers, and between the effectiveness of the four main types of legislative act is less clear in practice than it is in theory.

EXECUTIVE AND ADMINISTRATIVE FUNCTIONS

The executive and administrative functions of the USSR Council of Ministers are set out in detail in Art. 68 of the Constitution. The main ones are as follows:

(i) Directing the work of the economic plan and the state budget.

(ii) Supervising the individual Ministries, both all-Union and Union-Republican, and the State Committees.

(iii) Exercising general guidance in the sphere of foreign relations.

(iv) Organizing special committees and agencies for economic and cultural affairs and defence.

The Council of Ministers has probably always worked through inner committees. This has been necessary because of the size of the body. However, the actual nature of the inner committees—which are unspecified in the Constitution—has depended on a combination of factors including the international situation and the power position within the party leadership. Thus during the period June 1941–September 1945 the State Defence Committee exercised 'the full plentitude of state power'. This was clearly designed to provide a compact 'war cabinet' or a group of close advisers to Stalin.[10] At the outset it consisted of only five persons, Stalin (Chairman of the Council of People's Commissars and General Secretary of the Party), Molotov (Foreign Affairs), Voroshilov (Defence), Malenkov (Party Secretariat), and Beria (Internal Affairs). Later, Bulganin replaced Voroshilov and Kaganovich (Railways), Voznesensky (Gosplan) and Mikoyan (Foreign Trade) were added. With the end of the war the State Defence Committee was abolished and its functions transferred to the Council of People's Commissars.[11]

In March 1949 Molotov and Mikoyan were relieved of their Ministries but remained Deputy Chairmen of the Council of Ministers and members of the Party Politbureau. The purpose of this change seems to have been to relieve them of detailed administrative work to enable them to concentrate on general policy formulation. Whether it involved any establishment of a regular Presidium within the Council of Ministers is not clear. In any case they both resumed their Ministries in March 1953.

THE PRESIDIUM OF THE COUNCIL OF MINISTERS

The establishment of a regular Presidium within the Council of

Ministers seems to have occurred only in March 1953* as part of the immediate post-Stalin settlement. The agency is referred to in several works published in the period 1953–55. Thus M. P. Kareva and G. I. Fedkin in the 2nd edition of their book *Osnovy sovetskovo gosudarstva i prava*[12] state that: 'The USSR Council of Ministers includes in its structure the Presidium of the Council of Ministers, in which are included the Chairman and the four First Vice-Chairmen of the USSR Council of Ministers.' A. I. Denisov and M. G. Kirichenko in the 1954 edition of their book *Osnovy sovetskovo gosudarstva i prava*,[13] describe the Presidium of the Council of Ministers in similar terms and add that it is 'the internal operating organ of the government'.

The number of First Vice-Chairmen of the Council of Ministers has varied considerably since March 1953. In 1953–54 it was four, in the period from February 1955 to June 1957 it was five. Between March 1958 and 1962 there were only two First Vice-Chairmen. It is commonly assumed[14] that this Presidium functioned regularly at least up to the crucial plenum of the Central Committee in June 1957. If this is so its composition during February 1955–June 1957 would have been Bulganin (Chairman), Molotov, Kaganovich, Mikoyan, Saburov and Pervukhin, all of whom were members of the Presidium of the Central Committee. The only evidence I know to support the view that the Presidium of the Council of Ministers met regularly during this period is circumstantial.[15] If it did meet it perhaps excluded Mikoyan as he was the only Khrushchev supporter in the body. On the other hand works published in the Soviet Union between 1956 and 1960[16] make no mention of the Presidium of the Council of Ministers. Professor T. H. Rigby of Canberra has suggested that during this period the collective decision-making function of the Presidium of the Council of Ministers was largely taken over by its Current Affairs Commission and perhaps later (during 1956 and early 1957) by the State Economic Commission (*Gosekonomkomissia*) headed by Presidium-member Pervukhin.[17]

Just what the situation has been since June 1957 is not at all clear. There is some evidence for the view that full meetings of the Council of Ministers have become more frequent. But this would not obviate the need for some inner body, although none is acknowledged. This is confirmed by the fact that when Professor Robert C. Tucker, who accompanied Adlai Stevenson on his tour of the USSR during the summer of 1958 asked the then Chairman of the Council of Ministers of Uzbekistan if the Presidium of the USSR Council of Ministers still

---

* A Presidium and an inner body, The Bureau of The Presidium had been established during the Stalin period but it is not known whether either body functioned.

functioned he was told that it did and that it consisted of the Chairman, the two First Vice-Chairmen, the four Vice-Chairmen, the Minister of Agriculture and the Minister of Finance.[18] This would have given it a membership of nine.[19] However, the composition of this Presidium would perhaps render it unsuitable for the full consideration of questions of foreign policy. Perhaps the problem is solved by having the Chairman, First Vice-Chairmen and Vice-Chairmen form the core of the Presidium but with other Ministers attending by invitation according to the nature of the problem being examined. In any case the agency is flexible and its exact importance in comparison with the Council of Ministers or with the inner organs of the Central Committee is impossible to determine.

The complexity of economic and industrial administration has always required some system of inner co-ordinating agencies within the larger government. In the 1920s this task was performed partly by Gosplan but more by the Council of Labour and Defence. In 1937 this latter agency was reorganized into the Economic Council of the USSR Sovnarkom (Council of People's Commissars). This Economic Council comprised the Chairman and Vice-Chairmen of Sovnarkom as well as representatives of the trade unions. In 1940 six economic councils were organized, each headed by a Vice-Chairman of Sovnarkom. These six economic councils covered Machine Construction, Defence Industry, Agriculture, Purchasing, Power and Electricity. Each Economic Council co-ordinated the work of various Commissariats and departments relating to its sector of the economy. Additional special co-ordinating committees were established during the war years, 1941–45.[20] Since 1945 Gosplan has usually been the main agency for economic planning and co-ordination, although between 1955 and 1965 this function was shared with at least one other central agency.

NOTES

[1] A. Denisov and M. Kirichenko, 1960, p. 234.
[2] Ya. N. Umansky, 1959, pp. 284 ff.
[3] *Izvestia*, April 26, 1962; *Pravda*, August 4, 1966; July 16, 1970.
[4] Cf. Yu. M. Kozlov, 1956.
[5] An English text of this letter may be found in *Soviet Studies*, Vol. VII, July 1955, pp. 91–3.
[6] *Pravda*, August 28, 1956.
[7] *Izvestia*, April 15, 1958.
[8] *Izvestia*, July 1, 1958. Under the earlier system all farms sold a proportion of their crop at compulsory prices and any sales above that at higher (*zakupka*) prices. The new system involved payment for all state purchases at the same regional price which in most cases in 1958 was close to the old higher price.
[9] There is an extensive specialist literature on this problem but most general texts on Soviet law give some attention to it. See also articles in *S.G.i.P.* and

THE PRESIDIUM AND THE COUNCIL OF MINISTERS

I. N. Kuznetsov, 'K voprosu o yuridicheskoi prirode ukaza Presidiuma Verkhovnovo Soveta SSSR,' in *Voprosy sovetskovo gosudarstvennovo prava.* Akad. Nauk. SSSR., 1959, pp. 227–74.

[10] The State Defence Committee was established by a joint decree of the Presidium of the USSR Supreme Soviet, the Council of People's Commissars, and the Central Committee of the CPSU(B.), issued June 30, 1941. It was abolished by a decree of the Presidium issued September 4, 1945. *Sbornik zakonov SSSR i ukazov presidiuma verkhovnovo Soveta SSSR 1938-1958.* Gosyurizdat, Moscow, 1959, p. 119.

[11] For a brief description of the Committee see J. Towster, 1948, pp. 293–4.

[12] October 30, 1953. Gosyurizdat, Moscow. The quotation is from p. 230.

[13] Gosyurizdat, Moscow, 1954. Footnote to p. 180.

[14] For example H. McClosky and J. E. Turner, 1960, p. 368; D. J. R. Scott, 1961, pp. 119, 122.

[15] Cf. Bulganin's statement to the December 1958 plenum of the Central Committee:

'Being at the time the Chairman of the Council of Ministers I found myself not merely a participant but nominally their leader. The anti-Party group used to meet in my office to arrange their anti-Party work. Thus if at that time I conducted myself in a proper party fashion, in essence I shared all the anti-Party filth with them.' *Izvestia,* December 19, 1958.

[16] It has not been possible to make a complete check of all works published over this period. The Presidium is mentioned only by implication in Yu. M. Kozlov, *op. cit.*, p. 31. It is not mentioned at all by any of the following works: *Bolshaya sovetskaya entsiklopedia*, 1956.
Politichesky slovar, 2nd. edition, 1958.
Ya. N. Umansky, *Sovetskoe gosudarstvennoe pravo*, 1959.
V. A. Vlasov, *Sovetsky gosudarstvenny apparat*, 1959.
A. I. Denisov and M. G. Kirichenko, 1960.

[17] T. H. Rigby and L. G. Churchward, 1962, p. 11.

[18] 'Field Observations on Soviet Local Government', *American Slavic & East European Review*, Vol. xviii, Dec. 1959, p. 532.

[19] On the basis of the government elected in April 1962 it would have been ten, on that elected in August 1966, fourteen.

[20] A. E. Lunev, 'Improvement of the Legal Status of Ministries and Co-ordination of their Activities', *S.G.i.P.*, I, 1966, pp. 8–16.

SELECTED BIBLIOGRAPHY

Denisov and Kirichenko, 1960, Ch. 7.
Chkhikvadze, V. M., ed., 1972, pp. 124–32.
Gripp, R. C., 1963, Ch. 5.
McClosky and Turner, 1960, pp. 349–54, 360-76.
Schapiro, L., 1965, Ch. 6.
Scott, D. J. R., 4th edn., 1969, pp. 111–35.

Chapter 10

THE ECONOMIC ROLE OF THE SOVIET STATE

EXTENT OF STATE ECONOMIC ACTIVITY

In order to appreciate the economic role of the modern Soviet state it is first necessary to understand the scope of its economic activity. The economic activity of the Soviet state has been more extensive and more comprehensive than that of any capitalist state, including Fascist Italy, Nazi Germany and imperialist Japan. Even in wartime the economic activities of capitalist states have been confined to an increase in the normal regulatory activities. This has involved closer control over foreign trade, the extension of production activities in fields directly connected with the needs of the war machine, control of prices and profits, rationing of short consumer goods and raw materials, direction or partial direction of manpower, construction work directly connected with military needs, etc. In Nazi Germany these aspects of state control of the economy were well-established as early as 1936, but even here basic private ownership was not interfered with. In the Soviet Union most of productive property is directly owned by the state and its uses are determined by the state. The state has a near monopoly of investment, it determines the limits and the range of consumer goods produced and fixes prices. It has a complete monopoly of external trade and a near monopoly over internal trade. It exercises full control over banking, credit, transport and wholesale trade. Labour mobility operates strictly within the limits determined by the state.

The present extent of the economic activities of the Soviet state is the result of the systematic extension of activities over more than half a century. In the period of War Communism the economic activity of the Soviet state was not so vastly different from that of the British or the Australian state during the Second World War. It differed only in the fact that some of the extensions of governmental activity were of a revolutionary nature since they involved the transference of ownership from the landlords and the capitalists. But the limits of state control especially in agriculture and planning were obvious.

During the period of the New Economic Policy (1921–28) the state

145

consolidated its control over certain sectors of the economy (foreign trade, finance, transport, etc.) and also developed the concept of over-all economic planning. But economic planning could hardly become a reality until the collectivization of agriculture had been carried through and until the planning agencies had acquired a large group of experienced cadres. This was not finally achieved until about 1931 —the term Economic Plan was first used to describe the control figures for the economy in that year.

Following the achievements of the first Five-Year Plan, the rapid extension of heavy industry and the collectivization of agriculture, the economic role of the Soviet state has rapidly extended. In fact, it might be argued that the role of the state has undergone not merely a shifting of emphasis but a qualitative change, that the essential purpose of the central Soviet state is no longer the carrying out of traditional governmental activities but of economic and cultural development towards a planned future.

CHARACTERISTICS OF SOVIET ECONOMIC PLANNING

The essential characteristics of the Soviet system of direct general economic planning have been succinctly stated by Dr. R. W. Davies[1] as follows;

(a) The growth of the economy as regulated by the conscious aims of a central authority.

(b) The planning structure is such that these aims are embodied in specific investment or production plans.

(c) These plans are based on a more or less realistic knowledge of the present situation and future possibilities. To this end there has to exist a properly developed system of accounts and statistical reports; and the planners have to be able to distinguish which are the key planning tasks, and to link general aims with the actual situation.

(d) The plans must be applied and enforced by appropriate machinery. This may and probably will involve central control over the allocation of materials, equipment and labour.

(e) It will also involve the introduction of methods of providing incentives to replace those automatically provided by a competitive economy, so as to encourage the fulfilment of investment or production plans with respect to both output and costs. Planning methods must be devised which are sufficiently flexible to allow 'initiative from below' to find expression within the general aims of the plan, and to enable adjustments to be made for production of particular items in excess of or less than the plan. In general, the planning machinery must be so designed as to make possible a satisfactory compromise between centralization and decentralization.

PRINCIPLES AND OBJECTIVES OF PLANNING

The declared objectives of Communist economic planning have varied according to the place and the time of the statements but there is a basic continuity at least in the more general objectives. One of the first statements of the principle of economic planning to be made in Communist literature was probably the seventh point in the programme of the proletariat as outlined by Marx and Engels in the Communist Manifesto (1848):

Extension of factories and instruments of production owned by the State; the bringing into cultivation of waste lands, and the improvement of the soil generally in accordance with a common plan.

This early formulation might be compared with that contained in Art. 11 of the 1936 Constitution of the USSR:

The economic life of the USSR is determined and directed by the state national economic plan with the aim of increasing the public wealth, of steadily improving the material conditions of the working people and raising their cultural levels, of consolidating the independence of the USSR and strengthening its defensive capacity.

A more recent but somewhat fuller statement along the same lines is that given in the 1958 *Short Economic Dictionary:*

National economic planning proceeds from the imminent necessities of the material life of society, the all-round accounting of the achievements of science, technique and advanced methods of labour, the correct combination of the development of branches of the economy with the complex development of the economy of the Union Republics and the economic administrative regions on the basis of the rational utilization of all material and labour resources.[2]

Statements such as the above merely refer to the general principles of Soviet economic planning. In fact the several Five-Year Plans and Control Figures have emphasized various objectives, according to the needs of the period when they were introduced. Thus the first Five-Year Plan stressed collectivization of agriculture, the establishment of heavy industry, economic self-sufficiency and defence. The second Five-Year Plan continued these objectives but laid greater emphasis on improved technique and on light industry, transport and non-ferrous metallurgy. The Seven-Year Plan (1959–65) was the first plan to stress the rapid development of both capital

147

goods and consumer goods industry, foodstuffs, and cultural and social services. These more diverse objectives are certainly possible now but they were not in the early years of economic planning.

MACHINERY OF PLANNING

The original economic control agency of the Soviet state was the Supreme Economic Council (*Vesenkha*), which was merely one of the Commissariats but which was entrusted with supervising the industries which had been nationalized. Although the Supreme Economic Council was supposed to develop a unified economic plan this was never achieved.

The first specifically planning agency *Goelro*, the State Commission for Electrification, was established in March 1920. In 1922 this agency was merged into the newly established Gosplan (State Planning Commission). The original Gosplan was merely an advisory body without administrative powers. Its task was to draft plans and to pass judgment on departmental plans submitted to it. For some years Gosplan was merely a co-ordinating body and it did not attempt anything like an overall plan. Some of its members, including Strumilin, tried to push it towards general economic planning but it was not until August 1925 that Gosplan produced its first Control Figures. These 'control figures' were not intended to do more than to serve as guiding lines for the planning activities of the individual departments. The early Control Figures were much less detailed than the latter Economic Plans and they did not constitute a directive to the Departments. The original Control Figures were accepted, with some upward revision, by the 14th Congress of the CPSU (B) in December 1925. Gosplan produced further Control Figures each year up to 1930 with the figures becoming more and more detailed. The increasing comprehensiveness of the control was given official recognition in 1931 when the figures were re-named the Plan. This term remained in vogue until 1959. The Seven-Year Plan (1959–65) adopted at the 21st Congress in January 1959 was again officially described as 'Control Figures', presumably in order to indicate the greater flexibility and less detail of the new plan as compared with the earlier Five-Year Plans.

It is not necessary to trace through the history of Gosplan from the early twenties to today. The present organization is the direct descendant of the earlier body although its inner organizational structure, name and relationship to the government has been revised on several occasions. In recent years there has been a tendency towards the creation of two separate planning agencies, one concerned with short-term planning and the other with long-term planning. Thus in

May 1955 most of the traditional functions of Gosplan, including the control over the annual plan, were transferred to a new agency for short-term planning, the State Economic Commission (*Gosekonomkomissia*). Gosplan became concerned merely with long-range planning. The importance of the new organization was indicated by the fact that its Chairman, M. G. Pervukhin, introduced the Economic Plan to the Supreme Soviet in February 1957. Gosplan was renamed as a State Committee (instead of Commission) in 1956. *Gosekonomkomissia* was abolished in May 1957 along with the majority of the industrial Ministries. Khrushchev may have engineered the sudden ending of *Gosekonomkomissia* merely to remove an important agency from the control of a rival, Pervukhin. In any case the separation of long-range from short-range planning was re-established less than three years later. In April 1960 the State Scientific-Economic Council (*Gosekonomsovet*), which had been established in the previous year, was reorganized and given the responsibility for long-range planning. Gosplan continued to be responsible for short-term planning and for supervising the fulfilment of the annual plan by the individual republics and for the co-ordination of the republican plans.[3] In November 1962 the task of supervising the fulfilment of the annual plan was transferred to a new agency, the National Economic Council (*Sovnarkhoz*) of the USSR, while responsibility for long-range planning was again lodged in Gosplan. As before, the heads of both were included in the USSR Council of Ministers.[4]

During 1963 this reorganization was extended further. In March 1963 a new (or perhaps a revived) agency, the Supreme Economic Council (VSNKh–USSR) was established as 'the highest state organ for the management of industry and construction in the country'. The Supreme Economic Council was responsible to the Council of Ministers of which its chairman was a member. It was responsible for the immediate supervision and direction of the USSR National Economic Council, USSR Gosplan, *Soyuzselkhoztekhnika*, and a number of state committees which were previously directly represented in the Council of Ministers. Gosplan and the National Economic Council were reorganized as Union-Republican organizations during 1963. These changes were approved by the USSR Supreme Soviet in December 1963.

Between 1963 and 1965 each Union Republic and Autonomous Republic had its own Gosplan and Sovnarkhoz which were subjected to the dual subordination of the republican government and the central government agencies. From early 1963 until the end of 1964 four central Asian republics were included under one Central Asian Economic Council.

The September 1965 meeting of the Central Committee of the

CPSU reconstructed the planning machinery so that it was restored to something like its pre-1955 shape. The entire structure of regional economic councils was abolished. Twenty-eight industrial ministries were established, 11 at the All-Union Republican level. The Supreme Economic Council was abolished and Gosplan again became the central agency for both long-range and short-range planning and for plan fulfilment. USSR Gosplan supervises the work of lesser planning agencies, of the individual ministries, of republican Gosplans, and of Planning Sections of local Soviets. Besides Gosplan and lower planning agencies, industrial ministries and state committees, combines, trusts and individual plants have their own Planning Sections. These agencies are all involved in supervising the fulfilment of an existing plan as well as in drafting a new plan.

Besides the special planning agencies described above two other state agencies are integral parts of the Soviet planning machinery. These are the Central Statistical Administration of the USSR Council of Ministers and the USSR Finance Ministry and subordinate republican Finance Ministries and Budget-Finance Departments of local Soviets. Both agencies are directly concerned with the supply of statistical and other information without which the economic plan would be inoperable. The Economic Commission of the Soviet of Nationalities, although only an advisory agency, assumed increased importance as an agency for ventilating republican and regional proposals which might otherwise get overlooked by the central planning agencies. Finally, both government and party structures as a whole are jointly concerned with the plan fulfilment.

THE ECONOMIC PLAN

An annual plan may be said to be initiated by Gosplan preparing balances both in physical and financial terms. These indicate variants for production in different fields for the coming year. On the basis of these general projects and following consideration by the Central Committee of the Party, the government adopts a general directive, indicating the main targets for the planned year. This directive will fit in with the long-term perspectives of the Five-Year Plan. The directive consists of a series of interrelated production and investment targets based on the overall balances supplied by Gosplan. The directives adopted by the USSR Council of Ministers are then sent to the Councils of Ministers of the Union Republics and to the Ministries. Each Ministry then issues more detailed directives to the economic units subordinate to it. The amount of detail in these directives varies greatly from industry to industry. In general there is less detail in these directives today than there was before 1957[5] and the agricultural targets are put in terms of round figures only at the province (*oblast-krai*) level. The directives are then examined, discussed and revised at each level as they pass downwards, and at the level of the individual enterprise. Special measures adopted in 1958–59 were designed to make these criticisms and suggestions from below more efficient through the agencies of the trade union committee, the Permanent Production Conferences[6] and the Party primary organization.[7] Since 1965 many details in the enterprise plan have been filled out only by the individual enterprise. These modified directives are then passed upwards again through the same channels. The eventual plan is prepared by the USSR Gosplan and issued by the USSR Council of Ministers. It is this Plan which is normally ratified by the USSR Supreme Soviet although this is not required by law. Parallel with the Economic Plan (covering production, supply, labour, investment, etc.) is the financial plan which reaches its final form in the Unified State Budget which is usually adopted in December of the year preceding the budget year.

The Economic Plan is binding on all state agencies. It has the force of law, although individuals and plants cannot normally be prosecuted for non-fulfilment of the plan. However, the jobs and promotion prospects of industrial managers are closely related to their record of plan fulfilment and overfulfilment. During the period 1957–65 the main administrative agency for plan supervision and fulfilment was the Economic Council (*Sovnarkhoz*).[8] Today, industrial ministries again administer the bulk of Soviet industry although some local consumer goods industry and construction projects are controlled by local Soviets. In April 1973 industrial corporations to control production and production research in whole industries were established below the industrial ministries.

INDIVIDUALISM AND INCENTIVES IN THE SOVIET PLANNED ECONOMY

Private enterprise has not been entirely eliminated in the USSR but it has been rigidly circumscribed. There are still individual peasants, hunters, artisans and craftsmen in the Soviet Union but they are steadily declining and they contribute little to the national economy. The January 1959 census showed that these individual proprietors and their families numbered only 0·6 million, or 0·3% of the total population.[9] In 1970 they represented only 0·03% of the total population. Many professional people, doctors, dentists, lawyers, etc., carry on a subsidiary private practice for which they receive fees additional to their state salaries. Writers and musicians receive royalties on published works. But there is no individual ownership of the main means of production and individual ownership of the minor means of production is severely penalized by taxation, restrictions on marketing, inability to employ (and thus to exploit) labour. On the other hand it is worth remembering that until a few years ago more cows were individually owned than collectively owned.[10]

Despite earlier forecasts individual initiative has not disappeared in the USSR. On the contrary it has survived and has in a sense been further developed under the Soviet system of centralized economic planning. Individuals may exercise initiative in the selection of their profession or occupation, through assisting in the process of technical development by suggesting rationalizations or inventions and by using the incentive-bonus system which is incorporated into the Soviet economy. Many professional men seem to find it comparatively easy to change their place of employment or even their profession. Thus teachers and academics move fairly freely from teaching to research jobs and often move out of the teaching service to take appointments in journalism, translating or publishing agencies. Factory managers, collective farm chairmen and state farm directors have considerable scope for initiative and choice within the framework of the state plan. Once the collective farm chairman has met the quotas for grain, meat, milk and other main agricultural commodities established by the provincial authorities he can choose between a variety of agricultural activities on the basis of either selling the proceeds to state purchasing agencies or selling them through the *kolkhoz* market in the near-by town. Similarly, even before 1965 a factory director had considerable say over the use to which the Enterprise Fund was placed and he could undertake supplementary investment for technical improvement without higher approval up to 200,000 roubles in certain cases. He could alter the timing of the production programme as decided upon by higher authority within the limits of a quarterly division of the annual plan in order to meet urgent requirements of a customer. He could accept orders for products additional to the plan, provided it did not affect the fulfilment of the plan. Under the recent regulations on Soviet state industrial enterprises (October 4, 1965) the powers of the directors were considerably extended. Under these regulations higher organs direct the amounts of capital investment in the enterprises but the range and type of equipment is to be determined by the enterprise. The regulations extended the use to which the Enterprise Fund could be put and removed many restrictions on the power of the director to make bonus payments and to modify the wage pattern within the enterprise.[11]

Besides the legal avenues for individual incentive described above many forms of quasi-legal entrepreneurial activity are to be found in contemporary Soviet society. For example, factory directors in their effort to overfulfil the plans still make use of various funds (including the Enterprise Fund) to pay the services of sundry agents and *tolkachi* which are not covered by the Wages Fund for the factory. The *tolkach** system was not eliminated by the industrial reorganization in 1957.[12] Under the earlier system of centralized ministerial control *tolkachi* operated to cut through departmental barriers. Under the Khrushchev system of regional control *tolkachi* operated to bridge the barriers between different economic regions. Thus a factory manager who required urgent supplies from an adjoining or more remote region might use the services of a *tolkach* to secure them. The *tolkach* would establish a direct link with the supplying agency which was not possible through normal administrative channels. The system continues despite frequent official criticisms and decisions.[13] In fact it continues not because of the personal shortcomings of Soviet citizens but because the Soviet economy contains a built-in tendency to produce it.

A somewhat less respectable but still widespread practice is to use one's party or state position to enhance one's private fortune. *Blat*, or influence, is still a considerable problem in the Soviet system, especially in the sphere of consumer goods and services which are in short supply such as housing, furniture, equipment, holiday accommodation and (especially before the December 1958 Education Act) in admission to universities and other higher educational institutes.

At an even lower level and in fact strictly illegal are the activities of various black marketeers, professional beggars, thieves of public property, private distillers and *kustar* industrialists employing hired labour. Cases of the latter operating secret private 'factories' employing up to a score or more workers over several years without detection have been reported in the Soviet press. Legislation[14] passed between 1957 and 1961 designed to cope with these practices has been far from successful.

COMPULSION IN THE SOVIET ECONOMIC SYSTEM

It is usually assumed that there is much more compulsion in the Soviet socialist system than there is in a western capitalist system. The USSR Constitution in Art. 12 states that:

In the USSR work is a duty and a matter of honour for every able-bodied citizen, in accordance with the principle: 'He who does not work, neither shall he eat.'

However it is very difficult to enforce this as the legislation passed during 1957–61 indicates. There is no direction of labour in the

* The term comes from the Russian verb *tolkat* = to push, to shove. A *tolkach* is therefore a pusher or a fixer.

153

full sense of the term in the USSR today. Wartime Manpower Regulations in capitalist Australia provided for a more comprehensive direction of labour than does the Soviet planned economy. Soviet students in higher educational institutes are frequently required to serve a minimum number of years in particular employment after completing their courses but they are not normally directed to specific jobs. There is in fact considerable competition between enterprises for professionals, technicians and skilled workers and this is illustrated by the advertisements in Soviet local newspapers such as *Vechernyaya Moskva* as well as by direct approaches made by the managements of various enterprises to attract the services of students who are nearing completion of their courses. Communist Party members are subject to much closer direction than are the rest of the population. The Komsomol organization also enables many hundreds of thousands of youthful workers to be tapped for emergency jobs and projects such as the development of the virgin lands, assisting with harvesting, and assisting with various auxiliary and social service activities. By and large though the Soviet system, at least in peacetime, depends far more on indirect controls and incentives than on direct control over manpower. This is even more so since the rapid reduction of the reserve of prison labour after 1954. The normal methods of incentive rely on such material allies to patriotic enthusiasm as higher rates of pay and shorter hours for arduous jobs and difficult environments, special housing, rest homes and sanatoria, and more rapid promotion.

EFFICIENCY OF SOVIET ECONOMIC PLANNING

It is very difficult to answer the question 'How efficient is Soviet economic planning?' scientifically. This is so because the concept of efficiency is not purely an objective one. An economic system might be efficient in terms of capital investment and consumer goods and still not efficient in terms of cost. Efficiency is a relative term. Thus Soviet industry as a whole is much more efficient than tsarist industry was but its average performance is still considerably behind that of the USA when measured in terms of labour-time involved per unit of output. By the same measure Soviet agriculture is even further behind American agriculture.

Economic planning in the Soviet has certainly proved itself in general terms (in its capacity to accelerate the rate of industrial growth) but as it has operated to date it has had many shortcomings and deficiencies. These include over-centralization and bureaucracy, the tendency (probably endemic in the system) to fabricate results, especially in terms of agricultural outputs, and over-rigidity in fixing costs and targets.[15] Criticism by Soviet economists and managers, especially since the 20th Congress early in 1956 has become much sharper and much more realistic. As a result there has been considerable ventilation of proposals not merely for detailed reform but for basic reforms, including scientific costing and pricing of industrial products, linear programming, etc.[16] The views of reforming economists such as Liberman were given some official encouragement towards the end of the Khrushchev era. Thus the initial experiment with basing consumer goods factories on profitability was made in early 1964. By the decision of the Central Committee and the Council of Ministers of October 1965 the whole of consumer goods industry was to move over to the new system by the end of 1968.[17] Thus the restoration of industrial ministries did not represent the re-establishment of the overcentralized economy of the Stalin era but an attempt at combining central planning of the general direction and rate of economic growth with increased powers to factory managers. In other words the Soviet Union has moved a considerable way towards what the Yugoslavs refer to as 'market socialism'.

NOTES

[1] R. W. Davies, 1958, p. 96.

[2] *Kratky ekonomichesky slovar*, Gozpolizdat, Moscow, 1958, pp. 237–8.

[3] *S.G.i.P.*, No. 11, 1960, pp. 21–2.

[4] Decisions of the Central Committee Plenum, November 23, 1962.

[5] Cf. M. C. Kaser, 'Changes in Planning Methods during the Preparation of the Soviet Seven Year Plan', *Soviet Studies*, Vol. xi, April 1959, pp. 321–38.

[6] The extension of trade union functions and the role of the Permanent Production Conference were summarized by R. Schlesinger in *Soviet Studies*, Vol. x, October 1958, pp. 180–7.

[7] In June 1959 the plenum of the Central Committee of the CPSU decided to establish Party Control Commissions on the basis of Party primaries in all production and trading organizations for the purpose of exercising Party control over such matters as quality of production, automation and mechanization, and in some cases, plan fulfilment. *Izvestia*, June 30, 1959.

[8] 'Concerning Measures for the Improved Planning of the National Economy.' Decision adopted by the Central Committee of the CPSU and the USSR Council of Ministers, May 4, 1958. Text in *KPSS o Rabote Sovetov*, Gospolizdat Moscow, 1959, pp. 539–42. See also *Izvestia*, May 20, 1958.

[9] *Chislennost sostav i razmeshchenie naselenia SSSR*, Ts. S. U. Gosstatizdat, Moscow, 1961, p. 39.

[10] On October 1, 1955, 16,657,000 out of 29,237,000 cows, or 57%, were privately owned. Likewise at this date 41·6% of pigs, 21·7% of sheep and 83% of goats were privately owned. See *The USSR Economy*, A Statistical Abstract, USSR Council of Ministers, Central Statistical Administration, 1957, pp. 119–22. As late as 1960, 53·7% of cows were privately owned. In 1961 the figure was 47·1%, in 1964 it was 41·7%.

[11] For full details on the current powers of Soviet factory managers see, *Soviet Studies*, Vol. ix, October 1957, pp. 239–41; and *S.G.i.P.*, November, 1966, pp. 17–25.

[12] It is probable that the system has declined somewhat since May 1957. The 1959 census revealed that the number of 'agents and forwarding agents' declined from 176,400 in 1939 to 146,000 in 1959. *Chislennost sostav i razmeshchenie naselenia SSSR*, 1961, p. 52.

[13] See for example, *Sovetskaya Rossia*, November 16, 1961. In December 1961 the Bureau of the CPSU on the RSFSR took a decision relating to the elimination of *tolkachi*. This decision quoted a number of examples designed to underline the wastefulness of the system. Thus in 1961 the Magnitogorsk Metal Combine sent 3238 agents on trips to secure supplies, a Sverdlovsk factory sent 1703, and a Saratov factory 1427. *Sovetskaya Rossia*, December 12, 1961, and February 6, 1962.

[14] For example, 'The Draft Laws Against Parasites, Tramps and Beggars, and Against Home Brewing', *Sovetskaya Rossia*, May 5, 1961, *Izvestia*, May 16, 1961. Also, R. Beermann's summaries of this legislation in *Soviet Studies*, Vol. ix, October 1957, pp. 214–22; and Vol. xiii, October 1961, pp. 191–205.

[15] For good balanced analysis of this problem the reader might consult Alec Nove, 1961, Ch. 12; and Robert W. Campbell, 1960, Chs. 3–5.

[16] Cf. R. W. Davies, 'Industrial Planning Reconsidered', *Soviet Studies*, Vol. viii, April 1957, pp. 426–35.

[17] A summary of this decision was printed in Soviet newspapers on October 10, 1965.

SELECTED BIBLIOGRAPHY

Campbell, R. W., 1960, Ch. 5.
Fainsod, M., 1963a, pp. 403–10.
Hutchings, R., 1971.
Kaser, M. C., 1959.
Kaser, M. C., 1970.
Miller, Margaret, 1965.
Nove, A., 1961.
Nove, A., 1964.
Shaffer, H. G., 1965, pp. 145–65.

Chapter 11

SOVIET FEDERALISM

MEANING

Article 13 of the Soviet Constitution defines the USSR as 'a federal state, formed on the basis of a voluntary Union of equal Soviet Socialist Republics'. The Soviet *Political Dictionary* supplies a definition of federalism which is formally comparable with Western definitions. This work defines a federation as:

A Union of States, forming a new union state with a single citizenship. Entering into a federation the union states retain their legal and administrative organs, the activities of which are limited to specific groups of questions. Side by side with the organs of power of the different states belonging to the federation, there are established union (federal) legal, administrative and judicial organs, the acts of which are operative throughout the entire territory of the federal state.[1]

Fе￼ ￼alism, as it is understood in the West, is usually considered to involve the following characteristics:[2]

(*a*) Sovereignty is divided by the Constitution so that neither federal nor provincial government is supreme but each is supreme in its own sphere, the area of competency being set out in the Constitution.

(*b*) Financial powers are shared and both federal and state governments possess independent sources of revenue.

(*c*) Judicial review operates to determine constitutional disputes arising out of the federal system.

(*d*) States are equally represented in the federal Senate.

(*e*) The process of constitutional amendment is difficult and it often requires approval by either a majority of the population or by a majority of the states or even of the population in a majority of the states.

(*f*) States' boundaries cannot be changed without the consent of the states.

Only the last of these elements would be fully accepted by Soviet theorists. The Soviet conception of federalism is one which preserves the underlying principle of *democratic centralism* and which ensures the development of the socialist economy throughout the entire country on the basis of the national economic plan. This distinct conception of federalism is clearly recognized by Soviet jurists. Thus A. Y. Vyshinsky in his *The Law of the Soviet State* comments that:

Democratic centralism presupposes centralism in basic questions; in general guidance, in the maximum unification of all economic activity according to one state-wide plan in guiding production to the end of rational and economic utilization of all the country's material resources. Far from excluding, it presupposes local independence, upon conditions of developing the creative self-reliance and initiative of the local population (with its differing languages, ways of life; and economic relationships) for the best possible fulfilment of general plans and cultural building.

Soviet federalism, built on principles of democratic centralism, permitted all the diversity of ways of life, culture and economic conditions, of various peoples in different stages of development to be embraced. Its distinguishing feature is the elasticity of its forms, as applied (*a*) to concrete problems of the socialist state in raising the economic-cultural level of each people separately, and (*b*) the conditions of class struggle at each separate historical phase. The forms of federative bonds existing in bourgeois federations are alien to it.[3]

Although the principle of democratic centralism is not explicitly stated in the USSR Constitution it is there by implication. Thus Arts. 13–15 of the Constitution formally establish a federal state on traditional lines. Art. 13 declares that the USSR is a federal state composed of equal republics; Art. 14 defines the powers of the central government, while Art. 15 reserves to the Union Republics all those powers which are not listed in Art. 14. But the powers granted to the federal government are unusually wide if compared with those of the equivalent sections of other federal constitutions. They include the:

(*a*) determination of the national economic plans of the USSR;

(*b*) approval of the consolidated state budget of the USSR and the report of its fulfilment, determination of the taxes and revenues which go to the Union, the Republican and local budgets;

(*c*) determination of the basic principles in the spheres of education and public health;

(*d*) determination of the basic principles of labour legislation.

(*e*) The determination of the basic laws concerning the legal system and legal procedure, the basic civil, criminal and corrective labour codes.

158

Furthermore, Art. 20 established the supremacy of federal over state legislation while Art. 49 (f) empowers the USSR Presidium to annul decisions and orders of the Councils of Ministers of the Union Republics. All of this is consistent with the principle of democratic centralism and with the requirements of a socialist society but it obviously involves an altogether different relationship between central and state governments to that existing in a Western federal system. Not only does the Soviet system confer unusual powers on the central government but it makes no provision for judicial review of constitutional cases. The USSR Supreme Court is not empowered to handle constitutional cases but merely certain civil and criminal cases which come up to it on appeal. The structure of the federal house is different from that of Western federalisms since although it affords equal representation to the Union Republics it also represents Autonomous Republics, Autonomous Provinces and National Areas. In fact its function is to represent the various nationalities of the USSR and all nationalities which have administrative recognition; even those at the local government level are directly represented in it. Thus the 1970 Soviet of Nationalities (elected June 1970) included 750[4] deputies of national groupings, 480 elected by the Union Republics (32 each), 220 elected by the Autonomous Republics (11 each), 40 elected by the Autonomous Provinces (5 each) and 10 by the National Areas (1 each).

Constitutional amendment is peculiarly difficult in traditional federalisms. Only 24 amendments have been carried in the United States over a period of more than 170 years while in Australia only 6 amendments have been carried over seventy odd years. The Soviet Constitution (Art. 146) merely requires that a constitutional amendment be approved by a two-third's majority of both chambers. Since the practice is for all legislation to be approved unanimously this majority is no more difficult to secure than an absolute majority. Consequently constitutional amendments are carried at any session of the Supreme Soviet when required. During the 5th USSR Supreme Soviet (March 1958–March 1962) they were carried at five out of seven sessions.[5]

The Soviet Constitution (Arts, 17 and 18) provides that every Union republic has the right to freely secede from the federation and that the territory of a Union Republic may not be altered without its consent. In actual fact no Union Republic has ever seceded, although new states have joined the federation, and various changes have been made to the territories and territorial structures of Union Republics. There is no doubt that the federal government has the main say over boundary changes. In fact, until February 1957 even the administrative divisions within the Union Republics were altered by the central

159

government. This is done even now in the case of administrative divisions based on nationality groups (ASSRs and Autonomous Provinces). Formally, alterations to the territories of Union Republics have been carried through with their consent. Thus the liquidation of the Karelo–Finnish Union Republic was initiated by the Supreme Soviet of the Union Republic late in 1955 requesting the Russian Supreme Soviet for permission to join the RSFSR as an Autonomous Republic. This was approved in 1956 by both the Russian Supreme Soviet and the USSR Supreme Soviet.*

THE UNIFIED STATE BUDGET

Nowhere is the peculiar nature of Soviet federalism more evident than it is in the sphere of financial relations. In contrast with parliamentary federalism characterized by overlapping but separate budgets the USSR operates a uniform state budget in which the federal budget contains the budgets of the constituent states. The principles of the financial relations which operate in Soviet federalism might be stated thus:

(i) The consolidated State Budget is really the financial cover of the National Economic Plan and is in fact a pre-requisite for the effective realization of the plan.

(ii) There is no fixed and continuous division of taxing powers between the central and state governments in the USSR. Virtually all sources of revenue are included in the budget which is passed by the USSR Supreme Soviet.

(iii) The uniform budget enables the shifting of revenue from one part of the USSR to another in a much more comprehensive way than the grants system which is found in the USA and Australia.

The Soviet Budget is more decentralized today than it was before 1956. Until then the State Budget included not merely the details of the Union Republican budgets but local budgets also. The present system, which was regularized by the Budget Law of October 1959, provides for a national budget which merely lists the income and expenditure for each Union Republic in general terms. National expenditure is listed for main fields such as national economy, defence, social services, and administration. No break down of the income and expenditure of the Union Republics is given. The Union Republican budgets, adopted by the Supreme Soviets of the Union Republics some days after the federal Budget has been adopted, give the figures

* However the boundary between the RSFSR and Kazakhstan was altered unilaterally by the Presidium of the USSR Supreme Soviet in 1965. *Izvestia*, December 10, 1965.

for the allocations to local governments directly responsible to them. Thus the RSFSR Budget will give the figures for the expenditure for subordinate Autonomous Republics, Territories, Provinces, and for the cities of Moscow and Leningrad. The Union Republican Budgets also specify the amounts of the various revenues to be retained by the local governments. Details of lower level budgets are not shown in the Union Republican Budget but in the budget of the immediately superior local Soviet. Thus a District Soviet in the Moscow Province will have its own budget but the general figures for income and expenditure shown in this budget will form a part of the Moscow Oblast Budget. Similarly, a Village Soviet will have its own budget but it will form a part of the District Budget. Because of this interlocking of the budgets of all levels of government and their eventual inclusion within the Soviet Budget, it is not possible for any local Soviet to adopt its final budget until the budget of the next higher level Soviet has been formally adopted. In practice budget drafting by lower Soviets begins earlier, but they are often required to scale down their original estimates to fit into the more conservative estimates of the higher Soviet budgets. Although the central government spends the biggest share of the State Budget and (except for 1960–1970) more than the Republican and local Soviets together, it does not maintain a special organ for collecting the revenue. The USSR Ministry of Finance is organized as a Union-Republican Ministry and the fifteen Republican Departments of Finance supervise the Budget-Finance Departments of the local Soviets which are the actual tax-collecting and revenue-gathering agencies. Local agencies retain the percentage of each revenue or tax they are legally entitled to retain under the Budget and the remainder is passed upwards. The same process takes place at the level of the Union Republic where the Republican Finance Ministries retain the percentages of the revenues they are entitled to retain under the Budget. The financial powers of even the Union Republics are thus strictly limited. However, under the 1959 Budget Law they are entitled to allocate supplementary revenue provided capital investment is not involved. Revision of capital investment figures can only be done by the central government.

In practice the revenue from most sources is divided between local, republican and union (federal) governments, although the division varies from tax to tax and from revenue to revenue. In addition local Soviets have minor taxing powers, the income from which goes entirely to the local Soviet levying the tax. Even here, however, the central government fixes the rate of these taxes.

An illustration of this division is provided by the 1972 Budget.[6] The *turnover tax*, once the greatest single source of revenue in the Soviet Union, is now of declining importance. It contributed

46% of the revenue in 1959 but only 33% in 1972. The *turnover tax* is really a form of indirect tax which is levied on all commodities produced. It is like a sales tax in that its payment is reflected in the retail price of every commodity sold on the Soviet market, but unlike a sales tax in that it is usually paid by the producing organization, the wholesale organization, or in the case of agricultural commodities, by the procurement organization. The incidence of the tax is normally heavier on consumer goods than it is on capital goods where it is often a nominal 0·5–1 %. In most consumer goods it represents the difference between the cost of production plus the enterprise profit and the retail price of the commodity. In the case of certain commodities such as vodka, matches and salt, it is levied at a fixed rate and is comparable to an excise tax.[7] The percentage of the turnover tax retained varies from republic to republic. Thus in 1972 Kazakhstan retained 100% of the turnover tax collected in its territory whereas the RSFSR retained only 36·1%, the Ukraine 31·9% and Latvia 41·7%.

A second important source of Soviet revenue consists of *deductions from the profits of socialist industry*, and represents the state's share of the gross enterprise profit. In 1972 this source provided 34·9% of the total revenue. All the revenue collected from this source goes to the central government.*

Co-operative and collective farm taxes constitute the third source of revenue derived from the socialist economy. The incidence of these taxes varies according to the rate of profit and according to the source of the income. Under the 1972 RSFSR Budget, with few exceptions, 100% of the tax on collective farms and co-operatives went to the budgets of the Autonomous Republics and the local Soviets. With the turnover tax the percentage retained varied from 15·5% in the Voronezh *oblast* to 100% in the case of some Autonomous Republics. Moscow City retained 6·7% of this tax, Moscow *oblast* 8·6%, Leningrad city 10% and Leningrad *oblast* 60%. There would appear to be a rough correlation here between the amount of this tax collected in an area and the percentage retained—the percentage retained varying roughly in inverse ratio to the amount of industrialization.

Direct taxes are of declining importance in the Soviet budgetary system. Income tax, levied on incomes other than those of collective farmers, is of minor importance only. It provided only 8·6% of the revenue in 1972. Again the percentage of this tax retained by local governments varied from 5% in the case of the Moscow City Soviet to 100% in the case of many Autonomous Republics. On the other

---

* Local Soviets retain varying percentages of unplanned profits from socialist enterprises.

hand, most local Soviets received 100% of the revenue from the *agricultural tax* (paid by the collective farmers on their private holdings) and of the *forest tax*. The Union Republics retained 50% of the personal income tax collected (100% in the case of Uzbekistan, Lithuania, Tadjikistan and Turkmenia) and also 50% of loan money, another declining source of revenue.

Although each Union Republic, Autonomous Republic, Province, City, District and even Village Soviet is required to balance its budget the Soviet system of a Unified State Budget allows for rather more redistribution of income as between the various levels of government and between stronger and weaker units of the same administrative level than is possible in Western parliamentary federalisms. This is mainly achieved by two practices. First, the practice by which various units of the same administrative level retain varying percentages of a particular revenue allows an adjustment roughly according to needs. Thus in 1972 the RSFSR retained 36·1% of the turnover tax collected in its territory whereas the less developed republic of Kazakhstan retained 100%. Similarly, the Moscow City Soviet in 1972 retained 6·7% of the turnover tax collected whereas the Chuvash ASSR retained 28·3% and the Kalmyk ASSR 100%. Secondly, the Soviet budget regularly uses supplementary grants to stimulate the rate of economic development in the more backward regions. Both Kazakhstan and Turkmenia have received supplementary grants through the federal budget in recent years. In 1962 Kazakhstan received a supplementary grant of 1,030 million roubles and Turkmenia one of 62·9 million roubles to ensure plan fulfilment in 1962. In 1972 Kazakhstan received supplementary grants of over 456 million roubles.

ASSESSMENT OF THE SOVIET BUDGETARY SYSTEM

The advantages of the Soviet budgetary system are most clearly shown in the rapid development of the more backward regions of the federation, especially the central Asian republics. Over the period 1926–59 the number of teachers and cultural workers in the USSR increased 7 times; it increased 19 times in the Central Asian republics (Kazakhstan, Uzbekistan, Tadjikistan, Kirgizia and Turkmenia). The number of persons per 100 of population with a completed tertiary education in 1959 was 18 for the USSR as a whole. The figure was 12 for Kazakhstan, 10 for Tadjikistan, and 13 for the other 3 Central Asian republics. On the other hand, except for Kazakhstan, the rate of increase of graduates was greater in these republics than in the USSR as a whole.[8] The same trend is true for the development of medical services. Over the period 1926–59 medical personnel increased 8·5 times in the USSR but 21 times in the Central Asian republics.[9] Over the same period the number of wage and salary earners increased 10 times in the Central Asian republics compared with 6 times in the USSR.[10] On the other hand, the central control over capital investment and the interdependence of the budgets at the various administrative levels gives rise to a good deal of frustration and criticism from local and republican governments. This is partly because the USSR Ministry of Finance has not thoroughly varied its methods since the passage of the 1959 Budget Law and republican Finance Ministries still persist in detailed planning of local budgets to the disregard of present powers of local Soviets. The Soviet budgetary system would still appear to be insufficiently flexible.

THE ROLE OF UNION-REPUBLICAN GOVERNMENT

Some years go A. Y. Vyshinsky summarized the role of state government in the Soviet Union in these words:

Pursuant to its Constitution, each Union Republic carries into effect within its territory the following measures (i) it affirms the plan of national economy and the budget of its republic; (ii) it establishes in conformity with the USSR legislation, state and local taxes and levies; and other income; (iii) it manages insurance and savings; (iv) it establishes the order of using the land, the natural deposits, the forests and waters—guided therein by basic principles established by Union organs; (v) it actually controls and superintends the administration and conditions of enterprises subordinate to the Union (a particularly graphic illustration of the activity of Union Republics within the sphere of Union jurisdiction) and (vi) it accomplishes the building of roads and bridges and directs local transport and communications.[11]

This statement is still essentially correct although the role of state government in respect to many matters including economic planning, budgetary control and industrial management, has undoubtedly increased since 1955. But state governments still operate within the limits of the Economic Plan and the State Budget of the USSR and state governments may have their decisions countermanded by the Presidium of the USSR Supreme Soviet or by the central government.

In order to understand the extent of the enlargement of state powers in recent years it is first necessary to remember the peculiarities of the Soviet administrative structure. The general pattern of republican government is the same as that of the Union government. The highest state authority within each Union Republic is the unicameral Supreme Soviet. The relationship between the Presidium and the Council of Ministers of the Supreme Soviet and between these two agencies and the Supreme Soviet is broadly the same as it is in the central government. Republican Presidiums are perhaps more active than the USSR Presidium as it falls to their lot to supervise the work of lower Soviets.[12] But the main work of administration and decision taking is performed by the Council of Ministers. The Union-Republican Councils of Ministers are similarly structured to the USSR Council of Ministers. There are two categories of Ministries included in the Council, the Union-Republican and the Republican. The former are also included in the USSR Council of Ministers, the latter are not. The number of Ministries of both types varies from republic to republic. In the RSFSR in 1971 there were 18 Union-Republican Ministries and 9 Republican Ministries (See Chart. p. 168). The devolution of recent years has tended to increase the number of both sorts of Ministries as against the fully centralized All-Union Ministries of which only five had survived in 1963. Thus Republican Ministries in 1971 included not only such Ministries as Housing, Automobile Transport, Highways, Local Industry, but also that of Social Security. The Internal Affairs Ministry (renamed Defence of Public Order in December 1962) which was a key central Ministry until the end of 1956 was partly decentralized in February 1957 when it became a Union-Republican Ministry. It was fully decentralized in January 1960 when it became a Republican Ministry. This does not mean that the central government no longer had any control over internal affairs but merely that it had entirely entrusted the responsibility of administering the internal affairs department to republican and local government. The Ministry was re-established as a Union-Republican Ministry in 1966.

Over the past two decades the most important development of state government has been in the sphere of economic planning and industrial control. Since 1954 this has passed through five phases. First, during 1954–55 over 11,000 industrial enterprises were transferred from All-Union to Union-Republican control. New Union-Republican Ministries were established in the Ukraine, Kazakhstan and Azerbaidjan. Secondly, a large number of industrial ministries were decentralized and their industries transferred to republican control. In May 1956 nine such ministries were decentralized. Thirdly, in May 1957, following extensive public debate, the Supreme Soviet dissolved most of the industrial ministries. Industrial control passed to over a hundred regional economic councils or *sovnarkhozy*. In eleven Union Republics the Economic Council covered the entire republic but the RSFSR, the Ukraine, Kazakhstan and Uzbekistan were subdivided to form smaller economic regions. Only in the RSFSR did the Economic Councils run parallel to the existing administrative structure so that all territories and most provinces gained their own sov-narkhoz. This reorganization meant that roughly 70% of Soviet industrial establishments passed to the control of the *sovnarkhozy* while local Soviets increased their share to about 20% although it did not stay at that figure for long. Only about 10% of Soviet industrial establishments remained under the direct control of Ministries. By 1960 only three All-Union industrial ministries (Medium Machine Building, Construction of Electrical Power Stations, and Transport Construction) and no Union-Republican industrial ministry had survived. By the end of 1963 all industrial ministries had been abolished. A large number of State Committees controlling industries were established at both the All-Union and the Union-Republican levels but these were planning, supervisory and research rather than administrative agencies. The new system of industrial control resulted in certain anomalies especially in the fulfilment of inter-regional and foreign commitments. This resulted in an extension of the responsibilities of republican Gosplans in May 1958 and the establishment during 1960 of republican *sovnarkhozy* in the four larger republics which had not previously had them. The devolution of industrial control of recent years is clearly reflected in the increasing share of the state budget allocated to the Union Republics and local Soviets. This amount increased from 23·5% of the total budget in 1956 to 47·5% in 1959[13] to 55·7% in 1962.[14] Despite the restoration of industrial ministries during 1965 it was significant that 54·3% of the state budget was allocated to the Union Republics and to local Soviets in 1966.

The fourth phase, carried through in late 1962 and early 1963, represented a further restoration of central planning. It saw the consolidation of four Asian republics into a single Central Asian Economic Region and the reduction of the number of economic regions in Russia from 67 to 24, and in the Ukraine from 14 to 7. At the same time a USSR *sovnarkhoz* was established to co-ordinate the lesser economic councils and in March 1963 a Supreme Economic Council was established above this as the supreme agency of economic administration. At the same time several central state production committees were established with powers similar to those of the abolished ministries.

The fifth stage, which was carried through during 1965 after the fall of Khrushchev, represented the abandonment of the experiment of economic regionalism. Some industrial ministries were restored as early as March 1965. In September 1965 the Central Committee of the CPSU decided to abolish the entire structure of regional economic councils and to restore the industrial ministries. In October 1965 the USSR Supreme Soviet sanctioned the re-establishment of

28 industrial ministries, 11 All-Union and 17 Union-Republican ministries. At the same time Gosplan again became the central planning agency and reabsorbed the powers of the short-lived Supreme Economic Council.

The increase in the planning and industrial control powers of republican governments has necessitated some alteration of their budgetary powers. Decentralization of non-industrial ministries has also produced the same effect. Thus most of the Pensions Fund and the appropriations for higher and specialist educational institutes have formed part of the republican budgets since 1959–60.[15] The Budget Law of 1959 increased the budgetary powers of the Union Republics, especially in relation to the disposal of surplus revenue.[16]

The powers of the Union Republics have increased in recent years by other ways than ministerial decentralization. Thus Union Republics have controlled their internal administrative structure (excepting where national groups are concerned) since February 1957.[17] Likewise in February 1957 the powers of the USSR Supreme Court were reduced and its review powers restricted to cases which had already been reviewed by a Union-Republican Supreme Court and only then if the sentence, decision or resolution of the Union-Republican Supreme Court contradicted All-Union legislation or if it violated the interests of other Union Republics.

CONCLUSIONS

(1) The USSR is not a federalism in the normal Western sense of the term. It is better described as a multi-national unitary state. The system must remain unitary so long as the principles of democratic centralism continue to operate.

(2) The basis of the increased decentralization in recent years is largely economic. By 1955 a considerable measure of industrial decentralization was accepted as a pre-condition for the further advance of the Soviet economy. This was conceded even by leaders such as Kaganovich, Saburov and Pervukhin, who opposed the precise scheme for decentralization sponsored by Khrushchev.

(3) The restoration of centralized industrial ministries in 1965 was accompanied by the extension of the decision-making powers of industrial managers, especially decisions relating to investment and to the range and quality of goods produced. The 1965 reforms marked a different approach to the goal of economic devolution and not merely a return to the earlier pattern of centralized control of industry.[18]

167

Ministerial Structure within the Russian Republic (December 1971)

	Economic	Social and Cultural	Political-Administrative
	(22)	(4)	(5)
1 All-Union Ministries (27)			
2 Union-Republican Ministries (18*)	State Purchasing Light Industry Forestry Meat and Dairy Industry Food Industry Building Materials Industry Fishing Rural Construction Agriculture (9)	Higher and Secondary Specialist Education Health Culture Education (4)	Foreign Affairs Land Reclamation and Water Economy Trade Finance Justice (5)
3 Republican Ministries (9)	Automobile Transport Everyday Repairs Housing and Civil Construction Local Industry River Fleet Highways Fuel Industry (7)		Housing Social Security (2)
4 Autonomous Republican Ministries (8–16)	(4–7)	Health Culture Education	Internal Affairs Housing Social Security Trade Finance Justice

Rows 1–2 grouped as **USSR MINISTRIES**. All rows grouped as **REPUBLICAN MINISTRIES**.

* Does not include Ministries of Defence and Geology which do not operate in the RSFSR.

List of USSR Ministries, December 1971

All-Union Ministries:
  Aviation Industry
  Automobile Industry
  Foreign Trade
  Gas Industry
  Civil Aviation
  Machine Building
  Machine Building for Light Industry, Food and Appliances
  Medical Industry
  Merchant Marine
  Oil Industry
  Defence Industry
  General Machine Building
  Instrument-Making, Means of Automation and Control Systems
  Railways
  Radio Industry
  Medium Machine Building
  Machine Tool Building and Instrument Industry
  Construction, Road and Communal Machine Building
  Shipbuilding
  Tractor and Agricultural Machine Building
  Transport Construction
  Heavy, Power and Transport Machine Building
  Chemical and Oil Machine Building
  Chemical Industry
  Cellulose-Paper Industry
  Electronics Industry
  Electrotechnical Industry

Union-Republican Ministries:
  Higher and Secondary Specialist Education
  Geology
  State Purchasing
  Health
  Foreign Affairs
  Culture
  Light Industry
  Forestry
  Land Reclamation and Water Economy
  Meat and Dairy Industry
  Defence

Food Industry
Building Materials Industry
Education
Fishing
Rural Construction
Agriculture
Trade
Finance
Justice

Total Number of Ministries: All-Union 27
Union-Republican 20
                                                          ——
                                                          47
                                                          ——

NOTES

[1] *Politichesky slovar*, 2nd edition, Moscow, 1958, p. 607.
[2] Cf. K. C. Wheare, 1946, Ch. 1.
[3] A. Y. Vyshinsky, 1948, pp. 230–1.
[4] *Pravda*, June 16, 1970.
[5] December 1958, October 1959, May and December 1960 and December 1961.
[6] Based on the USSR Budget as printed in *Pravda*, November 27, 1971 and the RSFSR Budget as printed in *Vedomosti verkh. Soveta* RSFSR, No. 50, 1971.
[7] For an excellent short discussion of the Turnover Tax see Alec Nove, 1961 pp. 98–100.
[8] Based on the Table on p. 36 in *Chislennost, sostav i razmeshchenie naselenia SSSR.* TsSU. Moscow, 1961.
[9] *Ibid.,* p. 55.
[10] *Ibid.,* p. 54.
[11] A. Y. Vyshinsky, *op. cit.,* pp. 286–7.
[12] This is done much less by the Republican Councils of Ministers which legally may direct only the Executive Committees of local Soviets and not the Soviets themselves. Cf. Yu. A. Tikhomirov, I. M. Stepanov, 1960.
[13] N. G. Berdichevsky in *S.G.i.P.* No. 1, 1960 pp. 24–31.
[14] *Izvestia,* December 7, 1961.
[15] Budget Report by V. F. Garbuzov, *Izvestia,* October 28, 1959.
[16] Art. 41 of the October 1959 Budget Law empowers the Union Republics to use supplementary revenue for the financing of the national economy or social-cultural development 'excepting capital investment'.
[17] The Statute 'Concerning the transference to the jurisdiction of the Union Republics the handling of Questions of territorial and provincial administrative-territorial structure', February 11, 1957. However, it is clear that the decision to establish a new Territory (*krai*) in the Kazakh Republic in 1960 was taken centrally by the Central Committee of the CPSU. Cf. N. S. Khrushchev's Report to the Plenum of the Central Committee of the CPSU, *Izvestia,* January 22, 1961.
[18] Among the many articles in English on Soviet industrial decentralization the following are of particular value:
J. Miller, 'The Decentralization of Industry', *Soviet Studies,* IX, July 1957, pp. 65–83.

H. R. Swearer, 'Khrushchev's Revolution in Industrial Management', *World Politics*, October 1959, pp. 45–61.

Z. Mieczkowski, 'The 1962–1963 Reforms in Soviet Economic Regionalization', *Slavic Review*, XXIV, September 1965, pp. 479–96.

SELECTED BIBLIOGRAPHY

Chkhikvadze, V. M., ed., 1972, Chs. 4, 5.
Hazard, J. N., 4th edn., 1968, Ch. 6.
Lydolph, R. E., 1958.
Swearer, H. R., 1959.
Towster, J., 1948, Ch. 4.
Zlatopolsky, Chs. 2–5.

Chapter 12

SOVIET LOCAL GOVERNMENT

THE IMPORTANCE OF LOCAL GOVERNMENT

Soviet local government has received uneven attention from Western political scientists. It evoked strong interest in certain quarters in the thirties[1] but it was almost ignored in the fifties and sixties.[2] Today the picture is changing and several important works on Soviet local government have already been published in Britain, the United States and Canada.

At least three compelling reasons exist for a serious consideration of Soviet local government. First, it is mainly through the organs of local government that the ordinary citizen has direct contact with the Soviet state. Thus a collective farm chairman is scarcely troubled by Moscow but is continually supervised by the *raiispolkom* (Executive Committee of the District Soviet) and the *raikom* (District Party Committee). Even a Muscovite is seldom directly concerned with either federal or state government. The public transport he uses is controlled by the City Soviet. He buys his food, clothes, furniture and other commodities at emporia or shops run by the City District Soviets. His flat, the school he sends his children to, the hospital and medical services he uses, the militia he calls in in case of theft, are all managed by the City District Soviets. Even his payment of taxes and admission to the electoral roll are handled by the local Soviet authorities and not by the central authorities.

Secondly, it is mostly through the organs of local government that the most effective participation of the masses in the actual work of government occurs, and because of the importance of *mass participation* and *self-administration* in the Soviet concept of democracy it is impossible to give a complete answer to the question of how far the USSR is a democracy without including an assessment of local government. Thirdly, the important question of party–state relations in the USSR cannot be fully understood if the analysis stops short at central and republican levels of government.

172

STRUCTURE

At the outset it will be necessary to describe the structure and pattern of Soviet local government. In July 1971 there were 50,076 local Soviets ranging from village Soviets exercising authority over a few thousand people to the Moscow City Soviet (*Mossovet*) with 7 million people under its control.[3] These local Soviets fell into three different administrative levels. At the highest level were local Soviets directly subordinated to the Union Republican governments. These included 6 *krai* (Territorial) Soviets, 114 *oblast* (Provincial or Regional) Soviets, 8 Autonomous Oblast Soviets, 10 National *okrug* (Area) Soviets, and 84 large city Soviets. The latter included the city Soviets of Moscow, Leningrad, Kiev, Sevastopol, the capital cities of Union Republics, and also the more important cities in the case of the smaller republics which lacked the provincial administrative level. At the intermediate level of local government there were 3,031 rural *raion* (District) Soviets, 447 district Soviets in the larger cities and 756 town Soviets under territorial, province, autonomous province or national area supervision. At the third and lowest level were 40,915 village Soviets and 3,596 urban settlement Soviets. There were also several hundred town Soviets subordinated either to city Soviets or to rural district Soviets.

What I have described above is the state administrative structure. The party structure closely parallels this structure and at all levels and in all local Soviets the real leadership in local government and often the effective operation of local government comes from the parallel party committee or bureau. At the village level the Soviets are directed from the district committee of the party. The role of the party in local government will be discussed at greater length later in this chapter.

Until the end of 1962 the general pattern of Soviet local government had been fairly constant for upwards of two decades. What changes did occur were mainly in terms of the number of Soviets at various levels. Changes occurred partly as a consequence of urbanization, the development of new areas such as southern Siberia and northern Kazakhstan, and partly because of the official policy of improving and rationalizing the administrative structures so as to increase the chances of realizing planned targets. Thus the amalgamation of collective farms to form even larger agricultural units since 1955 has resulted in a parallel trend towards the enlargement of village Soviets. The establishment of economic regions under the industrial reorganization of 1957 resulted in some provinces being linked to neighbouring provinces to form economic regions. In the RSFSR and Uzbekistan this resulted in the reduction of the number of provinces. Government policy of reducing the complexity and expense of the administrative structure has resulted in many smaller rural Soviets being abolished and district Soviets in smaller cities (of from 100,000 to 200,000 population) have almost disappeared.[4] Thus between March 1, 1954 and January 1, 1963, the number of village Soviets fell from 73,730[5] to 40,480.[6] Between January 1, 1953, and July 1, 1971, the number of rural district Soviets fell from 4,418 to 3,031; the number of city district Soviets fell from 511 to 447; and province Soviets fell from 144 to 114.[7] However, increased industrialization tends to raise the number of both town Soviets and settlement Soviets. Thus 170 new town Soviets were established over the six years 1955–60 while none were abolished. While 1220 new village Soviets were established, mainly in the virgin lands areas, 10,396 village Soviets* were abolished.[8]

Although the administrative pattern of local Soviets varies considerably as between the different levels of local government and as between one part of the country and another, the basic pattern is constant. All local Soviets are now on a territorial basis.[9] This remained true even after the reorganization which followed the November 1962 Plenum of the Central Committee. This resulted in separate agricultural and industrial Soviets being established in most of the territories and provinces. Where the population was predominantly rural consolidated Soviets were retained. The former rural districts virtually ceased to exist. In place of the 3,374 rural districts which existed in October 1962, 1,883 enlarged rural and industrial districts were established. While these were not immediately referred to officially as *raiony* (districts) popular usage continued to regard them as such.

This structural alteration was supposed to represent reorganization according to the 'production principle'. In practice this meant the establishment of two hierarchies of Soviets from the village to the province level wherever urban development was significant. In principle village Soviets were to be supervised by the enlarged rural district Soviets which in turn were responsible to the province or territory (Rural) Soviet. Likewise, all urban Soviets, whether based on workers' settlements, towns or cities, were supposed to be hierarchically arranged under the control of the province or territory (Indus-

---

* The reduction in the number of village Soviets has been a steady process for many years. Its chief causes have been the enlargement (through consolidation) of the size of collective farms and the consequent enlargement of village Soviets; and campaigns to rationalize and to streamline the structure of village Soviets. Both processes have led to the elimination of smaller and weaker units of local government. For a brief summary of the main factors making for change in the structure of local government in the USSR, see L. G. Churchward, 'Soviet Local Government Today', *Soviet Studies*, XVII, April 1966, pp. 431–3.

trial) Soviet. In practice there were many anomalies and the resultant pattern was, to say the least, very messy. The new system put a premium on settlements being classified as urban. Many smaller town and urban-type settlements were brought together into industrial zones and placed under the control of the new Industrial District Soviets. While most urban units were separated off from the rural Soviets there were still over five hundred towns included in the rural districts and very frequently urban-type settlements remained subordinated to rural district Soviets. Not even all village Soviets were subordinated to the rural district Soviets. Thus Moscow City Soviet continued to control a village Soviet.

The appearance of the Soviets under the divided provinces is best illustrated in diagrammatical form. For this purpose I have constructed charts of the Soviets in two Russian *oblasts* of varying size and degree of urbanization, Kaluga and Rostov. Typically, the new industrial district figures only in the former example. In more urbanized *oblasts* such as Rostov, smaller towns and urban-type settlements were much more likely to be supervised by the City Soviets.

Examples of Divided Oblasts, April 1, 1963

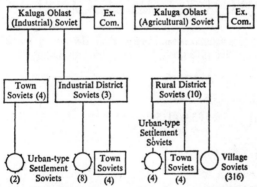

Source: *SSSR administrativno-territorialnoe delenie soyuznykh respublik na 1 aprelya 1963 goda*, Moskva, 1963, pp. 90–2.

KALUGA OBLAST, RSFSR

Population: 952,000
  Urban: 385,000 (40·5%)
  Rural: 567,000 (59·5%)

Administrative Divisions:

  10 Rural Districts
  3 Industrial Districts

175

16 Towns, of which 4 of oblast subordination;
        8 of industrial district subordination;
        4 within rural districts.
14 Urban-type Settlements
316 Village Soviets.

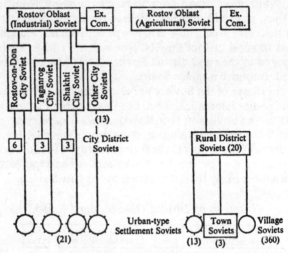

Source: *SSSR administrativno-territorialnoe delenie soyuznykh respublik,
na 1 aprelya 1963 goda, Moskva, 1963, pp. 157-9.*

ROSTOV OBLAST, RSFSR

   Population: 3,512,000

   Urban: 2,103,000 (59·8%)
   Rural: 1,409,000 (40·2%)

Administrative Divisions:

   20 Rural Districts
   12 City Districts
   16 Cities of oblast subordination
    3 Towns of District subordination
   34 Urban-type Settlements
  360 Village Soviets.

A month after Khrushchev's dismissal it was announced that the
consolidated Soviet structure was to be restored along with the consolidated party structure. Shortly afterwards articles began to appear
in the Soviet press criticizing the divided Soviets as producing confusion, inefficiency and over-government. The re-consolidation was
completed before the elections to local Soviets held in March 1965.

Deputies to local Soviets are elected for a two-year term on the basis of universal suffrage and of single member electorates which vary in size from 100–150 in the case of village Soviets to 1,000 and upwards in the case of city Soviets. The size of the Soviet varies from 20–50 deputies for village and settlement Soviets to 40–80 deputies for district Soviets to 50 or more for city Soviets.[10] The frequency of Soviet meetings is fixed by law and it varies somewhat from one republic to another. In the Russian Republic, village and district Soviets meet at least six times a year; provincial, territorial and city Soviets four times a year. Meetings are normally only a day in length but over recent years some larger Soviets have extended their normal sessions to two days. At the first meeting of a newly-elected Soviet an Executive Committee (*ispolkom*) consisting of a Chairman, Vice-Chairman or Vice-Chairmen, Secretary and other members, is elected. The main executive officials at the district and higher levels are paid officials, although ordinary executive members serve in a voluntary capacity. The Executive Committee appoints the heads of the various departments of local government (budget-finance, planning, education, health, etc.) and is chiefly responsible for carrying out the actual administrative work of local government. The reorganization of 1962 produced some complications which were solved rather differently in different parts of the country. While Industrial and Agricultural Provincial Soviets established separate administrations, in some cases such as Health, the Department of the Province Industrial Soviet served the entire population, urban and rural of the province. In some regions a single police organization continued but it was now jointly responsible to the Provincial Agricultural Soviet and the Provincial Industrial Soviet.[11]

Apart from attending sessions of the Soviet most of the deputies (those who are not members of the Executive Committee or Chairmen of local departments) are involved in working in one or other of the various Standing Commissions. These Standing Commissions (which number up to a dozen in the case of the larger Soviets) run parallel to the main Executive departments. Legally the job of the Standing Commissions is essentially advisory, investigatory, supervisory; they make recommendations to Executive Committees or the Soviets but they do not have any authority to issue orders. Nor are they in any sense controlling agencies.[12] Nevertheless, in recent years Standing Commissions have sometimes taken over administrative functions such as directing health and educational services.[13] Likewise over the past few years many local Soviets have assumed the responsibility, exercised through the Standing Commissions, of supervising all the various social organizations which assist in the work of local government. (See Chart.)

Scheme for Co-ordinating the Work of Volunteer Organizations of the Population of Anastasiev Village Soviet, Krasnodar Krai, RSFSR 1963

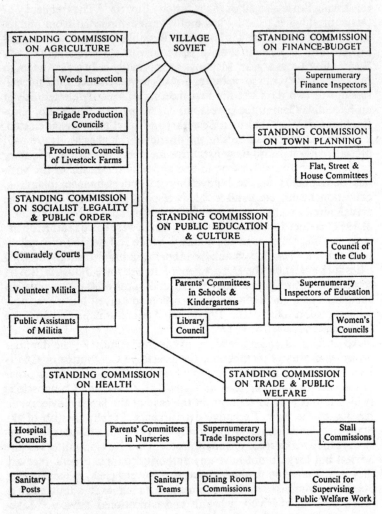

Source: *Sovety deputatov trudyashchikhsya*, No. 1, 1964, p. 44.

ROLE OF LOCAL SOVIETS

What then is the role of local Soviets? Legally, all local Soviets right down to the village Soviet have extensive powers, much more extensive powers than are possessed by local government bodies in Australia or even in the United Kingdom. These powers include the supervision of the economic plan in their area, the direction of industrial and agricultural development, direct control over a large number of industrial, construction and trading establishments (and control over the housing, cultural welfare, health and amenities of workers of all industrial establishments in their territory), control over health, education and other social services besides the conventionally local matters of roads, bridges, parks, water supply, transport, local markets, etc. However, despite these large powers, Soviet local government bodies are not autonomous bodies in any real sense of the term. They act much more as agencies of the central state than as independent units of government. Under the principle of democratic centralism all local Soviets are subjected to direction and control from the governments of a higher level. Thus the village Soviet will not act on most matters until it has an instruction from or approval of the *raiispolkom*. Similarly, the district Soviet is subordinate to the *oblast*, or *krai* Soviet, and these in turn to the Supreme Soviet of the Union Republic and to its Presidium. This line of supervision and direction is not limited to that between Soviets but covers their Executive Committees and departments. Thus the *raiispolkom* is subject to direction from the *oblispolkom* and this in turn from the Council of Ministers of the Union Republic. Likewise the Education Department of the District Soviet is subject to direction from the *oblast* Education Department and this in turn from the Republican Education Ministry. The quantity and quality of this supervision by higher administrative departments varies considerably—it is, for example, much tighter in the case of finance and planning departments than in the case of education and health departments.

The actual role of local government in the USSR depends less on the legal powers of local Soviets than on the degree of local autonomy which the central government permits. In fact, the actual power often falls short of the legal power. Thus local Soviets have always possessed wide powers over housing, both as to construction and control and supervision. But until the reorganization of industry in May 1957 local Soviets were handling only about 10% of housing construction. Since 1957 the bulk of housing funds have been controlled by local Soviets although in many cases the actual construction was done by the *sovnarkhozy* (regional economic councils) and

179

surviving industrial ministries rather than by local construction agencies.[14] Similarly, local Soviets have had wide general powers of control over local industry for many years but it was not until the industrial reorganization of 1957 that the bulk of local industry actually passed under the control of local Soviets. At the close of 1957 approximately one-fifth of all industrial establishments in the USSR[15] were under local Soviet control. The percentage is less today since in some republics several groups of local industries were reclassified and transferred to *sovnarkhoz* control.[16]

Recent extension (since 1954) of the powers of local Soviets, especially in regard to finance, industrial control, supervision of agriculture, etc., have not always been fully carried out because the surviving ministries continue to be highly centralized. Judging from the complaints made in the Soviet press, the Finance Ministry, the Ministry of Agriculture and Gosplan continue to be highly centralized organizations. In these fields the extent of decentralization is limited to the transference of some powers from the All-Union to the Union-Republican level. For example, *raion* Soviets are legally entitled to grant tax exemptions in cases of hardship and special distress.[17] In actual fact all such cases are decided by the *oblispolkom*. The *raion* Soviet may not modify the direction of its budget even if it decides that the same money might be spent differently.[18] Even the *oblispolkom* cannot vary the amounts provided in its budget for capital construction—only the Union Republican Finance Ministry can do that.[19] This sort of limitation is all the more irksome to local Soviets which have recently had more industry placed under their control and also had the amounts of the profits of local industry going to local budgets increased. These sorts of restrictions are greatest of all at the level of the village Soviet. Thus while the 1957–58 regulations on village Soviets enlarged the powers of village Soviets over *kolkhoz* agriculture, village Soviets can in fact exert little influence on the matter. *Kolkhoz* statutes and budgets are supervised by the *raion* Soviet, and *raion* agricultural officials often ignore village Soviets altogether and deal directly with the collective farmers.[20] The development of inter-kolkhoz organization since 1958 and the establishment in March 1962 of Inter-district Kolkhoz–Sovkhoz Boards represented a reduction of the agricultural role of *raion* authorities.[21] The rural *raion* Soviets recovered considerable powers over agriculture in 1965 and by 1970 they had absorbed the production boards.

In a country so vast as the Soviet Union one would expect to find the performance of local government uneven. This unevenness is not simply a consequence of variations in size (the contrast between the Moscow City Soviet and a remote village Soviet) but very often the weaker units of local government are so badly structured that the most efficient management could not make·them effective units of government. Thus many village Soviets are still too small to provide the sort of administration required to supervise the development of *kolkhoz* agriculture and industry. There are cases of collective farms being covered by two or more village Soviets and of more than one village Soviet being situated in the one village. Since the liquidation of the Machine Tractor Stations and the transference of the bulk of their agricultural equipment to the collective farms[22] there has been a rapid development of inter-kolkhoz industries such as food processing, bricks and other building materials, construction agencies and bread making. Such inter-kolkhoz co-operation sometimes brings in ten or more *kolkhozes*. Naturally village Soviets can do little to assist or to supervise such developments. Again, very many rural districts are uneconomical. Despite the reduction in the number of rural districts in recent years and their consequent enlargement 39·4 per cent of rural *raions* in existence on January 1, 1961, had less than 30,000 inhabitants.[23] Such small districts were expected to maintain not only a district apparatus but ten or more village Soviets! Until recently many medium-sized cities (of 100,000–200,000 population) established city district Soviets unnecessarily. Towns which happen to be simultaneously *raion* centres and town Soviets tend to produce an intricate parallel and overlapping administrative structure. On the other hand a village Soviet such as the Sofinsky Village Soviet (Moscow *oblast*), the winner of the Red Challenge Banner in the *oblast* in 1958, with a territory covering a dozen villages, two *kolkhozes* and including six schools, three clubs, three libraries, a hospital, two first aid centres, a maternity home and eleven food and retail stores, obviously had an adequate basis for effective local government.[24] Another example of a 'good achievement' by a local Soviet reported some years ago in the Soviet press was that of a settlement Soviet in a mining district which over the two years 1957–58 had built a new school, bath houses, two kindergartens, a multi-storied block of flats and also assisted workers to build scores of private homes. This same Soviet adopted a seven-year plan (1959–65) which provided for the opening of two new mines, the construction of two new hospitals, a new club, a school for 880 pupils, bath houses, many new shops, a bread factory, over 31,000 square metres of public housing and over 500 private houses.[25]

The same unevenness is to be found in the observance of democratic practices in the organization of Soviets. Over the last decade almost all local Soviets have become more correct in their formal procedure. Most of them hold meetings at regular intervals. Executives make regular reports to Soviets, deputies report back regularly to electorates and so on.[26] But in many cases formal observance of the rules of democratic procedure obscures the continued domination of the Soviet by the inner group of the Executive Committee.[27] Accurate assessment of such problems is rendered virtually impossible because of the exceedingly wide range of practice between individual Soviets. Soviet local government has always succeeded in involving millions of citizens. The restoration of formal Soviet democracy and the extension of the actual powers of local government in recent years has certainly resulted in the involvement of many millions more Soviet citizens in the process of self-administration. Prior to the March 1959 local government elections all local Soviets were enlarged resulting in almost 350,000 additional deputies being returned. This was officially explained as necessary for the better fulfilment of local government responsibilities. This meant the enlargement of the number of local deputies to close on 1·9 million. Even before the 22nd Congress decided that at least one-third of deputies should retire at each election there was a very high turnover in the membership of local Soviets.[28] In this way the number of persons with direct governmental experience in the community is steadily enlarging. In addition to deputies there are almost 2·7 million 'activists' (non-deputies) serving on the Standing Commissions of local Soviets.[29] Besides the activists engaged in helping the Standing Commissions many hundreds of thousands of citizens are involved in assisting the *ispolkoms* by serving in such agencies as Street Committees, House Committees, Library Councils, Social Courts, Voluntary Militia Squads, etc. The members of these organizations are more closely connected with administration than the mainly advisory Standing Commissions of local Soviets. Thus the Voluntary Militia Squads assist the local militia in controlling anti-social behaviour such as hooliganism, drunkenness and slander. Social and Comradely Courts are guaranteed assistance from militia and People's Courts in carrying out their decisions and they may impose petty fines and damages against people brought before them, although in all cases the accused is guaranteed the right of appeal to the *ispolkom*. House Committees exercise control over the maintenance of public housing and the upkeep and tidiness of flats. Above 9 million Soviet citizens are involved in the work of Electoral Commissions. The number of Soviet citizens directly involved in the work of local government was estimated at 27 millions in 1967. In addition there are over 38 millions involved at present in voluntary administrative work, supervision of amenities, and social services and safety of Soviet workers in Trade Unions.[30] Even allowing for considerable overlap between these two groups there must be at least 30 million persons directly involved in this process of 'self-administration' (*samoupravlenie*), a sizeable section of a population of 250 millions. It is a considerable achievement even if Standing Commissions are often ineffective because of the limitation on their powers and because in many local governments the *ispolkom* consistently ignores the recommendations of the Standing Commissions.[31]

PARTY CONTROL OF LOCAL SOVIETS

Before drawing any conclusions it is necessary to examine the role of the Communist Party in local government. On the surface the Communist Party domination of local Soviets is less evident than Communist Party domination of the Supreme Soviets. Thus while Communists (including candidate members) comprised almost 73% of the deputies of the USSR Supreme Soviet elected in June 1970[32] and 67·6% of the deputies of Union Republican Supreme Soviets elected in June 1971,[33] they represented only 41·3% (Estonia) to 47·5% (Moldavia) of the deputies of local Soviets elected in June 1971.[34] In most village, settlement and district Soviets, Communists are in the minority. However, the principle of Communist Party leadership operates in local government as elsewhere in the Soviet Union, irrespective of whether Communists hold a majority or a minority of the positions in the local Soviet.

Percentages of Communist* Deputies Returned to Local Soviets in Recent Years

	1965	1967	1969	1971	1973
RSFSR	45·0	46·1	44·3	43·3	42·7
Ukraine	46·3	47·0	47·4	47·0	46·5
Belorussia	41·6	43·5	43·9	43·9	43·6
Uzbekistan	46·0	46·3	46·4	45·6	45·3
Kazakhstan	44·4	44·6	42·8	41·8	41·2
Georgia	47·5	47·6	45·3	44·9	43·6
Azerbaidjan	49·9	50·5	44·4	46·5	44·5
Lithuania	38·9	42·3	43·5	44·2	45·3
Moldavia	41·7	47·7	47·3	47·5	47·0
Latvia	41·5	43·2	44·2	45·7	45·5
Kirgizia	45·4	46·5	45·5	44·3	44·1
Tadjikistan	46·1	46·1	46·2	44·9	44·3
Armenia	47·4	47·5	46·5	46·4	43·6
Turkmenia	43·4	43·3	43·3	42·9	42·9
Estonia	39·8	38·6	39·3·	41·3	42·9

* Including candidate members.

How then does this Communist Party guidance operate? What are its agencies and methods? First of all the Communist Party fractions still operate in the lower Soviets although they would not appear to be important in the Supreme Soviets. After an election the party fraction (or caucus of Communist deputies in a particular local Soviet) will meet, usually in advance of the meeting of the Soviet. This fraction, acting on the advice of the District Party Committee (*raikom*) in the case of district and village Soviets and of the *oblast* Party Committee (*obkom*) in the case of *oblast* Soviets, then adopts a slate of candidates for the election of the Executive Committee of the Soviet. The fraction will also consider the main lines of work for the Soviet over the coming period.[35]

Secondly, the Executive Committee of the local Soviet will normally have a Communist majority.[36] Its leading members, especially the Chairman, the Vice-Chairmen and the Secretary are almost always Party members from the district level upwards, and often even at the village Soviet level. There is a significant overlap between the membership of the leading Party Committee in the area and the *ispolkom*. Thus the Chairman of the *raiispolkom* is commonly a member of the *raikom* while the first secretary of the *raikom* is generally also on the *raiispolkom* although he is not likely to be either the chairman or the secretary of the latter body. Nevertheless he exercises Party leadership in the *raiispolkom*. Regularity of contact between *raiispolkom* and *raikom* is ensured not merely by overlapping membership but by the fact that the offices of the two committees are often situated in the same building—a physical symbol of the unity of party and state.

Thirdly, representatives of the *raikom* are generally invited to attend meetings of village and settlement Soviets in their district, even if they are not deputies of those Soviets. They exercise the right to speak at such meetings and often recommend candidates for the office of Chairman and, on occasion, ensure the removal of 'unsatisfactory' Chairmen, even against the wishes of the Soviet. Such practices were quite normal in the Stalin period and even today are not exceptional. However, it is perhaps worthy of note that over the past few years there has been a good deal of public criticism in the Soviet press[37] of such high-handed and undemocratic interference by District Party Secretaries in the affairs of village Soviets. I quote a recent example of this reported in the Soviet journal *Sovety*[38] under the heading *A Rough Violation of Soviet Democracy*.

From February 1950 I worked in the Chernotichi Village Soviet—at first as Secretary, and then (from April 1956) as Chairman of the Executive Committee. During all these years the Executive Committee of our Soviet received no special rebukes for its work. In the first half of 1959 our Village Soviet gained first place in the competition of Village Soviets in the Sosnitsky District.

Then at the beginning of October last year I was invited to attend the Bureau of the Party Primary of our kolkhoz 'Peremoga Zhovtnya'. The Secretary of the Sosnitsky *raikom*, comrade Kapran, was present and he proposed that I should go to work as leader of an irrigation brigade. In view of the poor state of my health and also because of strained relations with the Chairman of the kolkhoz, I declined this proposal. There was and is only one reason for the proposal—I have never worked directly in agriculture.

In answer to my request to be allowed to remain at my former work comrade Kapran suddenly announced,

'There is no place for you in the Village Soviet. You don't understand the policy of the Party.'

Just what produced such a statement I can't understand. I have been a member of the Party since 1944, I worked in a mine for several years, I studied at the Mining Industry School, I served in the Soviet Army, and before I was elected to the Village Soviet I was manager of the village club.

On the following day I was asked to attend the Bureau of the *raikom* where they decided to release me from working in the Village Soviet Executive Committee. A day later the Deputy Chairman of the Executive Committee of the District Soviet, comrade Leuta, came to our village of Chernotichi in order to attend the session of the Village Soviet called to discuss this organizational question. In the discussion he had with me he advised me to give up the position of Chairman of the Village Soviet and above all not 'to jib', otherwise it would be 'unhealthy' for me.

As a member of the Party I obeyed that demand and in my speech to the session I proposed that the Soviet should release me from my position. But the vote showed that the deputies did not want to gratify my request. Out of 20 deputies present at the session only 3 voted for relieving me; namely, the Chairman of the *kolkhoz*, the secretary of the Party Primary and the Manager of the Farm. Then the Deputy-Chairman of the *raiispolkom*, comrade Leuta, spoke again and urged the deputies to release me, since in any case it had already been decided by the *raikom*. However, on the second vote only 7 out of the 20 deputies voted to release me. Notwithstanding this comrade Leuta announced that I was released from the post as Chairman of the Executive Committee of the Village Soviet.

I consider that the leading workers of our Sosnitsky district organizations acted illegally in this case, for they did not consider the opinions of the deputies of the Village Soviet. They rode rough-shod over Soviet democracy.

I ask the editor of the journal to investigate this matter and to give his opinion on it.

N. KUZMENKO

Chernotichi,
Sosnitsky Raion,
Chernigov Oblast

The journal, having investigated the complaint and confirmed the facts mentioned in the letter, criticized the *raion* leadership for its actions which would 'dampen the enthusiasm of the people for self-government'. The follow-up by the party organizations indicated very clearly the relative strength of party and state organizations at this level of local government. Although the Sosnitsky *raikom* confirmed the complaint of comrade Kuzmenko it did not reinstate him. Although the *raikom* secretary and the *raiispolkom* officials were reprimanded for their 'intolerable administrative methods' their action in consigning Kuzmenko to work in an irrigation brigade was confirmed.[39]

A fourth method by which Party control over local Soviets operates is through the domination of the pre-selection meetings at which candidates for deputies are nominated. This sometimes extends to the *raikoms* deciding which candidate Party members in a particular factory or enterprise should nominate, a clearly undemocratic procedure, even within the Soviet concept of inner-party democracy.[40]

Fifthly, the Communist Party issues directives on economic and social policy and on many matters within the sphere of local government. This operates at all levels in the Soviet administrative structure. Just as the Central Committee of the CPSU issues directives to the USSR Council of Ministers, so the *obkom* issues directives to the *oblispolkom* and the *raikom* issues directives to the *raiispolkom* and to the village Soviets subordinate to it.

Finally, the Party exercises general supervision over the cadre policy of local Soviet Executive Committees and directly controls many key appointments. Party direction of cadres is mainly but not wholly confined to the direction of Party members into particular employment, while Cadres Sectors of Soviet *ispolkoms* are concerned with filling the general range of positions in local government administration with the best available persons, whether they be party or non-party. The process involves no clash between the two organizations as there is a clear division between the posts filled by the Party organization and those filled by the Cadres Sector of the *ispolkom*. Positions under Party control are listed in a 'nomenclature' or list. Party Organizations recommend appointments to those posts and the *ispolkom* invariably accepts the recommendations. The formal appointment is made by the *ispolkom*. It is probably a minority of positions[41] which are filled in this way but they include most of the key positions, including the Chairman, Vice-Chairmen and Secretary of the *raiispolkom* as well as the chiefs of the main departments.[42] This Party control over cadres is openly admitted. Thus in 1959 the secretary of the Kostroma *obkom* reported in *Izvestia* that the *obkom* had directed seventy-four persons into work in local Soviets over the previous three years, thirty of whom had been transferred from the Party apparatus.[43]

Party control over cadres is also maintained through Party control over training courses for workers in the state apparatus. The Central Committee of the CPSU established in 1946 basic courses for leading workers in the Soviets. These provided for a year's course for Chairmen and Vice-Chairmen of Executive Committees of territorial, provincial and city Soviets, and also for the heads of Executive Committee Departments of these Soviets, the course to be organized by the Party higher schools. Nine-month courses were provided for equivalent workers in the *raion* administration.[44] Also at the district level it is only the Party which maintains a complete system of instructors and these guide both the training of Party cadres and Soviet cadres. At the *oblast* level the Soviets have their own organizational-instructional departments but they are closely linked with those of the Party.

CONSEQUENCES OF PARTY CONTROL

How far does Communist Party Control over local government involve a restriction of Soviet democracy? An exact answer to this question is hard to give because Party control over local government has been both stimulating and encouraging and restrictive and stultifying. Quite obviously Party control has not prevented the involvement of millions of people in the work of local government. While Soviet citizens often think of the central government as being quite remote and out of their reach they do not recognize such a clear distinction between themselves and local authorities. Nor do they generally link their feeling of separation from the leadership to a rejection of its claim that the system is democratic. On the other hand it would seem likely (and it is occasionally conceded in the Soviet Union itself)[45] that close Party control has restricted the initiative of citizens as they tend to wait on the Communist Party coming out with its policy before bringing out suggestions on what should be done and how specific problems should be tackled.

Close Party supervision of local government has tended to increase local bureaucracy as Party committees and apparatus have not only paralleled local government, but at times, especially in rural districts, they have tended to outright duplication and even to the supplanting of Soviet apparatus.[46] Each administrative reorganization at the local level in recent years has been followed by the remodelling of the Party apparatus. Thus the establishment of the *sovnarkhozy* in 1957 was followed by the establishment of Party organization within the Economic Councils and between *oblasts* where this was necessary.[47] When, following the September 1953 Plenum of the Central Committee, the Machine Tractor Stations took over from the *raiispolkom* the main tasks of agricultural control the *raikom* instructional groups, previously based on a zonal system, were henceforth based directly on the Machine Tractor Stations. The dissolution of the Machine Tractor Stations in 1958 brought about another reorganization in the structure of the *raikom*. The establishment of Inter-district Kolkhoz–Sovkhoz Agricultural Boards in 1962 resulted in the establishment of a parallel system of Party instructors on an inter-district basis under *obkom* control.[48] On the other hand the reorganization of the Party along production lines at the end of 1962 was followed almost immediately by the reorganization of the Soviet structure into separate urban and rural organizations to keep it parallel to the new Party structure. In the same way the Central Committee decided on November 16, 1964 (a month after the fall of Khrushchev), to restore the consolidated party and state structures at all levels.

The implementation of the Party policy of systematically reducing the size of the administrative apparatus of local government has resulted in a reduction of the number of paid officials in both Party and state structures. Although precise figures on this trend are not available scattered evidence suggests that Party and state administrative structures were reduced between 15% and 20% between 1954 and 1962.[49] The evidence for the trend during 1963–64 is rather contradictory. At first glance it would seem that both Party and state apparatuses were reduced as the size of the district units was substantially larger and since the *raikom* apparatus was abolished and replaced by a simpler, less numerous apparatus.[50] However, after the fall of Khrushchev it was often asserted that the establishment of separate urban and rural organizations for both Party and state from the oblast level downwards had enormously inflated the administrative apparatus.[51]

Despite the shortcomings mentioned in the previous paragraph the available evidence suggests that public enthusiasm has increased over the last decade, partly through the general restoration of legal norms in the functioning of Soviets and even more because of the considerable increase in the power of local government over such matters as industry, agriculture, housing, construction, retail trade, public health and cultural services.[52] But it is still too soon to say if the increase in local Soviet powers and the expansion of the process of self-administration will result in any significant curtailment of the functions of the central state. This claim has been made by the Soviet leadership since early in 1959,[53] but the enhanced power of local Soviets has not resulted in any weakening of central control and the dismantling of various central agencies has been more than counterbalanced by the expansion of party control at every level of local government from the village to the province.[54]

NOTES

[1] For example, S. and B. Webb, 1935; B. W. Maxwell, 1935; Sir E. D. Simon, ed., 1937.

[2] Thus Merle Fainsod in *How Russia is Ruled*, 1954, devotes only two pages out of five hundred to the subject of local Soviets.

[3] The population of Moscow City (including settlement Soviets subordinated to the City Soviet) on July 1, 1971 was given as 7,061,000, of which 6,942,000 lived in Moscow itself. *SSSR Administrativno-territorialnoe delenie soyuznykh respublik* 1971, p. 128.

[4] Cf. R. A. Safarov, 1961, pp. 8, 14–15.

[5] *S.G.i.P.*, No. 1, 1960, p. 79.

[6] *Sovety* No. 4, 1963, pp. 96–97.

[7] 1953 figures given in *Izvestia*, January 11, 1953. 1961 figures from source quoted in Note 6 above. 1971 figures, cf. note 3 above.

[8] *S.G.i.P.* No. 5, 1961, p. 41.

[9] There are, however, vestiges of the earlier functional representation embedded in the present system of territorial Soviets. Thus settlement Soviets require that the majority of the inhabitants of the territory (it is 85% in the RSFSR) must belong to families of workers employed in the industrial establishments on which the Settlement Soviet is based. Legally, deputies of local Soviets report back to their electorate. In fact they often report back to the social group which nominated them (to the factory, workshop, mine, school, collective farm, etc.). Similarly in the rare cases where deputies are recalled the recall is initiated by the group which nominated them.

[10] The Moscow City Soviet elected March 1965 consisted of 1,104 deputies.

[11] *Sovety*, No. 2, 1963, pp. 9–14, 19–24; No. 3, 1963, pp. 19–25.

[12] Cf. A. Y. Luzhin, 1953; Yu. V. Todorsky, 1955; *Polozhenia o postoyannykh komissiyakh mestnykh Sovetov deputatov trudyashchikhsya*, Moscow, 1956.

Over recent years Standing Commissions have become more important as supervisory agencies and in this sphere their activities tend to duplicate those of the public organizations functioning under the Executive Committee. This has led to some criticism by those Soviet workers who feel that the Standing Commissions can do this job better. Cf. the article 'Standing Commissions or Public Departments?' in *Sovety*, No. 3, 1962, pp. 65–7.

[13] Cf. *Sovety*, No. 10, 1963, pp. 17–20.

[14] Cf. Yu. A. Tikhomirov, 1959, pp. 44–8.

[15] Immediately after the reorganization in 1957 the *sovnarkhozy* controlled 75% of all industry in the Russian Republic and 73% in Moldavia. *Izvestia*, May 9 and 10, 1957.

[16] *S.G.i.P.* No. 4, 1959, pp. 43–54. In Latvia during 1962 local industries were placed under dual control of local Soviets and the Sovnarkhoz. *Sovety*, No. 9, 1962, pp. 29–31.

[17] Cf. A. Kushnerova, 'Questions which should be decided locally', in *Izvestia*, March 7, 1957.

[18] Cf. V. Petrushka in *Izvestia*, May 11, 1958; V. Vasiliev in *Sovety*, No. 12, 1960, pp. 19–26. The 1968 Regulations on Village Soviets extended to the Village Soviets many powers given to district Soviets a decade earlier. *Sovety*, No 6, 1968, pp. 3–6. Once again the higher Soviet (in this case the District Soviet) often refused to relinquish these powers. Cf. *Sovety*, No 8, 1970, pp. 59–63.

[19] S. Kheifets in *Finansy SSSR*, No. 7, 1958, pp. 27–31.

[20] *Sovety*, No. 5, 1959, pp. 65–71.

[21] The decision to establish these inter-district agencies was taken at the March 1962 plenum of the Central Committee of the CPSU. *Izvestia*, March 25, 1962.

[22] The decision became law on March 31, 1958. Under this law the bulk of the Machine Tractor Stations were dissolved and their agricultural equipment transfered to the kolkhozes. Only those MTS serving very backward kolkhozes were temporarily preserved. Equipment not sold to the kolkhozes was placed in RTS (Technical Repair Stations) under *raion* control. *Izvestia*, April 1, 1958.

[23] *Sovety*, No. 3, 1961, p. 98. The average rural *raion* in the USSR on July 1, 1960, had 39,200 inhabitants. *Sovety*, No. 11, 1960, p. 98. For a recent Soviet criticism of irrationalities in the administrative structure see V. A. Nemtsev, *S.G.i.P.*, No 6, 1972, pp. 80–7.

[24] *Otvety na voprosy trudyashchikhsya*, No. 98 (1958–59).

[25] *Sovety*, No. 2, 1959, p. 36.

[26] In the RSFSR only 67·5% of Executive Committees reported back to their Soviets in 1955 but 87·7% reported back in 1959. Yu. A. Tikhomirov, I. M. Stepanov, *Rukovodstvo vysshikh organov vlasti soyuznykh respublik mestnymi Sovetami deputatov trudyashchikhsya*. Moscow, 1960, p. 94.

[27] Cf. *Izvestia*, January 24, 1958.

[28] Thus 49% of deputies elected to local Soviets in March 1961 were elected for the first time. *Sovety*, No. 6, 1961, pp. 102–3.

[29] In 1972 there were 327,991 Standing Commissions in local Soviets in which 1,754,000 deputies and 2,680,000 activists participated. *Sovety*, No. 5, 1973, pp. 74–7. The precise powers of non-deputy members of Standing Commissions varies from republic to republic. They have full powers only in the Baltic republics and in Belorussia.

[30] Yampolskaya, Ts. A., 1972.

[31] Cf. G. Nosach in *Izvestia*, March 18, 1959.

[32] Based on the analysis of the composition of the 8th USSR Supreme Soviet as given in *Pravda*, July 15, 1970.

[33] *Pravda*, June 20, 1971.

[34] *Vedomosti verkh. Soveta SSSR*, No. 25, 23 June, 1971.

[35] Cf. A. A. Askerov, 1953, pp. 174–82. Arutyunyan, N. Kh., 1970.

[36] In an earlier period when Communists were a smaller minority of local deputies party fractions functioned regularly within *ispolkoms* as well as within Soviets. Cf. A. I. Lepeshkin, 1959, Vol. 2 (1921–36), p. 17. The practice has been somewhat revived since 1962.

[37] See for example, the article by special correspondent M. Garin in *Izvestia*, September 25, 1958. 'Why do deputies remain unsatisfied?'

[38] *Sovety*, No. 2, 1960, pp. 67–8. See also the same journal Nos. 4, 6 and 7, 1960, for more on the same and similar cases.

[39] *Sovety*, No. 4, 1960, p. 90. A similar case with a like result was reported in *Sovety*, No. 3, 1973, pp. 66–9.

[40] Cf. my article in *Soviet Studies*, Vol. ix, July 1957, pp. 88–89.

[41] A. A. Askerov, *op. cit.*, p. 179, gives 3–4,000 posts of *oblast* and *raion* Soviet staffs as being on the Party nomenclature. Askerov (pp. 123–37; 174–82; 272) gives the fullest account I have seen in a Soviet text of this process.

[42] This process contains a contradiction between the principle of selection and promotion of cadres from above and the democratic principle of selection from below.

[43] *Izvestia*, March 28, 1959, p. 2.

[44] A. A. Askerov, *op. cit.*, p. 133.

[45] Cf. Yu. Feofanov in *Izvestia*, May 8, 1959, 'From Positions of Strength', who states that, '. . . in the localities they are overcautious; on each occasion they await instructions from some *raikom* or some higher organ, and this produces a great stream of papers, directives, and circulars. The monotonous gurgle of this

stream at times muffles the strong tumult of life. This fear of responsibility, this habit of guardianship, gives birth to bureaucratic–authoritarian methods of work.'

[46] Cf. A. A. Askerov, *op. cit.*, pp. 177–8. Cf. *Sovety dep. trud*, No.3, 1966, pp. 7–19.

[47] Cf. my article in *Soviet Studies*, Vol. ix, January 1958, pp. 267–8.

[48] See the speech by G. I. Voronov to the Plenum of the Central Committee. *Izvestia*, March 7, 1962, and the speeches by F. A. Surganov, *Izvestia*, March 8, 1962, and the decisions of the Plenum, *Izvestia*, March 10, 1962.

[49] Thus P. Bogdanov reporting on the Smolensk *gorkom*, *Sovetskaya Rossia* August 22, 1961, claimed that although Party organizations in that area had increased by one-third since 1957 the *gorkom* apparatus had been reduced from 119 to 38. As against the 38 paid functionaries there were 660 unpaid party workers in the party apparatus.

[50] Decisions of the November 1962 Plenum of the Central Committee November 23, 1962. *Izvestia*, November 24, 1962. At the time when this change was made there were 961 Inter-district Administrative Areas as compared with over 3,000 rural districts (*Raiony*).

[51] Cf. *Izvestia* editorial, November 19, 1964.

[52] For an examination of how far local Soviet powers over these and other matters have increased since 1956 see my article, 'Lokalverwaltung und Räte in der Sowjetunion seit dem XX Parteikongress', in *Osteuropa*, No. 1, 1960, pp. 5–14.

[53] Cf. N. S. Khrushchev's speech to the 21st Congress in which he stated that: 'It is already clear that many functions of our government agencies will gradually pass to public organizations. Take, for instance, certain aspects of our cultural services. It is not at all obligatory that they remain in the charge of government organizations. Public organizations can handle them just as successfully. Experience also suggests the need to modify the organization of our health services, including health resort facilities. Apparently we are approaching a point where more and more of our public health services in the towns should come under the trade unions and in the countryside, at the present stage, directly under the local Soviets.' Cf. N. S. Khrushchev, *O programme kommunisticheskoi partii Sovetskovo Soyuza. Doklad na XXII Sezde KPSS. 18 Okt. 1961. Moscow, 1961, pp. 80–8.

[54] For a more detailed evaluation of recent (1962–65) trends in Soviet local government see my article in *Soviet Studies* April 1966, 'Local Soviets Today'.

SELECTED BIBLIOGRAPHY

Braham, R. L., 1965, pp. 330–52.
Churchward, L. G., *Soviet Studies*, ix, 1958.
Churchward, L. G., 1966.
Denisov and Kirichenko, 1960, Ch. 8.
Frolic, B. M., 1971.
Morton, H. W., 1968.
Schapiro, L., 1965, Ch. 7.
Taubman, W., 1973.
Wesson, R. G., 1964.

Chapter 13

PARTY AND CLASS

THE COMMUNIST PARTY AS A WORKING-CLASS PARTY

The CPSU has always claimed to be a working-class party. Western critics often reject this claim and sometimes on irrelevant arguments. The purpose of this chapter is to examine the claims that have been made and are being made in the Soviet Union on the question of the relationship between the Party and the working class and to measure these claims against the political record of the Communist Party.

The claim that the CPSU is a working-class party means primarily that the party bases its political activities on the assumption that the working class provides the main class basis in the struggle to replace capitalism by socialism. This claim is made for a number of reasons. Firstly, the workers are held to be the most exploited class under capitalism and because of their everyday working experience they are in the best position to recognize the basis of exploitation under capitalism. They have nothing to lose by overthrowing capitalism and everything to gain by the establishment of socialism. Secondly, because the workers are already used to producing socially they can most easily be persuaded to accept socialization of property, i.e. social ownership and control. Thirdly, the working class is the only class capable of overthrowing capitalism even though they may well require allies to carry through their revolution to a successful conclusion. Neither the peasantry nor the petty bourgeoisie can provide the agency for the overthrow of capitalism because neither of these classes is opposed to private property as such.

The above notions are orthodox Marxist. The two chief modifications introduced by Lenin were firstly, his greater emphasis on the revolutionary role of the intelligentsia; and secondly, his stress on the peasants as indispensable allies of the industrial proletariat. As early as 1902 Lenin stated that:

> The history of all countries shows that the working class, exclusively by its own effort, is able to develop only trade union consciousness, i.e., it may itself realise the necessity for combining in unions, for fighting against the

192

employers and for striving to compel the government to pass necessary labour legislation; etc. The theory of socialism, however, grew out of the philosophical, historical and economic theories that were elaborated by the educated representatives of the propertied classes, the intellectuals. According to their social status, Marx and Engels, themselves belonged to the bourgeois intelligentsia. Similarly, in Russia, the theoretical doctrine of Social-Democracy arose independently of the spontaneous growth of the labour movement; it arose as a natural and inevitable outcome of the development of ideas among the revolutionary socialist intelligentsia.[1]

Thus Communists claim that the Communist Party is the result of the coming together of two great forces, the elemental mass movement of the proletariat and scientific socialism, Marxism.

The emphasis on the peasants as necessary allies of the working class was prompted by the fact that the modern industrial proletariat formed only a small minority in tsarist Russia while the peasants were the overwhelming majority. They were, moreover, natural allies in the first or bourgeois stage of the revolution, in the overthrowal of feudal landlordism and tsarist autocracy. This was recognized by Lenin and other Russian socialists even before 1900 and was much reinforced by the experiences of 1905. After the November Revolution the alliance with the peasantry was retained, but from 1918 onwards the strategy increasingly sought to ally the workers with the poor and middle peasants against the kulaks.

Because the CPSU bases its actions on the working class it has generally sought to recruit most heavily from among the workers. In January 1917 workers formed 60·2% of the membership of the Bolshevik Party. As a result of losses in the Civil War and the recruiting of peasants through the Red Army the working-class percentage fell to 41% by January 1921.[2] During the period of the NEP the leadership emphasized recruitment of workers into the Party, no doubt partly designed to safeguard against any undue peasant influence in Soviet politics. Mass membership drives conducted in 1924, 1927 and 1930 brought in tens of thousands of new working-class members. By 1930 workers comprised 68·2% of the party membership.* The percentage remained high during the early 1930s but dropped off rapidly after 1937 when the emphasis shifted more to the recruitment of intellectuals. This shift reflected the increasing complexity of Soviet administration and hence the need to increase the educational level of party members.

At various times in the history of the CPSU working-class persons have found it easier to secure admission to the Party than have other classes. Thus in the pre-1939 rules workers required a shorter period

* This really overstates the position as actual production workers represented only 48·6% of the Party membership in April 1930.

of candidate membership. In other periods, especially in 1924, 1927, 1930 and since 1954, working-class membership has been deliberately and rapidly extended. Very often workers have been given special emphasis in elections to higher committees. This was in line with Lenin's suggestion (made to the 11th Party Congress in December 1922) that more than half the members of the Central Committee should be workers. Many of the top leaders of the Party from 1917 right up to the present were originally workers, although almost all leaders in this period, irrespective of their social origin, have arrived at party leadership via a long career as professional revolutionaries or functionaries.

Since the middle 1930s recruitment patterns have changed several times. Intellectuals were favoured in recruitment between 1937 and 1941. The war reversed this trend and during the years 1941–45 most recruits came via the army and were drawn from workers and peasants. In the period 1945–52 intellectuals were again a favoured group in party recruitment. Since the 19th Congress, and increasingly since 1954, there has been greater emphasis on recruitment of industrial workers, collective farmers, and workers on state farms. Recruitment of peasants and agricultural workers has been facilitated by the consolidation of smaller farms into larger farms. The number of collective farms fell from 254,000 in January 1950 to 97,000 in October 1952, to 87,000 by January 1956 and to 39,500 by 1963. Communist Party organization in the farms has moved inversely. Thus in 1939 (at the time of the 18th Congress) party primaries existed in only 8% of collective farms whereas in January 1956 at the time of the 20th Congress party primaries operated in 92% of collective farms. At the 22nd Congress in October 1961 it was reported that 'almost all collective farms' had Communist Party organizations.[3]

The increase in the numbers of workers and farmers in the Party since 1954 is shown in other available statistics. Between January 1956 and October 1961 the number of primary party organizations based directly on industry, transport and construction rose from 46,894 or 12% of the total to 75,681 or 25·5% of the total number of primaries. The number of workshop party organizations* rose by one hundred thousand between the 22nd and the 23rd Party Congresses. In March 1966 there were 287,000 workshop party organizations. The percentage of workers in the Party rose from 32% in 1956 to 34·5% in 1960, and 40·1% in 1971.[4] More than half of the three million new members who joined the Party between the 23rd and 24th Congresses (1966–71) were workers. The percentage of collective farmers in the Party rose from 17·1% in 1956 to 17·5% in 1960 but

---

* Not all of these are classified as 'Primary Organizations'. There were 326,000 primary organizations in the CPSU in March 1966.

by 1971 it had fallen to 15·1%. The trend towards increased worker and collective farmer membership is also reflected in the composition of the delegates attending recent Congresses. Industrial workers formed 12·2% of delegates to the 20th Congress (1956), 23·3% of delegates to the 22nd Congress (1961) and 24·1% of delegates to the 24th Congress (1971). Working farmers from collective and state farms comprised only 4·6% of delegates to the 20th Congress, but 10·6% of delegates to the 22nd Congress and 17·5% of delegates to the 24th Congress. Conversely, the percentage of delegates who were Party functionaries fell from 36·6% at the 20th Congress, to 25·9% at the 22nd Congress and to 24·4% at the 23rd Congress. It rose to 25·9% at the 24th Congress.[5]

THE 'VANGUARD' PARTY

Linked with the concept of the Communist Party as being a proletarian party is that of it as a 'vanguard' party. This claim is not precisely the same as that it is an elite party. Stalin in *The Foundations of Leninism* (1924) categorized the concept as follows:

(a) The Party is the *vanguard of the working class*. The Party absorbs all the best elements of the working class, but in order to lead the workers it must be armed with revolutionary theory, with a knowledge of the laws of movement of society, for 'the Party cannot be a real party if it limits itself to registering what the masses of the working class think or experience'.[6] The Party is the general staff of the proletariat.

(b) The Party is *an organized detachment of the working class*. The Party must be a disciplined body based on strict conditions of membership and above all, a party of activists. This had been the chief distinguishing feature of Bolshevik organization since 1903. This concept of course tended to keep many sympathizers out of the Party, tended for many years to keep it, as Lenin stated, 'a more or less limited circle of leaders'. The Party numbered only 23,000 at the time of the March Revolution. It was estimated at more than 200,000 on the eve of the November Revolution but at only 115,000 in January 1918. It stood at 576,000 in January 1921 and 914,000 by January 1928. By January 1933 it had reached 2,204,000. Its membership fell during the purges and stood at under 1·5 million in January 1938. It was close on 4 million at the beginning of 1945. By October 1952 it stood at 6 million and reached 6,796,000 by January 1956.[7] At the time of the 21st Extraordinary Congress in January 1959 there were 7,622,356 full members and 616,775 candidate members, 8,239,131 in all. By the 22nd Congress in October 1961 there were 8,872,516 full members and 843,489 candidate members, or 9,716,005 in all. At the time of the 23rd Congress in March 1966 there was 11,673,676 full members and 797,403 candidate members, 12,471,079 in all. At the time of the 24th Congress the Party had 13,810,089 members and 645,232 candidate members, a total of 14,455,321.

The growth of the Communist Party since 1917 has involved the change from a relatively small revolutionary party to a mass party. This change pre-dated the November Revolution but the Bolshevik seizure of power undoubtedly facilitated it for a mass party is better suited both to maintaining power and to providing the disciplined manpower essential for administering the state and for running the socialist economy. Even today the CPSU is still considered as a vanguard organization with the duty of leading the masses towards a communist society. It is deliberately kept as a minority organization, as an association of 'the best elements of Soviet society', and admission to it is difficult, protracted and selective.[8] Party members (including candidate members) represented only 3·9% of the population in January 1959 (although they represented 10·5% of the population over twenty years of age) and 4·4% of the population in October 1961. At the time of the 24th Congress 6·0% of the entire Soviet population belonged to the Communist Party. The percentage of party members was highest in Georgia, Russia, the Ukraine and Kazakhstan. It was generally higher in urban than in rural areas. In Moscow roughly one out of every eight persons was a Party member.

(c) The Party is the *highest form of class organization of the proletariat*. The Party is considered to be higher than trade unions, co-operatives, Soviets and cultural organizations. The Party has the responsibility of determining the general or mass line of the revolution—i.e. its general direction, rate of development and strategy. Party members working in trade unions, co-operatives, Soviets, schools, hospitals, factories, farms, offices, etc., should 'persuade these non-Party organizations to draw nearer to the Party of the proletariat and to accept voluntarily its political guidance'.[9] This idea secured formal legal recognition in Article 126 of the 1936 Constitution where it is stated that:

... the most active and politically conscious citizens in the ranks of the working class and other sections of the working people unite in the Communist Party of the Soviet Union, which is the vanguard of the working people in their struggle to strengthen and develop the socialist system and is the leading core of all organizations of the working people, both public and state.

(d) The Party is *the essential instrument of the dictatorship of the proletariat*. It is not an instrument which can be dispensed with under any circumstances. Without it the working class could neither win nor maintain political power. Here Stalin was merely repeating what Lenin had said on many occasions. Thus writing in May 1920 in *Left Wing Communism* Lenin had conceded that:

Certainly almost everyone now realises that the Bolsheviks could not have maintained themselves in power for two and a half months, let alone for two and a half years, unless the strictest truly iron discipline had prevailed in our Party, and unless the latter had been rendered the fullest and unreserved support of the whole mass of the working class, that is, of all its thinking, honest, self-sacrificing and influential elements who are capable of leading or carrying with them the backward strata.[10]

In the same work Lenin stated that:

The dictatorship of the proletariat is a persistent struggle—bloody and bloodless, violent and peaceful, military and economic, educational and administrative—against the forces and traditions of the old society. The force of habit of millions and tens of millions is a most terrible force. Without an iron party tempered in the struggle, without a party enjoying the confidence of all that is honest in the given class, without a party capable of watching and influencing the mood of the masses, it is impossible to conduct such a struggle successfully.[11]

Again, on January 21, 1921, Lenin had forthrightly declared that, 'Were the Party to be set aside there would in fact be no dictatorship of the proletariat in Russia.'[12]

THE PARTY AND THE WORKING CLASS

Does this mean that the Communists recognize that the Party exercises a dictatorship over the Russian workers? This has occasionally been conceded. For example, a resolution of the 12th Party Congress, April 1923, stated that 'The dictatorship of the working class can only be assured in the form of the dictatorship of its vanguard, the Communist Party.' However, more often this has been denied. The term 'dictatorship' in Marxist theory is not commonly applied either to an individual tyrant or to a one-party state, but to all states. Any state is an instrument of class rule—a capitalist state is an instrument of the bourgeoisie and is therefore a bourgeois dictatorship; a socialist state is an instrument of the proletariat and is therefore a proletarian dictatorship. The Communist Party is a weapon of the proletariat, the essential agency by which it achieves and maintains its dictatorship, but it is the class as a whole that wields the dictatorship. Both Lenin and Stalin referred to such organizations as trade unions, the Young Communist League, co-operatives and Soviets, as 'levers' or 'transmission belts' in the dictatorship of the proletariat, because they connected the Party to the masses. The Party on the other hand was 'the main driving force'. Thus Stalin, in *On the Problems of Leninism* (January 1926), stated that:

The highest expression of the leading role of the Party, here, in the Soviet Union, in the land of the dictatorship of the proletariat, for example, is the fact that not a single important political or organizational question is decided by our Soviet and other mass organizations without guiding directions from the Party. *In this sense* it could be said that the dictatorship of the proletariat is *in essence* the 'dictatorship' of its vanguard, the 'dictatorship' of its Party, as the main guiding force of the proletariat.[13]

Relations between the Party and the masses were further defined as ones of 'mutual confidence', which meant, according to Stalin:

Firstly, that the Party must closely heed the voice of the masses; that it must pay close attention to the revolutionary instinct of the masses, that it must study the practice of the struggle of the masses and on this basis test the correctness of its own policy; that, consequently, it must not only teach the masses, but must learn from them.

It means, secondly, that the Party must day after day win the confidence of the proletarian masses; that it must by its policy and work ensure the support of the masses; that it must not command but primarily convince the masses, help them to realize by their own experience the correctness of the policy of the Party; that, consequently, it must be the guide, the leader and the teacher of its class.[14]

What this amounts to is an assertion that the Party does not use force against the working class. Of course this assertion is untrue. The Party and the government have used coercion against the working class on many occasions. Thus there was considerable working-class hostility to the replacement of the early workers' control of industry by one-man industrial management in 1918. There was almost as much opposition to the subordination of the trade unions to the requirements of state economic planning in 1928. Nor were the workers consulted when harsh labour regulations were adopted in 1929 and later years or when real income was reduced—as it was for the majority of industrial workers in 1929–34 and in the war and immediate post-war years. State police have also on occasions used military force to suppress striking workers. Socialist writers—Trotsky and Djilas for example—as well as non-socialist critics readily accept the proposition that a Party dictatorship has operated over the entire Soviet population, workers included. However, such a view ignores the fact that the industrial working class in the Soviet Union has always been handled more considerately than other sections of the

Soviet population. Thus until the late 1930s and since 1957 workers have received preferential treatment in the admission to tertiary educational institutes. Likewise workers have often enjoyed better housing, health and recreation facilities and social insurance than the rest of the population, particularly the peasants.*Again, while working-class consent has not been sought for many state policies affecting the working class the regime has generally sought and secured considerable working-class support and enthusiastic co-operation for the fulfilment of its more ambitious economic and social plans. Finally, specifically working-class organizations such as trade unions have not been suppressed but have been vastly extended. This might be contrasted with the fate of the equivalent Peasant Unions under collectivization—they have not been restored even to this day.[15] It is true of course that Soviet trade unions have experienced considerable modifications of their functions. This is as much a natural conse-quence of the socialist revolution as it is of deliberate debasing of these functions by the government. Trade unions must of necessity function differently under socialism than they do under capitalism. Thus while Soviet trade unions retained most of the characteristics of capitalist trade unions until 1928, including participation in wage struggles and strikes, they have not been permitted to operate in this way since the adoption of full-scale economic planning.† While cer-tain functions have been lost since 1928 other functions have been added and extended. Soviet trade unions are not now wholly or even primarily concerned with protecting the interests of their mem-bers but with assisting the Communist Party to rally the workers for the achievement of the targets of the economic plan.

SOVIET TRADE UNIONS

More specifically, Soviet trade unions are concerned with the follow-ing things:

(a) *Safety in industry*. This function has at times been neglected but for many years has been taken seriously and to good effect. Collec-tive agreements (abolished in 1933 but revived in 1947) contain de-tails on maintenance and improvement of working conditions over the given period. Special allocation of funds are made to each factory and industrial unit for this purpose. In addition to a limited number of paid trade-union officials concerned with safety inspection work

* Collective farmers were not included in state social security arrangements until July 1964.
† The reorganization of Soviet economic planning in late 1965 reintroduced the possibility of limited influence on wages by local trade unions.

hundreds of thousands of rank-and-file workers are drawn into the Labour Protection Commissions which operate in the factories, mines and workshops. The activities of such commissions are supervised by the trade-union committees and by the republican, regional and territorial Trade Union Councils.

(b) *Workers' health.* Many Soviet health services including specialized clinics, hospitals and sanatoria are operated by the trade unions. These give service, basically free of charge, to Soviet workers and in some cases to their families.

(c) *Social welfare.* Many state social insurance benefits are handled by Soviet trade unions. These include temporary disability benefits, pregnancy and post-confinement benefits, disability pensions, widow's pensions, burial expenses, and old age pensions for those continuing in employment. The basic agency here is the Social Insurance Commission which exists in all factories, workshops and offices.

(d) *Housing.* While Soviet trade unions do not as a rule directly construct homes, housing construction and allocation is covered by the collective agreements between managements and unions. Until 1958 it was often possible for factory managers to divert housing funds to other purposes, usually to augment the wages fund or to allow the overfulfilment of the industrial production plan. Present safeguards, as well as the official emphasis on increased housing construction over recent years, has greatly reduced this practice.

(e) *Cultural and sporting activities.* Trade unions not only maintain an impressive network of sporting, literary, dramatic and other cultural clubs for members but they have invested large funds in educational facilities for workers and their children. Trade unions organize clubs, holiday camps, excursions, film shows, dramatic performances, concerts, sports competitions, and so on, for the children of their members.

(f) *Labour disputes.* Soviet trade unions have not always provided adequate machinery for the handling of labour disputes. This fact was recognized when the 1958 Trade Union statute was drafted. Under this statute labour disputes are handled by three agencies; the Labour Disputes Boards, the Trade Union Committees and the People's Courts. A dispute is normally referred immediately to the Labour Disputes Board, a body which gives equal representation to the union and the management. If the Board cannot reach a decision the dispute can be referred to the Trade Union Committee, and in some cases to the Courts. No worker can be dismissed without the approval of the Trade Union Committee. Disputes over dismissal and reinstatement are handled directly by courts of law. This mechanism is proving increasingly effective over such matters as classification, specific wage rates and re-allocation of workers to lower paid jobs.

(g) *Wage rates.* Central unions are consulted in the determination of the size of the wages fund and in its allocation as between indus-tries. Local trade-union committees cannot influence the size of the wages fund allocated to their particular factory but they have a voice in distributing it between various workers and also in allocating bonus payments and spending the money accruing to the Factory Fund through unplanned profits and overfulfilment of the plan.

(h) *Fixing output norms.* Trade unions have proved ineffective as an agency to safeguard workers against excessive norms because of the overall stress on expanding production and overfulfilment of the plan. The establishment of Permanent Production Conferences in 1958 strengthened the safeguards against such abuses since although equally concerned with improving output their emphasis has been on improving technique rather than on speed-up. Furthermore, the fact that they directly represent the workers and not the trade unions no doubt increases their effectiveness in this direction.

The above list is by no means complete. Above all, Soviet trade unions are concerned with these three functions, plan formulation and supervision, plan fulfilment and promoting technical improve-ment in industry.

(i) *Plan formulation and supervision.* Trade unions have always been consulted in the formulation of the economic plan. In earlier years this consultation was mainly effective at the level of the All-Union Central Council of Trade Unions (AUCCTU), but the decentraliza-tion of economic planning and industrial administration since 1957 greatly extended the role of republican, regional and territorial trade union organizations. No factory or workshop plan is adopted until it has been discussed and endorsed by the workers themselves. The mechanism for consultation varies according to the size of the factory or shop. Where fewer than one hundred workers are employed a general meeting of workers and management discusses the draft plan and suggests amendments. In larger plants the Permanent Produc-tion Conference, directly elected by the production workers and comprising between 12% and 15% of the total work force, is the main agency for this purpose. Most revisions of draft plans are still upwards. This is a consequence not merely of Party pressure, but also of the fact that the entire factory has a vested interest in extend-ing production since it means higher bonuses and other rewards. It must also be recognized that the agencies which have the responsi-bility for drafting the original plans generally take a cautious view of production prospects for the coming year.

(j) *Plan fulfilment.* Both Trade Union Committees and Permanent

Production Conferences are regularly concerned with the plan fulfilment. The former agency still has the main responsibility for organizing socialist competitions between work brigades within the one workshop or between different workshops. Larger competitions between factories in a particular region are organized by the regional Trade Union Council. The Permanent Production Conference is mainly concerned with suggesting rationalization of work processes and technical changes likely to promote production.

(k) *Technical improvement.* This is the responsibility not merely of the management, the government and the Party, but of the trade unions and the workers in general. Permanent Production Conferences which meet twice a quarter are particularly concerned in this work.[16] Seven million Soviet workers were members of Permanent Production Conferences in 1959. More than a million Soviet workers belong to the USSR Society of Inventors and Rationalizers which functions under the auspices of the trade unions. It is claimed that 10 million inventions and improvements were suggested over the period 1950–58 many of which were adopted. Rationalizations and inventions adopted over 1956–58 resulted in a saving of 24 million roubles.[17]

Nothing I have written above should be taken as proof that Soviet trade unions are agencies of democratic working-class control of Soviet industry. They are not. Nor is it a complete description of Soviet trade unions to say that they are coercive and bureaucratic agencies of the state. They are semi-state agencies rather than state agencies. Their officials are paid out of trade union funds and are responsible to the trade union membership. But trade union posts are reserved for Party members and higher positions are included on the *nomenklatura* of the Central Committee apparatus. The unions themselves are entrusted with performing many services—such as health and insurance—which in a capitalist society are commonly the responsibility of the state. The trade union structure is certainly bureaucratic, especially in its central organs. But it is hard to see how an organization of upwards of 98 millions could avoid being bureaucratic. However, the surprising thing about Soviet trade-union organization is not the existence of bureaucracy but the extent to which rank and file participate in performing the various activities of trade unions. Millions of Soviet workers are regularly involved in voluntary unpaid service on such agencies as Trade Union Committees, Disputes Boards, Social Insurance Committees, Labour Protection Commissions, Permanent Production Conferences, Educational, Cultural and Sporting Committees. The number of paid officials is kept to a minimum. Plants of 500–2,000 employees may maintain one paid organizer, plants of 2–3,000 workers are allowed two paid organizers.

Membership in trade unions is not compulsory but strong social pressures and material incentives bring a high percentage of union membership. At the time of the 15th Trade Union Congress in March 1972 there were 98 million members, or over 95% of those eligible for membership. One-third of the membership in 1972 was serving on various trade-union and allied committees.[18] This high percentage of membership of Soviet trade unions is facilitated by the industrial basis of Soviet unionism. Whereas trade-union organization in most capitalist countries is complicated by the fact that many workers are still organized into craft unions and consequently many unions are involved in organizing workers in the one industry and sometimes in the one plant, Soviet unions are wholly organized on an industrial basis. All persons employed in the same factory or office belong to the same union and each trade union unifies the employees of one branch or of several related branches of industry. In 1959 there were only twenty-three unions.

The right to strike has not been formally revoked in the Soviet Union but strikes have been a rarity since the early thirties. In isolated cases in the post-war years strikes have been forcibly suppressed. Usually, however, strikes involve only a brief stoppage of a few hours and are quickly settled through negotiation under the aegis of the Party. Negotiation normally succeeds because both workers and management recognize that it is in their interests to fulfil and to overfulfil the economic plan. To continue production is not merely in the general interest of Soviet workers but is in the specific interest of the workers in the individual plant since their bonus payments depend on plan fulfilment and overfulfilment.[19]

My conclusion from this analysis of the relationship between the Communist Party and the working class is that the Soviet workers have a rather special relationship to the Communist Party and that while the Party still insists on leading the workers and interpreting their desires for them, the Party is continually seeking to involve the working class in the day-to-day administration of trade unions, social services and public welfare, and also in consultation and participation in the supervision if not in the actual management of industry. It is a real partnership again, although it is as yet an unequal one.[20]

NOTES

[1] 'What is to be Done?', *Selected Works*, Vol. 2, 1944, p. 53.

[2] Merle Fainsod, 1954, pp. 212–13.

[3] 'Report of the Credentials Commission' by V. N. Titov. *Izvestia*, October 22, 1961. The claim was repeated by I. V. Kapitonov in the Report of the Credentials Commission to the 23rd Congress. *Pravda*, April 1, 1966.

[4] Figures taken from *The Communist Review* (Sydney), May 1962. Based on an article which appeared in *Kommunist*. 1971 figures, *Pravda*, March 31, 1971.

[5] Based on the Reports of the Credentials Commissions to the 20th, 22nd, 23rd and 24th Congresses. A useful analysis of recruiting trends in the CPSU is given by T. H. Rigby in 'Social Orientation of Recruitment and Distribution of Membership in the Communist Party of the Soviet Union', *American Slavic and East European Review*, Vol. XVI, 1957, pp. 275–90. *See also*, Vernon V. Aspaturian, 'The Social Composition of the Communist Party', pp. 492–502 in Macridis and Ward, 1963.

[6] J. Stalin, 1945, p. 82.

[7] All figures given above are based on full members only.

[8] Under the present rules (as adopted at the 22nd Congress and revised at the 23rd Congress) prospective members must be 'politically conscious' and 'active workers, peasants and representatives of the intelligentsia'. Persons joining the Party must be twenty years of age, unless joining through the Young Communist League when they may join at eighteen. Persons joining below the age of twenty-three are admitted exclusively through the YCL. Persons must serve one year as a candidate member before being admitted to full membership. To be admitted to full membership a candidate requires to have his membership application supported by three party members of at least 5 years standing, or with the recommendation of the district or town committee of the YCL. Members are admitted on the basis of a two-thirds majority vote of the primary organization, subject to ratification by the district or town party committee.

[9] J. Stalin, *op. cit.*, p. 87.

[10] V. I. Lenin; *Selected Works*, 1946, Vol. 10, p. 60.

[11] *Ibid.*, p. 84.

[12] Quoted in J. Towster, 1948, p. 120.

[13] *Op. cit.*, p. 140.

[14] *Ibid.*, pp. 144–5.

[15] The restoration of Peasant Unions was openly canvassed during the 1958 public debate on agricultural reorganization and received support not only from collective farmers but from Party officials right up to *obkom* secretaries. See my article on 'The Agricultural Reorganization and the Rural District Soviets', in *Soviet Studies*, X, July 1958, pp. 94–7. The 3rd USSR Congress of Collective Farmers which met in Moscow in November 1969 established a Union Council of Collective Farms but it did not restore the Peasant Unions.

[16] See the articles in *Soviet Studies* X, July 1958, pp. 101–3; and X, October 1958, pp. 176–83. For a short summary of the work of Soviet trade unions based on an investigation in the Leningrad area, see, Mary Harris; Shop-Floor Relations in Industrial Countries; 'Soviet Union, 1963', *Co-existence*, 3, No. 1, January 1966, pp. 99–104.

[17] P. Petrov, 1959, p. 10.

[18] Report by A. N. Shelepin to 15th Congress of Soviet Trade Unions, *Pravda*, March 21, 1972.

[19] Very little empirical investigation of workers' attitudes has been done in the Soviet Union. Some recent investigations by Soviet 'concrete sociologists' suggest that there are significant differences between the attitudes to work of Soviet workers on the one hand and French and American workers on the other. Thus it has been found that Soviet workers adopt a more responsible attitude to work, are more concerned with improving technology and less with improving their status and earnings than are French or American workers. Cf. G. V. Osipov, ed., 1966, pp. 99–125, 261–9.

[20] Khrushchev suggested in his report to the plenary meeting of the Central

Committee on November 19, 1962 that elective Production Committees should be established in all factories and workshops. He did not make clear the exact relationship between these new committees and the existing Permanent Production Conferences. The decisions of the Plenum (November 23, 1962) merely contained the recognition of the need for 'more active participation by the working people in management of production'. Opportunities for such participation were unquestionably extended by the economic reorganization of October 1965.

SELECTED BIBLIOGRAPHY

Brown, E. C., 1966.
Fainsod, M., 1963a, Ch. 5.
McAuley, Mary, 1969.
Macridis and Ward, 1963, pp. 492–502.
Rigby, T. H., 1969.
Stalin, J. V., 1945, pp. 80–91, 136–56.
Towster, J., 1948, Ch. 6.

Chapter 14

THE COMMUNIST PARTY OF THE SOVIET UNION

THE THEORY OF COMMUNIST PARTY ORGANIZATION

The basic organizational principle of the CPSU is that of 'democratic centralism'. Rule 19 of the current (1961) rules states it thus:

> The guiding principle of the organisational structure of the Party is democratic centralism, which signifies:
>
> (a) election of all leading Party bodies from the lowest to the highest;
> (b) periodical reports of Party bodies to their Party organisations *and to higher bodies;*
> (c) strict Party discipline and subordination of the minority to the majority;
> (d) the decisions of higher bodies are obligatory for lower bodies.[1]

Recent criticism of the degeneration of the Party and state structure during the latter years of the Stalin period caused an addendum to this basic organizational principle to be included in the 1961 Rules. This is Rule 28 which states that:

> The supreme principle of Party leadership is collective leadership, which is an absolute requisite for the normal functioning of Party organisations, the proper education of cadres, and the promotion of the activity and initiative of Communists. The cult of the individual and the violations of inner-Party democracy resulting from it must not be tolerated in the Party; they are incompatible with the Leninist principles of Party life.
>
> Collective leadership does not exempt individuals in office from personal responsibility for the job entrusted to them.

In practice this has meant a determined though not wholly successful attempt at making committee leadership function at all levels in the Party structure.

The first part of the Rules (1–13) deals with the duties and rights of Party members. The ordering of these, duties ahead of rights, is significant. As for rights, a Party member has the right:

(i) to elect and be elected to Party bodies;
(ii) to discuss freely questions of Party policy and activities at Party meetings, Conferences, Congresses, etc.;

(iii) to criticise any Communist, irrespective of the position he holds, at Party meetings, Conferences, Congresses, at meetings of Party committees and in the Party press; to table motions; openly to express and uphold opinions as long as the Party organization concerned has not adopted a decision;

(iv) to attend in person all Party meetings and all Bureau and Committee meetings that discuss his activities or conduct;

(v) to address any question, statement or proposal, to any Party body, up to and including the Central Committee of the CPSU and to demand an answer on the substance of his address. (Rule 3).

Another 'right' listed in earlier rules, *criticism and self-criticism*, has since 1952 been listed as a 'duty'. Thus the present Rule 2(g) states that it is the duty of a Party member:

to develop criticism and self-criticism, boldly lay bare shortcomings and strive for their removal; to combat ostentation, conceit, complacency, and parochial tendencies; to rebuff firmly all attempts at suppressing criticism; to resist all actions injurious to the Party and the state, and to give information on them to Party bodies, up to and including the Central Committee of the CPSU.

Rules 10 and 11 safeguard individual Party members against unjust expulsion from the Party. These rules establish that:

(i) Members may be expelled on the basis of a two-thirds majority vote of the Party primary to which they belong.

(ii) Such a decision requires endorsement by the district or city Party committee.

(iii) An expelled member retains the right of appeal up to and including the Central Committee of the CPSU.

(iv) Members of all Party committees from the *raikom* to the Central Committee can only be expelled by a two-thirds majority vote of that committee. In the case of members of the Central Committee and the Central Control Commission the decision is made by the Party Congress and, in the intervals between two Congresses, by a full meeting of the Central Committee by a majority of two-thirds of its members.

INNER-PARTY DEMOCRACY

The theory of Communist Party organization takes as its central principle democratic centralism rather than democracy. The difference between democratic centralism and democracy in general can best be illustrated by reference to the position of minorities. Whereas most democratic political parties are content with formal observance of majority decisions, or of decisions of higher bodies, the Communist

Party insists on active conformity. This follows from the concept of Party unity, by which the Communist Party is held to be a party with one policy and one voice—i.e. *a monolithic party*. Thus the Rules oblige a Party member 'to put Party decisions steadfastly into effect' and also, 'to strengthen to the utmost the ideological and organisational unity of the Party'. This obligation extends to individuals who have opposed a decision. Again, lower bodies and rank and file must accept policy decisions of leading committees—this is so even if a majority of a Party Primary is opposed to this decision. This clearly conforms to the principle of democratic centralism, and it could not be otherwise or else there would be several centres and not one.

However, some modification of this rigid adherence to majority decision has been permitted in lower organs since 1956. Since then persons holding minority views on lower Party committees are not bound by committee decisions in a discussion on such decisions in a members' meeting but are permitted to express minority views and even to put motions in opposition to those of the committee.[2]

Does freedom of discussion operate within the CPSU? Formally the answer is yes, provided that the discussion does not go beyond certain limits. There is no toleration of non-Marxist or anti-Marxist views. Discussion must be conducted within proper Party bodies and through the Party press. The Party line must be determined in an organized way—not through the bringing together of resolutions from the primaries but by Congress, after the consideration of reports from the Central Committee. The role of lower organs and Party members as individuals is to apply this Party line to their own locality or workplace—for example, to a factory, mine, a farm, a school, a hospital or an office. Once the Party line has been formulated it is not open to unlimited debate. Only under special circumstances can widespread discussion occur. These circumstances are fully set out in Rule 26 which reads as follows;

The free and business-like discussion of questions of Party policy in individual Party organizations or in the Party as a whole is the inalienable right of every Party member and an important principle of inner-Party democracy. Only on the basis of inner-Party democracy is it possible to develop criticism and self-criticism and to strengthen Party discipline, which must be conscious and not mechanical.

Discussion of controversial or insufficiently clear issues may be held within the framework of individual organizations or the Party as a whole.

Party-wide discussion is necessary:

(*a*) if the necessity is recognized by several Party organizations at regional or republican level;
(*b*) if there is not a sufficiently solid majority in the Central Committee on major questions of Party policy;

(c) if the Central Committee of the CPSU considers it necessary to consult the Party as a whole on any particular question of policy.

Wide discussion, especially discussion on a country-wide scale, of questions of Party policy must be so held as to ensure for Party members the free expression of their views and preclude attempts to form factional groupings destroying Party unity and attempts to split the Party.

The Reorganized Party Structure 1962–64*

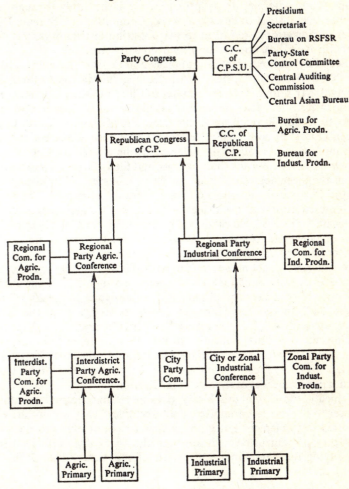

* A consolidated Party structure was re-established in November 1964. The Central Asian Bureau was abolished at the end of 1964, the Russian Bureau in April 1966.

In practice, since 1953 only the third alternative way of provoking a Party-wide discussion has operated. Normally Party policy will not be reviewed until the plenum of the Central Committee meets, perhaps not until the next Congress.

Some aspects of Communist Party organization as such restrict the operation of the fullest inner-Party democracy.

Firstly, the organizational structure is entirely a vertical or hierarchical one. There are no horizontal links between Party organizations. Thus adjoining Party primaries are linked only through the higher level district or city Conference, Committee and Bureau. District organizations are linked to neighbouring district organizations only through the territorial or provincial party structure.

Secondly, indirect elections, abolished in the state structure under the 1936 Constitution, have continued the rule in the Communist Party. Party primaries elect delegates to City or District Conferences; these in turn elect delegates to Provincial (Regional) Conferences and also to Union-Republican Congresses. Provincial-Territorial Conferences elect by secret ballot delegates to the Party Congress. In four republics the rules allow for delegates to be elected by Republican Congresses. This means that the rank and file is three steps removed from the delegates who attend the Party Congress. Representation at the Congress is determined by the Central Committee. The basis of representation was one delegate for every 2,000 members and one delegate for every 2,000 candidate members for the 22nd Congress. It was one delegate for every 2,900 members for the 24th Congress.

One effect of this system of indirect election of delegates is that the paid officials (functionaries) tend to be disproportionately represented in the Congress. Functionaries represent less than 3% of the Party membership but they comprised 36·6% of delegates to the 20th Congress, 34% to the 21st Congress, 25·9% of delegates to the 22nd Congress and 24·4% of delegates to the 23rd Congress.[3] This happens mainly because Party officials are usually considered more experienced and therefore more suitable for election to the Party Congress, and, being Party functionaries, they are likely to be better known than ordinary members at each stage in the election.

Thirdly, the Communist Party gives more than normal executive power to its leading committees and executives. They are not merely entitled to implement Party policy which has already been decided but they are entrusted with applying the Party line. This includes modifying the Party line on the basis of experience. Thus Rule 34 states that:

Between Congresses the Central Committee of the Communist Party of the Soviet Union *directs the activities of the Party*, the local Party bodies, *selects and appoints leading officials, directs the work of central government bodies* and public organizations of the working people through the Party groups in them, sets up various Party organs, institutions and enterprises and directs their activities, *appoints the editors of the central newspapers and journals* operating under its control, and distributes the funds of the Party budget and controls its execution.

The Central Committee represents the CPSU in its relations with other parties. (My italics—L.G.C.)

This means that Party committees and executives are accountable to rather than responsible to the Congress, Conference or members' meeting which elects them. The present Rules require that the Party Congress shall meet once in five years, and the rules which operated between 1939 and 1952 required a Congress once in three years. In fact Congress met only six times over the 31 years 1935–66; in 1939, 1952, 1956, 1959 (an Extraordinary Congress), 1961 and 1966. In any case Congress has been for many decades a large and unwieldy body. The 20th Congress had 1,355 full delegates, the 22nd Congress 4,394 full delegates and 405 delegates with a consultative vote. The 24th Congress had 4,740 full delegates and 223 delegates with a consultative vote, the former representing the full members, the latter the candidate members of the Party.

Fourthly, the Communist Party, while it insists that all members must be politically active, is really organized on the basis of two sorts of members, the paid Party officials or functionaries (the *apparatchiki*) who are the minority, and the majority of the members who serve the Party in a voluntary capacity. The Party functionaries today probably comprise no more than 2–3% of the total membership yet they dominate all Party committees from the District Committee upwards. This arrangement has certain advantages but it does involve some clash with democratic principles. Thus there is a direct clash between the principle of central control and appointment of leading functionaries and the democratic principle of the election of all Party Committees by the membership or by democratically elected Conferences or Congresses.

THE RECORD OF THE CPSU

The history of the CPSU shows many departures from democracy, even within the limits of the Communist definition of the term. Thus the first two elements of democratic centralism—election of all leading bodies and regular accounting back of leading bodies to their Party organizations—have often been ignored. Selection rather than election is widely practised at all levels from the Primary (Branch) secretary upwards. List or bloc voting is still practised, although the rules were deliberately changed as long ago as 1937 to exclude this practice. The practice is openly acclaimed in all but name. Thus the

Party journal, *Partiinaya zhizn* (Party Life) stated in October 1958 that:

Some comrades think that elections can be democratic only when the ballot contains more candidates than it is necessary to elect. But this is a profound misconception. Genuine democracy consists of giving Communists the chance of expressing their will, carefully to discuss the proposing of candidates and to choose for leading organs the most deserving and capable people to carry on their work on the basis of the contemporary demands of the Party. Therefore it isn't a bad thing but a good thing when as the result of broad and open discussion of candidates by the participants in a meeting or a conference they arrive at a unanimous opinion as to whom to trust the subsequent leadership of the organization to and whom to include on the list for the secret ballot. Such unanimity is a sign not of weakness but of strength of Communists, and of their cohesion, organization, and political understanding, and of their ability to place the interests of duty above all else.[4]

This attempt at editorial persuasion followed the general restoration of the official slate of pre-selected candidates for Party primary elections held during 1957–58. This reversion to earlier methods was extended in 1960 when the Central Committee approved of open voting for the election of group secretaries (within larger primaries) unless the members insisted on holding a secret ballot.[5]

Regular meetings of committees, although provided for in the rules, have not always been held. Over the period 1939–52 the Central Committee of the CPSU met at most four times although it was required to meet twice a year. *Raikoms* are obliged to meet monthly but there are cases reported even since 1953 of *raikoms* not meeting over periods of one year and more.

Criticism and self-criticism has often been denied. Complaints against the non-recognition of this principle by Party officials were made at the 18th Congress by Zhdanov, at the 19th Congress by Khrushchev and, in a milder form, by Kozlov at the 22nd Congress. In his report to the 19th Congress (1952) Khrushchev stated that:

Suppressors of criticism resort to the most diverse forms and methods of victimizing critics. We meet with cases of good and honest workers being dismissed only because they spoke up against shortcomings, cases of intolerable conditions being created for people who criticize executives. There are even instances where leading workers use intimidation against comrades who come forward with sound critical observations and compel them to recant and give an undertaking to refrain from criticizing shortcomings in future. . . .

It should be said in this connection that the pernicious opinion is prevalent among some Communists that Party members ought not to inform leading Party bodies on the plea that this interferes with their work. There are still among our leading executives bigwigs and bureaucrats who consider that rank and filers have no right to inform higher bodies of shortcomings in work, and must not do so. Some executives even go to the length of persecuting people who report shortcomings in work to leading Party bodies and to the Central Committee. The Party must naturally wage a merciless war on such high-handed potentates.[6]

Such criticisms led the 19th Party Congress to reformulate sections of the Party Rules and to make 'criticism and self-criticism' and appeals to higher Party bodies duties of Party members.

The provisions relating to expulsion of Party members have often been operated undemocratically. The main excesses were of course during the days when the mass purge operated, i.e. 1921–39. However, these struggles, at least up to 1934, were in the main principled, i.e. they were based on a struggle to develop a correct policy and to keep the Party united around it. They were also, at least in the twenties, fought out fairly openly. Thus Trotsky was only expelled from the Party in December 1927 after almost four years of deviation and factionalism.

The dangers of the mass purge were pointed out by Zhdanov, wise after the event, in his report to the 18th Congress in 1939:

The objectionable feature of the mass purges is that, bearing as they do the character of a campaign, they are attended by many mistakes, primarily by the infringement of the Leninist principle of an individual approach to people.

By establishing a definite standard and measuring everybody by one criterion, the method of the mass purge encourages a formal approach and does not permit the full observance of the Party principle that Party members, people, must be treated with careful attention, and in practice it often leads to the infringement of the rights of Party members.

The result of this was that during mass purges there were many cases of unwarranted expulsion from the Party, and of hostile elements who wormed their way into the Party, taking advantage of the purge to persecute and ruin honest people.[7]

What Zhdanov did not give sufficient emphasis to in 1939 (unlike Khrushchev in 1956) was the fact that the purge, through the involvement of the state police, ceased to be a purely internal Party matter. The worst abuses of the mass purge were the consequences of this fact. Nor did Zhdanov acknowledge that the responsibility for the purge rested on Stalin and the Politbureau rather than on local Party organs. Even Khrushchev did not fully concede this, because to date the responsibility for the mass purge has been extended beyond Stalin and Beria but only to the leaders of the so-called anti-Party group of 1956–57, i.e. to Molotov, Malenkov, Kaganovich, Bulganin and Voroshilov, but not to Khrushchev, Mikoyan and their supporters.

The mass purge was abolished in 1939 when the present rules on expulsion were adopted. Yet the purge was used extensively over the years 1939–53, and on a restricted scale against the Beria supporters in late 1953 and the supporters and alleged supporters of the anti-Party group in 1957–59.

A RETURN TO INNER-PARTY DEMOCRACY?

Such a cataloguing of non-democratic features requires some balancing by the considerable restoration of inner-Party democracy since 1953. The first democratic reform has been the considerable restoration of the principle of collective leadership and accountability at all levels. There is no doubt that there is more formal observance of these provisions now than there was a decade ago. Thus the Central Committee of the CPSU met infrequently between 1939 and 1952 but it has more than fulfilled its obligation to meet twice yearly since early 1953. Taking the record for the last few years only we find the following:

1957—5 plenums of the Central Committee
1958—6 plenums   1966—5 plenums
1959—2 plenums   1967—2 plenums
1960—2 plenums   1968—4 plenums
1961—4 plenums   1969—2 plenums
1962—3 plenums   1970—2 plenums
1963—2 plenums   1971—2 plenums
1964—3 plenums*   1972—2 plenums
1965—3 plenums

For a few years (from December 1958 to late 1964) full reports of the meetings of the Central Committee were published. These reports contained valuable information not only about the matters discussed but about how decisions are arrived at and about limits to formal collective leadership. They revealed the decisive role of Khrushchev while First Secretary. A single extract from the January 1961 plenum will suffice to illustrate this point. The morning session on January 13 opened as follows:

L. I. Brezhnev (Chairman). Comrades, we continue the work of the plenum. Cde. Zarobyan has the floor.

Report of the First Secretary of the C.C. of the C.P. of Armenia cde. Ya. N. Zarobyan.

Khrushchev It seems that you have a stench of sheep about you just as in Georgia and Kazakhstan.

* Counting the October 1964 meeting as a plenum.

Zarobyan There's no time to go into that question.
Khrushchev Do you like shashlyk?
Zarobyan Its too early to think about that. You don't eat shashlyk so early in the day.
Khrushchev Shashlyk isn't eaten at that time of the day but if he kills off all the rams when the time comes for eating shashlyk he won't have it in stock.
Zarobyan I'll say something on that.
Khrushchev Very well, we'll listen to your fresh young voice.[8]

Zarobyan was only interrupted once more by Khrushchev. After he had referred to the high milk and the wool yields gained by some individual workers, this interjection occurred:

Khrushchev Cde. Zarobyan, have these persons received supplementary remuneration or have they not?
Zarobyan They certainly have. .
Khrushchev Well, nobody said anything about supplementary remuneration. You don't move towards Communism on the basis of moral factors alone. Moral factors are good but one must give them a materialistic basis. The combination of these factors gives good foundation for the movement forward.
Zarobyan Quite right, Nikita Sergeyevich.[9]

There was scarcely a report which Khrushchev did not interrupt. Although there were occasional interjections from others the right to interrupt anyone on any occasion was clearly a prerogative of the First Secretary.

However, this same January 1961 plenum served to illustrate other characteristics about the Khrushchev Central Committee. The plenum was attended by many thousands, not only by members and candidate members of the Central Committee, but by representatives from district party and state organizations, by academics and agricultural scientists (including non-Party persons), as well as by leading farmers and farm managers. The number participating in the open discussion was limited. Only 43 persons, exclusive of rapporteurs, spoke, but they represented mainly the intermediate administrative level and those directly involved in agricultural production. Thus 20 out of these 43 participants came from the province-territory level; 19 out of 43 came directly from farms (including chairmen, directors and leading workers), and 2 were academics. Although the post-Khrushchev leadership criticized the inflated size of the Central Committee meetings under Khrushchev it made only minor changes to the Khrushchevian pattern. Thus the September 1965 plenum was attended not only by full and candidate members of the Central Committee but by first secretaries of oblast party committees, chairmen of Councils of Ministers of Union Republics, second secretaries of

Central Committees of the Party in the Union Republics, Chairmen and Ministers of State Committees of the USSR, responsible workers in the apparatus of the Central Committee of the CPSU and the USSR Council of Ministers, and chief editors of central newspapers. There were twenty-six speakers on the main report which was delivered by A. N. Kosygin. Seventeen of these speakers came from the USSR-Union Republican levels of the party or state structure; only nine came from the province-territory-city level and none from the lower levels of the party organization. Thus Central Committee meetings held since October 1964 may have been less inflated by the attendance of non-members but they have been less representative of the intermediate and lower levels of the Party structure and they have been less fully reported than they were over the years 1959–64.

The accountability of committees to membership and organizations has definitely improved at all levels of the party structure since 1953. Although some breaches to this principle still occur and are duly lamented in the party press, these would seem to be only in a minority of cases. The 22nd Congress sought to strengthen this accountability by insisting on the regular replacement of minimum percentages of Party Committees at each election. A new Rule (Rule 25) provided for:

The principle of systematic removal of Party bodies and continuity of leadership shall be observed in the election of those bodies.

At each regular election, not less than one-quarter of the composition of the Central Committee of the CPSU and its Presidium shall be renewed. Members of the Presidium shall not, as a rule, be elected for more than three successive terms. Particular Party officials may, by virtue of their generally recognized prestige and high political, organizational and other qualities, be successively elected to leading bodies for a longer period. In that case a candidate is considered elected if not less than three-quarters of the votes are cast for him by secret ballot.

The composition of the Central Committee of the Communist Parties of the Union Republics shall be renewed by not less than one-third at each regular election; the composition of the area, city and district Party committees, and of the committees or bureaus of basic Party organizations, by one-half. Furthermore, members of these leading Party bodies may be elected successively for not more than three terms, and the secretaries of basic Party organizations, for not more than two terms.

A Party meeting, conference or congress, in consideration of the political and professional qualities of an individual, may elect him to a leading body for a longer period. In such cases a candidate is considered elected if not less than three-quarters of the communists attending vote for him.

Party members not re-elected to a leading Party body due to the expiration of their term may be re-elected at subsequent elections.

This rule was clearly intended to preserve the dominant leaders of the moment but it was also concerned with preventing particular individuals or cliques from dominating Party organs of lower and intermediate levels. Rule 25 was clearly regarded by the *apparatchiki* as a threat to their right to indeterminate tenure of office. It was consequently deleted at the 23rd Congress in April 1966 and replaced by a statement of the general principle of 'the systematic renewal and replacement of the leadership' of all party organs from primary organizations right up to the Central Committee of the CPSU.*

Secondly, there has been a revival of criticism within the Party, although it is difficult to measure this in any exact way. It is probably true to say that inner-party critcism has been less sharp than it was in 1956 and early 1957. Khrushchev's reports to the 22nd Congress went further in their criticism of Stalin than did his official report to the 20th Congress. They were however moderate statements when compared with his secret speech to the 20th Congress.[10] There was no speech from an 'ordinary' delegate so scathing and merciless in its criticism as that of the writer Sholokhov to the 20th Congress.[11] Sholokhov, although by then enjoying the reputation of a spokesman for the literary establishment, nevertheless provided the most original contribution to the 22nd Congress debate. In this speech, after some obviously insincere praise of the qualities of the USSR Minister of Culture and then member of the Party Presidium, cde. Furtseva, Sholokhov declared that:

I am not a Minister and have no aptitude for diplomacy, and therefore I want, without any ceremony, without passing it over in silence, to reply to Ekaterina Alekseevna. Well it is good for you to say that out of 1,114 Soviet plays appearing in the theatres throughout the country, 780 deal with contemporary themes. You said that it was more than 70 per cent. But then I would like to ask, what percentage of this 70 per cent will stay on the stage? Leaving aside the percentage and dealing in absolute figures, God grant that out of 780 plays two or three dozen will last. (Applause.) And a second question; How many of these two or three dozen plays will the audience remember? I am not using any high-faluting phrases such as 'leave an indelible impression' but simply—how many will be remembered and will make the audience think? Even fewer! So the poor spectators have to pay for the artistic impotence of the play-wrights. That's the whole trouble.
Figures and percentages are sticky things, cde. Furtseva, and people come a cropper over them. (Applause.) Better for those figures to reside somewhere in the Central Statistical Administration, they'll be cosier there but they don't fit in art. (Laughter and applause.)[12]

His speech at the 23rd Congress contained only a single sally on the same matter. For the most part it was a careful defence of the official

---

* This was added to the end of Rule 24.

artistic credo although without any explicit use of the concept of 'socialist realism'.

The Party Congress is of course too large and rare a gathering for it to be an important forum for policy formulation or clarification. Besides the reports and replies (which involved 6 speeches given by 4 persons at the 22nd Congress) and the speeches by foreign delegates, there were only 85 contributors (86 speeches) to the 22nd Congress. This represented less than 2% of the delegates. Moreover, only 18 out of the 85 were 'ordinary members', the others were senior *apparatchiki* or holders of important state positions. It is doubtful if the holding of meetings of delegates on a republican and city basis outside of the general Congress sessions really provided an effective alternative to the limited debate in the general sessions. In many cases the numbers involved would also have been too great. The 23rd Congress conformed to the established pattern. There were two major reports (delivered by Brezhnev and Kosygin) and two minor, organizational reports (delivered by Muravieva and Kapitonov). Sixty-four (out of 4,620 delegates with a full voice) participated in the discussion on the two major reports; 47 on the Brezhnev report, the general report of the Central Committee, and 17 on the Kosygin report on the directives for the new Five-Year Economic Plan. Twelve of the speakers represented the inner organs of the Central Committee of the CPSU or the USSR government; 19 speakers came from the Central Committees or the Councils of Ministers of Union Republics; 21 represented the province-city level, but only 2 came from the district level of organization. There were 5 speakers from the branch (primary) level and 5 scientists and writers.

Self-criticism by the leadership has certainly improved since 1953. Thus Khrushchev's report on Soviet agriculture delivered to the Central Committee in September 1953 was the first major critical analysis of this subject coming from the Party leadership in over twenty years. The same might be said of the Bulganin report on Soviet technology in July 1955, and of many subsequent reports on various aspects of Soviet agriculture, industry, housing, education and public administration.

Finally, the factional struggles of recent years have been handled somewhat more democratically, at least in terms of formal observance of the Party Rules, than those of earlier years. Since the removal of Beria and his supporters deposed factional leaders have been subjected to demotion and in rare cases to expulsion from the Party but they have not been accused of treachery or treated as traitors. It is claimed that 309 persons (from the Central Auditing Commission as well as the Central Committee) attended the June 1957 plenum at which the inner-Party struggle of 1956–57 was resolved and that 60 persons spoke or submitted written statements.[13] Only four individuals were removed from the Central Committee by the June 1957 plenum—Molotov, Malenkov, Kaganovich and Shepilov. The decision of the plenum was virtually unanimous; only Molotov abstained and even he declared that the decision was correctly taken and that he would abide by it.[14] All four were given important state posts after their removal from the Central Committee. Others who were removed from or demoted in the Presidium in July 1957 or subsequently—Saburov, Pervukhin, Bulganin and Voroshilov—retained their membership of the Central Committee until 1961. Despite demands at the 22nd Congress for the expulsion of Molotov, Malenkov and Kaganovich from the Party this was not done until 1962. And this despite the fact that Molotov at least had continued his opposition to Party policy right up to the eve of the Congress. He is reported never to have referred to the decision of the June 1957 plenum in any subsequent public utterance and to have made a direct attack on the Draft Programme in the form of a circular letter sent to all members of the retiring Central Committee.[15]

However, this settling with the anti-Party group was done at the level of the Central Committee. As far as is known no statements of the 'opposition' were supplied to Party members during the inner-Party ratification of this decision in July 1957. Nor were oppositionists permitted to put their own views to Party meetings during this discussion. Nor was Molotov's circular letter made public, although it was subjected to detailed criticism at the 22nd Congress by Satyukov,* Chief Editor of *Pravda*.[16]

Much less is known about the precise manner of Khrushchev's dismissal in October 1964. The official statement (printed in *Pravda* October 16) merely recorded that the plenum of the Central Committee had accepted his request to be allowed to resign because of continued ill-health. Since the decision was not (as is usually the case) reported as being unanimous we may take it that it wasn't. In view of Khrushchev's proven ability to manipulate the Central Committee it seems unlikely that there was a full meeting of that body. It seems more likely that the meeting which dismissed him was an enlarged Presidium from which many of his supporters had been excluded.

Although there was a good deal of veiled criticism of Khrushchev and of his policies at the 23rd Congress he was not mentioned by name. Although still a member of the Party and of the Central Committee he was not a delegate to the Congress and consequently could not speak out in defence of his policies and his achievements. He was not re-elected to the Central Committee. However, there was no thorough reconstitution of the Party leadership at the 23rd Congress.

* Satyukov was dismissed from his position following the fall of Khrushchev.

Membership of the Leading Organs of the Central Committee of the CPSU
1964–1971

Presidium (Feb. 1964)	Politbureau (April 1966)	Politbureau (April 1971)
Full Members	**Full Members**	**Full Members**
Brezhnev, L. I.	Brezhnev, L. I.	Brezhnev, L. I.
Voronov, G. I.	Voronov, G. I.	Voronov, G. I.
Kirilenko, A. P.	Kirilenko, A. P.	Grishin, V. V.
Kozlov, F. R.	Kosygin, A. N.	Kirilenko, A. P.
Kosygin, A. N.	Mazurov, K. T.	Kosygin, A. N.
Kuusinen, O. V.	Pelshe, A. Ya.	Kulakov, F. D.
Mikoyan, A. I.	Podgorny, N. V.	Kunaev, D. A.
Podgorny, N. V.	Polyansky, D. S.	Mazurov, K. T.
Polyansky, D. S.	Suslov, M. A.	Pelshe, A. Ya.
Suslov, M. A.	Shelepin, A. N.	Podgorny, N. V.
Khrushchev, N. S.	Shelest, P. F.	Polyansky, D. S.
Shvernik, N. M.		Suslov, M. A.
		Shelepin, A. N.
		Shelest, P. E.
		Shcherbitsky, V. V.
Candidate Members	**Candidate Members**	**Candidate Members**
Grishin, V. V.	Grishin, V. V.	Andropov, Yu. V.
Rashidov, Sh. R.	Demichev, P. N.	Demichev, P. N.
Mazurov, K. T.	Kunaev, D. A.	Masherov, P. M.
Mzhavanadze, V. P.	Masherov, P. M.	Mzhavanadze, V. P.
Efremov, L. N.	Mzhavanadze, V. P.	Rashidov, Sh. R.,
Shelest, P. E.	Rashidov, Sh. R.	Ustinov, D. F.
	Ustinov, D. F.	
	Shcherbitsky, V. V.	

Secretariat		
(Feb. 1964)	(April 1966)	(April 1971)
Khrushchev, N. S.	Brezhnev, L. I.	Brezhnev, L. I.
(First Sec.)	(Gen. Sec.)	(Gen. Sec.)
Demichev, P. N.	Andropov, Yu. V.	Demichev, P. N.
Ilichev, L. F.	Demichev, P. N.	Kapitonov, I. V.
Kozlov, F. R.	Kapitonov, I. V.	Katushev, K. F.
Kuusinen, O. V.	Kirilenko, A. P.	Kirilenko, A. P.
Ponomarev, B. N.	Kulakov, F. D.	Kulakov, F. D.
Suslov, M. A.	Ponomarev, B. N.	Ponomarev, B. N.
Rudakov, A. P.	Rudakov, A. P.	Suslov, M. A.
Polyakov, V. I.	Suslov, M. A.	Solomentsev, M. S.
Andropov, Yu. V.	Ustinov, D. F.	Ustinov, D. F.
Titov, V. N.	Shelepin, A. N.	

N.B. In November 1971 Solomentsev was dropped from the Secretariat on his election to candidate membership of the Politbureau.

In May 1972 B. N. Ponomarev was elected to candidate membership of the Politbureau.

In April 1973 Voronov and Shelest were dropped from the Politbureau and Gromyko A. A., Grechko A. A., and Andropov elected. G. V. Romanov was elected to candidate membership.

Mikoyan's disappearance from the top circle of leaders seems to have involved no policy clash. He was presumably being honourably retired and he remained a member of the incoming Central Committee. New members to the top circle had in most cases held prominent positions during the Khrushchev era. The alteration of the titles of Presidium to Politbureau and of First Secretary to General-Secretary were made to emphasize a distinction between the new regime and the Khrushchev regime. Likewise the abolition of the Bureau of the Central Committee on the RSFSR (a Khrushchevian creation) was also a demonstration of the restoration of the earlier Leninist (and inadvertently Stalinist) organizational patterns.

In summary I would suggest that there has been a considerable improvement over recent years in the extent to which the CPSU practises its own conception of inner-party democracy. However, no attempt has been made to move towards a liberal democracy in inner-party politics.

NOTES

[1] *Rules of the Communist Party of the Soviet Union*. Adopted by the 22nd Congress of the CPSU, October 31, 1961. Soviet Booklet No. 82. London, 1961, p. 11. All subsequent translations from the rules are from this source. The italicized phrase in this rule was not in the previous rules.

[2] *Partiinaya zhizn*, No. 1, 1956, p. 65.

[3] These figures are based on information contained in the various Credential Committee Reports. They represent Party functionaries only and do not include delegates serving as officials in the YCL, trade union, or government structures.

[4] *Partiinaya zhizn* No 19, October 1958. Editorial.

[5] T. H. Rigby, 'Party Elections in the CPSU', Paper delivered to the ANZAAS Congress, Canberra, January, 1964.

[6] N. Khrushchev, *Amendments to the Rules of the CPSU(B.)* Report to the Nineteenth Party Congress. FLPH, Moscow, 1952, pp. 18, 20.

[7] A. Zhdanov, *Amendments to the Rules of the CPSU(B.)* Report to the 18th Congress of the CPSU(B.). FLPH, Moscow, 1939, p. 19.

[8] *Plenum tsentralnovo komiteta kommunisticheskoi Partii Sovetskovo Soyuza*, 10–18 Yanvarya, 1961 g. Stenografichesky otchet, Moscow, 1961, p. 233.

[9] *Ibid.*, p. 236.

[10] A reasonably authentic text of this speech to the secret session on February 25, 1956, is printed in *The Anti-Stalin Campaign and International Communism*, Columbia UP, 1956, pp. 1–89.

[11] The Russian text of this speech was printed in full in *Pravda*, February 21, 1956.

[12] *XXII Syezd Kommunisticheskoi Partii Sovetskovo Soyuza*. Stenografichesky otchet, Moscow, 1961, Vol. II, pp. 166–7. A full English translation of this speech was printed in *Soviet Literature*, No. 2, 1962, pp. 98–106.

[13] *Partiinaya zhizn*, No. 13, July 1957.

[14] A. I. Mikoyan, Speech to the 22nd Congress, *Izvestia*, October 22, 1961.

[15] See in particular the Report by Khrushchev on October 17, and speeches by E. A. Furtseva, N. G. Ignatov, L. F. Ilichev, P. A. Satyukov and O. V. Kuusinen to the 22nd Congress.

[16] *Izvestia*, October 27, 1961.

THE COMMUNIST PARTY OF THE SOVIET UNION

SELECTED BIBLIOGRAPHY

Armstrong, J. A., 1963, Chs. 3, 4.
Fainsod, M., 1963a, Chs. 7, 10.
Hazard, J. N., 4th edn., 1968. Ch. 2.
Macridis and Ward, 1963, pp. 473–91.
Reshetar, J. S., Jr., 1971, Chs. 4 and 5.
Rigby, T. H., 1969.
Schapiro, L., 1965, Ch. 3.
Willets, H. T., 1962.

Chapter 15

PARTY-STATE RELATIONS

THEORY

In theory the relationship of Party to State in the USSR is crystal clear. The Party is superior to the state because it is the directing force of the socialist revolution. State organs are regarded as one of the 'transmission belts' between the Party and the masses. As a standard Soviet textbook puts it:

> The unity and purpose of the activity of all organs of the Soviet state and especially of the activity of the leading organs of power, providing the leading and directing force of our state, is the Communist Party, which is the sole directing party in the Soviet state.[1]

However, the Communist Party is not considered as an alternative to the state organization. This was stated very clearly as early as the 8th Congress of the Party in March 1919:

> Soviets are the governing organizations of the working class and the poor peasantry, exercising the dictatorship of the proletariat until such time as the state itself shall wither away.
>
> Soviets unite in their ranks tens of millions of workers and they must strive to unite in their ranks all the working class and all the poor and middle peasants.
>
> The Communist Party is an organization which unites in its ranks only the vanguard of the proletariat and the poor peasants—that part of these classes which consciously aims at the realization in life of the Communist program.
>
> The Communist Party sets itself the task of conquering the decisive influence and the full leadership in all the organizations of the toilers; in the trade unions, co-operatives, rural communes, etc. The Communist Party strives especially for the realization of its program and for full control over contemporary state organizations such as the Soviets.
>
> In all Soviet organizations the establishment of party fractions, under strictest party discipline, is absolutely necessary. All members of the R.C.P. working in a given Soviet organization should be included in these fractions.
>
> By practical, daily, self-sacrificing work in the Soviets, by nominating for

all Soviet posts its staunchest and most devoted members, the R.C.P. must win for itself undivided political dominance in the Soviets and actual control over all their work.

In no circumstances must the functions of party collectives be confused with the functions of state organs such as the Soviets. Such confusion would produce fatal results, particularly in military affairs. The Party must carry out its decisions through the Soviet organs, *within the framework of the Soviet constitution.* The Party endeavours *to guide* the activities of the Soviets, not to supplant them.[2]

This leading and guiding role of the Communist Party has been repeated on numerous occasions since the 8th Party Congress. Scarcely a Congress has passed since then without it being re-emphasized.[3] The concept eventually found itself incorporated into Article 126 of the 1936 Constitution. Recent statements on this question, while emphasizing the present and future tasks of Communist Party leadership, tend to ignore the political-environmental changes that have occurred since 1919. Thus many Soviet texts infer that Party fractions function within Soviets much as they did in 1919.[4] This notion is cherished by the Party Rules which provide for Party fractions in all Soviets, trade unions, co-operatives and all other mass organizations having at least three Party members.[5] But clearly a Party fraction in a contemporary Soviet where all deputies are Communists or Communist supporters must function differently to one in a 1919 Soviet when Communist leadership was still challenged by remnants of other socialist parties and when Party majorities in the Soviets were less certain. Thus in present day Supreme Soviets nominations for important positions come directly from the Central Committee while those for less important positions come from the Councils of Elders[6] rather than from the Party fraction.

PRACTICE

In theory the Party leads the state organizations just as it leads various public and mass organizations. In practice no doubt exists that the Communist Party is the directing force of Soviet government but the exact relationship of Party and state organs is not the same at all levels. Nor has it been the same at all periods. Thus a factory manager is likely to be more independent of control by local Party organs than a Minister is of control by the Central Committee. However, at times, especially over the years 1939–53, the head of a central ministry had little to fear from interference by the Central Committee.

The organizational structures of Party and state are largely parallel. This can be illustrated most readily in diagrammatical form (see the accompanying Chart). At the top of the Party structure is the Party

Congress which in size and relative unimportance compares with the parallel state organ, the USSR Supreme Soviet. The Central Committee and its main organs parallel the Presidium and the Council of Ministers of the USSR Supreme Soviet. Lower down, the Supreme Soviet of a republic and its Presidium and Council of Ministers is paralleled by the Republican Party Congress and the Central Committee of the Republican Party. At the local level we have the City Soviet paralleled by the City Party Conference and the *gorispolkom* (Executive Committee of the City Soviet) by the *gorkom* (City Party Committee). Likewise the *oblispolkom* (Executive Committee of the Oblast Soviet) parallels the *obkom* (Oblast Party Committee) and the *raiispolkom* (Executive Committee of the District Soviet) parallels the *raikom* (District Party Committee). The only administrative level which does not automatically have an equivalent Party organization is the lowest level—i.e. the village and settlement Soviet level. This is because the basic organization of the Communist Party is the primary which wherever possible is established on an economic or functional basis rather than on a territorial basis as is the case with the village Soviets. There are of course some Party organs which do not exactly match state organs. Thus the Russian Bureau of the Central Committee of the CPSU* might be compared with the Council of Ministers of the Russian Republic. However, the Russian bureau is an agency of the Central Committee of the CPSU and is in no way responsible to or linked to a Congress of the republican Party. There is in fact neither a Russian Congress nor a Russian Central Committee. If the state structure were to parallel this it would require the Russian government to consist of a committee of the Council of Ministers of the USSR instead of a separate republican Council of Ministers.

The reorganization of the Party along production lines at the end of 1962 led to a similar reorganization of the Soviet structure. The new Party structure meant separate organization for agricultural and industrial members not merely at the level of the primary but right up to the regional or province level. For the Soviets it meant the enlargement of the rural districts and their re-classification into agricultural or industrial districts. Only at the regional level did the reorganizations produce a duplication of organs. Thus in those territories and provinces where separate Agricultural and Industrial obkoms were organized separate Agricultural and Industrial Oblast Soviets were also organized.

This parallelism between Party and state structures is not peculiar to the CPSU. It is to be found also in the organizations of political parties in parliamentary states. But what gives it its peculiar

* Abolished by decision of the 23rd Congress, April 1966.

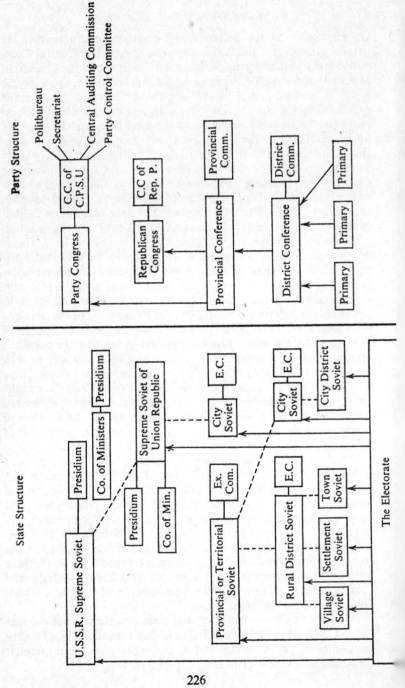

Parallel State and Party Structure, April 1971

significance in the USSR is the leadership of the political system from top to bottom by the one party. Furthermore, the CPSU maintains a Party bureaucracy which parallels the state bureaucracy. This bureaucracy consists not of the entire Party membership but of the Party functionaries, perhaps 2–3% of the total membership. Many of these serve not merely in the Party secretariats and committees but in such specialized agencies as Party Control Commissions, Propaganda Departments, Organizational-Instructional Departments, Agricultural Departments, etc. Many of these agencies parallel state agencies and if this is so we find the Party agency exercising the decisive policy-forming influence, although its actual relations with the parallel state organ will normally not be one of a separate Party organ supervising a separate state agency but one of interlocking of two agencies through overlapping membership.* Thus the parallel Cadres agencies functioning in a province or a district do not control appointments to the same positions. Each has its own list (*nomenklatura*) and although they are separate organs there will be some overlap in personnel. The same is true with other local Soviet departments which have parallels in the Party structure.

To fully appreciate the relationship of Party and state in the USSR it is necessary to consider a number of specific aspects of the Soviet state. In the following pages we will examine Party–state relations in these fields:

(*a*) Press, radio and publications;
(*b*) elections;
(*c*) Soviets;
(*d*) policy formulation;
(*e*) executive and administrative functions;
(*f*) the position of the army;
(*g*) law enforcement agencies.

PRESS, RADIO AND PUBLICATIONS

Formally Party and state agencies are separate. Thus *Izvestia* is a government newspaper, its full title being *Izvestia* of Soviets of Workers Deputies of the USSR. On the other hand *Pravda* is purely a Party newspaper, the organ of the Central Committee of the CPSU. Some newspapers are published jointly by the Party and the government. Thus while the Bureau of the Central Committee for the RSFSR existed *Sovetskaya Rossia* was published jointly by the Bureau and the RSFSR Council of Ministers.

* At the end of 1962 Party and State control agencies were united into a single Party—State Control Committee. Separate control organizations were re-established in December 1965.

Despite the formal separation between Party and government press there is no difference in policy. There are some differences in format and stress and even in reportage but not in policy. Important Party and government decisions are published in full in all newspapers. Moreover, Party control is maintained over the editorial boards of government newspapers. Thus the editorial board of *Izvestia* is included in the *nomenklatura* of the Central Party apparatus, while the editors of local newspapers are on the *nomenklatura* of the relevant Party Committees.

The Soviet radio and TV network is entirely state owned and operated. There is no separate Party radio. The news summaries which are broadcast over Radio Moscow are based on *Pravda* and *Izvestia* and other papers. But the state radio is fully at the disposal of the Party and the Party organization controls important appointments.

Separate Party and state publishing houses are operated and this means some division of labour as between Party publishing houses printing mainly Party material and government houses printing a wider range of official, semi-official and general material. State publishing houses are usually specialized. Thus *Yurizdat* concentrates on the publication of legal and constitutional books while *Politizdat* concentrates on the publication of political literature which ranges as wide as books on industrial management and economic geography. Literary publishing houses are similarly specialized. Again, key appointments to state publishing houses are under Party control.

ELECTIONS

The role of the Communist Party in Soviet elections has been discussed earlier in this book. The essence of the matter is that while other organizations may nominate candidates, the Communist Party as the sole political party, effectively controls the nominating procedure, the election campaign and the actual election. The same supervision is exercised over elections in non-state organizations such as trade unions, the *komsomol*, cultural and sporting organizations.

SOVIETS

Communist Party members are the decisive element in Soviets even if they happen to be in a minority. For many years the overwhelming majority of members of higher Soviets have been Communists. Thus almost 76% of the deputies of the USSR Supreme Soviet elected in March 1958 were Communists while 70·4% of deputies of Union Republican Supreme Soviets, 68·5% of the deputies of Supreme

Soviets of Autonomous Republics, and 45% of the deputies of local Soviets elected in March 1959 were members or candidate members of the Party.

Party rules still provide for Party fractions to operate throughout the Soviet structure, including within the Executive Committees of local Soviets. Party control of the Soviets is so complete that a local Soviet will not act on the most trivial local matter without first receiving a lead from the Party.

POLICY FORMULATION

Formally, this is done by the Supreme Soviet of the USSR and by its various organs, the Presidium and the Council of Ministers. In fact it is done mainly by the leading organs of the CPSU, although a certain amount of initiative on more technical matters undoubtedly comes directly from state bodies.

This Communist Party initiative and direction is formally acknowledged by such practices as the issue of important legislation under the joint authority of the Central Committee and of some state body and by reference to Party decisions in the legislation itself. Thus early in March 1962 the Central Committee met to hear a report from the First Secretary, N. S. Khrushchev, on the agricultural situation. The report recommended drastic changes to the administrative structure of Soviet agriculture and these were adopted in the decisions of the plenum. On March 22, 1962, a joint decision of the Central Committee of the CPSU and the USSR Council of Ministers on the reorganization of the agricultural administration was taken. This decision contained details of the reorganization of both the Party and the state structures.[7] Immediately following this decrees providing for these changes down to the district level were issued by the Presidiums of the Republican Supreme Soviets.[8] A further joint decision of the Central Committee and the USSR Council of Ministers relating to the increased use of agricultural specialists in the farms taken on April 12, 1962, was also based on the decisions of the March 1962 plenum.[9] Legislation issued in this way under the joint authority of the Central Committee and the Council of Ministers serves also as a Party directive and is binding on all Party members.

The overlapping of membership between the top Party and state bodies has traditionally served to symbolize the leading role of the Party and to ensure that state bodies carry out Party policy. However, the extent of this overlap is less today than it was some years ago. Thus if we take the USSR Council of Ministers elected in April 1962 we find that the Chairman, N. S. Khrushchev, was also First

Secretary of the Central Committee of the CPSU and a member of the Party Presidium. Both the First Deputy Chairmen, Mikoyan and Kosygin, were on the Party Presidium but none of the five Deputy Chairmen were. Of the remaining 63 members of the Council of Ministers, only one, D. S. Polyansky, was on the Party Presidium. Put in another way we may say that only four out of 16 members and candidate members of the Party Presidium were also in the Council of Ministers. Four other members and candidate members of the Party Presidium (Brezhnev, Kozlov, Podgorny and Mazurov) were on the Presidium of the USSR Supreme Soviet.

While it is obvious that basic policy decisions in all fields of domestic and foreign affairs are taken by the Communist Party rather than by state agencies acting on their own behalf it must be recognized that the role of state agencies is not uniform or constant. A state agency such as the USSR Gosplan has more initiative in decision-making than the Supreme Soviet or the Legislative Proposals Commissions of the Supreme Soviet. State agencies have tended to increase their importance relative to Party agencies only in certain fields since the end of 1957. At the Union and Union-Republican level agencies which are concerned with the more technical and specialized functions of planning have had their functions enlarged. On the other hand, actual industrial supervision at this level and at the lower level of the Economic Region became more than ever under the control of the corresponding Party organs. At the lower and intermediate levels of local government some state agencies have increased their role in the urban areas while in the rural areas the Party agencies have consolidated and extended their position relative to that of the local Soviets.

The increasing role of certain state agencies at various administrative levels is only partly the result of deliberate Party policy. It is perhaps more a response to the growing complexity of the Soviet economy, to the rapid growth of the size and range of the national product, and to its rising technical level. A safe generalization might be that Party control is cruder and tighter in areas of relatively retarded technique such as agriculture. The development outlined above has obvious repercussions on the number of persons involved in the taking of major decisions.

The above generalizations may be illustrated by reference to two important fields, economic planning and finance. In both fields the Party Presidium (or Politbureau) at present does little more than determine the major principles for investment, overall rates of expansion for the main branches of the economy, the main directions of expenditure and limits to expenditure in various fields, and the sources of revenue and any major change in the existing revenue structure.

The broad responsibility for the economic plan is at present borne by Gosplan, although at various times since 1955 Gosplan has lost control over essential aspects of economic planning to other central state agencies. For example, between November 1962 and October 1965 Gosplan handled long-range plans but the USSR Sovnarkhoz handled short-range perspectives and the fulfilment of the annual economic plan.[10] To these major central agencies must be added the Council of Ministers itself, the Central Statistical Administration, the Planning Departments of the centralized ministries and the Planning-Budget Commissions of the Supreme Soviet. In addition to these central agencies there is a network of agencies at the republican and regional level including Councils of Ministers, Republican Gosplans, planning departments within industrial ministries, and many other more specialized bodies. At the strictly local level we have planning agencies of local Soviets, Executive Committees of local Soviets, industrial managements in the individual economic units, and so on. Trade unions are also actively involved in the planning process at all levels from the All-Union Central Council of Trade Unions down to the trade-union committees in the workshops and to the Permanent Production Conferences where they operate. The role of these various intermediate and lower agencies is not unimportant since they determine the detail of the plan within a framework which has been determined only in broad outline by the highest Party authority.

The budget now as always is very much a monopoly of the experts in the Finance Ministry. Since 1956 the central budget has been less detailed, allowing more scope for Republican Finance Ministries and for Budget-Finance Departments of local Soviets. The formulation of the central budget involves planning, consultation, compromise and decisions over many months between central agencies such as the Finance Ministry other government departments and agencies, and the All-Union Central Council of Trade Unions. In its final stages it involves the Supreme Soviet. Although only a minority —usually less than 5%—of deputies participate in the budget debate, the 102 deputies who are members of the two Planning-Budget Commissions are actively involved in checking the departmental estimates and in suggesting modifications to these estimates for two or three months before they are presented to the Supreme Soviet. Even if we accept the fact that the majority of those taking part in deciding the budget are Communist Party members it must still be recognized that literally dozens of agencies are involved in determining the central budget and that hundreds of agencies and thus tens of thousands of persons are involved in the formulation of the final budget.

EXECUTIVE AND ADMINISTRATIVE FUNCTIONS

Party organizations have a responsibility for the implementation of both Party and government decisions. In fact, both Party and state organizations are expected to do the same job of supervising the carrying out of policy, of checking on the fulfilment of decisions. The decision taken in November 1962 to establish a single Party-State Control Committee was designed to increase the efficiency of the control system as well as to ensure firm Party control at all levels. However this system of unified control organs did not long survive the fall of Khrushchev. In December 1965 the Central Committee decided to again change the control organs. The party-state agencies were reorganized as People's Control organs under a USSR State Committee of People's Control. The main tasks of this new state agency were defined as the systematic verification of Party and government directives, the improvement of the work of communist construction and the struggle against bureaucracy and waste. However these new organs were not to be responsible for the supervision of Party organs. Party organs were to be subjected only to a system of inner-Party control on the basis of the Party Rules.

Economic administration is a state matter. Ministers are responsible to their Council of Ministers, factory directors to their Ministry or local Soviet. However, the Communist Party also keeps the main economic fields under its survey, and individual members of various Party committees are held responsible for various economic fields, even if they have no state position in these particular fields. Thus the First Secretary of a rural *raikom* is normally responsible for agriculture, the Second Secretary for industry. Legally, the District Soviet (or its Executive Committee) is the government agency in the district, but both District Soviets and District Party Committees are expected to see that the Economic Plan (especially those sections relating to agriculture) is fulfilled. However, only state agencies will eventually collect deliveries of agricultural products. Since 1962 all collecting agencies have been controlled by the Ministry of Agricultural Production and State Purchases. The Agricultural Departments of Krai and Oblast Soviets and the Agricultural Inspectorates of Raion Soviets were replaced by Boards of Agricultural Production and State Purchases at the *krai-oblast* level and by Interdistrict Kolkhoz–Sovkhoz Boards at the lowest level. Appeals in the Soviet press underline the joint responsibility of Party and state organs towards agriculture. Government reports and decisions often make specific reference to the responsibilities of both Party and state organs. As far as supervision of agricultural policy is concerned Party organization has often seemed more effective than government organization. This even extended to such functions as the supervision of ploughing, sowing, harvesting and deliveries. The fact that the District Party organization over the years 1953–58 was based on the Machine Tractor Stations gave Party organization a strategic advantage over the organization of the District Soviet in relation to agriculture. The recent trend seemed designed to strengthen the interdependence of Party and state agencies and to increase the direct responsibility of the Party in agriculture. Thus the State Agricultural Committee established in the RSFSR in 1962 included the following:

G. I. Voronov, Chairman (Voronov was First Vice-Chairman of the Bureau of the Central Committee of the CPSU on the RSFSR).

N. G. Smirnov, Vice-Chairman (Smirnov was First Vice-Chairman of the Russian Council of Ministers and Minister of Agricultural Production and Agricultural Deliveries).

I. S. Paukin (Chief of the Agricultural Department of the Bureau of the Central Committee of the CPSU on the RSFSR).

S. V. Shevchenko (Chairman of *Rosselkhoztekhnika*).

V. P. Sotnikov (RSFSR Minister of Agriculture).

V. P. Domrachev (Vice-Chairman of the RSFSR Gosplan on Agriculture).

K. S. Kornechev (Chairman of the RSFSR Committee on Irrigation).

It was also reported that D. S. Polyansky, Chairman of the RSFSR Council of Ministers and members of the Agricultural Department of the Bureau of the Central Committee on the RSFSR participated in the Committee.[11]*

Similar committees at the *krai-oblast* level were under the chairmanship of the First Secretary of the *kraikom* or the *obkom*. At the same time Communist Party organization in the rural areas was brought into line with the new agricultural administration. Thus Party instructors' groups were established in each inter-district administrative area. These groups were to directly assist Party primaries in their area and were to be responsible to the *kraikom* or to the *obkom* and not to the *raikoms*. Thus the 1962 administrative structure tended to weaken both the *raiispolkom* and the *raikom*.[12]

The role of the Party in industrial supervision has been somewhat less direct than in agriculture. In this sphere Party organs are essentially concerned with checking on decisions and their fulfilment rather than with actual management. Industrial managers are usually

* This Committee never seems to have got off the ground and has played no important role in agricultural supervision.

Party members and are likely to be also members of *obkoms* or *gorkoms*, and thus subject to Party discipline. If the manager flouts the decisions of the local Party organs, Party pressure can be applied through higher Party organs influencing the state agency to which the manager is responsible. The industrial reorganization in 1957 and following years increased the responsibility of Communist Party organs especially that of *obkoms*, *kraikoms* and *gorkoms*. Local Party influence was extended in June 1959 when the Central Committee established Party Control Commissions. These are based on the Party Primaries operating in individual industrial and trading establishments, the commissions being elected from among the members of the Party Primary. These commissions were concerned solely with the supervision of the plan fulfilment, with the quality of production, progress of automation, etc. They were not in any sense administrative agencies. The November 1962 decision to organize Party members working in industry, transport and construction into separate industrial primaries with separate higher bodies up to the regional level, was intended to bring industrial enterprises under more effective Party supervision.

THE POSITION OF THE ARMY

The Soviet Army is the creation of the Party and it has always been under strict Party control. Although the specific methods of maintaining Party control over the Army have varied, at all times the Party organization within the Army has been strong and much of the recruitment to the Party, especially during the Civil War and the Patriotic War, has been through the Army. Political Commissars are attached to each military division and political education is entirely in Party hands.

Party members in the armed forces are organized separately from the rest of the Party. Party primary organizations and Komsomol branches in the armed forces are not responsible to the adjacent regional Party Committee. They are responsible to the Main Political Administration (MPA) which is simultaneously an agency of the Central Committee of the CPSU and a part of the USSR Defence Ministry. MPA representatives are at present stationed at all levels of the army down to the battalion level. Until 1955 they existed right down to the company level. In April 1957 army officers were placed in charge of Party organization in the army and political study became optional for officers. This was reversed in November 1958 when compulsory study of Marxism–Leninism by officers was restored. Since 1959 the role of Party primaries in the army, including their right to criticize officers, has been restored and strengthened. Thus the principle of *edinonachalie* (one-man management) which Zhukov had sought to promote was preserved in regard to military matters but was disregarded as far as Party and political work in the army was concerned.[13] Party membership among officers is particularly high. It was 80% in 1939 and 86% in 1952.

Despite this the Party leadership has often been ultra-cautious of army leaders. Thus the Soviet High Command was drastically purged in 1936–37. The popular war hero Marshal Zhukov was rapidly demoted by Stalin in 1946 as he was by Khrushchev in October 1957. However, with the possible exception of Rokossovsky in 1956 there is no evidence of Soviet field commanders seeking to influence government policy. There is little evidence of professional soldier opposition to Party control such as developed at times in the German Army in 1939, 1941 and 1944.

LAW ENFORCEMENT AGENCIES

The Soviet police has proved the most difficult section of the state apparatus to keep under effective Party control. This is because from its very nature police work is highly specialized and its activities are always considerably obscured by secrecy requirements. Following Stalin's death the two separate police ministries, the Ministry of Internal Affairs (MVD) and the Ministry of State Security (MGB) were merged under the control of a single police chief, Beria. The removal of Beria and his personal machine in late 1953 soon resulted in a further reorganization. In March 1954 the MGB was abolished and replaced by a Committee of State Security (KGB), thus placing it more fully under the control of the Council of Ministers. The Ministry of Internal Affairs survived and a relatively junior figure (at first Kruglov and in 1956 Dudorov) was placed at its head. Efforts were made to bring it under collective control at all levels. During 1953–54 the MVD lost its right to exile political prisoners and the system of forced labour camps for political prisoners was drastically reduced. In January 1957 the MVD was partially decentralized, becoming a Union Republican Ministry. At the same time local militia and MVD police were amalgamated. In January 1960 the MVD was further decentralized and became a Republican Ministry.* It became a Union-Republican Ministry again in 1966.

The supervision of administration and justice in the USSR is done mainly by a special agency, the Procuracy. The USSR Procurator-General is appointed by the Supreme Soviet for a term of seven years. The Procurator's Office is fully centralized. Although branches exist down to the district level they are not subject to any

* Renamed the Ministry of the Defence of Public Order in August 1962.

control from republican governments or from local Soviets. Furthermore, they are designed to be immune from local Party influence. These offices are staffed mainly by law graduates, i.e. by experts rather than by Party functionaries. Their main role is the supervision of state organs (but not of Party organs or of higher state executive organs) and drawing attention to illegal actions of these bodies. They also serve an educational function, especially in regard to the local Soviets. Since April 1956 the Procurator's Office has maintained a special department to supervise investigations carried out by state security services. The Procuracy also acts as the prosecutor in law cases involving crimes against the state.

The basic Soviet court is the *People's Court*, which is established at the district level. A People's Court consists of a Judge (elected by universal suffrage for a term of five years) and two lay assessors (elected by general meetings of industrial, office and professional workers, peasants and servicemen for a term of two years). Higher level Courts are elected by the appropriate Soviet—that is, at the *krai*, *oblast* and autonomous *okrug* levels, and by the republican Supreme Soviets in the case of the republican Supreme Courts and by the USSR Supreme Soviet in the case of the USSR Supreme Court.

The Party does not maintain separate law courts any more than it does a police force. The Party Rules provide for the expulsion of a Party member for the commission of an offence punishable by Court of law and for his prosecution in conformity with the law.[14] It has been laid down by the Central Committee of the CPSU that local Party organs must never interfere to influence Court decisions. Some years ago the President of the USSR Supreme Court, Gorshenin, declared:

No one is entitled to dictate to the judges their decision in any criminal law case. Neither the agencies of government and of administration, nor those of the Ministry of Justice, nor social organizations, must interfere with the decision of individual cases.
. . . The interference of local Party organs with the decision of court cases violates the principle of the independence of judges established by the USSR Constitution.[15]

However, even the Supreme Court accepts guidance and direction from the Central Committee of the CPSU.

The conclusion to this chapter is brief. Party and state structures are not identical but they are closely related, inter-dependent, and overlapping. The role of the Party is to formulate basic policy in all fields, to guide and direct state organs at all levels, and to mobilize the people around the fulfilment of Party and state decisions. The

Party is not concerned with the direct administration of industry or agriculture but is concerned with checking the fulfilment of decisions. Both Party and state are considered as temporary agencies which will have no place in the mature international Communist society of the future.

NOTES

[1] A. Denisov and M. Kirichenko, *Osnovy sovetskovo gosudarstva i prava*, Moscow, 1954, p. 146.

[2] *KPSS o rabote Sovetov*, Moscow, 1959, pp. 39–40.

[3] Similar resolutions were carried at the 9th Congress (April 1920), at the 11th Congress (December 1921), at the 12th Congress (April 1923), at the October 1924 Plenum of the Central Committee, at the 14th Party Conference (April 1925), at the 15th Congress (December 1927), at the 16th Congress (July 1930), at the 17th Congress (February 1934) and at the 20th, 21st and 22nd Party Congresses.

[4] For example V. A. Vlasov, *Sovetsky gosudarstvenny apparat*, Moscow, 1959, pp. 72–3.

[5] Rule 67 of the 1961 Rules.

[6] Cf. Note 5 to Chapter 8. The composition of the Presidium elected by the Supreme Soviet April 24, 1962, was decided on by the Party Group in the Supreme Soviet and the Council of Elders, *Izvestia*, April 25, 1962.

[7] *Izvestia*, March 25, 1962.

[8] Cf. Decree of the Presidium of the RSFSR Supreme Soviet, *Sovetskaya Rossia*, March 25, 1962.

[9] Decision published in *Izvestia*, April 19, 1962.

[10] Decisions of the Plenum of the Central Committee, November 23, 1962. *Izvestia*, November 24, 1962.

[11] *Sovetskaya Rossia*, March 25, 1962.

[12] Decision of the Central Committee of the CPSU and the USSR Council of Ministers, March 22, 1962. *Izvestia*, March 25, 1962.

[13] Paul M. Cocks, 'The Purge of Marshal Zhukov', *Slavic Review*, September 1963, pp. 482–98.

[14] Rule 12 of the 1961 Rules. Cf. Rule 13 of the 1952 Rules.

[15] Quoted by Bob Davies in the *Marxist Quarterly*, July 1956, p. 193.

SELECTED BIBLIOGRAPHY

Fainsod, M., 1963a, Ch. 12.
Gripp, R. C., 1963, Ch. 9.
Hazard, J. N., 4th edn., 1968, Ch. 3.
Hough, J. F., 1969.
Schapiro, L., 1965, Ch. 8.
Scott, D. J. R., 1969, pp. 175–84.
Swearer, H. R., 1962.

Chapter 16

SOVIET FOREIGN POLICY

Soviet foreign policy is more a matter of international relations than of domestic politics. For that reason I will not attempt either a history of Soviet foreign policy since 1917 or a comprehensive analysis of the international politics of the contemporary Soviet state. In this chapter I am concerned with two aspects only of Soviet foreign policy, with the agencies of formulation and control of foreign policy, and with the role of ideology in the determination of foreign policy.

THE CONTROL OF FOREIGN POLICY IN THE USSR

At the outset I would like to stress two differences between the foreign policy process in the Soviet Union and parliamentary states. The first of these differences is the greater centralization of the process in the USSR. This is mainly a consequence of the differences between the Soviet and parliamentary political systems. In the former the Communist Party maintains strict control over all government agencies operating in the field of foreign policy, over the Foreign Affairs Department, over embassies and consulates, and over the armed forces. This strict Party control over Soviet foreign policy gives it greater cohesion. There is no visible antagonism between the various government agencies. There is nothing like the limited independence of the United States Department of State and, as has happened on several occasions during the post-war period, of the armed services. Nor is there any evidence of the sort of conflict which has occurred both in the US Department of State and in the British Foreign Office between different regional sections. This is so despite the fact that the various overseas agencies of the Soviet government are separate agencies which collect information and advise the Soviet government on foreign affairs independently of one another. The influence and degree of independence of generals such as MacArthur and Clay and of officials such as the two Dulles brothers and George Kennan cannot be matched in Soviet foreign policy.

Secondly, Soviet foreign policy is unaffected by pressure groups and rival parties. There is no possibility of different governmental agencies advising different policies for the handling of the same situation. Nor can armament makers, oil companies, business and labour groups, religious and national groups, influence the course of Soviet policy. Nor is the foreign policy formulated by the Communist Party government subjected to continuous challenge from the parliamentary or congressional opposition. There have been of course occasions when factional struggles within the CPSU and the international Communist movement have produced some uncertainties and contradictions in Soviet foreign policy—as for example, the reversal of the withdrawal of Soviet forces from Hungary early in November 1956. It is also certain that the opinions of military experts and strategists influence the choice of strategy and tactics followed by the Soviet government. This was frequently suggested as a factor in the Soviet withdrawal from the Summit Conference at Paris in May 1960,[1] although there is no precise information on what sort of advice the Soviet Defence Minister, Marshal Malinovsky, gave to Khrushchev at the time, nor is there any evidence to link Malinovsky's views to those of the 'tough' line foreign policy advocated by Molotov and his supporters.

The advantages of these features of Soviet foreign policy have been amply illustrated in the post-war years. For example, the Soviet Union emerged with a clear-cut policy towards Palestine in 1947–48, whereas the United States did not. The fact that the United States was unable to do this was a direct consequence of the antagonism between the American Jewish organizations seeking support for the establishment of Israel and oil companies operating through the State Department to keep the United States committed to a pro-Arab policy in the Middle East.[2] The Cuban crisis in October 1962 affords an even clearer illustration, especially as United States policy in the crisis was unusually prompt and definite. Despite this the President's control of the situation seemed somewhat uncertain as the crisis occurred at a late stage in the Congressional election campaign, and Republican critics sought to make it an election issue. Should American policy stop short at the naval blockade of Cuba and the insistence on the removal of Soviet missiles, or should an immediate armed invasion of Cuba be attempted? That Kennedy managed to follow a firm and consistent policy during the crisis was a measure of his political maturity and of his full control of the presidential office. As such it stood in marked contrast with the uncertainties of his policy during the earlier Cuban crisis of 1961. Unlike Kennedy, Khrushchev seemed to be in full control of Soviet foreign policy during the crisis. We do not of course know what views were expressed by the Soviet Defence Minister or by other military experts during the crisis. But there was no electoral pressure to ventilate what differences there may

239

have been within the leadership. For that reason Khrushchev was less tempted than Kennedy was to make his policy appear as tough and uncompromising. There are no obvious counterparts in Soviet politics to the domestic extremist groups and Cuban exiles of the United States. Khrushchev could therefore order the dismantling of the Cuban rocket bases and the withdrawal of Soviet experts from Cuba without provoking any challenge to his internal position. Immediately after the Cuban crisis he was able to launch into a domestic programme for administrative reorganization which he could never have attempted had his leadership been threatened because of the Cuba failure.

The disadvantages of the Soviet system of control of foreign policy are equally obvious. The essential centralization of decision-making results in frustration to the statesmen of other powers when complex negotiations are repeatedly held up to allow Soviet diplomats to consult with Moscow. It likewise produces, more frequently than in most countries, embarrassment to the Soviet diplomats when they have to hold a line against obvious evidence that it is false, simply because they have not been briefed on the 'new line' by Moscow. Thus Zorin on October 25, 1962, held to the line that the Soviet Union was not interested in acquiring overseas bases only to have Khrushchev two days later offer to remove Soviet bases in Cuba in return for the United States removing her missile bases in Turkey. More serious still is the complete abandonment in the Soviet system of any attempt at public debate and public control over foreign policy. This is not to say that public opinion is a negligible factor in Soviet foreign policy. Soviet public opinion, although it is conditioned in a more complete way by the leadership than is public opinion in the USA, Britain or Australia, is not a negligible factor. It does set ultimate limits and may exert a positive influence under certain circumstances on Soviet foreign policy. The universal opposition to war in the Soviet Union, a product of the extent of suffering of the Soviet people during the last world war, affords a considerable restraint to the Soviet government in its conduct of foreign policy. Again, on rare occasions, important segments of Soviet opinion may advocate the adoption of a particular policy in advance of its adoption by the Soviet government. Thus in 1957–58 the Soviet Society for General Disarmament and Peace urged the cessation of nuclear weapons tests some months before the Soviet government unilaterally ceased testing.

FORMULATING AGENCIES

The present-day formulating agencies of Soviet foreign policy may be listed as follows:

(*a*) the Central Committee of the CPSU and especially its Presidium (Politbureau);

(*b*) the USSR Council of Ministers and its Presidium;

(*c*) individual Ministries;

(*d*) the Presidium of the USSR Supreme Soviet;

(*e*) the Foreign Affairs Commissions of the USSR Supreme Soviet.

What follows immediately is an attempt at a statement of the actual role of these various agencies in the 1960s.

The Central Committee of the CPSU and its Presidium (*Politbureau*)

The Central Committee itself is certainly more a policy-crystallizing than a policy-formulating body. Foreign policy comes up fairly regularly to the Central Committee in the general reports from the Presidium of the Central Committee and also by means of special reports from special agencies of Soviet foreign policy such as the armed services, the Defence, Foreign Affairs and Foreign Trade Ministries, as well as from the Foreign Affairs Department of the Central Committee and from its Committees for Liaison with foreign Communist Parties. It is difficult to establish just how frequently foreign affairs has come up before the Central Committee. The evidence available would suggest that the Central Committee since 1953 has been primarily concerned with matters of domestic policy such as agricultural development, industrial development and technology, and educational reform. The only occasions when foreign policy issues are known to have been discussed and decided in the Central Committee over the ten years 1953–62 were in July 1955 when Molotov's opposition to *rapprochement* with Yugoslavia was overruled, in June 1957 when Molotov's opposition to the 'new line' in foreign policy was exposed and condemned, and in January 1961, when the Central Committee heard a report by M. A. Suslov on the International Communist Party Conference held in Moscow in November 1960.[3] On this last occasion the plenum adopted a resolution on the report although there was no discussion on the matter. There is some circumstantial evidence that foreign policy has been debated on some other occasions. Thus the Hungarian crisis was probably discussed at the December 1956 plenum of the Central Committee, Yugoslavia at the May 1958 plenum, the U-2 incident at the May 1960 plenum and international communism and the Chinese criticism of Soviet foreign policy at the July 1960 plenum.[4]

The Presidium (or Politbureau) of the Central Committee on the other hand is continuously involved in the formulation and reviewing of Soviet foreign policy. It was in the Presidium rather than in the plenum of the Central Committee that the 'new line' in foreign policy which emerged after the death of Stalin was hammered out. The reverses to Khrushchev's policy in Eastern Europe in 1956 led in turn to a strengthening of the opposition in the Presidium over the months November 1956–February 1957. It was the Politbureau which decided on the invasion of Czechoslovakia in August 1968.

The USSR Council of Ministers and its Presidium

The USSR Council of Ministers has considerable formal authority over foreign affairs. It exercises a general supervision over the conduct of foreign policy and external trade, grants or withdraws recognition of foreign governments, appoints and replaces diplomatic and trade representatives serving overseas, confirms treaties and agreements not requiring ratification and subjects all treaties and agreements to preliminary examination and approval. In fact its actions are taken mainly on the advice of the key Ministries which operate in the field of foreign affairs. It is a moot point as to how much the Council of Ministers as a whole is concerned with foreign policy. During the war years most of the government's powers of control over foreign affairs were exercised by an inner body, the State Defence Committee, a body of five (later eight) men under the chairmanship of Stalin. A similar concentration of foreign affairs powers in the hands of the Presidium of the Council of Ministers perhaps occurred during the years 1953–57. In more recent years it would appear that foreign affairs has been handled by the Presidium of the Council of Ministers with the addition of one or more of the Ministers of Foreign Affairs, Defence and Foreign Trade—that is, by a group of between eight and fifteen men.

Ministries

The key ministry is still the Foreign Affairs Ministry, although it is certain that the peculiar role of military strategy in modern foreign policy has enormously increased the role of the Defence Ministry in recent years. The Ministry of Foreign Affairs has always been headed by an important first-rank or second-rank Party leader—Trotsky, Chicherin, Litvinov, Molotov, Vyshinsky, Molotov, Shepilov and Gromyko. Of these men only Gromyko could be called a 'career' foreign office man and even he has been for many years a member of the Central Committee of the CPSU.* The Ministry of Foreign Affairs

* Gromyko was elected to full membership of the Politbureau in April 1973. Marshal Grechko, Soviet Defence Minister was also elected to the Politbureau in April 1973.

recruits its own staff on the basis of competitive exams. Many of its personnel are recruited relatively late in life after years of service in professions such as teaching, journalism and engineering. Because of the number of its officials serving overseas the Foreign Affairs Ministry is a very important agency for collecting information on overseas happenings, for processing and interpreting these happenings, and for suggesting policies. However, its advice on events and policy is invariably submitted to the Party Politbureau and to the Council of Ministers before becoming state policy. Moreover, the government is not dependent solely on information supplied by the Foreign Affairs Ministry. As a policy-formulating agency the Soviet Ministry of Foreign Affairs is undoubtedly less important than either the United States Department of State or the British Foreign Office. Likewise in the field of appointments the Ministry of Foreign Affairs shares its powers with the Defence Ministry and the Ministry of External Trade. All three ministries, individually or jointly, make recommendations on appointments to the government. This sharing of responsibility is also true of treaties so that trade treaties are more the province of the External Trade Ministry than of the Ministry of Foreign Affairs.

In addition to the three ministries mentioned above there are a number of state committees whose sphere of action extends into foreign affairs. The most important of these are the State Committee on External Economic Relations and the State Committee on Cultural Relations with Foreign Countries. The Chairman of each of these Committees is in the USSR Council of Ministers.

The Presidium of the USSR Supreme Soviet

The Presidium, as an agency of the Supreme Soviet, has extensive powers in the field of foreign policy, including the appointment and removal of the High Command of the Armed Forces; declaration of war (if the Supreme Soviet is not in session); ordering of general or partial mobilization; proclaiming of martial law in separate localities or throughout the USSR; ratification and renunciation of international treaties; the appointment and recall of plenipotentiary representatives of the USSR; and the receiving of foreign diplomats. These powers, most of which have occasionally been exercised, are not so much concerned with the formulation of foreign policy as with carrying out certain governmental actions to meet a particular international situation, and all such actions are presumably taken on the advice of the Soviet government. The only individual in the Presidium who has a clearly independent function in foreign relations is the Chairman or President, who as the formal head of the Soviet state, makes frequent goodwill visits to overseas countries.

The Foreign Affairs Commissions of the
USSR Supreme Soviet

These are perhaps not so much policy-forming agencies as control agencies of the Supreme Soviet. However, since they have the duty of exercising a continuous supervision over the conduct of Soviet foreign policy, they are brought more closely into contact with the Foreign Affairs Ministry than is the Supreme Soviet itself.[5] They do in fact play a minor and very subordinate role as policy-formulating agencies. This is achieved in the following ways. Firstly, the Commissions are often concerned with drafting policy statements on foreign affairs which are submitted to the Supreme Soviet, and on acceptance, become official documents of state policy. This was the case, for example, with the statement on the Principles of Soviet Foreign Policy adopted by the USSR Supreme Soviet on February 9, 1955. Secondly, texts of treaties negotiated by the USSR Council of Ministers are usually examined by the Commissions on Foreign Affairs before they are submitted to the Supreme Soviet or to its Presidium for ratification. This is also done with documents other than treaties. Thus the Council of Ministers statement on the results of the Conference of East European States held in Warsaw early in 1955 was discussed and endorsed by the Foreign Affairs Commissions prior to its submission to the Supreme Soviet for ratification on May 25.[6] Thirdly, representatives of the Foreign Affairs Ministry and other government departments and agencies attend meetings of the Foreign Affairs Commissions where they make statements and answer questions on foreign affairs. Fourthly, representatives of the Commissions on Foreign Affairs are usually included in Soviet teams whether negotiations are held in Moscow or abroad. Finally, the Foreign Affairs Commissions play a special part in receiving and assisting foreign parliamentary groups visiting the Soviet Union. No less than fifty-seven parliamentary groups visited the USSR during the Fifth Supreme Soviet (1958–61), thirty-five groups visited the Soviet Union over four years prior to March 1966.

The above outline of the formulation and control of Soviet foreign policy is far from complete. We have little reliable information on such crucial questions as the precise role of military experts in Soviet policy. Nor do we know the extent to which the Party leadership has been divided on foreign policy since 1953. There is considerable internal evidence to suggest that Molotov stood alone in the Party Presidium in his resistance to the 'new line' in foreign policy in 1953–57. The precise role of Khrushchev over the years 1955–64 is difficult to estimate. Although he was closely associated with the new stress on peaceful coexistence and negotiation this policy perhaps owed as much to Mikoyan as it did to Khrushchev.

RATIFYING AGENCIES

The Party Congress

Since the Report of the Central Committee to the Party Congress always contains a long analysis of the international situation and of Soviet foreign policy this enables the delegates to the Congress to discuss foreign policy. In fact most delegates restrict their speeches to domestic issues, leaving foreign policy to Politbureau members and to experts such as the Ministers of Foreign Affairs and Defence.

A feature of Soviet foreign policy as it is covered by the Party Congress is that an attempt is made at a Marxist appraisal of the international situation and of Soviet foreign policy on this basis. This theoretical basis is more thoroughly examined if Soviet foreign policy has recently undergone considerable modifications as may be illustrated by contrasting the relevant sections of the Central Committee Reports to the 19th Congress (Malenkov) and the 20th Congress (Khrushchev). Although modifications to the Party line in foreign affairs are quickly reflected in reports to and resolutions adopted by the Party Congress, the Congress has not in recent years been a forum for debate at which alternative foreign policies are advocated and canvassed. The latter was true only during the first few years of the regime.

The USSR Supreme Soviet

Despite extensive formal powers of control over foreign affairs the Supreme Soviet plays only a subsidiary role in policy-formulation (through its Standing Commissions on Foreign Affairs) and is largely confined to the role of a ratifying agency. Very few treaties are ratified by the Supreme Soviet although both the German–Soviet Pact (August 1939) and the Anglo-Soviet Treaty (May 1942) were. Most treaties, including such important treaties as the Sino-Soviet Treaty (February 1950) have been ratified by the Presidium of the Supreme Soviet.

Foreign policy may be brought before the Supreme Soviet in various ways. The submission of an important treaty for ratification may or may not be followed by a limited debate. Groups of deputies may ask questions on foreign affairs which will be answered by a foreign policy report and perhaps a short debate. The Foreign Minister or the United Nations representative may present a report on foreign affairs and this is often followed by a brief discussion. Statements on foreign affairs may be presented to the Supreme Soviet by the Standing Commissions on Foreign Affairs or even (as in the case of the 1956 Japanese Parliament's request that all parliaments should consider the problem of nuclear weapons tests) in reply to requests sent from a foreign Parliament. Finally, special reports on foreign affairs are sometimes given by the Soviet government after important international conferences or events. This happened in December 1955 after the Geneva Conference, in May 1960 after the abortive Paris Peace Conference and in December 1962 after the Cuban Crisis.

The limited nature of the actual debate on foreign affairs in the USSR Supreme Soviet is clear from the fact that in the five and a quarter years following the 20th Congress (i.e. from February 1956 to May 1960) foreign policy was brought before the Supreme Soviet on eleven separate occasions, that is at each session of the Supreme Soviet held during these years. Only 67 deputies (besides the Foreign Minister and the Chairmen of the Standing Commissions on Foreign Affairs) spoke in these debates—an average of six deputies per session. Even here the 67 deputies who spoke on foreign affairs included the Defence Minister and various members of the Party Presidium so that participation by the ordinary deputies was much less.

AGENCIES OF INFLUENCE ON WORLD OPINION

At the present time the greatest influence the Soviet Union exerts on the outside world is that of its achievement and example. However the agencies for exerting external influence are numerous and to some extent are peculiar to the Soviet Union.

The Red Army

The Red Army exerted a much greater influence during the war years than since. During the years 1941–45 the Red Army by its heroism and eventual success over the German military machine provided a fillip to the Communist Parties in many countries. Since the war the Soviet Army has exerted a direct influence only in a limited zone covering parts of Eastern Europe, Mongolia and North Korea. In 1944–46 the Soviet Army was the main agency for the destruction of feudal landlordism in several East European countries and also in the destruction of capitalism and parliamentary government in these countries in following years. While I hold it an exaggeration to claim that the regimes in Eastern Europe owe their existence solely to the presence of the Soviet Army it is abundantly clear that the presence of the Soviet Army is an essential ingredient in the security of the East European State system. It should be noted that the Soviet Army has been a decisive influence in the external policy of the USSR only in a limited number of East European Countries. It has not been the decisive influence in Finland or Yugoslavia or Albania since 1946 and has never been a factor in Greek, Scandinavian or Turkish politics. Nor has the Soviet Army ever been a worldwide agency of national power and influence in external affairs like the US Armed Forces have been since 1945. Finally, like US overseas bases, Soviet bases are in some ways more a liability than an asset at the present time.

Communist Internationals

The Communist International which existed over the years 1919–43 was dominated by the CPSU from its inception and served as a main agency for influencing the course of events abroad and for rallying overseas support for Soviet foreign policy. In 1947 a more limited organization, the *Cominform* or Communist Information Bureau, which included nine European Parties was established at a conference in Warsaw. This organization was liquidated in April 1956 following the resumption of diplomatic relations between the Soviet Union and Yugoslavia. Today the Soviet Union has no organizational link with foreign Communist Parties but it still has the'prestige of the leader of world Communism and in this way the 40 million foreign Communists in over eighty national Communist Parties still serve to spread Soviet influence throughout the world. This leadership is maintained through two main ways at the present time. Firstly, most Communist Parties continue to recognize the leadership of the Soviet Party and continue to send groups of functionaries for training in Soviet Party schools. Secondly, international Communist Conferences are frequently held in Moscow. Thus in November 1957, on the occasion of the Fortieth Anniversary of the November Revolution, two separate conferences were held in Moscow, one covering the countries with communist governments, the other being attended by representatives of sixty-four Communist Parties throughout the world. An even larger Conference was held in Moscow in November 1960. Representatives of eighty-one Communist Parties attended this Conference and signed the statement which was issued at the conclusion of the conference. While this statement included some compromises and possible inconsistencies (a reflection of differences between Soviet and Chinese Parties) it did in the main endorse the Soviet line on international relations. In contrast, fewer Parties attended the June 1969 Conference and not all Parties signed the resolution adopted by this Conference.

USSR Ministry of Foreign Affairs

As with other countries the embassies and legations maintained abroad by the Soviet government provide an avenue for the outlet of favourable information on Soviet achievements. Wherever embassies exist they assist the work of Friendship Societies with pamphlets, books, films, records, photographs, speakers and cultural exchanges. Friendship organizations also maintain regular contact with VOKS, the USSR Society for Cultural Relations with Foreign Countries with its headquarters in Kalinin Street, Moscow.

The USSR Ministry of External Trade

This ministry controls the network of Soviet consulates, trade missions and trade fairs abroad.

The East European Alliance

There are two chief organizations involved here, *Comecon*, the Council of Mutual Economic Assistance (established 1949) and the Warsaw Pact (established 1955). Conferences of both agencies include observers from non-European Communist states and in 1962 the People's Republic of Mongolia was admitted to full membership of *Comecon*.[7] Close liaison is also maintained between the Communist Parties of the bloc through frequent interchanges and through attendance at various Communist Party Conferences in the individual states.

Non-Party International Agencies

Agencies such as the World Peace Council, the World Federation of Trade Unions, the World Federation of Democratic Youth, the International Union of Students, the World Federation of Democratic Women and many others of like nature serve as excellent agencies for spreading Soviet influence abroad. This is achieved because the Soviet is the most important and in some cases the largest member of such organizations.

The United Nations

The Soviet Union, just as much as the United States, seeks to use the United Nations organs and agencies as forums of propaganda for the United Nations has become the major platform for the influencing of world opinion. Although the Soviet Union has kept out of some of the specialized agencies she obviously cherishes her role as leading member in the main agencies. Her absence from the Security Council in June 1950 when the Korean War broke out taught her a lesson of the dangers of boycotting the United Nations which she was quick to learn and will not readily forget.

THE ROLE OF MARXIST IDEOLOGY IN SOVIET FOREIGN POLICY

Having discussed at considerable length the formulating and ratifying agencies of Soviet foreign policy I intend now to discuss the difficult question of the role of Marxist ideology in the formulation of Soviet foreign policy. This is a difficult question and far too many writers have attempted to give a simple answer to it. We cannot categorically deny that communist ideology has an influence on Soviet foreign policy. Nor can we assume that ideology is the sole or main determinant of Soviet foreign policy. Yet even if we reject both of these extreme positions we still have to determine how far and through what processes Marxist ideology influences Soviet foreign policy. In order to clarify this problem I want to argue the following propositions.

(1) *Marxist ideology has at all stages since November* 1917 *exerted a determining influence on the tone of Soviet foreign policy.*

By this I mean not merely the language of its foreign policy statements but the basis of its analysis of international relations. Thus, as in domestic politics, the Soviet leaders insist that economic and social factors are the determining factors. This is done even in the assessment of Soviet strength at the present juncture. This assessment is made more in the terms of the present economic strength of the socialist camp and of its greater growth rate than in terms of quantity or quality of armaments.[8] The fact that Soviet analysis of international relations has at times been dogmatic, characterized by 'an attachment to the symbols and phrases of Marxism rather than to its analytical content',[9] does not belie this claim. Even the claim, which most Western writers make, that the Soviet Union has a distorted picture or image of the Western world, is a recognition of the fact that all Soviet analysis of international relations is related to the underlying theory of Marxism–Leninism. No doubt Soviet analysis of international events is sometimes distorted through the ignoring or minimizing of unsavoury evidence, although this is much less frequent today than it was in the Stalin period.* Bias exists in most analysis of international relations, governmental and non-governmental. What distinguishes Soviet analysis from, say, American analysis, is that the interpretation is more clearly related to an underlying theory of international relations and for that reason it is more uniform and more predictable.†

* A careful reading of recent publications of the Institute of World Economy and International Relations (USSR Academy of Sciences), Moscow, should convince anyone of the inaccuracy of the view that Soviet experts use only pro-Communist sources.

† Cf. the interesting discussion of this problem by Robert C. Tucker in 'Russia, the West, and World Order', *The Soviet Political Mind*, N.Y., 1972, Ch. 12.

A further aspect of the tone of Soviet foreign policy which is derived from Marxism is its unfailing optimism which is based on the belief that history is on the side of socialism. It is this belief which enabled Khrushchev to make his repeated pronouncements that socialism would soon catch up with capitalism. As the programme of the CPSU declares:

Not even nuclear weapons can protect the monopoly bourgeoisie from the unalterable course of historical development. Mankind has learned the true face of capitalism. Hundreds of millions of people see that capitalism is a system of economic anarchy and periodical crisis, chronic unemployment, poverty of the masses, and indiscriminate waste of productive forces, a system constantly fraught with the danger of war. Mankind does not want to, and will not, tolerate the historically outdated capitalist system.[10]

(2) My second proposition is that *Marxist ideology does not determine either the method or the immediate objectives of Soviet foreign policy* but only its ultimate expectancy of world socialism and eventually, of world communism. This follows from the nature of the Marxist theory as well as from the historical accident that Marx and Engels died many years before the establishment of the Soviet state. Marxism is a theory of social development rather than a detailed programme of how to produce a world communist order. Although much has been added to the original Marxist heritage by Lenin, Stalin, Khrushchev and others it is still a very general and uncertain body of theory.[11] The Soviet state has had to feel its way cautiously in foreign policy with little more than a general attitude towards society and international relations to assist it. It is because of this that policies as divergent as those of Trotsky and Stalin in the twenties or those of Khrushchev and Mao in the sixties could be equally argued as Marxist policies. It is also because of this fact that Soviet leaders have been able to make what appear to be contradictory pronouncements on particular issues. A good example of this are statements on the relations between capitalist and socialist states. Right from the beginning of the Soviet regime statements proclaiming peaceful relations were alternated with statements predicting non-peaceful, warlike relations. A common interpretation of these 'contradictory' statements is to accept the latter as genuine and to discount the former as insincere, or at best, tactical manoeuvres.[12] This is to mistake the nature of the Marxist approach to international affairs. A basic part of this approach is the need for policies to conform to the objective circumstances. Modifications in the expectancy of peaceful or non-peaceful relations have resulted from changes in the objective circumstances operating at particular times and from the degree of understanding of these objective circumstances. Thus throughout the

post-war years Soviet leaders proclaimed the possibility of peaceful coexistence of socialism and capitalism but they continued to argue the inevitability of wars between capitalist countries because imperialist rivalries and wars were regarded as an inevitable outcome of capitalism. Thus Stalin in his *Economic Problems of Socialism in the U.S.S.R.* argued that:

... Some comrades hold that, owing to the development of new international conditions since the Second World War, wars between capitalist countries have ceased to be inevitable. They consider that the contradictions between the socialist camp and the capitalist camp are more acute than the contradictions among the capitalist countries; that the USA has brought the other capitalist countries sufficiently under its sway to be able to prevent them going to war among themselves and weakening one another; that the foremost capitalist minds have been sufficiently taught by the two world wars and the severe damage they caused to the whole capitalist world not to venture to involve the capitalist countries in war with one another again—and that, because of all this, wars between capitalist countries are no longer inevitable.

These comrades are mistaken. They see the outward phenomena that come and go on the surface, but they do not see those profound forces which, although they are so far operating imperceptibly, will nevertheless determine the course of developments.[13]

Stalin then went on to analyse the signs of friction between the USA, Britain, France, West Germany and Japan, and to argue that the peace movement was strong enough to prevent the outbreak of particular wars but not of war altogether and that 'to eliminate the inevitability of war it was necessary to abolish imperialism.'[14]

However, a fuller assessment of these factors, made some years later, enabled Khrushchev to argue that war was no longer 'fatalistically inevitable', although he still argued that while capitalism remained the danger of war would continue.[15]

(3) My third proposition is that *Marxist ideology since 1956 has received a new emphasis as an integrating factor in the interstate relations of the socialist camp.* This is reflected in the Soviet statement issued on October 31, 1956, in the two international Communist Party Statements issued in November 1957, in the 81 Party Statement issued in December 1960, and even in the statement issued at the International Communist Parties Conference in June 1969. The renewed emphasis on Marxism in international Communist Party relations is not, as has been argued elsewhere,[16] because Marxist theory has no relevance to internal developments in the Soviet Union since the death of Stalin, and therefore the justification for the continued stress on Marxism for the Soviet citizen must be sought externally. It is more correctly understood as an illustration of a more flexible, less dogmatic, and I believe, a more intelligent application of Marxism

which has been a feature of the Soviet Union and, to some extent, of international Communism, since the 20th Congress of the CPSU. It is also a reflection of the growth of polycentrism within the Communist bloc resulting in a more genuinely international evaluation of the international situation and the determination of Communist policy.[17] In another sense ideology has served as a divisive force within the Communist bloc, especially since 1961.

SOVIET FOREIGN POLICY AND THE PURSUIT OF THE NATIONAL INTEREST

Explanations of Soviet foreign policy purely in terms of the national interest have been sought by at least two schools of thought, the dogmatic socialist internationalists and the realists. For the former, the Soviet Union under Stalin was guilty of a betrayal of the interests of the world revolution in favour of Russian national and imperial interests. For the latter, the Soviet Union like any other great power, has been concerned not with the pursuit of the Marxist ideal of world revolution but solely with the pursuit of state interests, with the strengthening of frontiers against attack and with improving the power-ratio of the USSR.

National interest is a central factor in Soviet foreign policy but this does not mean that the Soviet social structure, political system and ideology are unimportant. Each ruling class makes its own definition of the national interest. Even in a capitalist state historical development and realignments within the capitalist class may produce a reinterpretation of the national interest.[18] If we are prepared to make the assumption about the Soviet system that we make about other states, namely, that its preservation is essential for the national interest, I believe that Soviet foreign policy since 1917 can be largely explained in terms of the defence of the national interest. But this concept cannot be applied without a consideration of Marxist theory as Soviet statesmen ever since 1917 have always taken a Marxist approach to a definition of the national interest. Thus at the outset the entire Soviet leadership believed that if power could be retained for a few months or even years the world revolution would occur and bring succour and assistance to the Soviet revolution. Lenin could even accept the necessity for a surrender of large territories to Germany in 1918 in order that the regime itself might survive. After 1921 this policy became transformed into one of survival in order to guarantee the future of socialism. This made possible the identification of the security of the USSR with world revolution. This was a consistent policy objective from 1921–45, although the strategy and tactics of Soviet foreign policy were changed more than once over these years. Thus Soviet foreign policy during 1922–33 was based on a strategy of 'socialist isolation' (or 'socialism in one country') and non-aggression pacts were its main tactic. From 1933 to August 1939 socialist isolation was replaced by a policy of 'collective security'. This involved the recognition and utilization by the Soviet leaders of important secondary differences between capitalist states, between the aggressive imperialist Fascist states on the one hand and the defensive imperialist parliamentary states on the other.

From August 1939 to June 1941 Soviet foreign policy reverted to a policy of 'socialist isolation', which, despite its association with war, war preparation and territorial gains, was none the less essentially a policy of defensive isolation.[19] Molotov, in reporting on the Nazi–Soviet Pact to the USSR Supreme Soviet on August 31, 1939, declared:

Is it really difficult to understand that the USSR is pursuing and will continue to pursue its own independent policy, based on the interests of the peoples of the USSR and only their interests?

From June 1941 to September 1945 this strategy was replaced by one of collective security involving military alliances with Britain, the USA, France and China in the worldwide struggle against fascism. While the military defeat of the Axis powers was the first objective of the Soviet government during these years a second objective was to utilize the war and victory to consolidate Soviet defences against an outside world which was regarded—and perhaps not without reason —as basically hostile. This second objective had various undercurrents including ethnic factors (the desire to 'round out' Soviet frontiers in the west to include all Belorussians, Ukrainians and Moldavians), economic gains (initially, reparations), and the extension of socialism to Eastern Europe. These undercurrents were of minor significance, at least until 1944–45.

Soviet foreign policy since 1945 has gone through three main phases, 1945–53, 1953–62 and 1963 to the present. The chief objective of Soviet foreign policy in the first phase was to defend and enforce the war settlement, including not merely the revised frontiers in Eastern Europe and the Far East, but reparations, de-Nazification and the establishment of friendly governments in East European States bordering the Soviet Union. This last objective was clearly stated by Stalin in his interview with a *Pravda* correspondent immediately after Churchill's Fulton speech in March 1946. Stalin stated that:

. . The following circumstances should not be forgotten. The Germans made their invasion of the USSR through Finland, Poland, Rumania, Bulgaria and Hungary. The Germans were able to make their invasion through these countries because, at the time, governments hostile to the Soviet Union existed in these countries. As a result of the German invasion

253

the Soviet Union has lost irretrievably in the fighting against the Germans, and also through the German occupation and the deportation of Soviet citizens to German servitude, a total of about seven million people.* In other words the Soviet Union's loss of life has been several times greater than that of Britain and the USA put together. Possibly in some quarters an inclination is felt to forget about these colossal sacrifices of the Soviet people which secured the liberation of Europe from the Hitlerite yoke. But the Soviet Union cannot forget about them. And so what can there be surprising about the fact that the Soviet Union, anxious for its future safety, is trying to see to it that governments loyal in their attitude to the Soviet Union should exist in these countries? How can anyone who has not taken leave of his senses, describe these peaceful aspirations of the Soviet Union as expansionist tendencies on the part of our State?[20]

This purely defensive action became transformed in the process of the Cold War into the determination to consolidate and defend the socialist state system. While it is true that the socialization of the Peoples Democracies would hardly have stopped at the point reached in March 1946 even without the Cold War developing—for revolutions cannot stay still but must advance or retreat—the rate of revolutionary change increased in 1947–49.[21] In this sense the socialization of the satellites was as much a defence measure dictated by the Cold War as the inevitable consequence of Russian domination. In terms of underlying theory Stalin probably saw the development more as the defence of 'socialism in one country' than as a new step towards world socialism.

Although Soviet foreign policy has undergone important changes since mid-1953 it would be incorrect to equate these changes with any abandonment of the national interest. The new emphasis both on peaceful competition with the West and on the further development of the socialist system as a whole represents some transition from national to bloc planning and from national to international policy. In part this is a belated adjustment of Soviet foreign policy to meet the realities of the post-war international situation where rivalry between blocs has increasingly replaced rivalry between individual nation states. The only reasonable interpretation of both the Soviet and the American national interest today is in bloc terms. Neither power can afford to pursue the sort of isolationist policy which they both followed in the twenties. This shifting to a 'systemal' foreign policy is reflected not merely in the growing integration of the economies of socialist Europe and the USSR, not merely in communist bloc assistance to Cuba, Hanoi and to neutral countries,† but in

---

* Subsequently estimated at 20 million.

† Brezhnev reported to the 23rd Congress in March 1966 that the Soviet Union was assisting Asian and African states by the construction of about 600 industrial enterprises and 100 educational and medical institutes.

a re-examination of both the theory and practice of relations beween the capitalist and socialist world systems. Since 1963 Soviet foreign policy[22] has been concerned with defending the long Asian border of the USSR against Communist China. This has involved a search for *détente* with the West, a policy which reached a peak in 1972–73 with the visits of President Nixon to Moscow and L. I. Brezhnev to Washington. A series of political, economic, scientific and cultural agreements resulted. Soviet hostility towards China has led to renewed efforts to reach an arms limitation agreement with the United States and also to a narrower, more purely Soviet or East European interpretation of the principle of 'proletarian internationalism'. The principle was used to sanction the Soviet-led invasion of Czechoslovakia in August 1968 and the denunciation of China in June 1969.[23] Although called to consolidate support for the CPSU in its struggle with the CPC, the June 1969 Conference merely underlined the fact that the Communist world is now hopelessly divided.

NOTES

[1] Cf. A.A.P.-Reuter report from Paris, May 17, 1960, reported in the Melbourne *Age*, May 18, 1960. Cf. also R. Conquest, 1960, pp. 389–92.

[2] Cf. The *Nation*, June 26, 1948. The Secret ARAMCO Report.

[3] *Izvestia*, January 19, 1961.

[4] Cf. R. Conquest, *op. cit.*, pp. 292–4, 357, 389–92, 432–3.

[5] Each of the two Standing Commissions on Foreign Affairs elected in July 1970 had 32 members. The importance of the two Commissions is indicated by the persons elected to head them. Thus M. A. Suslov, a member of the Politbureau and the Secretariat of the C.C. of the CPSU, was re-elected Chairman of the Soviet of the Union Commission on Foreign Affairs, while B. N. Ponomarev, a member of the Secretariat of the C.C., was elected Chairman of the Standing Commission on Foreign Affairs of the Soviet of Nationalities.

[6] S. G. Novikov, 1962, pp. 45–6. For the work of the Foreign Affairs Commissions generally, see, pp. 44–50. See also V. Vladimov, 1958.

[7] Communiqué of C.E.M.A., *Izvestia*, June 10, 1962. Neither Albania nor China participated in this Conference.

[8] Cf. Khrushchev's speech in Moscow, January 6, 1961, Section 1, 'Our Epoch is the Epoch of the Triumph of Marxism–Leninism'. English text in *World Marxist Review*, January 1961, pp. 2–27. Cf. Programme of the CPSU, 1961. Part One.

[9] Adam Ulam, 'Soviet Ideology and Soviet Foreign Policy', *World Politics*, January 1959, pp. 153–72.

[10] *Programme of the Communist Party of the Soviet Union*. English text, FLPH, Moscow, 1961, p. 34. Cf. Khrushchev's reply to J. Reston of the New York *Times*, October 7, 1957:

'We proceed from the premise that wars are not necessary for the victory of socialism. We are convinced that in the peaceful competition of socialism and capitalism, victory will be on the side of socialism, while capitalism will inevitably vanish from the historical arena just as was the case with feudalism which gave way to capitalism.'

[11] For a summary of Soviet Marxist theory of international relations as it stood in 1960 see my article, 'Soviet Revision of Lenin's *Imperialism*', *The*

Australian Journal of Politics and History, Vol. VIII, No. 1, May 1962, pp. 57–65.

[12] Cf. George A. Morgan ('Historicus') 'Stalin on Revolution', *Foreign Affairs*, Vol. XXVII, January 1949, pp. 175–214.

[13] J. Stalin, 1952, pp. 37–8.

[14] J. Stalin, *op. cit.*, p. 41.

[15] N. S. Khrushchev, *Report of the Central Committee of the Communist Party of the Soviet Union to the 20th Party Congress.* February 14, 1956, FLPH, Moscow, 1956. espec. pp. 41–42. For a later, somewhat modified version, see N. S. Khrushchev, 'For New Victories for the World Communist Movement', Sect. 3 in *World Marxist Review*, January 1961.

[16] A. Ulam, *op. cit.*

[17] Cf. Z. K. Brzezinski, 1962, p. 152 ff.

[18] Cf. C. A. Beard, 1934.

[19] Contrast W. H. Chamberlin's term 'aggressive isolation' in 'Seven Phases of Soviet Foreign Policy', *Russian Review*, April 1956, pp. 77–84.

[20] J. V. Stalin, 1947, p. 5.

[21] Thus in Hungary by mid-1947 the state sector contained a total of only 32% of the employment in manufacture and was still only 40–50% of employment in industry at the end of 1947. Only in Yugoslavia did nationalization of industry approach 100% as early as 1945–46.

[22] A good indication of the present official Soviet 'global' view of foreign policy is the emphasis in the present textbook used in Party schools in the USSR, *Vneshnyaya politika SSSR* (V. L. Israelyan, ed.) Moscow, 1965. This book devotes one chapter (38 pages) to the analysis of intra-bloc relations but three chapters (115 pages) to the analysis of Soviet policy towards the countries of Asia, Africa and Latin America.

[23] L. Brezhnev, 'For Greater Unity of Communists, For a Fresh Upsurge of Anti-Imperialist Struggle'. Speech delivered at the International Communist Conference, Moscow, June 1969, Novosti, Moscow, 1969, pp. 31 ff.

SELECTED BIBLIOGRAPHY

Almond, G. A., Ch. 7
Armstrong, J. A., 1965.
Aspaturian, V. V., 1968.
Brzezinski, Z. K., 1962, Ch. 4, 5.
Chamberlin, W. H., 1956.
Crankshaw, E., 1963.
Dallin, A., 1960.
Hanak, H., 1972.
Jukes, G., 1973.
Kennan, G., 1958.
Tucker, R. C., 1972, Chs, 11, 12
Ulam, A. B., 1963, Ch. 3.
Wesson, R. G., 1969.

Chapter 17

SOVIET DEMOCRACY

The leaders of the Soviet Union have always described their political system as democratic. This claim has been made by Lenin, Stalin, Khrushchev and by subsequent leaders. It has been made irrespective of the different degrees of public criticism, inner-party debate, coercion and terror which have operated since November 1917. The claim has never enjoyed much support in the West, especially over the post-war years. At the present time the majority of Western political scientists firmly deny that the USSR is a democracy although a few concede that early Leninism included a democratic tradition which was contradicted by theoretical modifications to the theory of socialism after 1903 as well as by authoritarian political practice.[1] Many Western experts suggest that the claim by Soviet spokesmen that their system is democratic is not only spurious but is insincere.[2] My own view is that this is not so. It seems to me that the Soviet leadership throughout most of the period of its existence has sought to promote a belief in democracy.

This chapter will seek to explore two questions.

(i) What concept of democracy is held in the USSR and how is it related to that commonly held in the West?

(ii) How far does Soviet practice conform to the Soviet concept of democracy?

THE SOVIET CONCEPT OF DEMOCRACY

By official definition the Soviet Union is a socialist democracy which is moving towards communism. Until 1961 it was also described as a 'proletarian dictatorship', but since the 22nd Congress it has been described as 'a state of the whole people' (*obshchenarodnoe gosudarstvo*). The latter is held to represent a higher stage of democracy than the former, just as the former was considered to represent a higher stage of democracy than bourgeois (or parliamentary) democracy. Thus at the outset we may notice that the Soviet Union, like

257

most parliamentary democracies, claims to be evolving in the direction of greater democracy. It may of course be found that the system itself, the direction of its development, and its democratic ideal are vastly different to those of the West.

The origins of the Soviet theory of democracy are to be found in Marxism. Marx and Engels both participated in the revolutionary movements of Western Europe in 1848 and afterwards. These revolutions were influenced by the dual forces of economic development and the French Revolution. The chief beneficiary of these revolutions was expected to be the bourgeoisie, because a parliamentary democracy was considered by Marx and Engels to be the most satisfactory political system for the development of capitalist society. However, they believed that the working class should support the general movement for democratic constitutions. They held political democracy to be a desirable goal for the workers because it enhanced their chances of organizing to defend their interests and eventually to challenge and overthrow the capitalist state. Marxism was influenced by political liberalism to a far lesser extent than non-Marxist socialist and labour movements were. Political democracy under capitalism was regarded as deficient in many respects, especially in its denial of social and political equality. Furthermore, Marx and Engels regarded a democracy, like any other form of state, as an instrument of class domination. Hence bourgeois democracy was a bourgeois dictatorship exercised by and in the interests of the minority, the bourgeoisie, over the majority, the proletariat. Marx and Engels viewed democracy historically, but unlike their liberal contemporaries, their historical perspective extended into the future. They acknowledged that nineteenth-century democracy was more advanced than the democracy of classical Greece because it was based on free labour and the capitalist mode of production whereas the former was based on slavery. But they held that bourgeois democracy would in turn be superseded by a higher form of democracy, proletarian democracy. This higher form of democracy would be based on socialism.

The early Russian Marxists were distinguished by their orthodoxy. They took over from Marx not merely his critique of capitalist society, historical materialism and his revolutionary socialism, but also his partial acceptance of bourgeois democracy. Right up to 1917 both the Bolshevik and the Menshevik wings of Russian Social Democracy accepted a common platform which included the destruction of tsarist autocracy and its replacement by a constitutional republic. Even the theories of 'permanent revolution' and 'uninterrupted revolution' developed by Trotsky and Lenin in 1905–6 retained the notion of the bourgeois revolution preceding the proletarian revolution. It was, however, to be foreshortened and was to be carried out not by the bourgeoisie but by the proletariat (with some assistance from the peasantry) in the interests of the future socialist revolution. Lenin was also influenced by Russian revolutionary traditions, especially in his scheme for a relatively small, highly centralized, revolutionary organization. But despite contradictory elements in these two traditions Lenin retained his Marxist theory of democracy. Indeed the experience of revolution in 1905 and 1917 forced him to undertake a re-examination of this part of the Marxist tradition. This re-examination is reflected in such works as *Two Tactics of Social-Democracy in the Democratic Revolution* (written in June–July 1905), *The Tasks of the Proletariat in Our Revolution* (April 1917), *The State and Revolution* (September 1917) and *The Proletarian Revolution and the Renegade Kautsky* (November 1918). This restatement of the Marxist theory of democracy still provides the basis of the present-day Soviet theory of democracy. Because of this it is necessary to look at Lenin's 1917–18 position on this matter more closely.

The work *The State and Revolution* was written while Lenin was in temporary hiding in Finland after the failure of the July Insurrection in 1917. The date is significant because by this date Lenin had already accepted the Soviets as superior organizations to parliaments for representing the workers and the peasants in a socialist state. He found justification for this view in Marx's 1871 analysis of the Paris Commune (*The Civil War in France*). Lenin found many similarities between the Soviets and the Commune. He also claimed that the weaknesses of the Commune, especially its isolation from the rest of France, were not repeated in the Soviets. The fact that the book was written before the Bolshevik seizure of power is also significant. It represented the highest level of Lenin's optimism and indeed contains many naïve assumptions about the innate capacity of the ordinary workers to run a state without the need for a complex administrative structure.

Lenin considered democracy in its literal, classical meaning. For him democracy represented the 'rule of the people'. But inasmuch as all advanced societies contained conflicting classes and all states involved suppression a really democratic state would involve the rule of the majority over the minority. Unlike liberal democracy, minorities were not considered to have any inherent rights, although they might enjoy limited toleration if such concessions proved in the interests of the ruling majority.

Democracy for the vast majority of the people, and the suppression by force, i.e., exclusion from democracy of the exploiters and oppressors of the people—this is the change democracy undergoes during the *transition* from capitalism to communism.[3]

The second proposition Lenin made about democracy was that it involved representative institutions, although not parliaments or parliamentarism. Soviets he said were superior representative institutions to parliaments because they represented more directly and more fully the majority classes, the proletariat and the peasantry, and because they excluded the bourgeoisie. The keynote to the rejection of parliamentarism was the notion that Soviets were 'working institutions', not merely 'talking institutions'. The usual distinction between legislative and executive-administrative functions must be abandoned. The bourgeois state apparatus must be smashed and replaced by Soviets which were to combine legislative and administrative functions.

The old, i.e., bourgeois democracy and parliamentarism were organised in such a manner that it was precisely the toiling masses who were mostly alienated from the apparatus of administration. The Soviet government i.e., the dictatorship of the proletariat, on the contrary, is organised in such a way as to bring the masses of the toilers closer to the apparatus of administration. The same aim is pursued by the unification of the legislative and executive authorities under the Soviet organisations of the state and by the substitution of production units, like the factories and works, for the territorial electoral constituencies.[4]

Not only were ordinary workers directly represented in the Soviets but they were themselves frequently drawn into assisting the work of Soviets by serving in Soviet agencies in a voluntary capacity.

The third proposition Lenin made about Soviet democracy was that its socialist basis enormously enhanced the freedom of ordinary people because it removed them from economic exploitation by the capitalist and landlord classes and made them the owners of the means of production. The Soviet socialist state not only gave them political liberties but provided the material conditions for the exercise of these liberties—the use of buildings for meetings, the use of printing presses and paper for their propaganda, etc.

Lenin's fourth proposition, based directly on Marx, was that only the proletarian state sought its own elimination. The purpose of its dictatorship was to build a communist society which would make possible the gradual withering away of the state, i.e. its disappearance as an agency of coercion although not of economic administration. The achievement of this objective would represent both the attainment of full democracy and the abandonment of democracy for it would be the democratic state which would wither away:

Only in communist society, when the resistance of the capitalists has been completely broken, when the capitalists have disappeared, when there are no classes (i.e., when there is no difference between the members of society as regards their relation to the social means of production), *only then* does 'the state . . . cease to exist', and it *'becomes possible to speak of freedom'*. Only then will really complete democracy, democracy without any exceptions, be possible and be realised. And only then will democracy itself begin to *wither away* owing to the simple fact that, freed from capitalist slavery, from the untold horrors, savagery, absurdities, and infamies of capitalist exploitation, people will gradually *become accustomed* to the elementary rules of social life that have been known for centuries and repeated for thousands of years in all copy-book maxims; they will be accustomed to observing them without force, without compulsion, without the *special apparatus* for compulsion which is called the state.[5]

The more complete democracy becomes the nearer the moment approaches when it becomes unnecessary.[6]

The key to the above contradiction lies partly in the acceptance of a dual definition of democracy, as a form of government (majority rule), and as a set of political beliefs or ideals. This dualism is also present in liberal democratic theory. Thus Lenin could predict the elimination of organized democratic government under communism but at the same time argue that individual freedom would continue and become fully effective for the first time in history. The other side to this contradiction is the persistence—following Marx—in drawing a distinction between state (i.e., coercive) functions and administrative and welfare (non-state) functions. These latter Lenin expected to survive under communism.

Lenin's theory of Soviet democracy was taken up by Stalin at various times over the years 1924–52. Stalin's additions to the theory were important but were mostly logical developments from Lenin's theory. Thus Stalin,[7] far more than Lenin, was forced to justify or to rationalize the continuation of the political monopoly of the Communist Party in the Soviet Union. His justification is still fully accepted, although it has become a little more sophisticated in recent years. I will discuss it later in this chapter. His second modification, logical in terms of the situation if not of the theory, was his modification of that section of the theory relating to the withering away of the state under communism. This has already been discussed in an earlier chapter. Related to this was a third modification to Lenin's theory. This was the theory of the increasing severity of class struggle as socialism develops. This was a dubious proposition in terms of the underlying theory and was formally abandoned in the Soviet Union in the mid-1950s. Stalin's fourth modification related to a specific section of Lenin's theory, namely the explanation of the Soviet electoral system. The replacement of functional or vocational representation by territorial electorates in 1936 necessitated some restatement of Lenin's theory at this point and an abandonment of the claim that Soviet representative institutions were superior because of their irregular and indirect election and because they were based directly on economic enterprises.

What is the present-day concept of Soviet democracy* and how far has it advanced from that developed by Lenin and Stalin? The definition of the state as no longer a 'proletarian dictatorship' but a 'state of the whole people' was adopted at the 22nd Party Congress in October 1961. It did not involve any substantial alteration to the argument about Soviet democracy. It did however remove one of the verbal difficulties, namely, the necessity of arguing that the Soviet Union was at once a democracy and a dictatorship. It also constituted a sort of pledge that the new Soviet leaders were seeking to reduce direct coercion and to emphasize consent and public participation in Soviet politics.

CONTEMPORARY THEORY OF SOVIET DEMOCRACY

The present-day Soviet theory of democracy contains the following propositions:

(1) Soviet democracy is socialist democracy. This in itself ensures that it is a higher form of democracy than parliamentary bourgeois democracy, irrespective of any shortcomings in its political institutions. Thus a Soviet scholar, F. Burlatsky, has recently stated that:

The yardstick of genuine democracy is not so much the form of the political machinery but, chiefly and mainly, who owns the national wealth, what the class substance of power is, which classes rule, what policy the state authority conducts and in whose interests it does it.[8]

(2) Soviet democracy, being based on a socialist society, guarantees individual social and political rights more effectively than any capitalist democracy. Public ownership and control of the economy ensures full employment, freedom from exploitation, equal opportunity and rising living standards for all members of Soviet society. Unlike under capitalism, workers play a direct part in the direction of the economy. As one Soviet writer puts it:

Real democracy, which actually obtains, is expressed not merely in democratic forms of state organisation. It is also expressed in that the working people manage production both through their representatives and directly by taking part in production conferences, meetings of workers and collective farmers.[9]

Furthermore, improved material and cultural standards under socialism provide the most favourable conditions for the development of personal abilities and talents for millions of people.

* See Appendix VI.

In Soviet society all those rights and liberties which are usually inscribed in the constitutions of the democratic countries—e.g., recognition of freedom of speech, press, meetings, inviolability of the person, inviolability of the homes of citizens, and so on—really exist for the working people.[10]

(3) Soviet society, unlike bourgeois society, is fully united— 'Soviet democracy is now based on the complete moral and political unity that has been achieved in Soviet society,'[11] wrote a senior Soviet philosopher in the latter days of Stalin. The claim is still made, although less stridently. Thus a 1964 book states that:

The differences between classes are becoming more conventional than real, more relative than essential. There is a distinct community among them. Soviet society has no class fences. There are no barriers or restrictions to prevent a citizen going from one social stratum to another. It is often hard to determine what social bracket a person belongs to. A worker innovator, for example, is at once a worker and an intellectual. The demarcation between social groups is becoming less distinct. The various groups are gradually blending into a classless association of people of labour in socialist society.[12]

(4) The political monopoly of the Communist Party does not belie but confirms the claim that the Soviet state is democratic. Since antagonistic classes are held not to exist in the Soviet Union (workers and collective farmers are regarded as separate but non-antagonistic classes) there is no need for more than one party. The Communist Party is now said to represent all sections of Soviet society, as is evidenced not only from its social composition but from its policies and from its electoral support. A further rationalization of the monopoly position of the Communist Party is the historical argument. This runs something like this. At the outset (in 1917–18) there were competing parties. However, these soon compromised themselves by supporting counter-revolution and were consequently either suppressed or atrophied through members and supporters transferring their allegiance to the Bolsheviks. Since the early 1920s the Communist Party has enjoyed a monopoly but only because it has proved itself by its policies and achievements both in domestic and foreign affairs to be a party representing the interests of the people. If it occasionally erred and followed incorrect policies this was because of the historical accident of the personality cult of J. V. Stalin and was rapidly corrected after his death. Furthermore, if socialist democracy is to continue to develop and not to atrophy it requires the continuation of party control. For only the party can understand and interpret the real interests of the masses and guide social development in the shortest possible time to a fully fledged communist society. The following quotations, all from recent works, cover the salient points of this argument:

263

The essence of democracy does not consist of there being one or more parties in a given society but in the deeds of the political system and in the leadership of the party, in the worth of its power to the liberty and fundamental interests of the majority of the people, to the interests of the workers. As was shown above all the internal and external policies of the Soviet State, of the leadership by the Communist Party of the Soviet Union, proclaims that the Soviet system is fully democratic, is a fully popular system, for the highest aim and the daily care of the Soviet state is the general raising of the living standard of the population, the safeguarding of the peaceful existence of its people. There are not several parties in the USSR because there are no antagonistic classes here, the interests of which might be expressed by corresponding parties. Consequently, in the circumstances of victorious socialism, there is no ground for the existence of a multi-party system so as to provide the basis for oppositional struggle in the political arena.[13]

Only the Party can give correct political direction to the activities of all forms of organizations of the public, hasten the development of socialist democratism in the work of Soviets and raise their role as mass organizations. Thus the transformation of socialist statehood into communist social self-administration is impossible without the development of the leading role of the Party in the work of all mass organizations of workers—as in state so in social organizations.[14]

The Party exists for the people; in serving the people it sees the purposes of its activities. It continually advises the people on important questions of internal and external policy and widely draws the non-Party masses into participation in all its work.

The deeply democratic methods of its activities correspond to the all-people's character of the Communist Party. Its leadership rests on its moral authority, on the recognition of the correctness of its policy and on its leadership by the broadest sections of the people.[15]

(5) Soviet democracy, like any system claiming to be democratic, accepts the concept of popular sovereignty.

In the Soviet state all power derives from the people. All organs of state receive their power either directly from the hands of the electors or from the representative organs of the people.[16]

Soviet democracy recognizes the need for democratic representative institutions, for democratic elections, and for the accountability of state bodies and of individual deputies to their electorates. However the Soviet concept of representative government is very different from that commonly accepted in a parliamentary democracy. Firstly, it rejects the notion of professional parliamentarism on the grounds that parliamentarians are notoriously easy at making promises to their electors and difficult to control. Soviet deputies, unless they belong to the small minority of members of leading executive bodies, are unpaid amateurs.* Most of their time is spent in working in their normal occupations as factory workers, collective farmers or in professions. Secondly, it rejects the notion of the separation of powers between executive and legislative agencies. All Soviets are simultaneously empowered to legislate and to administer laws. Thirdly, it insists on mass participation in actual administrative work. This is achieved by a combination of curtailing the number of paid administrators, especially in local government, by inflating the size and membership of Soviets, by the practice of involving millions of non-deputies (the *activ*) in the work of Soviets as well as by practising a rapid rotation of membership of Soviets.[17] Fourthly, it rejects the view that electors should be permitted to form rival political parties and that political competition in the sense of open competition between rival parties or factions is essential for democratic government. On the contrary, it replaces the conventional notion of political representation by a notion of social representation.

The composition of Soviets reflects the social structure of Soviet society. Soviet deputies are workers, collective farmers, intellectuals, Communist and non-Party people of different nationalities. Through their composition Soviets of Workers' Deputies constitute fully representative organs.[18]

This is the basis for the Soviet claim that their system of representation is more democratic than those operating in parliamentary democracies.

The composition of the Soviets of Working People's Deputies reflects quite accurately the national, social and professional composition of the country's population.

Official statistics published in capitalist countries show that the proportion of workers and peasants in the population by no means corresponds to their representation in parliament where usually most of the M.P.s come from the propertied minority.[19]

(6) The Soviet concept of democracy insists that representative government must be supplemented by the direct participation of the people in the work of government, especially as advisers and critics in legislation, as supervisors of state agencies, and as petty administrators. In this sense the Soviet concept of democracy, like that of Athens, is one of 'direct democracy':

In distinction to representative democracy which means people's power through elected people's representatives in the organs of government, direct democracy supplements representation, gives to the people the possibility of direct participation in the work of state administration.[20]

Popular participation is cherished because it is held to provide checks

* Members of the Supreme Soviets receive free travel to the capital and a token payment during sessions.

against the development of bureaucratic practices and because it enables the size of the bureaucracy to be limited. It is also cherished because unless there is a spectacular increase in popular non-official participation in the immediate future the objective of replacing the socialist state by communist self-administration must remain a utopian pipe-dream.

(7) The Soviet concept of democracy includes the principle of accountability and removability of representatives and office holders. This principle is not altogether the same as that found in parliamentary democracies. Accountability of executive bodies to Soviets is considered fulfilled if executive committees make regular reports to their Soviets which normally happens only once or twice each year. Accountability of deputies to their electors is given far greater stress. Deputies are expected to report frequently to their electors and unsatisfactory deputies may be recalled. However the Soviet notion of accountability (*podotchetnost*) differs enormously from the British notion of Cabinet responsibility because it does not include provision for the replacement of the government in response to an electoral defeat. The Soviet theory of democracy requires a democratic electoral system but this requirement is held to be met if universal adult suffrage operates and if the electoral system provides for all recognized collectives and organizations having the right to nominate candidates and thus ensure the representation of all important sections of society in the organs of state power.[21] Finally, the Soviet notion of accountability covers only state or governmental organs. Communist deputies are accountable to the electorate as are non-Communist deputies, but the leading organs of the Communist Party, which are the main political organs in the country, are accountable only to the Party Congress.

My purpose is analysing the Soviet concept of democracy at such length has been to show its historical relationship to Western democratic theory and also the extent to which it has diverged from it. I have argued that while Soviet and Western theories of democracy share a common historical origin the contemporary theories (and of course practice) differ widely. While Soviet theorists still define democracy as majority rule and place considerable emphasis on individual rights they do not recognize minority rights except in peculiarly circumscribed conditions as within a primary party or social organization. Secondly, Soviet theory rejects many theoretical concepts found in the Western theory of democracy, such as 'separation of powers', 'division of powers', 'ministerial responsibility', 'the rule of law', etc. These principles are of course largely derived from the practice of parliamentary government or from English common law. Thirdly, while Soviet theory includes principles of electivity and accountability and removability of office holders, it couples the concept of 'direct democracy' to the concept of representative democracy. It is not my purpose here to go beyond this and to undertake a philosophical discussion of the Soviet theory of democracy. That there are deficiencies in this theory is obvious and an examination of the practice of Soviet democracy will bring some of these to light.

DOES SOVIET PRACTICE CONFORM TO THE SOVIET CONCEPT OF DEMOCRACY?

It is patently obvious that the Soviet state under Stalin was not a democracy even in the Soviet sense of the term. The mass purge, police terror, non-observance of established norms and Stalin's personal power, all involved breaches of Soviet democracy. Many other practices such as the absence of competing parties, the Communist Party monopoly of leadership, democratic centralism, etc., which are often attacked by Western writers as being undemocratic, are not inconsistent but are in conformity with the Soviet concept of democracy.

The following features occupy a central place in the Soviet concept of democracy:

(1) Soviet democracy is based on socialism.

(2) Mass participation in the governmental process, including criticism of administration and policy, participation in administration, supervision of administrative agencies, etc.

(3) A governmental structure which is based on popular election and which is accountable and ultimately responsible to the electorate and which allows for accommodation and adjustment and evolutionary change.

(4) Guarantees of individual rights.

(5) A Communist Party which is popularly based and which enjoys widening mass support.

SOVIET DEMOCRACY IS BASED ON SOCIALISM?

The claim that the Soviet state is a socialist state rests on four grounds. Firstly, that the former exploiting classes of capitalists, landlords and kulaks have been liquidated and that Soviet society now consists of two friendly classes of workers and peasants, and a steadily expanding intellectual stratum which is drawn chiefly from the workers and the peasants. Secondly, that the Soviet state is controlled by and in the interests of the working people. Thirdly, that the state owns all the main means of production and that the economy is operated according to a central plan for the good of the entire community. Fourthly, that the Soviet political system is democratic and that its democracy is steadily improving. Only the third of these claims is readily conceded and then only in part. Many Westerners, including Marxists (such as Trotsky and Djilas) have refused to accept the official description of Soviet society. Few Westerners would concede the second and fourth claims which are concerned with the relationship between Soviet society and democracy. Only this aspect of the problem will be examined here.

It is difficult to test the proposition that the policies of the Soviet state are in the interests of the Soviet people. Many policies adopted and implemented over recent years have obviously been in the public interest—the raising of pensions payments in 1956 and 1964, the extension of pensions to collective farmers in 1964, higher prices for agricultural products delivered to the state, wage increases for lower paid workers, increased allocations for public education, health, housing, and the production of consumer goods, etc. But was collectivization in the public interest in 1930? Is it in the public interest today? Were the reductions in the Soviet armed forces undertaken in 1959–60 in the public interest? On the last issue Khrushchev thought so but apparently the generals thought otherwise. What the ordinary people thought on the matter we really don't know, as there is no mechanism for allowing conflicting policies to be freely presented to the public. Even if there were it would not be possible to argue that all policies securing majority electoral support were in the public interest. The same difficulty arises with the proposition that general plans are invariably for the good of the community. They are in a sense but the Party leadership, top planners and administrators, at most a few thousand people, decide the perspectives of the economic plans. And clearly many perspectives are compromises necessitated by the problem of distributing the available means over different and often conflicting claims.

Soviet workers and collective farmers do not automatically work harder because they are legally joint owners of the enterprises they work in. As far as the collective farmers are concerned they generally work less efficiently on the collective farm than on their private plots. But this is perhaps as much a consequence of inadequate incentives provided for work performed in the collective farm economy than a rejection of the principle of collective farming. Where wages are directly linked to the quantity and quality of work performed both workers and farmers respond. Furthermore, from my own observation as well as from my reading, I believe that Soviet workers have often acted as if they felt themselves the owners of their resources. This may be a 'false consciousness' but it is nevertheless there. Thus during the war Soviet workers performed many acts of heroism not merely in defending their homes but in defending their collective property. Such heroism as the removal under enemy fire of several hundred major industrial plants and their re-establishment in the rear[22] can be only partly explained as due to patriotism and it owed little to fear and coercion. The feeling of common ownership is an important ingredient in Soviet campaigns for 'socialist competition', for securing volunteers for the development of Kazakhstan and Siberia, and for enlisting the support of workers in the general process of rationalization and automation of industry. Rank and file workers do not directly run the factories but they share in the control of factories through their participation in Soviets to which all industries are responsible, through trade unions, production conferences and production committees. The latter two agencies have developed mainly since 1959. Until 1965 their role was largely to assist in technological development and rationalization of production processes. The industrial reorganization of late 1965 led to some extension of their activities and to an increased say in the allocation of factory profits.

The various forms of worker participation and 'worker democracy' discussed above are of course all closely guided by the Communist Party. However, the very complexity, number and scope of these organizations (trade unions, shop committees, production conferences, production committees, etc.) does seem to have produced more than elsewhere in Soviet society the democratic practices of free discussion, variety of opinion and individual and group initiative.

MASS PARTICIPATION

Democracy of any sort requires some degree of mass participation. But whereas in parliamentary democracy this is primarily concerned with participation through the political parties and through elections, in Soviet democracy mass participation goes much further. In addition to the nearly universal participation of Soviet citizens in elections* to local, republican and all-Union Soviets, the Soviet Union develops mass participation through at least four other ways— through public debate of policy and legislative proposals; through popular involvement in administration; through participation in the running of social organizations such as trade unions, co-operatives and collective farms, comradely courts, volunteer militia and fire brigades, street and house committees, parents' councils, pensioners'

---

* Soviet authors view Soviet elections as simultaneously acts of *representative government* and of *direct democracy*. Mass participation is required to provide the canvassers (the agitators) and to man the complex network of electoral commissions.

councils, women's councils, etc.; and through socialist competition.

Many parliamentary systems have sought to involve the public directly in the process of legislation by means of popular initiative and referenda. Since 1956 the Soviet Union has made a regular practice of holding public discussions on important legislation and Party policy. Such public discussions serve to rally mass support for newly-formulated Party policy. They also provide criticism of the detail of central policy and allow for its modification before adoption. This happened, for example, during the 1956 discussion on the Pensions Law, during the 1957 discussion on industrial reorganization, and during the 1958 discussion on the Education Act. These periodic public debates also stimulate and facilitate criticism of administrative failures since they provide a sort of 'open season' for this type of criticism. Such public discussions are of course conducted as Party campaigns and no doubt many of the meetings held during such campaigns are deadly formal. It is also noteworthy that the proposal contained in the Party Programme (adopted October 1961) for frequent referenda, under which new policies would be submitted to the entire electorate for approval or rejection, has not been implemented.

The intricate governmental system of the USSR requires many millions to run it. Thus at present there are over 2 million deputies of local Soviets alone, more than half of them serving their first term of office. At the local level more than 1·5 million deputies are members of Standing Commissions of local Soviets together with 2·7 million non-deputies. Hundreds of thousands of citizens are engaged as voluntary workers in the departments of Executive Committees of local Soviets. The same practice operates at the level of the Supreme Soviets. Thus while only 62 deputies of the USSR Supreme Soviet served on the Legislative Proposals Commissions during 1963, 450 persons were members of the sub-commissions of these Legislative Proposals Commissions and a further 350 persons were consulted as advisers.[23]

If the operation of local Soviets directly involves 4–5 million citizens the operation of the network of social organizations involves many more people. Electoral Commissions (an intermittent responsibility) require some 8–9 million citizens. Trade union committees and production conferences involve over 20 millions—there were 470,000 primary trade union committees alone in 1963.[24] Allowing for overlapping membership perhaps 25–30 million persons are directly involved in local government, trade union and social organizational work at any one time. The total number of 'activists' directly and indirectly involved in local government was estimated at 20 million at the time of the 22nd Congress and at 23 million in 1963.[25] This represents about one in six of the adult population. Many provinces claim a one in five participation. Since most of the positions are rotated every few years there can be few Soviet adults who escape the responsibility of direct participation in government.

Socialist competition is designed to promote the fulfilment and over-fulfilment of the economic plan, but it also stimulates mass participation in production committees, production conferences, and trade union work generally. It was estimated in October 1963 that 26 million Soviet workers were involved in the movement of Communist Labour, and that this competition was a main factor in many enterprises fulfilling the Seven-Year Plan in under five years.

Western critics of the Soviet Union are apt to discount the process of mass participation on the grounds that it is not spontaneous but is prompted and supervised at all levels by the Communist Party. Soviet writers on the other hand seldom see any contradiction between Party control and the objective of developing democracy. Thus the authors of a recent textbook remark that, 'The control of the Party over the work of all links of the state apparatus develops Soviet democracy, strengthens the regime of Socialist legality and state discipline.'[26] More recently several Soviet writers have criticized various elements in the present campaign for increased mass participation. Thus Executive Committees of local Soviets have been criticized for developing non-staff departments under Executive control rather than transferring administrative functions to Standing Commissions of Soviets,[27] official statistics on the number of social organizations have been rejected as misleading,[28] unnecessary duplication between executive and Soviet-based agencies has been criticized, excessive enthusiasm leading to the formation of useless agencies has been lampooned,[29] and even the stifling effect of too-detailed Party control has been conceded.[30] My own view on the matter, based on a careful reading of a wide range of material over many years and some direct investigation of the problem during 1965, is that the Soviet system has achieved considerable success in its development of mass participation, especially in the countless petty tasks of local government. This has enabled a substantial reduction of paid officials but it may not have reduced Soviet bureaucratism. The Party has been directly responsible for much of this development so that the so-called 'voluntary organizations' are not voluntary in the full sense of the term. Furthermore, Party control, while it has often encouraged new activities and organizations, has sometimes curbed local initiative and enthusiasm.[31]

DEMOCRATIC ELEMENTS IN THE GOVERNMENTAL SYSTEM

Several elements of the Soviet governmental system have clearly improved over recent years. The electoral system continues under the

271

control of the Communist Party but it does provide for the ventilation of local grievances and gives some encouragement to local initiative. The extended activities of Standing Commissions of local
Soviets and the development of deputies' groups (either on a territorial basis or within factories and workplaces) has undoubtedly
strengthened the ties between deputies and electors. Reporting back
of individual deputies has been improved by the above developments
as well as by such practices as itinerant Executives and Standing
Commissions.* While complaints against the negligent deputy are
still frequent the situation is clearly improving. This improvement is
perhaps more the result of increased leisure and opportunity for
governmental work than of a heightened social consciousness.[32] A
further measure of this improvement is the increasing exercise of the
right of recall of deputies. Revived in 1959 this practice soon reached
up from local Soviets to Supreme Soviets. Over 400 deputies were recalled from local Soviets between March 1963 and the end of 1964.

The evidence also suggests that the majority of Executive Committees now make regular reports to their Soviets, and often directly to
their electors. The same trend may be observed in Supreme Soviets.
This suggests that there has been a considerable advance towards
regularity in government and that this has been accompanied by some
development of democratic forms. At all levels leadership has ceased
to be arbitrary and individual and has become regular and collective.

On the other hand the Communist Party leadership continues to
exercise a firm control over the process of democratic development.
So far it has been able to determine the direction of its development
and to establish its limits. While the scope of individual criticism has
been enlarged the impact of this has been felt only at the lowest level
in social and state, and perhaps, although we know little about it, in
Party primary organizations. Between this 'grass-roots' level and the
top there is a great gap which ordinary people accept with varying
degrees of resignation. Decisions relating to major policy changes
and appointments are taken within a small group of Party leaders.
At this level even the Central Committee of the Party and the USSR
Supreme Soviet are powerless. The most that can be said of the Soviet
leadership over recent years is that it has made some slight advance
towards curbing the concentration of power into the hands of one
individual and towards realizing the principle of collective leadership,
that it has improved existing ways and means of consulting informed
opinion in the community on specific issues, and that it has become
increasingly sensitive to public opinion.

* The itinerant Executive Committee or Standing Commission varies its
meeting place, meeting frequently in factories, schools or farms to enable
different sections of the electors to witness its work.

GUARANTEES OF INDIVIDUAL RIGHTS

Many of these in the past were more honoured in the breach than in the observance. Political rights apart, social rights were partially established and were generally extended even during the Stalin regime. Thus rights such as the right to work, equality of sexes, equality of nationalities, equality of citizens to education, to health and to leisure, were more nearly secured in the Soviet Union in the post-war period than they were in many parts of the capitalist world. These rights today are fairly completely enjoyed and redress can be had through the courts.* The political and religious rights, while considerable, are limited and in many respects are less than those enjoyed under capitalist democracies. Thus Art. 125 of the 1936 Constitution limited the basic civil liberties of freedom of speech, press, assembly and demonstration, to persons acting 'to strengthen the socialist system'. Similarly, Art. 124 of the same Constitution limited religious freedom by granting merely 'freedom of religious worship' while granting 'freedom of anti-religious propaganda'. Nor are these constitutional qualifications to political and religious liberty an empty letter. Political freedom is restricted by many parts of the Criminal Code as well as by lack of opportunity for organizing against the ruling party. The Criminal Code provides severe penalties for anti-Soviet (i.e., anti-Communist) propaganda. This section of the Criminal Code (Art. 70 of the RSFSR Code) was effectively used to convict two Soviet writers, A. D. Sinyavsky and Yu. M. Daniel, to terms of seven and five years' imprisonment with hard labour because they had published literary works outside the Soviet Union which the RSFSR Supreme Court held to be 'anti-Soviet propaganda' and slander.[33] Religious freedom has also been narrowly interpreted, especially during periods of active anti-religious campaigning and during the campaign against economic crimes which was carried on over the years 1961–64. Mosques, churches and above all synagogues, were publicly censored as habouring criminal elements and in some cases closed to religious worship.[34]

Again, the rights of individuals against arbitrary arrest and imprisonment are even now not so adequate as those guaranteed in Anglo-Saxon countries. This is so even under the Basic Criminal Code and Code of Criminal Procedure adopted in December 1958. While the latter guarantees that all court cases shall be tried in public and that

---

* However, complaints by individual workers and collective farmers against wage injustices are very common. They form a large part of cases handled by Labour Disputes Boards. In 1964 69% of appeals to the Procuracy under the 'general supervisory power' concerned breaches to *kolkhoz* law and to labour law. *Sovety dep. trud.*, No. 1, 1966, p. 12.

273

all accused persons have the right to defence,[35] it does not include the principle of *habeas corpus*. However, it is clear that there has been a considerable improvement of Soviet legal practice in recent years and fewer departures from a vastly improved law. Rights of appeal are not only guaranteed to individuals in criminal cases but in civil cases also. This extends to such matters as workers' appeals against adverse decisions of Labour Disputes Boards. In short, the Soviet concept of 'socialist legality' has at length been given some meaning, although it remains true that the institutional guarantees of civil rights are still very inadequate.

THE POPULAR BASIS OF THE COMMUNIST PARTY?

The degree of support for the Communist Party cannot be measured by the near unanimous verdict of Soviet elections. However, there is some evidence that the Communist Party not only enjoys continuing support but is extending its support. The Party membership is growing steadily and millions of non-Party persons are regularly involved in party campaigns. Both these facts are not new and have characterized periods of the Stalin era. However, the sustained expansion of membership of the Party since 1956 does suggest that support for the Party extends far beyond the limits of Party membership.

The Communist Party claim to be able to know the real needs of the people as distinct from their present wishes is often criticized by Western writers. However, this claim does not mean that the Communist Party ignores public opinion in the formulation of its policy. The bulk of recent evidence suggests that public opinion is an important factor in the determination of Communist Party policy. Public opinion certainly modified the leadership's educational reform measures in 1958. Again, the housing targets adopted by the Party and Government since 1956 have been increasingly subjected to upward revision as a result of public pressure.[36] Perhaps more significant than the overpublicized national discussions is the growing frequency with which sectional and expert opinion is consulted in the formulation of policy. The usual mechanism here is the conference or 'consultation' (*soveshchanie*). Such conferences are held on a national, republican, or zonal basis and consist of representatives of a particular speciality or profession or economic sector. The method was much favoured by Khrushchev. Thus 65 All-Union conferences and congresses involving 95,000 persons were held over the years 1953–59, while 103 involving 145,000 persons were held over two years 1960–61. In some cases such conferences took the initiative in suggesting new policy to party or state bodies. But, as Kotok correctly observes in reporting on these developments:

In the majority of cases the initiative in formulating new major questions of state, economic and cultural construction was taken by the Central Committee of the Communist Party of the Soviet Union.[37]

These developments notwithstanding, the one-party system has certain inherent weaknesses as an agency for expressing and formulating public opinion. Minority opinions are liable to be ignored since they are not permitted any independent organization.

CONCLUSIONS

My conclusions on the matter of Soviet democracy are as follows:

(i) The USSR is an unfinished socialist state, more advanced in its material and technological basis than in its political superstructure.

(ii) The USSR is a Communist state with some democratic elements. Democracy is a part of its ideology but this concept of democracy is in some respects deficient. In practice the Soviet system has been more undemocratic than democratic. The degree of Soviet democracy has not been constant and has varied widely since 1917. The periods of greatest democracy have been 1917–18, 1921–27 and since 1953.

(iii) In the last analysis the extent of Soviet democracy depends neither on the rights guaranteed in the Constitution nor on the activity of citizens through the Soviets but on the degree of inner-Party democracy and on the willingness of the Party leadership to exercise a voluntary self-restraint. This is an incomplete and an inadequate basis for democracy.

NOTES

[1] Very few Western books on Soviet politics include a discussion of the general Soviet theory of democracy. Among the exceptions are those by John N. Hazard, 1957, Ch. 1; and, Alfred G. Meyer, 1957, Ch. 3.

[2] Cf. Richard C. Gripp, 1963, p. 39: 'Lenin cannot be treated as a believer in democracy in either its theoretical or practical versions.' Cf. the explanation of the 1936 Constitution as mainly for the purpose of making propaganda abroad; Merle Fainsod, 1954, pp. 313–15. Herbert McClosky, John E. Turner, 1960, p. 292.

[3] V. I. Lenin, 'The State and Revolution', *Selected Works*, Vol. 7, 1946, p. 81.

[4] V. I. Lenin, 'Theses and Report on Bourgeois Democracy and the Dictatorship of the Proletariat' (Submitted to the 1st Congress of the Communist International, March 4, 1919). *Selected Works*, Vol. 7, 1946, pp. 231–2.

[5] 'The State and Revolution', *Selected Works*, Vol. 7, 1946, p. 81.

[6] *Ibid.*, p. 93.

[7] See in particular J. V. Stalin, *On the Draft Constitution of the USSR*, November 1936; and Speech to the 19th Congress of the CPSU, October 14, 1952.

[8] F. Burlatsky, author of the famous article advocating a Soviet political science which appeared in *Pravda*, January 10, 1965, 'Politics and Science'. The

quotation here is from the article 'The Development of Socialist Democracy at the Present Stage of Communist Construction'. English translation included in G. Glezerman, *Democracy in the U.S.S.R.*, Soviet News Booklet, London, 1958, pp. 76–96.

⁹ G. Glezerman, *op. cit.*, p. 40.

¹⁰ *Ibid.*, p. 74.

¹¹ M. B. Mitin, 1950, p. 32.

¹² F. Burlatsky, 1965, p. 84.

¹³ V. F. Kotok, 'Socialist Democratism and the Soviet State', in *Voprosy sovetskovo gosudarstva i prava 1917–1957*, USSR Academy of Sciences Press, Moscow, 1957, p. 165.

¹⁴ G. V. Barabashev, K. F. Sheremet, Ch. 2 of *Sovetskoe gosudarstvo i obshchestvennost v usloviyakh razvernutovo stroitelstva kommunizma*. Moscow University Press, 1962, p. 57.

¹⁵ A. S. Fedoseev, ed., 1964, p. 52. The statement is from Chapter 2 written by Fedoseev.

¹⁶ V. F. Kotok, 'Fundamentals of Soviet Constitutional Law.' Ch. 4 in Fedoseev, *op. cit.*, p. 97.

¹⁷ Cf. V. F. Kotok, 'Fundamentals of Soviet Constitutional Law', in Fedoseev, *op. cit.*, pp. 184–5:
'Soviets of Workers' Deputies constitute a new higher type of representative organ, where the deputies not only discuss important questions of state leadership and take decisions on them, but carry these decisions into life. Thanks to this their Soviets are working organs which concentrate in their hands full state power.

'The order of work of Soviets has accommodated itself to the fact that the deputies have not turned into professional parliamentarians as in bourgeois states but have remained workers in production, and in economic and cultural construction, in daily close contact with the popular masses. For this reason Soviets are convened periodically in short sessions for discussion and decision of questions of state but in the remaining time all the deputies carry into practice the decisions adopted, organize the masses for the fulfilment of the tasks of communist construction.

'The system of elections to Soviets also forms a guarantee against the transformation of deputies into a narrow caste of professional parliamentarians. With the aim of enlisting in the representative organs the widest section of all workers, and also in order to exclude the possibility of abuse of power from the side of securely elected persons, the Programme of the CPSU has adopted the principle of systematic rotation in the composition of leading organs.'

¹⁸ V. F. Kotok, 'Socialist Democratism and the Soviet State,' pp. 118–69 of *Voprosy sovetskovo gosudarstva i prava 1917–1957*, Moscow, 1957, p. 145.

¹⁹ G. Glezerman, *op. cit.*, 1958, p. 26.

²⁰ V. F. Kotok, *Sezdy i soveshchania trudyashchikhsya–forma neposredstvennoi demokratii*, Moscow, 1964, p. 3.

²¹ V. F. Kotok, *Sovetskaya predstavitelnaya systema*, Moscow, 1963.

²² Thus in August–September 1941 the workers of the Zaporozhe Steel Plant assisted the Soviet Army to hold up the German advance for 45 days while the plant was dismantled and the equipment (8,000 van loads of it) sent to the rear. Ralph Parker, *Moscow Correspondent*, F. Muller, London, 1949, p. 63. Cf. the series of stories collected by K. Simonov in *Shtrikhi epopei*, Tashkent, 1960.

²³ G. Vorobev, *Sovety dep. trud.*, No. 8, 1963, pp. 27–30.

²⁴ V. V. Grishin, Report to the 13th Congress of Soviet Trade Unions, *Izvestia*, October 30, 1963.

²⁵ V. Kotov, *Sovety* No. 10, 1963, pp. 10–16. There were 966,412 public

organizations in the RSFSR in 1964 with 9,724,372 members. *Sotsializm i narodovlastie.* Moscow, 1965, p. 88.

[26] K. F. Sheremet, G. V. Barabashev, 1961, p. 65.

[27] V. I. Razin, ed., 1965, pp. 114–15. Cf. S. V. Soloveva, 1963, pp. 64 f. L. Karapetyan, V. Razin, 1964, Ch. 3.

[28] A good example of the occasional scepticism to be found in local newspapers is the report, 'What the speaker didn't mention' which appeared in *Severnaya Pravda* (Kostroma) January 16, 1965.

[29] Cf. V. I. Razin, *op. cit.*, pp. 111–12.

[30] Yu. Feofanov in *Izvestia*, May 8, 1959, p. 2, 'From Positions of Strength'.

[31] See my article 'Local Soviets Today', *Soviet Studies*, April 1966.

[32] 81·1% of deputies of local Soviets elected March 1963 reported back to their electorates during 1964 compared with 48·2% during 1955. On the connection between leisure and governmental and public work see V. I. Razin, *op. cit.*, pp. 29 f. This view is certainly confirmed by a recent sociological survey of deputies in Estonia reported in *S.G.i.P.*, No. 10, 1965, pp. 65–70. This survey was based on a questionnaire sent to 994 deputies (8·5% of all deputies) of local Soviets in Estonia. On the matter of the level of activity of deputies correlations were found with urbanization, age, occupation and education. Only 38·9% of deputies reported spending more than four hours per week on deputy's work.

[33] *Pravda*, February 11 and 15, 1966.

[34] Cf. John Lawrence, 'Soviet Policy towards the Russian Churches, 1958–64', *Soviet Studies*, January 1965, XVI, pp. 276–84.

[35] Arts. 11 and 12 of the Basic Code of Judicial Procedure of the USSR, Union and Autonomous Republics, approved by the Supreme Soviet of the USSR, December 25, 1958.

[36] The 20th Congress in February 1956 adopted a target for public urban housing of 205 million square metres. On July 31, 1957, the Central Committee of the CPSU and the USSR Council of Ministers raised this target to 215 million square metres. Additional funds were allocated to enable this higher target to be realized. At the same time the target for private housing was raised from 84 to 113 million square metres. The 21st Party Congress in February 1959 adopted a target of 650–660 million square metres (or 15 million flats) for public housing over the seven years 1959–65 and 7 million homes in the rural areas, while housing funds were to be increased 80% over the previous seven years. The Supreme Soviet in December 1964 increased the housing construction target for 1965 by 13% above 1964.

[37] V. F. Kotok, 1964, p. 86.

SELECTED BIBLIOGRAPHY

Bayanov, B., *et al.*, 1968.
Boffa, G., 1960, Ch. 14.
Braham, R. L., 1965, pp. 391–406.
Glezerman, G., 1958.
Hazard, J. N., 1968, Chs. 1, 13.
Karpinsky, V., 1948, Chs. 2, 6, 7.
Lenin, V. I., 1943–46, Vol. 7, pp. 1–264.
Shaffer, H. G., 1965, Ch. 8.
Stalin, J. V., 1945, pp. 540–68.

Chapter 18

THE POST-STALIN ERA

Soviet politics since the death of Stalin has undergone many changes both in leaders and in policies. There is however no general agreement as to how far the changes have gone or on the significance of the various changes. For some each new round of change is acclaimed as the latest proof of the steady progress of the Soviet system towards greater democracy and socialism. Others acknowledge these same changes as further evidence that the Soviet system is an 'enduring despotism'.

THE SOVIET POWER STRUGGLE

The struggle for power between opposing groups and persons is a basic element in any political system. Yet this obvious truism does not in itself explain the peculiar stress of Western writers on power struggles in the Soviet Union. This derives from the unusual ruthlessness of the Soviet power struggle as well as from the fact that the death of Stalin removed a main stabilizer of the Soviet political system and increased the inherent instability of its political leadership. Since so much of this power struggle takes place behind the scenes Soviet citizens as well as Western Kremlinologists have had to pay close attention to such mute witnesses of changes in the leadership as the sudden removal of a portrait from a gallery of leaders, the dropping of a name from a list or the sudden variation in the printed order of the names of the Party leaders attending an important social function. This preoccupation with Soviet power struggles is strengthened by the models which Western writers use for the interpretation of Soviet politics. Soviet politics is generally seen as the competition within an elite or between dependant elites from which the masses are completely excluded.

For several years after Stalin's death many Western writers considered that the basic element in Soviet politics was the struggle for personal power between the leaders. The period March 1953–June 1957 was regarded as a sort of interregnum comparable to that which existed in the Soviet Union for five years after the death of Lenin.

278

The power conflict during this interregnum was said to have passed through several stages. Thus the months of March–July 1953 saw the domination of the triumvirate of Malenkov–Beria–Molotov. From July 1953 to February 1955 there was the triumvirate of Malenkov–Khrushchev–Molotov. From February 1955 to June 1957 there was the Khrushchev–Bulganin duumvirate. In June 1957 the Soviet Union reverted to a personal dictatorship under Khrushchev.

This sort of explanation is far too schematic even when it is given an institutional basis and the swing from oligarchy to autocracy between 1953 and 1957 is seen as a natural response to the imbalances of the system rather than as the outcome of a purely personal lust for power on the part of Khrushchev.[1] Not only was Khrushchev not a second Stalin but his position was not identical with that of Stalin. A further weakness of this approach is that it does not allow for a proper evaluation of policy differences in the political process. At most, policy differences are seen as providing a device by which individuals and factions within the leadership seek to legitimize the crudities of the power struggle. But this provides only a partial explanation. Not only are the leaders conditioned by the ideology but many if not all of the policy disputes in past decades have sprung from the underlying social structure. It is a myth of Western political scientists that Soviet society is simply the creation of Soviet politics and that politics is not a reflection and an adjustment of Soviet society.[2] It was partly in recognition of this fact that Western political scientists since the mid-fifties have been moving over to some sort of group explanation of Soviet power struggles. Thus Professor Hazard of Columbia in his important work *The Soviet System of Government* (first published in 1957) argued that a major factor in the Soviet political system today was the pressure of intellectuals seeking a greater share in the formulation of party policy. This is an interesting hypothesis but as originally advanced by Professor Hazard it suggested a greater degree of cohesion and group consciousness on the part of Soviet intellectuals than existed in fact. It also suggested that they were capable of acting as a group within the Party to force concessions from reluctant central leadership.

A later writer, Roger Pethybridge, in *A Key to Soviet Politics* (1962) argued that the clash of leaders reflected the clash between the rival interest groups of the party apparatus, the government bureaucracy, the technical elite, the army and the secret police. Still later, Dr. T. H. Rigby of Canberra, distinguished twelve types of internal conflict within the Soviet system,[3] including those between the principal leader and secondary leaders who have a common interest in setting limits to the former's powers; those between different individuals and groupings within the secondary leadership competing for influence over the

279

principal leader; conflicts between different aspirants for the position of principal leader; between the interests of one area and another; between 'masses' and party or regime, and so on. While this classification recognizes the existence of groups in Soviet politics it doesn't go far towards classifying them. A more recent book by two American scholars does precisely this. Brzezinski and Huntington in their *Political Power: USA/USSR* (1964) recognize three levels of 'group' politics in the Soviet Union. At bottom there are the 'amorphous social forces', including peasants, manual workers, 'white-collar' workers, technical intelligentsia, etc., which exert a social pressure but which are not capable of exerting direct political pressure. Secondly, there are the 'specific interest groups' such as the intellectuals, scientists, Jews, etc., which operate purely defensive strategies in order to retain their limited autonomy. Thirdly, there are the 'policy groups' which advocate to the leadership certain courses of action. These include the military, heavy industry managers, light industry managers, agricultural experts, cultural experts, state bureaucrats, and so on.[4]

These recent attempts to apply a modified group theory to Soviet society offer scope for a more realistic interpretation of Soviet politics than was possible on the basis of a rigid totalitarian model. However, much less information and less exact information is available on Soviet group conflicts than is available on pressure groups in parliamentary states. There is moreover a danger that interest-group theory might be transferred too mechanically to a distinctive society. Certainly some writers in recent years have exaggerated the independence of Soviet political groups and consequently ignored the continued cohesion of the political leadership as a whole. So far the major changes to the Soviet political system have been initiated from above, not in response to pressure from intellectuals, technical bureaucrats, military or any other group. And the leadership has initiated these changes not merely to preserve its own power but out of recognition of the fact that the authoritarian controls of the early industrialization period are no longer necessary, or even possible, because the complex industrial and agricultural processes of the Soviet Union today require more flexible, more decentralized, and more democratic forms of management.

One qualification is perhaps necessary to the above generalization. On two occasions in recent years, in the first months after Stalin's death and in the first months after Khrushchev's removal, the leadership obviously made concessions to particular interests which were dictated partly by the uncertainty of how the population at large would react to the change in leadership. Thus in 1953 not only Malenkov but Beria competed to offer more consumer goods and more liberal controls. After Khrushchev's removal the new leaders immediately announced concessions to the collective farmers in relation to their private plots and in December 1964 announced substantially increased allocations for public housing, schools, nurseries and kindergartens, and improved living conditions.

STALINISTS VERSUS ANTI-STALINISTS

It is fairly common both in the West and in the Soviet Union to interpret Soviet power conflicts as between Stalinists and anti-Stalinists, or Conservatives and Progressives. That these trends have operated since 1953 is clear enough; the difficulty is to attach the terms accurately to any of the political divisions that have occurred. If Molotov and Kaganovich deserve the title 'Stalinist' do Malenkov and Beria? Again, what is the basis of the common Western evaluation of Malenkov as a 'liberal', as the initiator of a consumer-directed policy? Part of the evidence quoted for this interpretation is Malenkov's speech to the Supreme Soviet on August 8, 1953.[5] Yet in this speech Malenkov said:

We shall continue in every possible way to expand our heavy industries—metallurgical, fuel, power, chemical, timber, machine construction and building industries—and to develop and perfect our transport system. We must always remember that heavy industry is the foundation of foundations of our socialist economy, for without its development it is impossible to guarantee the further development of light industries, the growth of the productive forces of agriculture, or to strengthen the defensive power of our country.

Now on the basis of the successes achieved in the development of heavy industry, we have all the conditions necessary for the organization of a sharp increase in the production of articles of popular consumption.

We have every possibility of doing this, and we must do it. In the past 28 years the output of means of production in our country has increased approximately 55 times; the output of consumer goods on the other hand has increased only 12 times in this period. Comparison of the 1953 level of production with the pre-war 1940 level shows that in this period the output of means of production has increased 3 times but the output of consumer goods by only 72 per cent.

The volume of production of consumer goods cannot satisfy us.

Hitherto, we had no possibility of developing light industries and food industries at such a tempo as heavy industry. At the present time we can, and consequently, we are obliged in the interests of securing a more rapid rise in the material and cultural standards of the people, to force the development of light industry.[6]

However, neither in this speech nor elsewhere during the years 1953–55 did Malenkov explicitly urge a higher rate of investment for consumer goods industry than for capital goods industry.[7]

The increased emphasis on consumer goods industry was generally accepted in 1953–54 and has been resumed with new emphasis since the 20th Congress early in 1956. When Malenkov was demoted in February 1955 it was on grounds of inefficiency and errors in agriculture rather than on grounds of investment policy.[8] Nor did the long statement issued by the Central Committee in July 1957[9] make any reference to Malenkov's supposed divergency on industrial development policies, although Kozlov, in an article in *Leningradskaya Pravda*, July 5, 1957, explicitly accused him of this.[10] It is sometimes suggested that Malenkov's policy resulted in a reduction of amounts appropriated for defence (the expenditure on defence declining from 23·6% of the total budget in 1952 to 17·8% in 1954), while the removal of Malenkov in 1955 reversed this trend.[11] Yet the downward trend was resumed in 1956 and between 1956 and 1961 the defence expenditure fell from 18% of the total budget to 11·9%.

On this question the weight of available evidence suggests that the Party leadership was united in following the 'new course' in 1953–54, but that divisions developed over the extent to which it was to be carried and over the methods of realizing it. Thus Malenkov's leadership in 1953–54 resulted in a virtual levelling of the growth rates of capital goods and consumer goods industries, notwithstanding formal approval by all leaders of the priority for capital goods industry. Malenkov also seems to have favoured a more reckless financial policy for realizing his targets for consumer goods, including the diversion of funds and the use of foreign exchange to secure imports.[12] On agriculture, Malenkov favoured improving old farming areas whereas Khrushchev favoured the 'crash programme' of cultivating the virgin lands. Molotov, it is said, opposed the opening up of virgin lands altogether.[13]

The labels 'Stalinist' and 'anti-Stalinist' are not altogether apt. The labels 'conservatives' and 'progressives' are perhaps more accurate, recognizing that these labels must be understood in a Soviet context. The label 'conservative' was in fact officially applied to the 'anti-Party group' by the July 1957 Central Committee statement. This statement made two sorts of charges against the opposition. Firstly, they were accused of using factional methods of struggle to oppose the Party line decided on by the 20th Congress. Secondly, they were said to have resisted the application of new policies in the spheres of agriculture, administrative decentralization and the reorganization of industry. It was this second charge which earned them the label of 'conservatives':

The basic position of comrades Malenkov, Kaganovich and Molotov, taking them away from the Party line, rested on the fact that they stood to one side and supported in the plenum old decisions and methods divorced from the life of the Party and the country. Not seeing new developments, new positions, they took a conservative stand and an irresponsible attitude to the development towards Communism.[14]

Over the years since 1957 this charge has been repeated on numerous occasions,[15] and some detail has been supplied. Thus Khrushchev, in an interview given to the American publicist, Gardner Cowles, on April 20, 1962, stated that:

Molotov, Kaganovich, Voroshilov and Malenkov, considered themselves all-powerful. . . . We said that what had happened under Stalin could not happen in the future. They replied, 'as it was, so it will be.' Then they announced, 'We'll get rid of you.' But our Party, our people, took over and they themselves were removed because they prevented the Party and the people from correcting all the wrongs and ills that were perpetrated by Stalin and themselves during the period of the personality cult.[16]

A RECONSTRUCTION OF THE POWER STRUGGLE SINCE 1953

I would suggest the following as a reconstruction of the inner-Party struggle since the death of Stalin.

The People Involved

Only four persons were mentioned in the July 1957 statement, Molotov, Kaganovich, Malenkov and Shepilov. The statement explicitly said that 'there wasn't anyone else who supported this group in the plenum of the Central Committee'. This statement was only formally true of the June 1957 plenum. The certain involvement of Saburov and Pervukhin and the probable involvement of Bulganin was pointed out by many Western commentators at the time. If these men were not involved in the opposition how could the demotion of Saburov and Pervukhin in June 1957 be explained and how could so many members of the government Presidium be involved and Bulganin not be a party to it? This supposition was confirmed by subsequent Soviet statements. Bulganin was replaced by Khrushchev as Chairman of the Council of Ministers in March 1958 and was removed from the Party Presidium by the Central Committee plenum in September of the same year. At a subsequent plenum in December 1958 Bulganin admitted his involvement in the anti-Party group.[17] At the 21st Congress early in 1959 Saburov[18] and Pervukhin[19] admitted their support for the group. The 22nd Congress extended the list by adding Voroshilov.[20]

The Nature of the Opposition

The opposition was essentially a top-level affair. There is no indication that the anti-Party group in the top leadership attempted to organize support outside the Central Committee. Nor did the opposition at any time issue a programme. The nearest approach to this was the belated issue by Molotov of a circular letter to members of the Central Committee on the eve of the 22nd Congress.[21] There is no evidence of any opposition organization outside of the Party Presidium and the Council of Ministers. It is therefore perhaps more accurate to describe the 'anti-Party group' as an incipient faction rather than as a faction.

The Basis of the Opposition

The opposition began as a power struggle which developed immediately after Stalin's death. In the first instance this had nothing whatever to do with policy differences. Thus the March 6, 1953, deal between Malenkov and Beria was designed solely to prevent the further division of Stalin's power. Within days some details of this deal became known to the rest of the Party command who succeeded in allying with Beria to cut down Malenkov's powers. On March 14 he was forced to relinquish the post of First Secretary of the Central Committee. The ousting of Beria in July 1953 was also mainly a power struggle since his individual control over the entire police apparatus threatened to make him the head of a state within a state. Only the united front of the rest of the Presidium and the assistance of the army, enabled the arrest and removal of Beria. Power struggles within the leadership continued throughout 1953–57 but policy differences were increasingly involved. How important were these policy differences? It is impossible for an outsider to determine this accurately. In fact even the CPSU leaders differ among themselves on this matter. Thus while some speakers at the 22nd Congress stressed the role of policy differences, Kuusinen,* a member of the Presidium and Secretariat, declared that:

During my long life I have more than once had the opportunity of participating in the struggles of the Party against various kinds of factions —Trotskyists, Zinovievites, Bukharinites, and others. Usually each of these factions began the struggle against the Party with proclamations of political differences. But it soon transpired that the most important thing for them wasn't political differences but how to seize power. They placed their personal ambition and power higher than their devotion to the working class, to socialism and to communism.[22]

While conceding that the anti-Party group had certain differences with the rest on the handling of the personality cult and other matters Kuusinen declared that their main concern was to remove Khrushchev from the Party leadership and to seize power for themselves.

* V. O. Kuusinen, born 1881, died 1964.

Over the period July 1953–December 1956 Khrushchev's opponents were in a minority within the Party Presidium. In this period the opposition consisted only of three persons, Molotov, Malenkov and Kaganovich, with a fourth, Voroshilov, becoming involved only after the 20th Congress. They were probably only united in their opposition to the de-Stalinization campaign. Molotov had also opposed various foreign policy changes in 1953–55, in particular, the Peace Treaty on Austria in 1954 and the *rapprochement* with Yugoslavia in 1955. Molotov had opposed the virgin lands campaign while Malenkov had favoured alternative policies of agricultural reform. Shepilov, a candidate member of the Presidium and for a time Minister of Foreign Affairs, moved over to support the opposition group late in 1956 although precisely what caused him to desert his patron Khrushchev is not at all clear.[23]

The question of industrial reorganization which came to a head in 1956–57 at once enlarged the opposition and consolidated it. This happened because this was the most drastic of the administrative changes carried through to date and because it involved a direct threat to the power position of several top leaders including Kaganovich, Bulganin, Malenkov, Saburov and Pervukhin. Yet even here the opposition of these party industrial bureaucrats to the policy of industrial decentralization favoured by Khrushchev must have been supported by a good deal of rational argument in favour of a more cautious and less reckless approach to industrial reform.[24]

The Failure of the Opposition

The first reason for the failure of the opposition group is that they were hopelessly outmanœuvred by Khrushchev. By June 1957 the opposition had a majority both in the Party Presidium and in the Presidium of the USSR Council of Ministers. This enabled them to call a special meeting of the Party Presidium on June 18 and to demand Khrushchev's resignation. Apparently Khrushchev refused to resign from the First Secretaryship until the matter had been put to the Central Committee. The Presidium then detailed Voroshilov and Bulganin to put the recommendation to a special plenum of the Central Committee and Khrushchev and Mikoyan to put the case against. The opposition had to concede this because many Central Committee members, tipped-off by Khrushchev and brought up to Moscow by special army planes, were clamouring for a meeting. In any case the Central Committee invariably endorsed the recommendations of its Presidium, so the opposition felt they had little to fear from submitting the matter to the Central Committee. In the end a joint meeting of the Central Committee and the Party Auditing Commission met

(June 22–27) and decided against the opposition. It is said that no one voted against the resolution carried at the end of this meeting although Molotov abstained.[25]

The second reason for the failure of the opposition was the considerable popular support for Khrushchev's policies. This applied not merely to the de-Stalinization campaign but to his other policies. The bumper harvest in the virgin lands areas in 1956 was the crucial factor in producing a Union grain harvest 55% above the 1949–53 level.[26] The defeat of the opposition in the Central Committee was not simply due to Khrushchev's successful 'packing' of the Central Committee in 1956. At most one-third of the members can be considered as his 'nominees'. The strong representation of the intermediate level of Party organization in the Central Committee since the 20th Congress produced a natural support for Khrushchev's decentralization policy. It is also probable that most of the rank and file of the Party supported Khrushchev's policies and this support is a part of the reason for the rapid expansion of party membership since 1956. While party membership (including candidate members) rose by less than 5% between the 19th and 20th Party Congresses it rose by more than 14% between the 20th and 21st Congresses and by almost 18% between the 21st and the 22nd Congresses.

THE FALL OF KHRUSHCHEV

The key to Khrushchev's fall lies in an appreciation of the strengths and weaknesses of his position over the period 1957–64. After the crucial June 1957 plenum Western experts were fairly evenly divided between those who saw it as the decisive act in the restoration of individual autocracy and those who saw it as a temporary and incomplete victory for Khrushchev over his peers. Both groups could marshal some evidence to support their interpretation. The former group argued that the Soviet system could not survive long as an oligarchy because prolonged personal and factional struggles within the leadership would threaten the security of the regime. The rule was for an intense but relatively brief period of power struggles within the collective to be replaced by the domination of one leader. The June plenum saw the election of an enlarged Presidium and an enlarged Secretariat in which Khrushchev's supporters had a clear majority. In March 1958 Khrushchev became Chairman of the Council of Ministers while continuing to hold the position of First Secretary to the Central Committee. While plenums of the Central Committee continued to be held at regular intervals they served either as sounding boards for checking on the fulfilment of current policies in particular sectors or as platforms from which the First Secretary launched new policies.

Central Committee plenums and Party Congresses were increasingly marked by adulation and praise for the leader. Khrushchev's dominance was seen to be clearly demonstrated by his ability to launch without prior warning a complete reorganization of the Party and state structure from the regional level downwards at the very time when his foreign policy in Cuba had demonstrated its rashness and ineffectiveness.[27]

On the other hand, the hardened Kremlinologists heralded each minor change in the personnel of the Party leadership and each new tack in domestic or foreign policy as clear evidence of continued opposition to Khrushchev. This opposition was most frequently lodged in the military or the heavy industrialists who were said to be fierce opponents of Khrushchev's policies of reducing defence expenditure, de-emphasizing steel in the Soviet economy and increasing allocations for consumer goods.[28] Khrushchev's fall in October 1964 was naturally enough hailed as clear proof of the correctness of the latter group's position.[29]

Why then did Khrushchev fall? The official statement issued in *Pravda*, October 16, states that he was relieved from his three leading posts by the plenum of the Central Committee on October 14 because of 'advancing age and continued worsening health'. This implies that the initiative came from Khrushchev himself and that the collective of the Central Committee endorsed it. This is obviously untrue and has been tacitly admitted in subsequent official statements. Thus *Pravda*, October 17, 1964, published an editorial which indirectly accused the former leader of 'subjectivism and spontaneity in communist construction', and of 'bureaucratic methods and individual decisions ignoring the practical experience of the masses'. When the delegation of the British Communist Party visited Moscow early in November they were assured by the Soviet leaders that Khrushchev was dismissed because of differences over internal policy and:

because in recent years there had been more and more defects in his methods of leadership. The principles of collective leadership were violated. When an idea entered his head he hurried to put it into operation without due thought and without discussion with others. This applied especially to agriculture.

There had been many discussions and disagreements with Khrushchev in the Presidium, which finally felt that his methods had exceeded all possible limits and had become an obstacle. Part of the problem was his age and the fact that he was suffering from sclerosis. This contributed to his wrong methods of work.[30]

Foreign experts have added considerably to this list of differences and failures. Thus agricultural policies, foreign policy, defence policy,

287

inter-bloc relations, investment policy, industrial administration and party organization, have all been held to have produced the revolt against Khrushchev.[31] It is worth noting that Western writers have emphasized policy differences more than power factors while Soviet statements have sought to minimize policy differences and to emphasize differences over methods of leadership. In 1957 on the other hand, the Soviet statement emphasized policy differences as between the Khrushchev forces and the 'anti-Party group'.

How important then were policy differences in producing Khrushchev's fall? There is clear evidence of differences existing within the Soviet leadership both before and after October 14, 1964, on many elements of domestic policy. It is not however possible to identify either Khrushchev or his successors with firm positions on these matters. Take the question of the ratio of investment as between capital goods industry and consumer goods industry. This is a fairly fluid matter and most of the leaders involved have made what appear to be different statements from time to time even over a limited period. Closer examination, however, often shows these individual statements to have been guarded, qualified, and even contradictory. Thus Khrushchev made repeated attacks during 1960 and 1961 on 'certain comrades' with 'an appetite for metals that could only unbalance the economy'. In May 1961 he went so far to assert (as Malenkov had in August 1953) that, 'Now we consider our heavy industry as built. Light industry and heavy industry will develop at the same pace.'[32] However, this was not, and has never yet been presented as an objective realizable under any circumstances. The increase in the United States military budget in January 1961, the Bay of Pigs affair in April and the failure to make any headway with President Kennedy in the Vienna talks, led to a quick re-emphasis on defence needs and on heavy industry.

The debate within leading Party and government organs over investment strategy has never been abandoned at any period since 1953 but it has been intensified not only in response to changes in the international situation but whenever plans were nearing fulfilment and new long-range plans being drafted. Thus it welled up in 1955, 1959–61, and, towards the end of 1964 when the final year of the Seven-Year Plan was under discussion. Khrushchev's last stand on this matter was made at the enlarged meeting of the Party Presidium and the USSR Council of Ministers called to consider the economic guidelines for the next long-range plan at the beginning of October 1964. The fact that Khrushchev's speech was not printed in full as well as certain ambiguities in the summary (printed in *Izvestia*, October 2) suggests that there may have been differences of opinion at this conference. *Izvestia* summarized current policy in this way:

In composing the long-range plans for the next period comrade N. S. Khrushchev emphasized, it is necessary to be guided by the fact that the chief task of this plan is a further rise in the living standards of the people. Whereas during the period of the first five-year plans we laid chief stress on the development of heavy industry as the basis for an upsurge of the economy of the entire country and on strengthening its defence capacity, now, when we have a mighty industry, when the defence of the country is at the proper level, the Party is setting the task of the more rapid development of the branches that produce consumer goods.

We now have powerful metallurgy, modern machine building and highly developed power, fuel and other branches of heavy industry. At the present stage of communist construction our task consists in the further development of the means of production for the wider branches that produce consumer goods.

Basing ourselves on what has already been achieved and continuing to develop at steady tempos the production of the means of production, we should in drawing up the plan stipulate the acceleration of the means of consumption and a further rise in the well-being of the people. Of course, in doing so we must always keep the country's defences at the proper level, because there may yet be adventures by the imperialist powers against the countries of the socialist commonwealth.

Our country is now at the stage of its development when we should advance the satisfaction of the growing material and spiritual requirements of man into first place in working out the long-range plan for the development of our economy.[33]

This policy was not only in line with Khrushchev's utterances from 1960 onwards but with the decisions of the 22nd Congress.

Despite considerable speculation in the Western press in October 1964 and since that Khrushchev's fall would be followed by a re-emphasis on defence and heavy industry this has not happened. The economic plan adopted by the USSR Supreme Soviet in December 1964 provided for capital goods industry to increase production by 8·2% and for consumer goods industry by 7·7% over 1964.[34] Housing construction was to increase by 13% and expenditure on living conditions to increase by 18·7%. On the other hand defence expenditure was reduced from 14·5% to 12·9% of national expenditure.* We know far too little about the way individuals have argued in the debates over investment policy to be able to make much of it. Certainly the formula generally accepted since 1953 allows for considerable variations of emphasis within the common policy. But not all speeches seeming to record differences may be taken as evidence of their existence. An investment policy which contains more than one priority (e.g., defence, capital goods industry producing producer goods for capital production, capital goods industry producing producer

---

* Defence expenditure rose to 13·5% of the budget in 1968 but it had dropped to 10·3% by 1972.

goods for consumer production, consumer goods, agriculture, social services) will vary not merely because different speakers give different emphasis to different elements of the policy but also because of occasion and circumstance. Thus the Defence Minister speaking at the November rally always emphasizes the defence industry and its continued rapid development. This is a tradition and the occasion demands it. Likewise this happens with addresses delivered on Red Army day. When a leader addresses a rural gathering consisting of farmers and rural townspeople he naturally emphasizes the government's determination to increase investment in agriculture and to raise rural incomes and living standards.

In view of the minimal changes in Soviet foreign policy since Khrushchev's departure it seems unlikely that there were major differences over foreign policy. What seems more likely is that there were serious differences within the leadership not over the general direction of Soviet foreign policy but over some of the tactics followed by Khrushchev. The chief examples are two, the unbalanced emphasis given by Khrushchev to the importance of the 1963 agreement on nuclear weapons testing and the stubborn insistence of the former First Secretary on the holding of an international Communist Party Conference in Moscow in December 1964 when it was obvious that such a meeting could only worsen the relations within the communist world. On both matters the new leaders brought about a quick reversal of tactics.

Much of Soviet agricultural policy over the years 1953 to 1964 bore the Khrushchev stamp. However the leadership as a whole, especially after June 1957, accepted this policy and shared responsibilities for its failures and its successes. And at the time of the ousting of Khrushchev it was already obvious that the 1964 harvest was a good one, much better than those of the two previous years. There is some evidence of differences over policy especially in respect to the treatment of the individual plots and the new government quickly made concessions here. But apart from this the main complaint against Khrushchev on the agricultural question seems to have been directed at his recklessness on organizational questions. He did in fact put through five major reorganizations to the agricultural administration between September 1953 and the end of 1962. And while he no doubt consulted various colleagues and experts before he adopted a new reorganization they did seem to appear suddenly as if the First Secretary had had a brainwave so good that it couldn't wait.

The more I consider the question the more I lean towards accepting the basic explanation advanced in Moscow, namely, that Khrushchev fell more because of his methods of work and his temperament than because of policy differences with the other leaders. He had a mad genius for extemporizing administrative solutions to basic social problems that were no solutions at all. This streak of genius (or was it madness?) seemed to assert itself with increasing frequency over the last few years of his career. The frequent reorganizations in administration of industry and agriculture made the Soviet administrators at all levels from the central government to the rural *raion* insecure and uncertain. The changes, while they sometimes brought unexpected promotion, often brought added insecurity and made it increasingly difficult for the lower and middle-level administrators to fulfil the conflicting directives which came from the complex of central, republican and regional agencies.[35] And plan fulfilment is the key not only to promotion but to survival for such people.

The reorganizations which went through prior to November 1962 were disturbing but not disastrous. The reorganization to the Party and state structures which Khrushchev rushed through in November 1962 was ostensibly designed to improve Party direction and supervision and state management of both industry and agriculture. Khrushchev seems to have seized upon the obvious fact that Party organizations at the district and provincial-territorial levels were trying to do too many things at once and doing none of them properly. Thus *obkoms* neglected agriculture when the pressure was on to fulfil the quarterly industrial targets, but had to put the whole emphasis on to agriculture during the brief ploughing, sowing and harvesting periods. Party leadership became a series of campaigns or 'drives' rather than steady all-the-year-round direction of affairs. As the chief *apparatchik* Khrushchev could hardly find a solution by abandoning some of the jobs to purely state agencies. His solution was to remodel the Party organization according to the 'production-principle'. This meant that party members in industry (and as it turned out most urban party members) were organized into industrial branches. They were supervised by specialized Zonal Industrial-Production Party Committees or by City Party Committees. These in turn were supervised by Oblast or Krai Party Committees for Industrial Production. Similarly, all agricultural workers, collective farmers, agricultural scientists and technicians, and villagers were organized into agricultural party branches, supervised by Party Committees of Kolkhoz-Sovkhoz Production Management Boards which in turn were supervised by the Oblast or Krai Party Committee for Agricultural Production. State organizations—local Soviets and their Executive Committees—were organized along parallel lines (cf. p. 209).

This reform sounded all right on paper but it produced near administrative chaos and it also halved the orbit of responsibility and power of the territorial Party and state officials. Within months their power was further cut away by the enlargement of the *sovnarkhozy* which meant that no longer did the *sovnarkhoz* in the RSFSR usually coincide with an *oblast* or *krai*. The group of administrators affected by this reorganization numbered only a few thousand but this group held slightly more than half of the positions in the Central Committee. Thus if at first sight it may appear strange that Khrushchev, who had assisted between a quarter and a third of the Central Committee to their seats, and who had received such overwhelming support from the Central Committee in June 1957 should lose that support in October 1964, it is not strange when reconsidered. He lost the support after 1962 because he had forfeited it.

Nor must we consider that this group of important intermediate level Party *apparatchiki* reacted only to the reduction of their personal power and promotion prospects. As loyal Party men, albeit careerists, they were no doubt upset over the increasing difficulties they experienced after the division of the Party and governmental structures.

The evidence of the administrative confusion resulting from the implementation of the November 1962 decision consists of many articles, letters and pamphlets published during 1963 and 1964, which, while guarded in their criticism, nevertheless reflect the difficulties and the uneasiness of the local apparat.[36] The dismissal of Khrushchev was followed a month later by a decision of the Central Committee to re-establish a consolidated Party and state structure. The *Pravda* editorial of November 18, 1964 declared that: 'Life has shown the practical impossibility of bringing about a separation into spheres of the activities of the industrial and agricultural party organizations,' while the *Izvestia* editorial of November 19 claimed that:

The division of the Party, Soviet, trade union and Komsomol organs greatly complicated their work, called forth countless difficulties, resulted in a confusion of functions in the localities, limited the possibilities of rendering efficient help to the villages from the side of the industrial centres, and created distinct inconveniences for the population. The administrative apparatus during the past two years didn't become either simplified or more economical, but on the contrary, was inflated. Through this the *raion* link was noticeably weakened. In short, the reorganization not only did not bring the desired results but in relation to the most important parts of economic construction it led to the weakening of the influence of Party organizations in production activities.

The November 16 decision and official admission of the failure of the 1962 reorganization led to a spate of revealing articles in Soviet newspapers and periodicals.[37] Particular criticisms made included the complaint that the reorganization of the Party structure along production lines had resulted in increased Party interference in administration. Thus the Party Committee of the Karatalsk Sovkhoz-

Kolkhoz Administration in Alma-Ata Oblast, had 'interfered in the economic and operational-managerial activities of the board, examining and deciding questions which called for everyday and concrete examination by the specialists and directors of the administration', while at the same time the Party primaries suffered from neglect and inadequate assistance. The same article claimed that in Alma-Ata and in other *oblasts* 'the petty guardianship of the Party Committee froze the initiative of Soviet and economic cadres, inflicting obvious damage to their work'.[38] A secretary of the Industrial Production Party Committee of the Central Committee of the C. P. Ukraine, gave a graphic example of the confusion which resulted when the separation of Party and Soviet organs did not run strictly parallel. In the Mirgorod *raion* Party organizations within town-based agricultural agencies and establishments were placed under the control of the Agricultural Raikom. But under the reorganization of the Soviets these agencies and establishments were attached to the Town Soviet which was subordinated to the Poltava Industrial Oblast Soviet. In the town there were a number of non-agricultural agencies such as the industrial combine, the food combine, auto park, post office, printery, polyclinic, hospital, etc. Party organizations in these agencies also came under the control of the agricultural Party organization. However, in many cases the higher organs of these agencies came under the control of the Industrial Oblispolkom. The key to this muddle is no doubt that Mirgorod was regarded as the centre of a rural administration board by the Party but as an urban centre by the Soviets. How the confusion operated in practice is shown by the example quoted. The Industrial Oblast Party and Soviet Executive Committees took a decision relating to improving the living conditions of the population. However such a decision was not operative over those town-based agencies (such as the Mirgorod District House of Culture) which happened to be controlled by the Rural District Soviet.[39]

The precise method of Khrushchev's removal cannot yet be established. Early reconstructions by Western commentators[40] varied considerably as might be expected when there was so little information to go on. We don't know the role played by individual Presidium members, the extent of the involvement of the security police, or even whether there was a full meeting of the Central Committee. And while we know how the vote went we do not know how many supported and how many opposed the motion that Khrushchev should be relieved of his responsibilities. It does seem that Khrushchev was caught off guard. The decisive steps to remove him were taken while he was holidaying in the Crimea. He seems to have received a late summons to attend a meeting of the Party Presidium on October 13, after the Presidium had already been in session for some days presumably after it had already taken the decision to remove him. It seems likely that Khrushchev, having failed to alter this decision, then sought to repeat his June 1957 move of appealing to the full Central Committee. No doubt the Presidium had anticipated this move and had already directed sufficient members of the Central Committee to provide a quorum to attend an emergency meeting on October 14. We may take it that Khrushchev had no time to mobilize his strongest supporters and that he therefore lost the appeal. Thus for the third time in a decade the holder of the undefined and in a sense unconstitutional position of leader of the Soviet political system was decided through the agency of the Central Committee. Khrushchev's removal demonstrated a possible mechanism for solving succession questions within the Soviet system. However, the survival of the Party collective would seem to require some formalization of the procedure and perhaps the adoption of rules to prevent the same individual from simultaneously holding the top positions in the party and state structures and also some limit to the terms of office.*

Khrushchev helped to establish the conditions for his own removal. Not only did he re-establish the principle of the Central Committee as the final arbiter of leadership disputes but he established strict limits to the use of the purge and the police in solving these disputes. Finally, the anti-Stalin campaign, as well as personal memories of the Stalin period, must have made members of the Presidium particularly sensitive to any apparent threat of a new dictator. Khrushchev was not another Stalin but he was too much of an individualist for the cult of the collective.†

A PERSPECTIVE ON RECENT CHANGES IN THE USSR

The first thing to be said about recent changes in the Soviet Union is that the changes pre-date the death of Stalin by several months. The difficult and lengthy operation of restoring inner-Party democracy was begun at the 19th Congress in October 1952. Again, the Party Presidium was established at the 19th Congress, not as is sometimes imagined, after the death of Stalin. The significance of Stalin, his

* Some tentative suggestions along these lines were made by Soviet writers in 1963–65. However, the decision of the 23rd Congress to delete the rotational retirement rule in elections of Party committees at all levels would seem to indicate the resistance of the Party leadership to strict rules of rotation of office.

† Since this chapter was written a few full-length studies of the Khrushchev era and the post-Khrushchev era have been published. The most useful are: Robert Conquest; *Russia after Khrushchev*, Pall Mall, London, 1965; and, Roger W. Pethybridge; *A History of Postwar Russia*, Allen & Unwin, London, 1966.

death and denunciation, can easily be exaggerated. While these have been important elements in the Soviet political pattern over recent years the modernization of the Soviet economic, political and administrative structures goes much beyond curtailing individual dictatorship. It is probable that the material advances in Soviet industry and technology would have forced some tentative modifications to the Stalinist system even had Stalin survived beyond March 1953. It is certain however that his death provided a necessary condition for rapid reform and reorganization. This view is reinforced by the fact that at the time of his death Stalin was preparing for a new mass purge.

In my opinion the starting point for an explanation of the changes occurring in Soviet politics over the past two decades is a recognition of the fact that by 1950–52 the Soviet economy had matured, had come of age. By 1950 the Soviet economy had made good the major losses of the war and was producing at a rapidly expanding rate in almost all branches save agriculture. The physical volume of gross industrial production in 1950 was 72% greater than that of 1940, the production of producer goods was almost 105% above 1940 and that of consumer goods 23%.[41] By 1953 there were close on 200,000 state-owned industrial enterprises in the USSR and industrial and office workers and their families constituted over half of the total population. This development of the industrial system was accompanied by a rapid improvement in the educational and cultural standards of the people. Numbers of students attending Soviet tertiary educational institutes increased by 67% between 1940 and 1951 and 221,000 specialists graduated in 1952. By 1952 there were 5·5 million persons in the USSR with a university or senior technical school education, 120% more than in 1940.[42]

Since 1952 the political and legal superstructure has been adjusted to this material basis. But this adjustment has not been automatic. Although Soviet industry was producing at above the 1940 level by 1950 it was only in 1953–54 that there was a decisive shifting of emphasis towards the production of consumer goods and this emphasis was again reversed in 1955. Clearly, the majority of the Party leadership considered that industrial production had to be much more than that of 1940 before any significant improvement could be made in the output of consumer goods. This estimate was influenced not only by devotion to the dogma of a higher rate of investment for capital goods industry than for consumer goods industry and by the determination to overtake the United States as soon as possible, but also by the experience of the war as well as by the uncertainties of the international situation during 1950–54. The nearness of Soviet defeat during the Second World War combined with the development of the qualitative arms race after 1945 led to the continued stress on capital goods industry and defence. Production in consumer goods industry was 116% above the 1940 level by 1955 but production in capital goods industry was 289% above the 1940 level.[43] Soviet defence expenditure represented 20·1% of the USSR budget in 1950, 23·9% in 1952 and 18% in 1956. It had fallen to 11·9% in 1961 before the Berlin crisis and increases in Western military expenditures brought about a reversal of the downward trend. Linked with this was the uncertainty of the agricultural situation. The agricultural crisis of 1950–51 was not seriously grappled with until after the September 1953 plenum of the Central Committee and the impact of the new policies was not immediately evident. In addition to the above factors it is clear that factional struggles within the leadership over the period March 1953 to June 1957 delayed the adjustment of the political system to the changed material basis. Several of the inner group of leaders showed an understandable preference for old methods of industrial control and administration. Despite this resistance it was becoming increasingly clear by 1955–56 that the continued rapid expansion of the Soviet economy required drastic changes in the administrative and planning systems, including considerable decentralization of management, industrial supervision, finance and planning. Industry required rationalization while agriculture required substantially increased investment and genuine incentives. Yet it was only after the resolution of the factional struggle (roughly between the 'conservatives' and the 'progressives') within the Party Presidium in 1956–57 that the opportunities of directing the process of modification from primitive socialism to advanced socialism were fully realized.[44]

Although the political changes referred to above represent a readjustment to underlying social and economic changes they are not concessions that have been forced from a retreating ruling group, but are changes that have been decided upon by the Party command and carried out under Party control and direction. Nor can it be said that these changes represent a response to group pressures since Soviet social groups are not permitted anything approximating to autonomous organizations. However, it is clear that the present leadership does recognize special sectional and class interests and that it has made or permitted some tentative moves towards giving organizational expression to these groups. Thus during the agricultural reorganization debate in 1958 there was open canvassing of support for Peasant Unions. While the suggestion was not given official approval many changes since 1958 bear witness to the fact that collective farmers and allied agricultural workers are securing something like controlled group agencies. Thus inter-kolkhoz construction agencies developed rapidly from 1958 onwards and early in 1962 Inter-district Kolkhoz-Sovkhoz Administrative Boards were established under the control of provincial and republican agricultural administrations. In November 1962 the Central Committee approved a reorganization of the Party apparatus which provided for separate organization of agricultural and industrial personnel. Such a reorganization was designed to provide better Party supervision of both industry and agriculture, but it also strengthened the representation and weight of agricultural interests within the Party. However, this separation within the Party structure lasted for only two years before being reversed. Similarly, reforms to Soviet Trade Unions since 1958 have not only improved the efficiency of trade unions as agencies for worker protection but have extended the role of workers in industrial supervision and plan fulfilment. Professional groups such as lawyers and school teachers proved their capacity to influence the details of government legislation in 1958 during the passage of the new Criminal Code and the Education Act.

THE SPEED OF POLITICAL CHANGE

It is sometimes said that reform slowed down in 1955–56, or after the Hungarian uprising late in 1956, or since June 1957. Closer examination suggests the need for caution on this matter. Take the consequences of Malenkov's fall in February 1955. The rate of increase of consumer goods industry fell. This is evident from the official figures published by the Central Statistical Administration in 1956. Over the years 1953–54 the annual average increase of physical output of consumer goods industry was 13·25% as against 13·5% for capital goods industry. In 1955 the output of consumer goods industry rose by only 8% above 1954 but that of capital goods industry rose by 15%. However, the breakthrough in housing construction occurred only in 1957 and the basic decisions relating to this problem were taken in July 1957.[45] Similarly, important decisions relating to improving the supply of furniture and household requisites, establishing a network of public cleaning and repair shops,[46] improving the amount and quality of clothing and footwear, public catering, etc.,[47] were taken in 1958 or later. As far as the Polish and Hungarian crises are concerned they probably contributed to the anti-liberalism which was evident in several sectors of Soviet policy during late 1956 and early 1957. Thus there was a tightening up of controls over Soviet writers. This resulted in the reconstruction of the editorial boards of several journals including *Voprosy istorii* (1956) and *Novy mir* (1957), and the increasing insistence on *partiinost* (party-mindedness) in literature. Writers and students—perhaps because of their role in both the Polish and Hungarian revolts—were clearly under suspicion. There was some censorship of critical novels. However, Dudintsev's *Ne khlebom edinym* ('Not by Bread Alone'), serialized in *Novy mir* in late 1956 was eventually published in book form without major change in March 1957 but in a limited edition of 30,000. Despite the suppression of Pasternak's novel *Dr. Zhivago* in 1958 many critical novels, stories and poems have continued to be published. In fact the thaw in Soviet literature has continued, notwithstanding a temporary freezing over in 1956–57. If there was some reduction in the public criticism of Stalin during the early months of 1957[48] this undoubtedly reflected the state of the inner-Party struggle as much as external events. The June 1957 Central Committee plenum ended the situation in which a group of top leaders could effectively sabotage Congress decisions. Thus change in agricultural policy, industrial administration, education and even foreign policy proceeded more rapidly after June 1957 than before it. At the same time the establishment of Khrushchev's supremacy within the leadership resulted in such frequent administrative changes that both economic managers and administrators were kept in a state of uncertainty as to their powers and responsibilities.

SOME SIGNIFICANT CHANGES IN SOVIET DOMESTIC POLICIES SINCE 1953

This is a selective rather than a comprehensive list. Its purpose is to outline some of the main directions of political change, an essential preliminary operation to any general assessment of the extent and significance of the changes.

(1) There has been an obvious change towards a more equitable distribution of income. The material basis of this change was reached by 1952 if not earlier but the implementation was delayed until 1956 and later. The July 1956 Pensions Act raised basic pension rates and also extended their coverage. Pensions were further increased in December 1959 and extended to collective farmers in July 1964. Minimum wage rates were raised in September 1956 (to 270–350 roubles a month—old style). Successive increases brought the minimum wage to 70 roubles a month by the end of 1972. In July 1964 new basic rates of pay were established for teachers, doctors and other public health workers, for workers in retailing and catering, workers in house servicing and for local government employees. Eighteen million wage and salary earners benefited from these increases. At the same time margins for skill were lowered under the Seven-Year Plan (1959–65) to roughly 2 : 1 compared with 2·8 : 1 several years earlier. Bonuses were likewise reduced. The abolition

of income tax on lower incomes (under the Law of May 7, 1960) while never fully implemented did contribute towards the levelling of incomes. Peasant incomes, while still lower on the average than industrial incomes, have been systematically raised since 1953. Higher prices paid by the government for agricultural products, especially the increased prices of July 1958 and June 1962, have resulted in increased peasant incomes. By the end of the sixties most collective farmers received the bulk of their income in monthly wage payments and their living standards were steadily improving.

(2) The move towards a more equitable distribution of income has been accompanied by a reduction of the working week. The seven-hour working day (six-hour day for arduous occupations) which had been removed in June 1940 was restored in March 1956. The May 7, 1960, Law on the Transition to a shorter Working Day established a 36–41-hour working week for all workers by the end of 1960 and provided for a 30–35-hour working week by the end of 1965. Most Soviet workers had moved to a five-day working week by 1967.

(3) Since 1953 there has been a general improvement in both the quantity, range, and quality of foodstuffs and consumer goods. Agricultural production increased on an average 60% between 1953 and 1961, most of the increase being realized by 1958. The output of milk and milk products, meat and meat products, fish, fruit and vegetables, eggs and other foodstuffs, increased substantially. The fall in grain production over 1962–63 resulted also in lower production of milk and meat. Footwear, clothing, furniture, household requisites, refrigerators, radio and television sets, washing machines and many other consumer durables, are in rapidly increasing supply although the supply is still inadequate to meet demand. Thus in 1972 the production of refrigerators rose by 10%, watches and clocks by 5%, TV sets by 3%, light cars by 38% and furniture by 9% over 1971.[49]

(4) Public housing has received a high priority in government planning since 1956. Almost seven million flats and 1·5 million homes were completed during the first three years (1959–61) of the Seven-Year Plan. The Soviet Union had the highest level of flat construction in the world over 1958–63. While this haste has often resulted in poorly finished housing it has certainly brought about a substantial improvement in Soviet housing. However, continued expansion of the urban population (which increased by 29 millions between 1953 and 1962) and some dropping off in the rate of housing construction during 1963–64 produced a good deal of feeling around this issue, which was reflected in many speeches at the USSR Supreme Soviet in December 1964. The 1965 economic plan provided for a 13% increase in public housing construction over 1964.

(5) Since 1953 and especially since 1955 there has been a new stress

on technical progress and on industrial and agricultural efficiency. Khrushchev's report to the September 1953 plenum of the Central Committee was the first genuinely critical report on Soviet agriculture for more than two decades. Among other things it revealed the technical and scientific backwardness of Soviet agriculture. A similarly critical report on Soviet industrial technology was given by Bulganin to the Central Committee in July 1955. Since then there has been a continued effort to improve technology, increase investment in science and research, to increase the output of trained scientists and engineers of all types, and to raise labour productivity in industry and agriculture. Workers are increasingly involved in this process through their trade union committees, Permanent Production Conferences and Production Committees, as well as through such agencies as the All-Union Society of Inventors and Rationalizers.

(6) Although contradictory trends exist the general line of Soviet political development since 1953 has been towards greater democracy, in the Soviet sense of the term. Thus in inner-Party affairs and in the functioning of state agencies, there has been a continued stress on socialist legality, i.e. on the search for norms, rules, regularity in performance, and on the ending of arbitrariness. The period 1953–60 saw an impressive reduction of police powers. It is sometimes suggested that this was counterbalanced by an extension of the scope of the police through such agencies as Volunteer Militia units and Comradely Courts. Yet while these agencies work in close liaison with the militia they are closely supervised by local Soviets* and trade unions. These agencies handle mainly petty crimes and non-criminal anti-social behaviour. Since May 1955 the general supervisory powers of the Procurator-General's Office have been extended. In April 1956 a special department was established in the Procurator-General's Office for the purpose of supervising investigations conducted by the Committee on State Security (KGB). The reform of the Criminal Code in 1958–1959 also reflected a move towards liberalism and humanism in Soviet law. Yet this reform of the Criminal Code has not been uniformly liberal. The Basic Criminal Code of December 1958 established capital punishment for six categories of crime— high treason, espionage, terrorist acts, sabotage, banditry, and premeditated murder under aggravating circumstances.[50] Yet within four years this list had been more than doubled.[51] The only encouraging thing about such extensions of the death penalty was that they were openly criticized by many persons in the Soviet Union, especi-

---

* The present regulations on Volunteer Militia place them under the aegis of the District Party Committee and in many cases this has reduced the local Soviets to exercising merely a supervisory power. This has recently come under heavy criticism. Cf. *Sovety*, No. 3, 1966, pp. 69–74.

ally within the legal profession. Apart from the extension of the death penalty to many categories of 'economic crimes' there is also evidence that many courts responded to the political campaign against such crimes (mainly during the years 1962–63) by dubious practices including retrospective application of laws.

Decentralization is neither intrinsically democratic nor an irreversible trend in Soviet policy. This is indicated by the failure of the 1957 industrial reorganization to stimulate at the enterprise level the initiative of either managers or workers. It did strengthen 'localism' (*mestnichestvo*) and temporarily increased the powers of City and Provincial Soviets, as well as those of regional economic councils. But by 1960 the trend was steadily towards centralism again by strengthening Gosplan controls and by establishing *sovnarkhozy* at the republican level in the larger republics (1960) and at the USSR level (November 1962), and by the establishment of the Supreme Economic Council in March 1963. The confusion inherent in a regional structure which was combined with a centralized superstructure was soon realized and it was ended during 1965. In October 1965 the pre-1957 system of industrial ministries was re-established. However, the pursuit of local initiative was continued although it was transferred to another level. Henceforth it was to rest on the economic enterprise and not on the regional economic council.

The reduction of the size of the Soviet bureaucracy is one of the most obvious trends of recent years. This applies to the Party as well as to the state bureaucracy. In both cases administrative structures are being rationalized and streamlined and officials and functionaries are being replaced at many levels by amateurs. Over the six years 1954–59 the number of persons employed in administrative and managerial work fell by 568,000 and the percentage of this group in the total Soviet workforce fell from 14% to 9·7%.[52] While the appropriation for administration in the USSR budget has sometimes increased in recent years its percentage of the total budget has fallen since 1954 to reach an all-time low level of 1·0% of the budget in 1972 and 1973. Although the general tendency for several years now has been for the reduction and rationalization of the administrative structure it has nevertheless become more complex at certain levels. This is true of the republican and provincial levels as far as the planning and industrial administrative apparatus is concerned. It is also probable that the separation of Soviets into industrial and rural Soviets in most provinces and territories (during the years 1962-64) resulted in an absolute enlargement of the number of paid officials employed in local government.

Although it is difficult to measure there has undoubtedly been a great deal of discussion, criticism and consultation in the Soviet

Union in the clarification of policy over recent years. Public discussions of policy have been a regular feature of the Soviet system since the discussion on the sixth Five-Year Plan early in 1956. While I would not go so far as Giuseppe Boffa and claim that, 'Each time there was a refinement of method, so that the last debates have been those most productive of ideas',[53] I do think that this process has a genuine consultative value and that it is not merely designed as a substitute for self-government. Indeed, the close study of all these public discussions since 1956 would be a rewarding exercise. Of those which I have studied in any detail I would select the public discussions on industrial reorganization early in 1957, on agricultural reform early in 1958, and on educational reform late in 1958, as the most fruitful in terms of detailed amendments to government policy. Later national discussions such as those which preceded the 22nd Congress (1961) and the discussion on the Collective Farm Statute (April–November 1969) produced fewer modifications to the policies drafted by the leadership.

Consultation does not stop at nationwide discussions. Perhaps even more significant is the increasing use of conferences of experts. Over the eight years 1953–61 more than eighty All-Union Conferences involving over 100,000 participants were held.[54] Many similar conferences have been held at republican and regional levels. In addition, press discussion and criticism has become wider and more common. This is even truer in the case of much of the specialist periodical press. Further developments of this process will probably be in terms of less rigid Party control of lower-level local Soviets. This problem has been raised several times in the Soviet press in recent years.[55] The expansion of the actual functions of higher Soviets is likely to continue but this will not involve competitive politics in the Western sense. Any movement towards greater democracy in the Soviet Union is towards a fuller exercise of Soviet democracy and not in the direction of capitalist parliamentary democracy.

(7) Many of the above reforms have been carried through as part of the general de-Stalinization campaign. This campaign began as a cautious and concealed movement by Stalin's heirs to restore collective leadership within the Party and state systems. At the 20th Congress early in 1956 it was extended to a public criticism of Stalin's ideological domination, a criticism that was openly linked to a drive for the restoration of Leninist principles in Party leadership. Khrushchev's secret speech to the 20th Congress (February 25, 1956)[56] took the campaign further and involved a direct attack on the police terror of the Stalin era. Although the campaign slumped somewhat in late 1956 and early 1957 it was later revived. By the 22nd Congress in October 1961 the responsibility for the terror had been extended be-

yond Stalin and his police chiefs to all the leaders of the anti-Party group. This of course was an illogical apportioning of responsibility but it was as far as the 1961 leaders could go without accepting the responsibility themselves. The campaign was dropped in 1965.

The anti-Stalin campaign was deliberately organized by Stalin's successors to emphasize the difference between present and past in Soviet politics. After 1957 it was obviously used by Khrushchev and his supporters to discredit the anti-Party group. At the same time the general direction of the campaign since 1956 and particularly the re-lease and re-instatement of loyal Communists who had suffered under Stalin unquestionably had mass support. And while the Party leadership has developed the campaign to suit its own purposes its public impact has been such that it provides considerable restraints against any complete reversion to the methods of the Stalinist regime.

(8) Although many Western experts[57] have forecast a decline in the importance of the Communist Party in the Soviet political system, especially since June 1957, the present trend seems to be rather in the reverse direction. While the role of specific Communist Party agencies has not been constant since March 1953 (for example, the Presidium–Secretariat relationship), these generalizations might safely be made:

(a) The Central Party agencies, especially the Central Committee, the Presidium (Politbureau) and Secretariat, have exercised a much greater role in policy formulation and policy implementation than they did over the years 1934–53.

(b) The supervisory as distinct from the hectoring role of the Party organization has been extended. At the top this has seen the consolidation of the Party Control Committee. At the bottom it is reflected in the establishment of Party Control Commissions in the factories (since 1959) and in the extension of control powers of Party primary organizations from industrial and economic agencies to research and educational establishments after 1968, a change formally sanctioned by amendments to the Party Rules carried at the 24th Congress in April 1971.

(c) The educational and general 'cultural-enlightenment' role of the Communist Party has been vastly expanded. But in order to keep the Party to the forefront in a period of rapid technological advance, the stress has been increasingly on Party members securing specialist secondary and higher education.

(9) The greatest achievement of the Soviet regime since October 1964 has been the striving for a stable leadership. This has been attempted through separating the top Party and State positions, through sharing of top positions and responsibilities, by restricting the patronage powers of the General Secretary and by limiting the

powers of the central State bureaucracy through extending the role of the Supreme Soviet Presidium and of the Standing Commissions.[58]

CONCLUSION

Soviet politics like Soviet society has entered a period of rapid and far-reaching change. It is important to emphasize this fact as many Western political scientists still write of the Soviet system in terms of models constructed in the Stalin period. These models are not all static[59] but they tend to ignore, to underestimate, and not to explain the changes that have occurred over recent years. Communist writers on the other hand, still tend to confuse official legal theory with the reality of Soviet politics. I have sought to give careful consideration to official Soviet theory while at the same time examining this theory against the actual practice of the changing Soviet system. This has necessitated a detailed examination of the way Party and government bodies function and of their inter-relationships. My conclusion here is that the formally leading agencies of both the Party and the State structures—the Party Congress, Central Committee, Politbureau and Secretariat; the Supreme Soviet and the Council of Ministers—are becoming increasingly important, although the key national decisions in both domestic and foreign affairs are still taken by a small body of leaders in which one person may have a decisive influence. My analysis has further required an exploration of the changes which have taken place in the structure, role and tone of various institutions since the death of Stalin. These changes include such things as new methods and styles in leadership, new and more beneficial and more popular policies, and a broadening of the process of consultation and discussion in decision-making. It has involved the extension of the powers of republican and local government, the whittling down of the police and a genuine enlargement of citizens' rights. It has involved the attempt to establish government on the basis of legal norms and to make it less arbitrary, less personal and more collective in its decisions. Yet in these changes the directing role of the Communist Party has been maintained and strengthened.

Finally, I have attempted at various stages in this work, to make overall generalizations and appraisals of the Soviet system. While these are linked to my general assessment of the Soviet system they are not dependent on any elaborately constructed artificial model. I have not been satisfied with old designations such as dictatorship, totalitarian, bureaucratic dictatorship, or even democracy.

Like most political systems in existence today the Soviet is a mixed one which contains elements of democracy. While some may dispute this I believe that it is nearer the truth than the view that the Soviet system is an unpopular and enduring despotism.

NOTES

[1] Cf. T. H. Rigby, L. G. Churchward, 1962, pp. 5–8.

[2] See in particular Zbigniew Brzezinski, Samuel P. Huntington, 1964.

[3] T. H. Rigby, 'The Extent and Limits of Authority', *Problems of Communism*, XII, No. 5, September–October 1963.

[4] *Op. cit.*, Ch. 4. See also Skilling and Griffiths, 1971.

[5] Herbert McClosky, John E. Turner, 1960, p. 175.

[6] G. M. Malenkov, 1953, pp. 8–9.

[7] Malenkov's position was sufficiently ambiguous to encourage some Soviet writers to openly advocate a higher rate of development for consumer goods industry than for capital goods industry. See the editorial in *Voprosy ekonomiki* No. 1, 1955. Cf. R. Conquest, 1961, pp. 250–6, 262.

[8] An English translation of Malenkov's letter of resignation is printed in *Soviet Studies*, VII, July 1955, pp. 91–3. It is probable that Malenkov's responsibilities to agriculture and his alliance with Beria in March 1953 were also reasons for criticism at the January 1955 plenum of the Central Committee. Cf. G. Boffa, 1960, pp. 29–30.

[9] *Pravda*, July 4, 1957.

[10] R. Conquest, *op. cit.*, p. 321.

[11] Herbert McClosky, John E. Turner, *op. cit.*, p. 175.

[12] Cf. G. Boffa, *op. cit.*, pp. 29–30. This explanation was also given to me personally by various people in Moscow in August 1957.

[13] *Pravda*, July 4, 1957.

[14] *Ibid.*

[15] For example, the speeches by Mikoyan and Satyukov to the 22nd Congress, *Izvestia*, October 22 and 27, 1961.

[16] *Izvestia*, April 28, 1962.

[17] *Izvestia*, December 19, 1958.

[18] Saburov's statement was printed in the *Stenografichesky otchet* of the XXI Party Congress but not in the newspaper summaries of the Congress. An English summary of this statement is given in *Soviet Studies*, XI, October 1959, pp. 220–2.

[19] *Izvestia*, February 4, 1959.

[20] See the Report of the Central Committee to the 22nd Congress by N. S. Khrushchev, *Izvestia*, October 18, 1961. Voroshilov's statement to the Congress was printed in *Izvestia*, October 29, 1961.

[21] This letter has not been published but it was referred to several times during the Congress, particularly by Satyukov, *Izvestia*, October 27, 1961.

[22] *Izvestia*, October 27, 1961.

[23] He was accused in the June 1957 statement of liberal tendencies in regard to cultural matters but he could hardly have found much support for his views from the leaders of the anti-Party group.

[24] None of these leaders contributed to the public discussion on industrial reorganization during March–May 1957 but the cautious and even conservative views of various administrators in the central Ministries which were printed probably reflected their views.

[25] This analysis is based mainly on the revelations made by various speakers to the 22nd Congress in October 1961.

[26] Frank A. Durgin Jr., 'The Virgin Lands Programme 1954–60', *Soviet Studies*, XIII, January 1962, p. 261.

[27] Cf. T. H. Rigby in T. H. Rigby, L. G. Churchward, *op. cit.*

[28] Cf. Carl Linden, *Problems of Communism*, XII, No. 5, September–October 1963.

[29] Cf. Victor Zorza, 'The Kremlinologists Vindicated', *The Guardian*, December 11, 1964. Robert Conquest; 1965.

[30] *The Guardian*, November 17, 1964.

[31] Cf. articles by Victor Zorza in *The Guardian* November 17 and 20, December 2, 4, 10 and 11, 1964 and articles in the *Observer* over the period October–December 1964.

[32] Z. Brzezinski, S. P. Huntingdon, *op. cit.*, pp. 272 f. The statement was made at the British Fair, May 20, 1961.

[33] Translation from *Current Digest of the Soviet Press*, XVI, No. 4, 1964.

[34] Law on the Economic Plan for 1965, adopted December 11, 1964. *Izvestia*, December 12, 1964.

[35] The Soviet press has printed many complaints on this matter written by officials of local Soviets. For example I. Sinitsyn, 'Oblispolkom and Sovnarkhoz', *Izvestia*, September 5, 1964; M. Onipko, 'Hand in Hand', *Izvestia*, November 4, 1964.

[36] Cf. Ts. A. Yampolskaya, 'On the Development of the State and Administration Structural and Organizational Forms', *S.G.i.P.* No. 6, 1964, pp. 31–40; S. E. Borisyuk, 'Industrial and Agricultural Executive Committees and Common Activity Forms of their Organs', *S.G.i.P.* No. 7, 1964, pp. 115–17; and I. Sinitsyn, *Izvestia*, September 5, 1964.

[37] For example, the article by G. Kiselev, Chairman of the Council of Ministers, Belorussia, in *Izvestia*, November 27, 1964.

[38] Foreword to *Partiinaya zhizn*, No. 21, November 1964. This issue went to press November 2, a fortnight prior to the decision of the C.C. to restore the old organizational structure.

[39] D. Rukavets, 'Stones on the Road', *Partiinaya zhizn* No. 22, November 1964, pp. 41–2. This issue went to press November 17 so that the article must have been written prior to the November 16 Central Committee decision.

[40] Compare, for example, the account by Richard Growald in *The Guardian*, October 19, 1964, with that published in the *Observer*, November 29, 1964.

[41] Based on figures in *The USSR Economy: A Statistical Abstract* (USSR Council of Ministers, Central Statistical Administration, 1956) English trans. London, 1957, p. 46.

[42] G. M. Malenkov, *Report to the 19th Party Congress*. Moscow, 1952, pp. 95–6.

[43] *The U.S.S.R. Economy*, 1957, p. 46.

[44] Cf. G. Boffa, *op. cit.* Part Two.

[45] Decision of the Central Committee of the CPSU and the USSR Council of Ministers, 'On the Development of Housing Construction in the USSR', July 31, 1957. *Izvestia*, August 2, 1957.

[46] Decision of the C.C. of the CPSU and the USSR Council of Ministers, 'On Measures for Improving Repair Services', *Izvestia*, March 13, 1959: This provided for the opening of 29,000 shoe repair shops over the next three years, 22,200 new clothing repair shops and 12,100 other repair shops for household goods and 262 new dry cleaning factories.

[47] Decision of the C.C. of the CPSU and the USSR Council of Ministers 'On the Further Development and Improvement of Social Provisioning', *Izvestia*, February 28, 1959.

[48] One of the first public acknowledgements of Stalin's ideological leadership after the 20th Congress was in an article by Professor A. Denisov on 'Soviets—the fully democratic organs of the Masses', which appeared in *Pravda*, March 1, 1957.

[49] Central Statistical Administration, Results of the 1972 Economic Plan. *Pravda*, January 30, 1973.

[50] Art. 22 of the Basic Criminal Code for the USSR and the Union-Republics, December 25, 1958.

[51] A decree of the USSR Presidium, May 5, 1961, added three further crimes; embezzlement of state or social property 'of a particularly large scale', counterfeiting, and organized terrorism among persons undergoing prison sentence. A decree of July 1, 1961, added large-scale speculation in currency or securities. A decree published on February 27, 1962, added capital punishment for repeated convictions for bribery, for attempts on the life of a militia man, and for certain categories of rape.

[52] *Finansy SSSR* No. 1, 1961, p. 1. 8·8% of the state workforce was employed in administration 1963. *Finansy SSSR*, No. 12, 1964, p. 10.

[53] G. Boffa, *op. cit.*, p. 206.

[54] F. Kalinychev, 'Era of People's Power', *Sovety*, No. 11, 1962, p. 14.

[55] For example, *Izvestia* May 7 and 8, 1959. Cf. I. Korshunov, 'Party leadership to Soviets', *Sovety*, No. 3, 1966, pp. 7–19.

[56] A full English text of this speech is printed in *The Anti-Stalin Campaign and International Communism*, N.Y., 1956, pp. 1–89.

[57] Cf. T. H. Rigby in T. H. Rigby, L. G. Churchward, *op. cit.*, espec. pp. 13–14; and 'Political Forces and Soviet Reality' *A.P.S.A. News* (Bulletin of the Australian Political Studies Association), May 1962, pp. 14–16.

[58] Cf. T. H. Rigby, 1970.

[59] Contrast for example, the static model used by McClosky and Turner, 1960 with the more flexible model used by Professor John N. Hazard, 1957. The latter model allows for a more realistic assessment of the extent and quality of the changes that have occurred in Soviet politics while the former book takes little account of the changes and offers no basis for an explanation of them.

SELECTED BIBLIOGRAPHY

Boffa, G., 1960.
Brzezinski and Huntingdon, 1964, Chs. 3, 4 and Conclusion.
Brzezinski, Z. K., 1966.
Churchward, L. G., 1973.
Dallin, A., 1960, pp. 262–81.
Dallin, A., and Larsen, T. B., eds., 1968.
Deutscher, I., 1966.
Deutscher, I., 1967.
Fainsod, M., 1965.
Leonhard, W., 1962.
Linden. Rigby, Conquest, *Problems of Communism*, xii, 1963.
Osborn, R. J., 1970.
Pethybridge, R. W., 1961.
Pethybridge, R. W., 1966, Chs. 5, 6.
Rigby, T. H., *World Politics*, xvi, 1964.
Rigby, T. H., 1970.
Skilling, H. G., and Griffiths, F., eds., 1971.
Swearer, H. R., 1966.
Tucker, R. C., 1963, Ch. 3.
Tucker, R. C., 1965.

Appendix I

MARXISM–LENINISM

(Translated from *Politichesky slovar*, Moscow, 1958, pp. 337–8)

The science of the laws of development of nature and society, of the revolution of the exploited masses, of the victory of socialism, of the construction of communist society; the ideology of the working class and its Communist Party.

The founders of Marxism were the brilliant thinkers and leaders of the working class K. Marx and F. Engels. Generalizing, criticizing and reworking all that was valuable and progressive, all that had been created by public opinion over the stretch of many centuries of human development, they armed the proletariat with the revolutionary theory of struggle for the construction of a classless communist society. Having shown the motive forces of social development and disclosed the objective laws on the basis of which this development happens, Marxism accomplished a revolutionary transformation in the history of social thought.

Marx and Engels lived and worked in a period when capitalism was still advancing, when only the preconditions for a proletarian revolution had matured. At the close of the nineteenth and the beginning of the twentieth century capitalism entered into its final monopoly stage (cf. *Imperialism*). In this epoch, when the centre of the world revolutionary movement shifted to Russia, the leader of the Russian proletariat, V. I. Lenin, defended Marxism from attacks from the side of revisionism and opportunism and creatively developed Marxism further in conformity with new historical circumstances. Leninism is Marxism in the epoch of imperialism and proletarian revolutions, Marxism in the epoch of the victory of socialism.

The basic constituent parts of Marxism are: Marxist philosophy, Marxist political economy and the theory of scientific communism. The philosophy of Marxism–Leninism—dialectical materialism, involving the unity of the *Marxist dialectical method* and *Marxist philosophical material-ism*—is the most profound and comprehensive theory of development. Marxist philosophical materialism is the highest form of materialism which scientifically discloses the laws of development of the objective world. *Historical materialism* is the application of dialectical materialism to the study of the life of society. Dialectical and historical materialism are the theoretical basis of communism, the only true method of scientific investigation and revolutionary transformation of the world in the interests of the working masses. Questions of Marxist philosophy are most fully and comprehensively treated in the works: *The Communist Manifesto* by Marx and Engels, Marx's *A Contribution to the Critique of Political Economy*, Engels' *Anti-Duhring*, and Lenin's *Materialism and Empirio-Criticism*.

Marxist-Leninist political economy studies the social-production, i.e. the economic relations of people. The corner stone of the economic theory of Marx is the theory of *surplus value*, exposing the nature of capitalist exploitation, the source of the enrichment of the bourgeois class. Marxism-Leninism teaches that the production relations of capitalism, which at first promote the growth of the productive forces, the creation of large-scale social production, at length change into fetters to the development of the productive forces. In every possible way the existing contradictions between the social character of production of material goods under capitalism and the individual mode of appropriation are intensified. The necessity for the revolutionary destruction of capitalist productive relations matures. Marxist economic theory scientifically substantiates the inevitability of the destruction of capitalism and the victory of *communism*. The main works on Marxist political economy are Marx's *Capital* and Lenin's *Imperialism: the Highest Stage of Capitalism*.

Teachings which propagated the necessity of establishing socialism existed before Marx and Engels but they were unscientific and utopian. Although sharply criticizing the capitalist system, *utopian socialism* was not able to show the correct path to Socialism, not seeing the force which has the capacity to liquidate the capitalist system and to build a Socialist society. Marxism-Leninism changed socialism from a utopia into a science and showed that capitalism itself creates the circumstances for its own overthrowal in the shape of the proletariat—the most revolutionary class in history, which was called to be the grave-digger of capitalism and the creator of communism. The theory of scientific communism is most fully set out in the works: Marx's *Critique of the Gotha Programme*; Lenin's *Two Tactics of Social-Democracy in the Democratic Revolution, The State and Revolution, Economics and Politics in the Period of the Dictatorship of the Proletariat*, and *Left-Wing Communism: An Infantile Disorder*.

Marxism-Leninism teaches that the motive power of each antagonistic society is the class struggle, the struggle between exploiters and exploited. In order to fulfil its historical mission the proletariat must accomplish in alliance with the working peasantry and other exploited sections of the population a socialist revolution, expropriating from the bourgeoisie the means of production and transforming them into communal property. The Marxist-Leninist science of communism scientifically substantiates the certainty of the proletarian revolution and the dictatorship of the proletariat, showing the concrete ways of constructing communist society.

The considerable degree of socialization of production, the growth of the proletariat and the raising of its class consciousness and organization creates the objective circumstances for the revolutionary transformation of the capitalist system. In solving the question of the socialist reorganization of society Marxism–Leninism eschews schematic blueprints. Lenin stated that:

All nations will arrive at socialism, that is inevitable; but they won't all get there in the same way—each brings its own peculiarity in one or other form of democracy, in one or other variant of the dictatorship of the proletariat, in one or other tempo of socialist transformation of the different sides of social life.

The proletarian revolution is not restricted to the taking over of power by the proletariat. Having gained power the proletariat uses it for the construction of a socialist society. Therefore the study of the *dictatorship of the proletariat* as the main content of the period of the transformation from capitalism to communism is the essence of Marxism–Leninism. The Marxist–Leninist theory of the party of the proletariat as the highest form of working-class organization, as its fighting vanguard, is of greatest significance for the successful decision of all the tasks of the socialist revolution. Communist and workers' parties, which are supported in their activities by Marxist–Leninist theory, are the leading and directing force in the preparation for and the carrying out of revolution, in the construction of socialism and communism.

Marxism–Leninism is a creative science which is eternally developing and enriching itself in the process of development and generalizing on the experience of the international working-class movement, of socialist construction and the development of science.

Appendix II

MARXISM-LENINISM AS A POLITICAL WEAPON

(*History of the Communist Party of the Soviet Union*. FLPH., Moscow, 1960, pp. 748-52)

The history of the CPSU teaches us that the Party would not have been able to secure the historic gains of socialism in the USSR if it had not been guided in all its activity by the *theory of Marxism-Leninism*.

Bolshevism [wrote Lenin], arose in 1903 on the very firm foundation of the theory of Marxism. (*Collected Works*, Vol. 31, p. 9.)

Marxism-Leninism is an integral and consistent dialectical materialist world outlook, and the theory of scientific communism. It is the science of the laws of development of society, the science of the Socialist revolution and the dictatorship of the proletariat, the science of the building of socialist and communist society. From Marxist-Leninist theory the Party draws its strength and its confidence in the triumph of communism. This theory enables the Party to ascertain the laws governing social life, to find the right orientation in any situation, to understand the inner connection of events and the trend of their development. It helps to find the answer to the basic questions posed by the revolutionary struggle and communist construction.

The absolute demands which the Communist Party makes on theory are:

(*a*) fidelity to Marxism-Leninism, defence and support of its principles, an uncompromising attitude towards any kind of deviation from it, and a determined struggle against all attempts to revise it;

(*b*) a creative approach to theory; the mastering of theory; its development in keeping with the changing conditions of the life of society and the tasks confronting the Party at different stages of the struggle for the triumph of the proletariat and the building of communism; a resolute struggle against dogmatism, against divorcing theory from practice, from the Party's revolutionary struggle;

(*c*) the indissoluble connection of theory and practice; organic unity between theory and practice in the Party's entire activity.

Throughout their entire activity, Lenin and his comrades-in-arms, the Party as a whole, carried on a resolute struggle against overt and covert opponents of Marxism, and against revisionists of all hues both in Russia and in the international arena. As a result of this struggle the revolutionary theory of Marx and Engels triumphed, in spite of bitter attacks, spread throughout the world, and today serves as a powerful ideological weapon in the building of communism in the USSR, and in strengthening and developing the world socialist system and the international liberation movement. The history of the Party is the history of uncompromising struggle for the purity of Marxist–Leninist theory, both against revision and against dogmatism.

The struggle of Lenin and his followers for the purity of Marxist theory went hand in hand with a *creative* elaboration of this theory. Mastering Marxist theory does not at all mean learning its various conclusions and propositions by heart. Marxist theory must not be regarded as something set and fossilized, as a collection of dogmas. Like any other science, it develops, advances and is enriched with new experience, new knowledge, new conclusions and propositions. Mastering Marxist theory means assimilating its essence and learning to apply it in solving practical problems of the revolutionary movement and communist construction. The Communist Party's fidelity to the spirit of Marxism has ever been combined with the replacement of some of its obsolete propositions and the elaboration of new fundamental theoretical propositions conforming to the changes that have come about in the life of society, and to the requirements of the practical struggle for the interests of the working class, for the cause of socialism and communism.

Proceeding from the essence of Marxist theory, Lenin made a number of brilliant discoveries, and drew new conclusions that are of decisive importance for the proletariat and its revolutionary Party in the new conditions of the epoch of imperialism and socialist revolution.

An example of the creative development of Marxism, and the replacement of obsolete propositions by new ones that meet the requirements of the political struggle of the proletariat, is the theory of socialist revolution worked out by Lenin.

Marx and Engels, who discovered the laws of capitalism in its premonopoly stage, arrived at the conclusion that socialist revolution could not triumph in one country taken singly, that it would triumph simultaneously in all or most of the capitalist countries.

This conclusion, which was correct in the period when capitalism was on the ascent, became a guiding principle for all Marxists. But the situation had changed radically by the beginning of the twentieth century: capitalism had grown into imperialism, which intensified all the contradictions of capitalism to the utmost and brought mankind to the threshold of the transition to socialism; ascendant capitalism had turned into moribund capitalism. The proposition of Marx and Engels that socialism could not triumph in one country taken singly no longer corresponded to the new situation, and Lenin did not hesitate to revise it. Analysing capitalism at its new stage, he showed that the uneven development of capitalism becomes especially marked in the epoch of imperialism, and that this development assumes a spasmodic, catastrophic character. He arrived at the conclusion that in the conditions of imperialism, socialism cannot triumph simultaneously in all the capitalist countries and that, on the contrary, the world imperialist chain can be broken at its weakest link, that socialism can triumph at first in one capitalist country taken singly.

The Party upheld this brilliant discovery of Lenin's in its struggle against the opportunists. It became a guiding principle for the whole of revolutionary Marxism, enriched the revolutionary struggle, opened up new prospects for it and unfettered the initiative of the proletariat in its revolutionary onslaught against its own bourgeoisie in each particular country. The victory of the Great October Socialist Revolution and the building of socialism in the USSR furnished irrefutable proof of the correctness of the Leninist theory of socialist revolution.

Had Lenin not made his brilliant discovery in time, had he not had the courage to replace one of the obsolete propositions of Marxism by a new proposition, and the only correct one for the new historical situation, and had the Communist Parties not mastered and adopted this proposition as a guiding principle, the revolutionary initiative and activity of the proletariat of the various countries would have been fettered, and they would not have had a clear perspective or confidence in the success of their revolutionary undertaking.

Another instance of the creative elaboration of Marxism was Lenin's discovery of Soviet power as a state form of the dictatorship of the proletariat, now firmly established in the USSR. Had Lenin not discovered the Soviet form of the dictatorship of the proletariat, the Republic of Soviets, the Party would have groped in the dark, the proletariat would have lost, the bourgeoisie would have won and Marxist theory would have suffered a severe setback.

Still another illustration of the creative development of Marxism is the discovery by Marxist–Leninists of a new form of the dictatorship of the proletariat, in the shape of People's Democracy. Only one form of the dictatorship of the proletariat, the Soviets, was known before the Second World War. The experience of the Soviet Union, which acquired all the more significance as a result of the establishment of a socialist society and the victory of the USSR in the Second World War, attested the vitality of the Soviets. However, taking into account the international situation during and after the Second World War and the actual course of revolutionary development in the countries where a people's revolution was unfolding, and drawing upon the Leninist proposition that different forms of the dictatorship of the proletariat were possible and upon the experience of the masses, Marxist–Leninists advanced a new form of the dictatorship of the proletariat—People's Democracy. It was applied in the Chinese People's Republic and in all the socialist countries that came into being after the Second World War.

The decisions of the 20th Congress of the CPSU serve as a vivid example of creative development of Marxism–Leninism. N. S. Khrushchev's report and the Congress decisions were a development of Lenin's doctrine of the peaceful co-existence of the two social systems, and contained the theoretically and politically important proposition as to the possibility of averting wars in our epoch. They dealt with the forms of the transition to socialism in a number of capitalist countries and with the ways of establishing working-class unity in the capitalist countries.

The 21st Congress of the CPSU made a further contribution to the theory of scientific communism. Its decisions and N. S. Khrushchev's report theoretically substantiated and elaborated, on the basis of Marxism-Leninism, major problems of the new stage of Communist construction in the USSR—the laws governing the development of socialism into communism, the ways of developing and bringing closer together the collective farm and nationally-owned forms of socialist property; the distribution of material values among the members of society, the political organization of society, the state system and administration in the period of the full-scale construction of communism. The Congress stated that in the USSR the victory of socialism was not only complete but final. Of tremendous importance is the conclusion drawn by the 21st Congress that the successes of the Socialist countries, the growth and strengthening of the peace forces throughout the world, will make it really possible to exclude war from the life of society even before the complete victory of socialism on earth, with capitalism still existing in a part of the world.

The decisions of the 21st Congress and the report delivered by N. S. Khrushchev were an example of the creative application and elaboration of Marxism-Leninism. The propositions elaborated by the Congress are of immense theoretical and practical importance to the activity of the CPSU and to all brother Marxist-Leninist parties.

Leninism teaches us that he who takes no account of the changes in the development of society, ignores concrete historical conditions, defends obsolete propositions and conclusions, and substitutes a simple repetition of old Marxist formulas for a scientific analysis of new historical conditions and a theoretical generalization of new experience in the class struggle of the proletariat, remains true only to the letter of Marxism, distorts its revolutionary substance and, in fact, deviates from Marxism.

The Communist Party has never dissociated the theory from revolutionary practice. The invincibility of the Communist Party lies in the organic unity of its theory and practice.

The Communist Party has always been guided by the proposition of Marx and Lenin that Marxism is not a dogma but a guide to action.

Appendix III

RULES OF THE COMMUNIST PARTY OF THE SOVIET UNION

(Adopted by the 22nd Congress of the CPSU October 1961 and incorporating changes made at the 23rd and 24th Congresses)

The Communist Party of the Soviet Union is the tried and tested militant vanguard of the Soviet people, which unites on a voluntary basis, the more advanced, politically more conscious section of the working class, collective-farm peasantry and intelligentsia of the USSR.

Founded by V. I. Lenin as the vanguard of the working class, the Communist Party has travelled a glorious road of struggle, and brought the working class and the working peasantry to the victory of the Great October Socialist Revolution and to the establishment of the dictatorship of the proletariat in the USSR. Under the leadership of the Communist Party, the exploiting classes were abolished in the Soviet Union, and the moral and political unity of Soviet society has taken shape and grown in strength. Socialism has triumphed completely and finally. The Communist Party, the party of the working class, has today become the party of the Soviet people as a whole.

The Party exists for, and serves, the people. It is the highest form of social and political organization, and is the leading and guiding force of Soviet society. It directs the great creative activity of the Soviet people, and imparts an organized, planned and scientifically-based character to their struggle to achieve the ultimate goal, the victory of communism.

The CPSU bases its work on unswerving adherence to the Leninist standards of Party life—the principle of collective leadership, the promotion, in every possible way, of inner-Party democracy, the activity and initiative of the Communists, criticism and self-criticism.

Ideological and organizational unity, monolithic cohesion of its ranks, and a high degree of conscious discipline on the part of all Communists are an inviolable law of the CPSU. All manifestations of factionalism and group activity are incompatible with Marxist–Leninist Party principles, and with Party membership. The Party rids itself of persons who infringe the Programme and Rules of the CPSU, and who compromise by their behaviour the high name of Communist.

In all its activities, the CPSU takes guidance from Marxist–Leninist theory and the Programme based on it, which defines the fundamental tasks of the Party for the period of the construction of communist society.

In creatively developing Marxism–Leninism, the CPSU vigorously com-

315

bats all manifestations of revisionism and dogmatism, which are utterly alien to revolutionary theory.

The Communist Party of the Soviet Union is an integral part of the international Communist and working-class movement. It firmly adheres to the tried and tested Marxist–Leninist principles of proletarian internationalism; it actively promotes the unity of the international Communist and working-class movement as a whole, and fraternal ties with the great army of the Communists of all countries.

I

Party Members, Their Duties and Rights

1. Membership of the CPSU is open to any citizen of the Soviet Union who accepts the Programme and the Rules of the Party, takes an active part in Communist construction, works in one of the Party organizations, carries out all Party decisions and pays membership dues.

2. It is the duty of a Party member:

(a) to work for the creation of the material and technical basis of communism; to serve as an example of the Communist attitude towards labour; to raise labour productivity; to display the initiative in all that is new and progressive; to support and propagate advanced methods; to master techniques, to improve his skill; to protect and increase public socialist property, the mainstay of the might and prosperity of the Soviet country;

(b) to put Party decisions firmly and steadfastly into effect; to explain the policy of the Party to the masses; to help strengthen and multiply the Party's bonds with the people; to be considerate and attentive to people; to respond promptly to the needs and requirements of the working people;

(c) to take an active part in the political life of the country, in the administration of state affairs, and in economic and cultural development; to set an example in the fulfilment of his public duty; to assist in developing and strengthening Communist social relations;

(d) to master Marxist–Leninist theory, to improve his ideological knowledge, and to contribute to the moulding and education of the man of Communist society. To combat vigorously all manifestations of bourgeois ideology, remnants of a private-property psychology, religious prejudices and other survivals of the past; to observe the principles of Communist morality, and place public interests above his own;

(e) to be an active proponent of the ideas of socialist internationalism and Soviet patriotism among the masses of the working people; to combat survivals of nationalism and chauvinism; to contribute by word and deed to the consolidation of the friendship of the peoples of the USSR and the fraternal bonds linking the Soviet People with the peoples of the countries of the socialist camp, with the proletarians and other working people in all countries;

(f) to strengthen to the utmost the ideological and organizational unity of the Party; to safeguard the Party against the infiltration of people unworthy of the lofty name of Communist; to be truthful and honest with the Party and the people; to display vigilance, to guard Party and state secrets;

(*g*) to develop criticism and self-criticism, boldly lay bare shortcomings and strive for their removal; to combat ostentation, conceit, complacency and parochial tendencies; to rebuff firmly all attempts at suppressing criticism; to resist all actions injurious to the Party and the state, and to give information of them to Party bodies, up to and including the Central Committee of the CPSU;

(*h*) to implement undeviatingly the Party's policy with regard to the proper selection of personnel according to their political qualifications and personal qualities. To be uncompromising whenever the Leninist principles of the selection and education of personnel are infringed;

(*i*) to observe Party and state discipline, which is equally binding on all Party members. The Party has one discipline, one law, for all Communists, irrespective of their past services or the positions they occupy;

(*j*) to help, in every possible way, to strengthen the defence potential of the USSR; to wage an unflagging struggle for peace and friendship among nations.

3. A Party member has the right:

(*a*) to elect and be elected to Party bodies;

(*b*) to discuss freely questions of the Party's policies and practical activities at Party meetings, conferences and congresses, at the meetings of Party committees and in the Party press; to table motions; openly to express and uphold his opinion as long as the Party organization concerned has not adopted a decision;

(*c*) to criticize any Communist, irrespective of the position he holds, at Party meetings, conferences and congresses, and at the full meetings of Party committees. Those who commit the offence of suppressing criticism or victimizing anyone for criticism are responsible to and will be penalized by the Party, to the point of expulsion from the CPSU;

(*d*) to attend in person all Party meetings and all bureau and committee meetings that discuss his activities or conduct;

(*e*) to address any question, statement or proposal to any Party body, up to and including the Central Committee of the CPSU, and to demand an answer on the substance of his address.

4. Applicants are admitted to Party membership only individually. Membership of the Party is open to politically conscious and active workers, peasants and representatives of the intelligentsia, devoted to the Communist cause. New members are admitted from among the candidate members who have passed through the established probationary period.

Persons may join the Party on attaining the age of eighteen. Young people up to the age of twenty-three may join the Party only through the Leninist Young Communist League of the Soviet Union (YCL).

The procedure for the admission of candidate members to full Party membership is as follows:

(*a*) Applicants for Party membership must submit recommendations from three members of the CPSU who have a Party standing of not less

317

than five years and who know the applicants from having worked with them, professionally and socially, for not less than one year.

Note 1.—In the case of members of the YCL applying for membership of the Party, the recommendation of a district or city committee of the YCL is equivalent to the recommendation of one Party member.

Note 2.—Members and alternate members of the Central Committee of the CPSU shall refrain from giving recommendations.

(*b*) Applications for Party membership are discussed and a decision is taken by the general meeting of the basic Party organization; the decision is taken if not less than two-thirds of the members present at the meeting vote for it, and it comes into force after endorsement by the district Party committee; or by the city Party committee in cities with no district divisions.

The presence of those who have recommended an applicant for Party membership at the discussion of the application concerned is optional;

(*c*) citizens of the USSR who formerly belonged to the Communist or Workers' Party of another country are admitted to membership of the Communist Party of the Soviet Union in conformity with the rules established by the Central Committee of the CPSU.

Former members of other parties are admitted to membership of the CPSU in conformity with the regular procedure, except that their admission must be endorsed by a regional or territorial committee or the Central Committee of the Communist Party of a Union Republic.

5. Communists recommending applicants for Party membership are responsible to Party organizations for the impartiality of their description of the moral qualities and professional and political qualifications of those they recommend.

6. The Party standing of those admitted to membership dates from the day when the general meeting of the basic Party organization decides to accept them as full members.

7. The procedure of registering members and candidate members of the Party, and their transfer from one organization to another is determined by the appropriate instructions of the Central Committee of the CPSU.

8. If a Party member or candidate member fails to pay membership dues for three months in succession without sufficient reason, the matter shall be discussed by the basic Party organization. If it is revealed as a result that the Party member or candidate member in question has virtually lost contact with the Party organization, he shall be regarded as having ceased to be a member of the Party; the basic Party organization shall pass a decision thereon and submit it to the district or city committee of the Party for endorsement.

9. A Party member or candidate member who fails to fulfil his duties as laid down in the Rules, or commits other offences, shall be called to account, and may be subjected to the penalty of admonition, reprimand (severe reprimand), or reprimand (severe reprimand) with entry in the registration card. The highest Party penalty is expulsion from the Party.

In the case of insignificant offences, measures of Party education and influence should be applied—in the form of comradely criticism, Party censure, warning or reproof.

When the question of expelling a member from the Party is discussed, the maximum attention must be shown, and the grounds for the charges preferred against him must be thoroughly investigated.

10. The decision to expel a Communist from the Party is made by the general meeting of a basic Party organization. The decision of the basic Party organization expelling a member is regarded as adopted if not less than two-thirds of the Party members attending the meeting have voted for it, and is subject to endorsement by the district or city Party committee.

Until such time as the decision to expel him is endorsed by a regional or territorial Party committee or the Central Committee of the Communist Party of a Union Republic, the Party member or candidate member retains his membership card and is entitled to attend closed Party meetings.

An expelled Party member retains the right to appeal, within the period of two months, to the higher Party bodies, up to and including the Central Committee of the CPSU.

11. The question of calling a member or alternate member of the Central Committee of the Communist Party of a Union Republic, of a territorial, regional, area, city or district Party committee, as well as a member of an auditing commission, to account before the Party is discussed by basic Party organizations.

Party organizations pass decisions imposing penalties on members or alternate members of the said Party committees, or on members of auditing commissions, in conformity with the regular procedure.

A Party organization which proposes expelling a Communist from the CPSU communicates its proposal to the Party committee of which he is a member. A decision expelling from the Party a member or alternate member of the Central Committee of the Communist Party of a Union Republic or a territorial, regional, area, city or district Party committee, or a member of an auditing commission, is taken at the full meeting of the committee concerned by a majority of two-thirds of the membership.

The decision to expel from the Party a member or alternate member of the Central Committee of the CPSU, or a member of the Central Auditing Commission, is made by the Party congress, and in the interval between two congresses, by a full meeting of the Central Committee, by a majority of two-thirds of its members.

12. Should a Party member commit an indictable offence, he shall be expelled from the Party and prosecuted in conformity with the law.

13. Appeals against expulsion from the Party or against the imposition of a penalty, as well as the decisions of Party organizations on expulsion from the Party shall be examined by the appropriate Party bodies within not more than one month from the date of their receipt.

II

Candidate Members

14. All persons joining the Party must pass through a probationary period as candidate members in order to familiarize themselves more

thoroughly with the Programme and the Rules of the CPSU and prepare for admission to full membership of the Party. Party organizations must assist candidates to prepare for admission to full membership of the Party, and test their personal qualities.

The period of probationary membership shall be one year.

15. The procedure for the admission of candidate members (individual admission, submission of recommendations, decision of the primary organization as to admission, and its endorsement) is identical with the procedure for the admission of Party members.

16. On the expiration of a candidate member's probationary period the basic Party organization discusses and passes a decision on his admission to full membership. Should a candidate member fail, in the course of his probationary period, to prove his worthiness, and should his personal traits make it evident that he cannot be admitted to membership of the CPSU, the Party organization shall pass a decision rejecting his admission to membership of the Party; after endorsement of that decision by the district or city Party committee, he shall cease to be considered a candidate member of the CPSU.

17. Candidate members of the Party participate in all the activities of their Party organizations; they shall have a consultative voice at Party meetings. They may not be elected to any leading Party body, nor may they be elected delegates to a Party conference or congress.

18. Candidate members of the CPSU pay membership dues at the same rate as full members.

III

Organizational Structure of the Party

Inner-Party Democracy

19. The guiding principle of the organizational structure of the Party is democratic centralism, which signifies:

(*a*) election of all leading Party bodies, from the lowest to the highest;

(*b*) periodical reports of Party bodies to their Party organizations and to higher bodies;

(*c*) strict Party discipline and subordination of the minority to the majority;

(*d*) the decisions of higher bodies are obligatory for lower bodies.

20. The Party is built on the territorial-and-production principle: basic organizations are established wherever Communists are employed, and are associated territorially in district, city, etc., organizations. An organization serving a given area is higher than any Party organization serving part of that area.

21. All Party organizations are autonomous in the decision of local questions, unless their decisions conflict with Party policy.

22. The highest leading body of a Party organization is the general meeting (in the case of basic organizations), conference (in the case of district, city, area, regional or territorial organizations), or congress (in the case of the Communist Parties of the Union Republics and the Communist Party of the Soviet Union).

23. The general meeting, conference or congress, elects a bureau or committee which acts as its executive body and directs all the current work of the Party organization.

24. The election of Party bodies shall be effected by secret ballot. In an election, all Party members have the unlimited right to challenge candidates and to criticize them. Each candidate shall be voted upon separately. A candidate is considered elected if more than one-half of those attending the meeting, conference or congress have voted for him. In elections to all Party organs—from basic organizations to the Central Committee of the CPSU—the principle of systematic renewal of their composition and continuity of leadership shall be observed.

25. A member or alternate member of the Central Committee of the CPSU must by his entire activity justify the great trust placed in him by the Party. A member or alternate member of the Central Committee of the CPSU who degrades his honour and dignity may not remain on the Central Committee. The question of the removal of a member or alternate member of the Central Committee of the CPSU from that body shall be decided by a full meeting of the Central Committee by secret ballot. The decision is regarded as adopted if not less than two-thirds of the membership of the Central Committee of the CPSU vote for it.

The question of the removal of a member or alternate member of the Central Committee of the Communist Party of a Union Republic, or of a territorial, regional, area, city or district Party committee from the Party body concerned is decided by a full meeting of that body. The decision is regarded as adopted if not less than two-thirds of the membership of the committee in question vote for it by secret ballot.

A member of the Central Auditing Commission who does not justify the great trust placed in him by the Party shall be removed from that body. This question shall be decided by a meeting of the Central Auditing Commission. The decision is regarded as adopted if not less than two-thirds of the membership of the Central Auditing Commission vote by secret ballot for the removal of the member concerned from that body.

The question of the removal of a member from the auditing commission of a republican, territorial, regional, area, city or district Party organization shall be decided by a meeting of the appropriate commission according to the procedure established for members and alternate members of Party committees.

26. The free and business-like discussion of questions of Party policy in individual Party organizations or in the Party as a whole is the inalienable right of every Party member and an important principle of inner-Party democracy. Only on the basis of inner-Party democracy is it possible to develop criticism and self-criticism and to strengthen Party discipline, which must be conscious and not mechanical.

Discussion of controversial or insufficiently clear issues may be held within the framework of individual organizations or the Party as a whole.

Party-wide discussion is necessary:

(a) if the necessity is recognized by several Party organizations at regional or republican level;

(*b*) if there is not a sufficiently solid majority in the Central Committee on major questions of Party policy;

(*c*) if the Central Committee of the CPSU considers it necessary to consult the Party as a whole on any particular question of policy.

Wide discussion, especially discussion on a country-wide scale, of questions of Party policy must be so held as to ensure for Party members the free expression of their views and preclude attempts to form factional groupings destroying Party unity, attempts to split the Party.

27. The supreme principle of Party leadership is collective leadership, which is an absolute requisite for the normal functioning of Party organizations, the proper education of cadres, and the promotion of the activity and initiative of Communists. The cult of the individual and the violations of inner-Party democracy resulting from it must not be tolerated in the Party; they are incompatible with the Leninist principles of Party life.

Collective leadership does not exempt individuals in office from personal responsibility for the job entrusted to them.

28. The Central Committees of the Communist Parties of the Union Republics, and territorial, regional, area, city and district Party committees shall systematically inform Party organizations of their work in the interim between congresses and conferences.

29. Meetings of the active of district, city, area, regional and territorial Party organizations and of the Communist Parties of the Union Republics shall be held to discuss major decisions of the Party and to work out measures for their execution, as well as to examine questions of local significance.

IV

Higher Party Organs

30. The supreme organ of the Communist Party of the Soviet Union is the Party Congress. Congresses are convened by the Central Committee at least once in five years. The convocation of a Party Congress and its agenda shall be announced at least six weeks before the Congress. Extraordinary congresses are convened by the Central Committee of the Party on its own initiative or on the demand of not less than one-third of the total membership represented at the preceding Party congress. Extraordinary congresses shall be convened within two months. A congress is considered properly constituted if not less than one-half of the total Party membership is represented at it.

The scale of representation at a Party Congress is determined by the Central Committee.

31. Should the Central Committee of the Party fail to convene an extraordinary congress within the period specified in Article 30, the organizations which demanded it have the right to form an Organizing Committee which shall enjoy the powers of the Central Committee of the Party in respect of the convocation of the extraordinary congress.

32. The Congress:

(*a*) hears and approves the reports of the Central Committee, of the

Central Auditing Commission, and of the other central organizations;

(*b*) reviews, amends and endorses the Programme and the Rules of the Party;

(*c*) determines the line of the Party in matters of home and foreign policy, and examines and decides the most important questions of Communist construction;

(*d*) elects the Central Committee and the Central Auditing Commission.

33. The number of members to be elected to the Central Committee and to the Central Auditing Commission is determined by the Congress. In the event of vacancies occurring in the Central Committee, they are filled from among the alternate members of the Central Committee of the CPSU elected by the Congress.

34. Between congresses, the Central Committee of the Communist Party of the Soviet Union directs the activities of the Party, the local Party bodies, selects and appoints leading officials, directs the work of central government bodies and public organizations of working people through the Party groups in them, sets up various Party organs, institutions and enterprises and directs their activities, appoints the editors of the central newspapers and journals operating under its control, and distributes the funds of the Party budget and controls its execution.

The Central Committee represents the CPSU in its relations with other parties.

35. The Central Committee of the CPSU shall keep the Party organizations regularly informed of its work.

36. The Central Auditing Commission of the CPSU supervises the expeditious and proper handling of affairs by the central bodies of the Party, and audits the accounts of the treasury and the enterprises of the Central Committee of the CPSU.

37. The Central Committee of the CPSU shall hold not less than one full meeting every six months. Alternate members of the Central Committee shall attend its full meetings with consultative voice.

38. The Central Committee of the Communist Party of the Soviet Union elects a Politbureau to direct the work of the Central Committee between full meetings and a Secretariat to direct current work, chiefly the selection of cadres and the verification of the fulfilment of Party decisions. The Central Committee elects the General Secretary of the C.C. of the CPSU.

39. The Central Committee of the Communist Party of the Soviet Union sets up the Party Control Committee of the Central Committee.

The Party Control Committee of the Central Committee of the CPSU:

(*a*) verifies the observance of Party discipline by members and candidate members of the CPSU, and takes action against Communists who violate the Programme and the Rules of the Party or state discipline, and against violators of Party ethics;

(*b*) considers appeals against decisions of Central Committees of the Communist Parties of the Union Republics or of territorial and regional Party committees to expel members from the Party or impose Party penalties upon them.

323

40. In the period between Party Congresses the Central Committee of the CPSU, in cases of necessity, may call an All-Union Party Conference for the discussion of impending questions of Party policy. The agenda of the All-Union Party Conference shall be determined by the C.C. of the CPSU.

V

Republican, Territorial, Regional, Area, City and District Organizations of the Party

41. The republican, territorial, regional, area, city and district Party organizations and their committees take guidance in their activities from the Programme and the Rules of the CPSU, conduct all work for the implementation of Party policy and organize the fulfilment of the directives of the Central Committee of the CPSU within the republics, territories, regions, areas, cities and districts concerned.

42. The basic duties of republican, territorial, regional, area, city and district Party organizations, and of their leading bodies, are:

(*a*) political and organizational work among the masses, mobilization of the masses for the fulfilment of the tasks of Communist construction, for the maximum development of industrial and agricultural production, for the fulfilment and over-fulfilment of state plans; solicitude for the steady improvement of the material and cultural standards of the working, people;

(*b*) organization of ideological work, propaganda of Marxism–Leninism, promotion of the Communist awareness of the working people, guidance of the local press, radio and television, and supervision over the activities of cultural and educational institutions;

(*c*) guidance of Soviets, trade unions, the YCL, the co-operative and other public organizations through the Party groups in them, and increasingly broader enlistment of working people in the activities of these organizations, development of the initiative and activity of the masses as an essential condition for the gradual transition from socialist statehood to public self-government under communism. Party organizations must not act in place of government, trade union, co-operative or other public organizations of the working people; they must not allow either the merging of the functions of Party and other bodies or undue parallelism in work;

(*d*) selection and appointment of leading personnel, their education in the spirit of Communist ideas, honesty and truthfulness, and a high sense of responsibility to the Party and the people for the work entrusted to them;

(*e*) large-scale enlistment of Communists in the conduct of Party activities as voluntary workers, as a form of social work;

(*f*) organization of various institutions and enterprises of the Party within the bounds of their republic, territory, region, area, city or district, and guidance of their activities; distribution of Party funds within the given organization; the provision of systematic information to the higher Party body and accountability to it for their work.

Leading Bodies of Republican, Territorial and Regional Party Organizations

43. The highest body of regional, territorial and republican Party organizations is the respective regional or territorial Party conference or the congress of the Communist Party of the Union Republic, and in the interim between them the regional committee, territorial committee or the Central Committee of the Communist Party of the Union Republic.

44. Regular regional and territorial conferences are convened by the regional and territorial committees once in two or three years. Regular congresses of the Communist Parties of the Union Republics are convened by the Central Committees of the Communist Parties at least once in five years. Extraordinary conferences and congresses are convened by decision of regional and territorial committees, by the Central Committees of the Communist Parties of Union Republics, or by the demand of one-third of the total membership of the organizations belonging to the regional territorial and republican Party organization.

The scale of representation at regional and territorial conferences of the Communist Parties of the Union Republics is determined by the respective Party committees.

Regional and territorial conferences and congresses of the Communist Parties of Union Republics hear the reports of the respective regional or territorial committees, or the Central Committee of the Communist Party of the Union Republic, and of the Auditing Commission; discuss at their own discretion the matters of the Party, economic and cultural development, and elect the regional or territorial committee, the Central Committee of the Union Republic, the Auditing Commission and the delegates to the Congress of the CPSU.

In the period between congresses of Communist Parties of Union Republics the Central Committees of the Communist Parties may, in cases of necessity, convene a Republican Party Conference for the discussion of the activities of Party organizations. The agenda of the Republican Party Conferences shall be determined by the Central Committees of the Communist Parties of the Union Republics.

45. The regional and territorial committees and the Central Committees of the Communist Parties of the Union Republics elect bureaus, which also include secretaries of the committees. The secretaries must have a Party standing of not less than five years. The full meetings of the committees also confirm the chairmen of Party commissions, heads of departments of these committees, editors of Party newspapers and journals.

Regional and territorial committees and the Central Committees of the Communist Parties of the Union Republics may set up secretariats to examine current business and verify the execution of decisions.

46. The full meetings of regional and territorial committees and the Central Committees of the Communist Parties of the Union Republics shall be convened at least once every four months.

47. The regional and territorial committees and the Central Committees of the Communist Parties of the Union Republics direct the area, city and district Party organizations, inspect their work and regularly hear reports of area, city and district Party committees.

Party organizations in Autonomous Republics, and in autonomous and other regions forming part of a territory or a Union Republic, function under the guidance of the respective territorial committees or Central Committees of the Communist Parties of the Union Republics.

Leading Bodies of Area, City and District (Urban and Rural) Party Organizations

48. The highest body of an area, city or district Party organization is the area, city and district Party conference or the general meeting of Communists convened by the area, city or district committee at least once in two years, and the extraordinary conference convened by decision of the respective committee or on the demand of one-third of the total membership of the Party organization concerned.

The area, city or district conference (general meeting) hears reports of the committee and auditing commission, discusses at its own discretion other questions of Party, economic and cultural development, and elects the area, city and district committee, the auditing commission and delegates to the regional and territorial conference or the congress of the Communist Party of the Union Republic.

The scale of representation to the area, city or district conference is established by the respective Party committee.

49. The area, city or district committee elects a bureau, including the committee secretaries, and confirms the appointments of heads of committee departments and newspaper editors. The secretaries of the area, city and district committees must have a Party standing of at least three years. The committee secretaries are confirmed by the respective regional or territorial committee, or the Central Committee of the Communist Party of the Union Republic.

50. The area, city and district committee organizes and confirms the basic Party organizations, directs their work, regularly hears reports concerning the work of Party organizations, and keeps a register of Communists.

51. The full meeting of the area, city and district committee is convened at least once in three months.

52. The area, city and district committee has voluntary officials, sets up standing or *ad hoc* commissions on various aspects of Party work and uses other ways to draw Communists into the activities of the Party committee on a voluntary basis.

VI

Basic Party Organizations

53. The basic Party organizations are the basis of the Party.

Basic Party organizations are formed at the places of work of Party members—in factories, state farms and other enterprises, collective farms, units of the Soviet Army, offices, educational establishments, etc., wherever there are not less than three Party members. Basic Party organizations may also be organized on the residential principle in villages and in blocks of flats.

Under special circumstances, with the consent of the regional committee, the territorial committee, or the Central Committee of a Union Republic, basic Party organizations may be formed within the framework of some enterprises which have entered into production unions and extend, as a rule, over the territory of one or several districts of a city.

54. At enterprises, collective farms and institutions with over fifty Party members and candidate members, shop, sectional, farm, team, departmental, etc., Party organizations may be formed as units of the general basic Party organization with the sanction of the district, city or area committee.

Within shop, sectional, etc., organizations, and also within basic Party organizations having less than fifty members and candidate members, Party groups may be formed in the teams and other production units.

55. The highest organ of the basic Party organization is the Party meeting, which is convened at least once a month.

In Party organizations having shop organizations a general Party meeting shall take place at least every two months.

In large Party organizations with a membership of more than 300 Communists, a general Party meeting is convened when necessary at times fixed by the Party committee or on the demand of a number of shop or departmental Party organizations.

56. For the conduct of current business the branch, shop or departmental Party organization elects a bureau for the term of one year. The number of its members is fixed by the Party meeting. Branch, shop and departmental Party organizations with less than fifteen Party members do not elect a bureau. Instead, they elect a secretary and deputy secretary of the Party organization.

Secretaries of branch, shop and departmental Party organizations must have a Party standing of at least one year.

Basic Party organizations with less than 150 Party members shall have, as a rule, no salaried officials released from their regular work.

57. In large factories and offices with more than three hundred members and candidate members of the Party, and in exceptional cases in factories and offices with over one hundred Communists by virtue of special production conditions and territorial dispersion, subject to the approval of the regional committee, territorial committee or Central Committee of the Communist Party of the Union Republic, Party committees may be formed, the shop and departmental Party organizations at these factories and offices being granted the status of basic Party organizations.

The Party organizations of collective farms may set up Party committees if they have a minimum of fifty Communists.

In Party organizations with more than 500 Communists Party committees may be formed, with the approval of the regional or territorial committee or of the Central Committee of the Union Republic, in large workshops, but the Party organizations of production divisions retain the powers of basic Party organizations.

327

The Party committees are elected for a term of two or three years. Their numerical composition is fixed by the general Party meeting or conference.

58. Party committees of basic organizations with more than 1000 Communists, with the approval of the Central Committee of the Union Republic, may exercise the powers of a district Party committee on questions of admissions to the CPSU, keeping account of members and candidate members of the Party, and examining the personal activity of Communists.

59. In its activities the basic Party organization takes guidance from the Programme and the Rules of the CPSU. It conducts its work directly among the working people, rallies them round the Communist Party of the Soviet Union, organizes the masses to carry out the Party policy and to work for the building of communism.

The basic Party organization:

(*a*) admits new members to the CPSU;

(*b*) educates Communists in a spirit of loyalty to the Party cause, ideological staunchness and communist ethics;

(*c*) organizes the study by Communists of Marxist–Leninist theory in close connection with the practice of communist construction and opposes all attempts to introduce revisionist distortions of Marxism–Leninism or a dogmatic interpretation of Marxism–Leninism;

(*d*) ensures the vanguard role of Communists in the sphere of labour and in the social and political and economic activities of enterprises, collective farms, institutions, educational establishments, etc.;

(*e*) acts as the organizer of the working people for the performance of the current tasks of communist construction, heads the socialist emulation movement for the fulfilment of state plans and undertakings of the working people, rallies the masses to disclose and make the best use of untapped resources at enterprises and collective farms, and to apply in production on a broad scale the achievements of science, engineering and the experience of front-rankers; works for the strengthening of labour discipline, the steady increase of labour productivity and improvement of the quality of production, and shows concern for the protection and increase of social wealth at enterprises, state farms and collective farms;

(*f*) conducts agitational and propaganda work among the masses, educates them in the communist spirit, helps the working people to acquire proficiency in administering state and social affairs;

(*g*) on the basis of extensive criticism and self-criticism, combats cases of bureaucracy, parochialism and violations of state discipline, thwarts attempts to deceive the state, acts against negligence, waste and extravagance at enterprises, collective farms and offices;

(*h*) assists the area, city and district committees in their activities and is accountable to them for its work. The Party organization must see to it that every Communist should observe in his own life and cultivate among working people the moral principles set forth in the Programme of the CPSU, in the moral code of the builder of communism:

loyalty to the Communist cause, love of his own socialist country, and of other socialist countries;

conscientious labour for the benefit of society, for he who does not work, neither shall he eat;

concern on everyone's part for the protection and increase of social wealth;

lofty sense of public duty, intolerance of violations of public interests;

collectivism and comradely mutual assistance: one for all, and all for one;

humane relationships and mutual respect among people: man is to man a friend, comrade and brother;

honesty and truthfulness, moral purity, unpretentiousness and modesty in public and personal life;

mutual respect in the family circle and concern for the upbringing of children;

intolerance of injustice, parasitism, dishonesty, careerism and money-grubbing;

friendship and fraternity among all peoples of the USSR, intolerance of national and racial hostility;

intolerance of the enemies of communism, the enemies of peace and those who oppose the freedom of the peoples;

fraternal solidarity with the working people of all countries, with all peoples.

60. Basic Party organizations of industrial enterprises, transport, communications, construction, material-technical supply, trade, public catering, cultural and communal services, collective farms, state farms and other agricultural enterprises, planning organizations, construction bureaus, scientific research institutes, educational establishments, cultural enlightenment and medical establishments, shall exercise the right of control over administrative activities.

Party organizations in Ministries, State Committees and other central and local Soviet economic agencies and departments, exercise control over the work of the apparatus for the fulfilling of directives of the Party and government, for the observance of Soviet laws. They must actively seek the improvement of the work of the apparatus, educate employees in the spirit of high responsibility for the entrusted duty, take measures for the strengthening of state discipline, for the improvement of service to the people, to carry on a decisive struggle with bureaucracy and red-tape, timely to inform the responsible Party organs of shortcomings in the work of institutions and of individual workers, irrespective of the importance of their positions.

VII

The Party and the YCL

61. The Leninist Young Communist League of the Soviet Union is an independently acting social organization of young people, an active helper and reserve of the Party. The YCL helps the Party educate the youth in a communist spirit, to draw it into the work of building a new society, to

train a rising generation of harmoniously developed people who will live and work and administer public affairs under Communism.

62. YCL organizations enjoy the right of broad initiative in discussing and submitting to the appropriate Party organizations questions relating to the work of enterprises, collective farms and offices. They must be active levers in the implementation of Party directives in all spheres of Communist construction, especially where there are no basic Party organizations.

63. The YCL conducts its activities under the guidance of the Communist Party of the Soviet Union. The work of the local YCL organizations is directed and controlled by the appropriate republican, territorial, regional, area, city and district Party organizations.

In their Communist educational work among the youth, local Party bodies and primary Party organizations rely on the support of the YCL organizations, and uphold and promote their useful undertakings.

64. Members of the YCL who have been admitted into the CPSU cease to belong to the YCL the moment they join the Party, provided they do not hold leading posts in YCL organizations.

VIII

Party Organizations in the Soviet Army

65. Party organizations in the Soviet Army are guided in their work by the Programme and the Rules of the CPSU and operate on the basis of instructions issued by the Central Committee.

The Party organizations of the Soviet Army carry out the policy of the Party in the Armed Forces, rally servicemen round the Communist Party, educate them in the spirit of Marxism–Leninism and boundless loyalty to the socialist homeland, actively further the unity of the army and the people, work for the strengthening of military discipline, rally servicemen to carry out the tasks of military and political training and acquire skill in the use of new technique and weapons, and to carry out irreproachably their military duty and the orders and instructions of the command.

66. The guidance of Party work in the Armed Forces is exercised by the Central Committee of the CPSU through the Chief Political Administration of the Soviet Army and Navy, which functions as a department of the Central Committee of the CPSU.

The heads of the political administrations of military areas and fleets, and heads of the political administrations of armies must be Party members of five-years' standing, and the heads of political departments of military formations must be Party members of three-years' standing.

67. The Party organizations and political bodies of the Soviet Army maintain close contact with local Party committees, and keep them informed about political work in the military units. The secretaries of military Party organizations and heads of political bodies participate in the work of local Party committees.

IX

Party Groups in Non-Party Organizations

68. At congresses, conferences and meetings and in the elective bodies of Soviets, trade unions, co-operatives and other mass organizations of the working people, having at least three Party members, Party groups are formed for the purpose of strengthening the influence of the Party in every way and carrying out Party policy among non-Party people, strengthening Party and state discipline, combating bureaucracy, and verifying the fulfilment of Party and government directives.

69. The Party groups are subordinate to the appropriate Party bodies: the Central Committee of the Communist Party of the Soviet Union, the Central Committees of the Communist Parties of the Union Republics, territorial, regional, area, city or district Party committees.

In all matters the groups must strictly and unswervingly abide by decisions of the leading Party bodies.

X

Party Funds

70. The funds of the Party and its organizations are derived from membership dues, incomes from Party enterprises and other revenue.

71. The monthly membership dues for Party members and candidate members are as follows:

Monthly earnings	Dues	
up to 50 roubles	10 kopeks	
from 51 to 100 roubles	0·5 per cent	
from 101 to 150 roubles	1·0 per cent	
from 151 to 200 roubles	1·5 per cent	of monthly
from 201 to 250 roubles	2·0 per cent	earnings
from 251 to 300 roubles	2·5 per cent	
over 300 roubles	3·0 per cent	

72. An entrance fee of 2% of monthly earnings is paid on admission to the Party as a candidate member.

Appendix IV

ON SOVIET ECONOMIC DEVELOPMENT AND THE REORGANIZATION OF PARTY GUIDANCE OF THE NATIONAL ECONOMY

(Excerpts from the Decision adopted by the Plenum of the Central Committee of the CPSU, November 23, 1962)

. . . . .

The 22nd Congress of the CPSU has advanced as a primary and most important task of the Party the further improvement of national economic guidance. It is now necessary to bring Party guidance of industry, construction and agriculture into line with the demands of the time. The reorganization of the guidance of the national economy is of great political importance in the conditions of full-scale Communist construction, when the role of the Party has immeasurably grown.

Nowadays the Party is required not only to possess an ability to advance the proper slogan at the right time but to efficiently guide production and the development of industry and agriculture and all branches of the economy constantly and concretely.

The rate of development of the national economy depends chiefly on the labour efforts of millions, on the ability to organize the implementation of the Party's policy and plans for economic advance.

However, the organizational forms of guidance of the national economy, which took shape earlier and which in their time played a positive role, do not now enable all branches of industry and agriculture to be run in a more concrete and smooth manner, do not permit timely and effective steps to be taken to remove existing shortcomings. They give rise to fondness for declarations and spasmodic campaigns in the guidance of the economy and prevent the proper distribution of Party cadres and better use of their knowledge and experience.

In order to overcome the above-mentioned failings and to improve the guidance of the national economy, it is necessary to go over to the production principle of organizing leading bodies of the Party from top to bottom.

The organization of Party organs on the production principle makes it possible to ensure more concrete and smooth guidance in industry, construction and agriculture, and to concentrate the main attention on production matters. Such a reorganization will help activize all aspects of Party work and link organizational and ideological work still closer to

332

the tasks of creating the material and technical basis for Communism and moulding the new man.

. . . . .

Proceeding from the Party's general policy of reducing the administrative machinery and improving its work, the plenum of the Central Committee of the CPSU emphasizes that the radical reorganization of the Party, government and economic agencies, far from increasing the number of the executives, will on the contrary decrease it and reduce the administrative maintenance expenses.

The Soviet people, who have the honour to be the first to pave the way to communism, have accumulated vast experience in economic development. In reorganizing the management of the national economy, the Communist Party proceeds from Lenin's instructions on the need to constantly improve the forms of organization of the new society and of management of the socialist economy.

The Plenum of the Central Committee of the Communist Party of the Soviet Union resolves:

I

In the field of Party guidance of the national economy:

1. To approve the measures for the reorganization of Party guidance of the national economy, worked out by the Presidium of the CPSU Central Committee and set forth in the report of N. S. Khrushchev at this plenum of the Central Committee.

2. To recognize the need to reorganize the leading Party bodies from top to bottom on the production principle, thus ensuring more concrete guidance of industrial and agricultural production.

To set up, as a rule, two independent Party organizations within the limits of the present existing Territories and Provinces (Regions):

A Territorial, Regional Party organization uniting Communists working in industry, construction and transport, at educational and research institutes, and projecting, designing and other establishments working for industrial production and construction;

A Territorial, Regional Party organization uniting Communists working in collective farms and state farms, at experimental stations, agricultural educational establishments and research institutes, at enterprises processing agricultural raw materials, procurement and other establishments and organizations connected with agricultural production.

To have in a Territorial, Regional Party organization correspondingly:

A Territorial, Regional Party Committee for Industrial Production;
A Territorial, Regional Party Committee for Agricultural Production.

3. With a view to improving national economic guidance to acknowledge the advisability of setting up a Bureau of the Central Committee for Industrial Production and a Bureau of the Central Committee for Agricultural Production in the Central Committee of the CPSU and the Central Committees of the Communist Parties of the Union Republics.

For the settlement of questions of Republican importance and for the co-ordination of the activities of the specialized bureaux to elect a Central Committee Presidium in the Central Committees of the Union Republics.

4. To consider it advisable for collective farm and state farm management boards to be formed on the basis of the enlargement of the now existing rural districts, and for Party Committees of production management boards to be set up instead of Rural District Party Committees.

For the guidance of Party organizations of enterprises and construction sites on the territory of the agricultural production management boards that are to be set up, to have zonal industrial production Party Committees where there are no City Party Committees.

5. To lay down that the new Party organs for the guidance of industrial and agricultural production should be governed in all their activities by the corresponding provisions of the Rules of the CPSU on Territorial and Regional Party organizations, while the Party Committees of collective farm and state farm production management boards must be governed by the provisions of the Rules of the CPSU on City and District Party organizations.

6. With a view to electing new Party organs, to hold Conferences of Party organizations of collective farm and state farm production management boards and also City, District (in cities), Regional and Territorial Conferences of industrial and agricultural Party organizations, in December 1962 and January 1963.

. . . . . .

III

In the field of Party-state control:

1. To reorganize the system of control in the country, using as its basis Lenin's behest that Party and state control be merged and a uniform, permanently operating control system set up with broad sections of the working people participating in it.

2. To form a single organ of Party and state control—the Committee of Party-State Control of the Central Committee of the CPSU and the Council of Ministers of the USSR, and corresponding organs locally.

To consider the most important task of the Party-state control organs to help the Party and the state implement the CPSU programme, organize systematic check-ups on the fulfilment of the directives of the Party and the government, improve still further the guidance of Communist construction and to observe Party and state discipline and socialist laws.

3. To reorganize the now functioning Party Control Committee of the Central Committee of the CPSU into a Party Commission of the Central Committee of the CPSU, giving it the duty of considering appeals against decisions of the Central Committees of the Communist Parties of the Union Republics, and territorial and regional Party Committees on expulsion from the CPSU and on Party penalties.

4. To consider it inexpedient to retain in the future the State Control Commission of the Council of Ministers of the USSR and its local organs,

Appendix V

DECISION OF THE PLENUM
OF THE C.C. OF THE CPSU
CONCERNING THE UNIFICATION
OF INDUSTRIAL AND RURAL OBLAST
AND KRAI PARTY ORGANIZATIONS
NOVEMBER 16, 1964.

(*Pravda* November 17, 1964)

1. With the aim of strengthening the leading role of the Party and its local organs in Communist construction, the more rapid solution of the tasks of economic and cultural development in each Oblast, Krai and Republic, to consider the necessity to return to the principle of constructing Party organizations and their leading organs according to the territorial-production principle which comprised a most important part of the Rules of the CPSU adopted by the 22nd Party Congress.

2. To restore in Oblasts and Krais where Party organizations were divided into industrial and rural, united Oblast and Krai Party organizations, uniting all Communists in the Oblast or Krai whether workers in industry or agriculture.

Krai and Oblast Party organizations to have united Krai and Oblast Party Committees.

3. To recognize the necessity to reorganize Party Committees of Kolkhoz-Sovkhoz Production Boards into Raion Party Committees having concentrated into their hands all Party organizations including those in industrial enterprises and construction sites situated on the territory of the given Raion.

To abolish the Industrial Production (Zonal) Party Committees established earlier on the territories of the rural Raions and in Oblast and Republican centres.

4. To hold in December 1964 in all Krais and Oblasts where united Krai and Oblast Party Committees are being restored, Party Conferences to elect the corresponding Party organs.

5. To approve the proposals elaborated by the Presidium of the C.C. of the CPSU concerning the method of consolidating Krai and Oblast Industrial and Rural Party organizations. To commission the Presidium of the C.C. to examine and to decide all organizational questions connected with the creation in Krais and Oblasts of united Party organizations and leading organs and also with the restoration of united Soviet organs.

335

Appendix VI

A SOVIET DEFINITION OF DEMOCRACY

(Translated from *Politichesky slovar*, Moscow, 1958, pp. 163–5.)

DEMOCRACY (Lit. people's power) is a political system in which power belongs to the people. Democracy always has a class character and is nothing less than the political form of the dictatorship of the ruling classes.

In capitalist society democracy represents a particular form of the class domination of the bourgeoisie, under which the equality of citizens before the law is declared, personal and democratic freedoms are proclaimed by law: freedom of speech, press, meeting, etc. However, these freedoms have a limited character as there cannot be in reality equality between exploiters and exploited, between capitalists and workers. The state apparatus of bourgeois democracy defends the interests of property owners using thousands of tricks in order to prevent the workers from participating in administration, hindering their access to the highest representative organ of the bourgeois state—the parliament.

The establishment of bourgeois democracy, notwithstanding its restricted character, had a progressive significance since it led to the liquidation of serfdom and promoted the growth of the productive forces. In so far as the development of capitalism strengthened the power of the bourgeoisie, the bourgeoisie retreated from the conquests of the bourgeois revolution and transforming itself by force of circumstances retarded the further progress of society.

In the epoch of imperialism, the turning from democracy to political reaction in the political superstructure of capitalist society is continued. The bourgeoisie begins to attack the democratic rights of the workers. However, this policy of the imperialists meets resistance from the side of the proletariat of the capitalist countries, headed by the Communist and Workers' Parties. The struggle for democracy is the school in which the consciousness and solidarity of the proletariat and its political maturity are nurtured. V. I. Lenin showed that the working class which is not educated in the struggle for democracy is unable to accomplish economic revolution, to take state power into its hands. In contemporary circumstances, as a result of radical changes in favour of socialism, in the ranks of capitalist countries, the working class, the leading toilers, peasantry and all patriotic forces, have the possibility of capturing a firm majority in parliament and of turning it from an organ of bourgeois democracy into a weapon of real people's power.

Proletarian socialist democracy represents a new, historically higher type of democracy. The *dictatorship of the proletariat* forms the basic political content of the period of transition from capitalism to socialism; the essence of which is the power of the people, for the people, and in the interests of the people. Carrying out the political leadership of society the working class and its Communist Party draw all workers into the administration of the state, create the circumstances for the development of economic and political independent activity of the masses in the interests of building socialism and communism.

In the socialist state the broad popular masses take a direct part in deciding state matters through a system of representative working organs of power. The apparatus of the socialist state is constructed in conformity with the principle of *democratic centralism*. The organs of executive power are accountable to the corresponding elected organs; the control of the masses over the activity of the state apparatus is also provided for in the elected people's judges and assessors, and their accountability to the electors.

A brilliant example of the breadth of democratism of socialist society is the general public discussion of questions concerning the further perfecting of the organizations of administration of industry and construction in 1957. In enterprises and construction sites, in scientific organizations and institutes, in collective farms, MTS and state farms, in units of the Soviet Army and in academic institutions, more than 514 thousand meetings took place in which over 40·8 million workers participated, of which more than 2 million 300 thousand presented their views and proposals. More than 68 thousand persons put forward proposals in central and local newspapers.

Marxist–Leninist theory teaches that each nation in carrying out the socialist revolution has its peculiarity in one or other form of proletarian democracy, in one or other variant of the dictatorship of the proletariat. In the Soviet Union socialist democracy found its realization in the practical construction of the *Soviet State*, legally consolidated by the Constitution of the USSR. In the countries of people's democracy proletarian democracy was realized in the form of *People's Democracy*.

Appendix VII

TEXT OF CERTAIN ARTICLES OF THE
USSR CONSTITUTION

(As amended to December 1973)
Article 70

The Council of Ministers of the USSR is appointed by the Supreme Soviet of the USSR and consists of:

The Chairman of the Council of Ministers of the USSR.

The First Deputy-Chairmen of the Council of Ministers of the USSR.

The Deputy-Chairmen of the Council of Ministers of the USSR.

The Ministers of the USSR.

The Chairman of the State Planning Committee of the Council of Ministers of the USSR.

The Chairman of the State Committee on Construction Affairs of the Council of Ministers of the USSR.

The Chairman of the State Committee on Material-Technical Supply of the Council of Ministers of the USSR.

The Chairman of the USSR Committee of People's Control.

The Chairman of the State Committee of the Council of Ministers of the USSR on Questions of Labour and Wages.

The Chairman of the State Committee of the Council of Ministers of the USSR on Science and Technology.

The Chairman of the State Committee of the Council of Ministers of the USSR on Inventions and Discoveries.

The Chairman of the State Committee on Prices of the Council of Ministers of the USSR.

The Chairman of the State Committee on Standards of the Council of Ministers of the USSR.

The Chairman of the State Committee of the Council of Ministers of the USSR on Professional and Technical Education.

The Chairman of the State Committee of the USSR Council of Ministers on Radio and Television Broadcasting.

The Chairman of the State Forestry Committee of the USSR Council of Ministers.

The Chairman of the State Committee of the USSR Council of Ministers on Foreign Economic Relations.

The Chairman of the Committee on State Security of the Council of Ministers of the USSR.

338

The Chairman of the All-Union organization 'Soyuzselkoztekhnika' of the Council of Ministers of the USSR.

The Chairman of the Board of the USSR State Bank.

The Chief of the Central Statistical Administration of the Council of Ministers of the USSR.

The Council of Ministers of the USSR includes the Chairmen of the Councils of Ministers of the Union Republics by virtue of their office.

Article 77

The following Ministries are All-Union Ministries:

Aviation Industry.
Automobile Industry.
Foreign Trade.
Gas Industry.
Civil Aviation.
Machine Building.
Machine Building for Cattle-rearing and Fodder Production.
Machine Building for Light and Consumer Goods Industry.
Medical Industry.
Shipping.
Oil Industry.
Defence Industry.
General Machine Building.
Means of Automation and Systems of Management.
Railways.
Radio Industry.
Medium Machine Building.
Machine and Instrument Making.
Construction, Road and Communal Machinery.
Construction of Enterprises for the Oil and Gas Industries.
Shipbuilding.
Tractor and Agricultural Machine Building.
Transport Building.
Heavy, Power and Transport Engineering.
Chemical and Oil Machine Building.
Chemical Industry.
Cellulose-Paper Industry.
Electrical Industry.
Electro-Technical Industry.

Article 78

The following Ministries are Union-Republican Ministries:

Internal Affairs.
Higher and Secondary Specialist Education.

Geology.
State Purchasing.
Health.
Foreign Affairs.
Culture.
Light Industry.
Timber and Wood-Working Industry.
Irrigation and Water Conservation.
Assembly and Specialized Building Works.
Meat and Dairy Industry.
Oil Extracting Industry.
Defence.
Food Industry.
Industrial Construction.
Building Materials Industry.
Education.
Fisheries.
Communications.
Agricultural Construction.
Agriculture.
Construction.
Construction of Heavy Industrial Plants.
Trade.
Coal Industry.
Finance.
Non-Ferrous Metallurgy.
Ferrous Metallurgy.
Electric Power Development and Electrification.
Justice.

Bibliography

The sources used in preparing this book are clearly indicated in the Notes to each chapter, in the Selected Bibliographies and in the main Bibliography. Some gaps in the sources are a consequence of the author's preferences; others reflect the geographical isolation of Australia, and the inadequacies of Australian libraries in Soviet material. Thus I have not had regular access to the indispensable *Current Digest of the Soviet Press*. Instead I have had to rely on a narrower selection of Russian newspapers, chiefly *Izvestia, Pravda* and *Sovetskaya Rossia*. Soviet journals, which I have used more or less steadily over the past decade, include the following (listed roughly in order of importance):

> *Sovety deputatov trudyashchikhsya* (cited as *Sovety*),
> *Sovetskoe gosudarstvo i pravo* (cited as *S.G.i.P.*),
> *Partiinaya zhizn,*
> *Kommunist,*
> *Finansy SSSR,*
> *Vedomosti verkhovnovo Soveta SSSR,*
> *Voprosy ekonomiki,*
> *Voprosy filosofii,*
> *Voprosy istorii.*

During two trips to Europe (1957 and 1964–65) I had access to a much wider range of material in specialized libraries at St. Antony's College (Oxford), the Centre for Russian and East European Studies (Birmingham), the Institute of Soviet and East European Studies (Glasgow), and at the Institute of State and Law (Moscow), and the Fundamental Library of the Social Sciences (Moscow).

The following list of references includes all the main works used in the preparation of the book, including the titles of books and pamphlets in Russian. It includes all articles in English referred to in the text, Notes and Selected Bibliographies. It does not include articles written in Russian although these have been used extensively. However, many specific references to Russian periodicals are cited in the Notes.

The Selected Bibliographies which follow each chapter are intended mainly for students using *Contemporary Soviet Government* as a textbook. The references are selected so as to provide both supplementary material and alternative interpretations to those contained in the book.

ABRAMOVITCH, RAPHAEL R. (1962) *The Soviet Revolution*, London; Allen & Unwin.

BIBLIOGRAPHY

AFANASYEV, V. *Marxist Philosophy*, Moscow, n.d.

A History of the Communist Party of the Soviet Union (Bolsheviks), Moscow, 1938. Sydney, 1942.

ALBITSKY, P. D. (1956) *Voprosy obshchevo nadzora v praktike sovetskoi prokuratury*, Moscow.

ALEKSANDROV, N. G. (1961) *Gosudarstvo i Kummunizm*, Moscow, 1961.

ALLAKHVERDYAN, D. A., ed. (1966) *Soviet Financial System*, Moscow.

ALMOND, GABRIEL A. (1950) *The American People and Foreign Policy*, New York.

ANANOV, I. N. (1958) *Razvitie organizatsionnykh form upravlenia promyshlennostyu v SSSR*, Moscow.

ANANOV, I. N. (1960) *Ministerstva v SSSR*, Moscow.

ANDREWS, WILLIAM J. (1966) *Soviet Institutions and Policies; Inside Views*, New York.

APTHEKER, HERBERT, ed. (1965) *Marxism and Democracy:* A Symposium, New York.

ARAGON, LOUIS (1962) *A History of the USSR*, London; Weidenfeld & Nicolson.

ARENDT, HANNAH (1951) *The Origins of Totalitarianism*, New York.

ARMSTRONG, JOHN A. (1959) *The Soviet Bureaucratic Elite*, New York.

ARMSTRONG, JOHN A. (1961) *The Politics of Totalitarianism;* The Communist Party of the Soviet Union from 1934 to the Present, New York.

ARMSTRONG, JOHN A. (1963) *Ideology, Politics and Government in The Soviet Union*, New York.

ARMSTRONG, JOHN A. (1965) 'The Domestic Roots of Soviet Foreign Policy', *International Affairs* (London), xli, pp. 37–47.

ASKEROV, A. A. (1953) *Ocherki sovetskovo stroitelstva*, Moscow.

AZOVKIN, I. A. (1956) *Kulturno-vospitatelnaya rabota raionnovo Soveta deputatov trudyashchikhsya*, Moscow.

AZOVKIN, I. A. (1959) *Organizatsia raboty v ispolkom raionnova Soveta*, Moscow.

AZOVKIN, I. A. (1962) *Oblastnoi (kraevoi) Sovet deputatov trudyashchikhsya*, Moscow.

BACHULO, I. L. (1959) *Rol mestnykh organov gosudarstvennoi vlasti v razvitii narodnovo obrazovania i kultury*, Moscow.

BAKHRAKH, D. (1960) *Pravo zaprosa deputatov mestnykh Sovetov*, Moscow.

BARGHOORN, FRED C. (1966) *Politics in the USSR*, New York.

BAYKOV, ALEXANDER (1947) *The Development of the Soviet Economic System*, Cambridge University Press.

BEARD, CHARLES A. (1934) *The Idea of National Interest*, New York.

BELL, DANIEL (1961) *The End of Ideology*, New York.

BESPALY, I. T. (1959) *Prezidium verkhovnovo Soveta soyuznoi respubliki*, Moscow.

BLACK, C. E. (1958) 'Soviet Political Life Today', *Foreign Affairs*, xxxvi, pp. 569–81.

BLAKE, PATRICIA, and HAYWARD, MAX, (1964) *Dissonant Voices in Soviet Literature*, London, Allen & Unwin.

342

BOFFA, GIUSEPPE (1960) *Inside the Khrushchev Era*, London: Allen & Unwin.

BORKENAU, FRANCZ (1962) *World Communism*, Michigan.

BOTTOMORE T. B., and RUBEL M., ed. (1956) *Karl Marx: Selected Writings in Sociology and Social Philosophy*, London: C. A. Watts.

BOTTOMORE, T. B. (1964) *Elites and Society*, London: C. A. Watts.

BOTTOMORE, T. B. (1965) *Classes in Modern Society*, London: Allen & Unwin.

BRINKLEY, G. A. (1961) 'The Withering Away of the State under Khrushchev', *The Review of Politics*, xxiii, pp. 37–51.

BRYANOV, E. (1964) *Poselkovye i selskie Sovety deputatov trudyashchikhsya*, Moscow.

BRZEZINSKI, ZBIGNIEW K. (1962) *Ideology and Power in Soviet Politics*, New York.

BRZEZINSKI, Z. K., and HUNTINGTON, S. P. (1964) *Political Power: USA/USSR*, London: Chatto & Windus.

BRZEZINSKI, Z. K. (1966) 'The Soviet Political System: Transformation or Degeneration?', *Problems of Communism*, xv, pp. 1–15.

BULGANIN, N. A. (1956) *Report on the Directives of the 20th Congress of the C.P.S.U. for the Sixth Five Year Plan for the development of the USSR 1956–1960*, Moscow.

BURKOV, B. (1959) 'Soviet Trade Unions', *New Times*, No. 12, pp. 5–6.

BURLATSKY, F., *The State and Communism*, Moscow, n.d.

BURNHAM, JAMES (1945) *The Managerial Revolution*, London: Penguin Books.

BURNS, EMILE, ed. (1935) *A Handbook of Marxism*, London: Gollancz.

CAMPBELL, ROBERT W. (1960) *Soviet Economic Power*, Harvard University Press.

CARR, E. H. (1946) *The Soviet Impact on the Western World*, London: Macmillan.

CARR, E. H. (1950) *Studies in Revolution*, London: Macmillan.

CARR, E. H. (1964) *A History of Soviet Russia*, 7 vols., London: Macmillan.

CARSON, GEORGE B. (1955) *Electoral Practices in the USSR*, New York.

CHAMBERLIN, W. H. (1956) 'Seven Phases of Soviet Foreign Policy', *Russian Review*, xv, pp. 77–84.

CHEKHARIN, I. M. (1966) *Postoyannye komissii mestnykh Sovetov*, Moscow.

CHEREMNYKH, P. S., ed. (1965) *Sochetanie gosudarstvennykh i obshchestvennykh nachal v upravlenii obshchestvom*, Moscow.

CHESNOKOV, D. I. (1960) *Ot gosudarstvennosti k obshchestvennomu samoupravleniu*, Moscow.

Chislennost, sostav i rasmeshchenie naselenia SSSR, Central Statistical Administration, Moscow, 1961.

CHURCHWARD, L. G. (1957) 'Some Aspects of Republican and Local Government before the Decentralization', *Soviet Studies*, ix, pp. 84–91.

CHURCHWARD, L. G. (1958) 'Continuity and Change in Soviet Local Government', *Soviet Studies*, ix, pp. 256–85.

CHURCHWARD, L. G. (1958) 'The Agricultural Reorganization and the Rural District Soviets', *Soviet Studies*, x, pp. 94–7.

CHURCHWARD, L. G. (1961) 'Contemporary Soviet Theory of the Soviet State', *Soviet Studies*, xii, pp. 404–19.

CHURCHWARD, L. G. (1962) 'Soviet Revision of Lenin's *Imperialism*', *Australian Journal of Politics and History*, viii, pp. 57–65.

CHURCHWARD, L. G. (1966) 'Soviet Local Government Today', *Soviet Studies*, xvii, pp. 431–52.

CHKHIKVADZE, V., and ZIVS, S. (1959) *Protiv sovremennovo reformizma i revizionizma v voprose o gosudarstve*, Moscow.

COATES, W. P., and ZELDA K. (1944) *A History of Anglo-Soviet Relations*, London: Lawrence & Wishart.

COCKS, PAUL M. (1963) 'The Purge of Marshal Zhukov', *Slavic Review*, xxii, pp. 482–98.

COLE, G. D. H. (1937) *Practical Economics;* or Studies in Economic Planning, London: Penguin Books.

COLE, G. D. H. (1954) *Marxism and Anarchism*, Vol. II of *A History of Socialist Thought*, London: Macmillan.

COLE, G. D. H. (1964) *The Meaning of Marxism*, Michigan.

CONQUEST, ROBERT (1960) *Common Sense About Russia*, London: Gollancz.

CONQUEST, R. (1961) *Power and Policy in the USSR*, London: Macmillan.

CONQUEST, R. (1963) 'After Khrushchev: A Conservative Restoration?', *Problems of Communism*, xii, pp. 41–6.

CONQUEST, ROBERT (1965) *Russia After Khrushchev*, London: Pall Mall.

CRANKSHAW, EDWARD (1956) *Russia Without Stalin*, London: Michael Joseph.

CRANKSHAW, EDWARD (1963) *The New Cold War: Moscow v Pekin*, London: Penguin Books.

CRANKSHAW, EDWARD (1966) *Khrushchev*, London: Collins.

CRICK, BERNARD (1964) *In Defence of Politics*, London: Penguin Books.

DAHL, ROBERT A. (1963) *Modern Political Analysis*, Princeton.

DALLIN, ALEXANDER, ed. (1960) *Soviet Conduct in World Affairs*, New York.

DANIELS, ROBERT V. (1964) *Russia*, Princeton.

DAVIES, R. W. (1956) 'The New Stage in Soviet Democracy', *The Marxist Quarterly*, iii, pp. 184–204.

DAVIES, R. W. (1957) 'Industrial Planning Reconsidered', *Soviet Studies*, viii, pp. 426–36.

DAVIES, R. W. (1958) *The Development of the Soviet Budgetary System*, Cambridge University Press.

DENISOV, A. I. (1947) *Sovetskoe gosudarstvennoe pravo*, Moscow.

DENISOV, A. I., and KIRICHENKO, M. G. (1954) *Osnovy sovetskovo gosudarstva i prava*, Moscow.

DENISOV, A., and KIRICHENKO, M. (1960) *Soviet State Law*, Moscow.

DEUTSCHER, I. (1949) *Stalin: A Political Biography*, London: Oxford University Press.

DEUTSCHER, ISAAC (1950) *Soviet Trade Unions*, London: Royal Institute of International Affairs.

DEUTSCHER, ISAAC (1953) *Russia after Stalin*, London: Hamish Hamilton.

DEUTSCHER, ISAAC (1954) *The Prophet Armed: Trotsky 1879–1921*, London: Oxford University Press.

DEUTSCHER, ISAAC (1959) *The Prophet Disarmed: Trotsky 1921–1929*, London: Oxford University Press.

DEUTSCHER, ISAAC (1960) *The Great Contest: Russia and the West*, London: Oxford University Press.

DEUTSCHER, ISAAC (1965) *The Prophet Outcast: Trotsky 1929–1949*, London: Oxford University Press.

DEUTSCHER, ISAAC (1966) 'The Failure of Khrushchevism', *The Socialist Register 1965*, Miliband, R., and Saville, J., ed., London: Merlin Press, pp. 11–29.

DMYTRYSHYN, BASIL (1965) *USSR: A Concise History*, New York.

DOBB, MAURICE (1948) *Soviet Economic Development Since 1917*, London: Routledge & Kegan Paul.

DROBYAZKO, S. G. (1961) *Komissii verkhovnovo Soveta soyuznoi respublik*, Moscow.

DURGIN, FRANK A. (1960) 'The Growth of Inter-Kolkhoz Cooperation', *Soviet Studies*, xii, pp. 183–9.

DURGIN, FRANK A. (1962) 'The Virgin Lands Programme 1954–1960', *Soviet Studies*, xiii, pp. 255–80.

ELLISON, H. S. (1961) 'The Decision to Collectivise Agriculture', *American Slavic & East European Review*, xx, pp. 189–202.

ENGELS, F. (1932) *Socialism Utopian and Scientific*, London: Allen & Unwin.

ENGELS, F. (1942) *The Origins of the Family, Private Property and the State*, Sydney.

ERLICH, A. (1960) *The Soviet Industrialization Debate, 1924–1928*, Harvard.

FAINSOD, MERLE (1958) *Smolensk Under Soviet Rule*, Harvard University, Press.

FAINSOD, MERLE (1963a) *How Russia is Ruled*, Harvard University Press, 1954, Revised Edition Enlarged.

FAINSOD, MERLE (1965) 'Khrushchevism', *Marxism in the Modern World*, Drachkovitch, M. M., ed., Stanford University Press, pp. 108–35.

FEDEROV, V. A. (1957) *Pervy period revolyutsionnovo dvizhenia v Rossii (1825–1861gg.)*, Moscow.

FEDOSEEV, A. S., ed. (1964) *Osnovy sovetskovo gosudarstva i prava*, Moscow.

FEIFER, GEORGE (1964) *Justice in Moscow*, London, Bodley Head, 1964.

FEUER, LEWIS S., ed. (1959) *Marx & Engels: Basic Writings on Politics and Philosophy*, New York.

FILONOVICH, YU. K. (1958) *Sovetsky deputat*, Moscow.

FISCHER, LOUIS (1965) *The Life of Lenin*, London: Weidenfeld & Nicolson.

FLORINSKY, MICHAEL T. (1939) *Toward an Understanding of the USSR*, New York.

FRANKLAND, MARK (1966) *Khrushchev*, London: Penguin Books.

FRIEDRICH, CARL J. (1954) *Totalitarianism*, Harvard University Press.

FRIEDRICH, C. J., and BRZEZINSKI, Z. K. (1956) *Totalitarian Dictatorship and Autocracy*, Harvard University Press.

FURAEV, V. K. (1964) *Sovetsko-Amerikanskie otnoshenia 1917–1939*, Moscow.

GABRICHIDZE, B. N. (1963) *Organizatsionno-instruktorskii apparat ispolkom mestnykh Sovetov*, Moscow.

GAIDUKOV, D. A., and STAROVOITOV, N. G., ed. (1965) *Mestny Sovety na sovremennom etape*, Moscow.

GARTHOFF, RAYMOND L. (1958) *Soviet Strategy in the Nuclear Age*, New York.

GERTH, H. H., and MILLS, C. WRIGHT (1947) *From Max Weber: Essays in Sociology*, London: Routledge & Kegan Paul.

GLEZERMAN, G. (1958) *Democracy in the USSR*, London: Soviet News Booklet.

GLEZERMAN, G., and UKRAINTSEV, B. (1958) 'Socialism and the State', *World Marxist Review*, i, pp. 22–31.

GLEZERMAN, G., *The Laws of Social Development*, Moscow, n.d.

GRANICK, DAVID (1960) *The Red Executive*, London: Macmillan.

GRIFFITH, WILLIAM E. (1964) *The Sino-Soviet Rift*, Harvard University Press.

GRIPP, RICHARD C. (1963) *Patterns of Soviet Politics*, Dorsey, Illinois.

HARPER, SAMUEL N. (1937) *The Government of the Soviet Union*, New York.

HARPER, SAMUEL N., and THOMPSON, RONALD (1949) *The Government of the Soviet Union*, 2nd Edition, New York.

HARRIS, MARY (1966) 'Shop-Floor Relations in Industrial Countries; Soviet Union 1963', *Co-existence*, iii, pp. 99–104.

HAZARD, JOHN N. (1958) *Law and Social Change in the USSR*, London: Stevens & Sons.

HAZARD, JOHN N. (1964) *The Soviet System of Government*, Chicago, 1957. 3rd Edition, Revised and Enlarged.

HENDEL, SAMUEL, ed. (1959) *The Soviet Crucible: Soviet Government in Theory and Practice*, New York.

HILL, CHRISTOPHER (1947) *Lenin and the Russian Revolution*, London: Hodder & Stoughton.

HOOK, SIDNEY (1955) *Marx and the Marxists*, New York.

HUDSON, G. F., LOWENTHAL, R., and MACFARQUHAR, R. (1961) *The Sino-Soviet Dispute*, London: The China Quarterly.

HUNT, R. N. CAREW (1957) *The Theory and Practice of Communism*, London: Geoffrey Bles.

IOIRYSH, A. I., ed. (1957) *Voprosy sovetskovo gosudarstvennovo prava*, Moscow.

IOIRYSH, A., and ROZHDESTVENSKY, P., ed. (1965) *Sotsializm i narodovlastie*, Moscow.

ISRAELYAN, V. L. (1965) *Vneshnyaya politika SSSR*, Moscow.

346

JACOBS, DAN N., ed. (1962) *The New Communist Manifesto and Related Documents*, New York.

JASNY, NAUM (1949) *The Socialized Agriculture of the USSR*, Stanford University Press.

JASNY, NAUM (1957) *The Soviet 1956 Statistical Handbook: A Commentary*, Michigan.

JASNY, NAUM (1965) *Khrushchev's Crop Policy*, Glasgow: Outram.

KALINYCHEV, F. I., ed. (1961) *Sovety deputatov trudyashchikhsya v period razvernutovo stroitelstva kommunizma*, Moscow.

KAMENKA, EUGENE (1962) *The Ethical Foundations of Marxism*, London: Routledge & Kegan Paul.

KARAPETYAN, L. M. (1960) *Razvertyvanie demokratii v usloviyakh stroitelstva kommunizma*, Moscow.

KARAPETYAN, L. and RAZIN, V. (1964) *Sovety obshchenarodnovo gosudarstva*, Moscow.

KAREV, D. S., ed. (1960) *Yuridichesky spravochnik deputata mestnykh Soveta*, Moscow.

KAREVA, M. P., and FEDKIN, G. I. (1953) *Osnovy sovetskovo gosudarstva i prava*, Moscow.

KARPINSKY, V. (1948) *The Social and State Structure of the USSR*, Moscow.

KASER, M. C. (1959) 'Changes in Method during the Preparation of the Soviet Seven Year Plan', *Soviet Studies*, x, pp. 321–37.

KENNAN, GEORGE F. (1958) *Russia, the Atom and the West* (BBC Reith Lectures, 1957), London: Oxford University Press.

KENNAN, GEORGE F. (1960) *Soviet Foreign Policy 1917–1941*, New York.

KERENSKY ALEXANDER (1965) *Russia and History's Turning Point*, New York.

KHIMICHEVA, N. I. (1964) *Byudzhetnykh prava mestnykh Sovetov deputatov trudyashchikhsya*, Saratov.

KHLYABICH, I. A. (1960) *V chem opasnost sovremennovo revizionizma*, Moscow.

KHRUSHCHEV, N. S. (1952) *Report to the Nineteenth Congress on Amendments to the Rules of the CPSU(B.)*, Moscow.

KHRUSHCHEV, N. S. (1956) *Report of the Central Committee of the Communist Party of the Soviet Union to the Twentieth Party Congress*, Moscow.

KHRUSHCHEV, N. S. (1957) *O dalneishem sovershenstvovanie organizatsii upravlenia promyshlennostyu i stroitelstvom*, Thesis of speech to C.C. of CPSU, February, 1957, Moscow.

KHRUSHCHEV, N. S. (1957) *Improvement of Industrial Management in the USSR*, May, 1957. London: Soviet News Booklet.

KHRUSHCHEV, N. S. (1959) 'On Peaceful Coexistence', *Foreign Affairs*, xxxviii, pp. 1–18.

KHRUSHCHEV, N. S. (1959) *Control Figures for the Economic Development of the USSR for 1959–1965*, Moscow.

KHRUSHCHEV, N. S. (1961) 'For New Victories for the World Communist Movement', *World Marxist Review*, iv, pp. 2–27.

KHRUSHCHEV, N. S. (1961) *O programme Kommunisticheskoi Partii Sovetskovo Soyuza*, Doklad na XXII Sezde KPSS, 18 Okt., 1961, Moscow.

KIRICHENKO, M. G. (1958) *Vysshie organy vlast soyuznykh respublik*, Moscow.

KIRICHENKO, M. G. (1962) *Verkhovnovo Sovet SSSR*, Moscow.

KIRICHENKO, M. G., ed. (1963) *Formy uchastia obshchestvennosti v rabote mestnykh Sovetov*, Moscow.

KISH, GEORGE (1960) *Economic Atlas of the Soviet Union*, Michigan.

KOCHAN, LIONEL (1966) *Russia in Revolution 1890–1918*, London: Weidenfeld & Nicolson.

KOLARZ, WALTER (1952) *Russia and her colonies*, London: George Phillip.

KOLARZ, WALTER (1964) *Communism & Colonialism*, London: Macmillan.

KORNHAUSER, WILLIAM (1959) *The Politics of Mass Society*, New York.

KORSCH, KARL (1938) *Karl Marx*, London: Chapman & Hall.

KOSMENNIKOV, V. M. (1958) *Ekonomicheskie raiony SSSR*, Moscow.

KOSSOI, A. I. (1957) *Osnovy cherty perekhodnovo perioda ot kapitalizma k sotsializmy v SSSR*, Moscow.

KOTOK, V. F. (1963) *Sovetskaya predstavitelnaya sistema*, Moscow.

KOTOK, V. F. (1964) *Sezdy i soveshchania trudyashchikhsya—forma neposredstvennoi demokratii*, Moscow.

KOZLOV, G. A., and PERVUSHIN, S. P., ed. (1958) *Kratky ekonomichesky slovar*, Moscow.

KOZLOV, YU. M. (1956) *Kollegialnost i edinonachalie v sovetskom gosudarstvennom upravlenii*, Moscow.

KOZLOV, YU. M. (1961) *Upravlenie v oblasti administrativno-politicheskoi deyatelnosti sovetskovo gosudarstva*, Moscow.

KOZLOV, V. I. (1962) *Vmeste s massami pod kontrolem mass*, Moscow.

KOZLOVA, E. I. (1960) *Ispolnitelnye komitety gorodskikh Sovetov*, Moscow.

KPSS o rabote Sovetov (1959) sbornik dokumentov, Moscow.

KRENGEL, ROLF (1960) 'Soviet, American and West German Basic Industries: A Comparison', *Soviet Studies*, xii, pp. 113–25.

KUDRYASHOV, R., and CHUDINOVICH, L. (1956) *Sostavlenie i ispolnenie byudzheta raiona*, Moscow.

KUUSINEN, O. V., ed. (1959) *Osnovy Marksizma–Leninizma*, Moscow.

LABEDZ, LEOPOLD, ed. (1962) *Revision:* Essays on the History of Marxist Ideas, London: Allen & Unwin.

LAIDLER, HARRY W. (1948) *Social-Economic Movements*, London: Routledge & Kegan Paul.

LAQUEUR, WALTER Z. (1956) *Communism and Nationalism in the Middle East*, London: Routledge & Kegan Paul.

LAQUEUR, WALTER Z. (1959) *The Soviet Union and the Middle East*, London: Routledge & Kegan Paul.

LAQUEUR, W., and LABEDZ, L. (1962) *Polycentrism:* The New Factor in International Communism, New York.

LASKI, H. J. (1963) *Reflections on the Revolution of Our Time*, London: Allen & Unwin.

LAURAT, LUCIEN (1960) *Marxism and Democracy*, London: Gollancz.

LAWRENCE, JOHN (1965) 'Soviet Policy Towards the Russian Churches', *Soviet Studies*, xvi, pp. 276–84.

LEFF, G. (1961) *The Tyranny of Concepts*, London: Merlin Press.

LENIN, V. I. (1946) *Selected Works*, 12 vols. London: Lawrence & Wishart.

LENIN, V. I. (1950) *The State* (July 1919), Moscow.

LENIN, V. I. (1956) *The Development of Capitalism in Russia*, Moscow.

LEONHARD, W. (1962) *The Kremlin Since Stalin*, London: Oxford University Press.

LEPESHKIN, A. I. (1958) *Fazy razvitia i funktsii sovetskovo gosudarstva*, Moscow.

LEPESHKIN, A. I. (1959) *Mestny organy vlasti sovetskovo gosudarstva*, 2 vols., Moscow.

LEPESHKIN, A. I. (1961) *Kurs sovetskovo gosudarstvennovo prava*, Vol. I, Moscow.

LESSNOI, V. M. (1955) *Osnovy printsipy sovetskovo gosudarstvennovo apparata*, Moscow.

LEWIS, JOHN (1965) *The Life and Teaching of Karl Marx*, London: Lawrence & Wishart.

LICHTHEIM, GEORGE (1961) *Marxism: a historical and critical study*, London: Routledge & Kegan Paul.

LINDEN, CARL (1963) 'Conflict and Authority: A Discussion', *Problems of Communism*, xii, pp. 27–35.

LIPPMANN, WALTER (1959) *The Communist World and Ours*, London: Hamish Hamilton.

LOCKHART, SIR ROBERT BRUCE (1950) *Memoirs of a British Agent*, London: Penguin Books.

LUZHIN, A. Y. (1953) *Postoyannye komissii Sovetov deputatov trudyashchikhsya*, Moscow.

LYADOV, M. (1956) *Iz zhizni partii v 1903–1907 godakh (vospominania)*, Moscow.

LYDOLPH, PAUL E. (1958) 'The Soviet Reorganization of Industry', *American Slavic and East European Review*, xvii, pp. 293–301.

MCCLOSKY, HERBERT, and TURNER, JOHN E. (1960) *The Soviet Dictatorship*, New York.

MACKINTOSH, J. M. (1962) *Strategy and Tactics of Soviet Foreign Policy*, London: Oxford University Press.

MCNEAL, ROBERT, ed. (1963) *Lenin, Stalin, Khrushchev: Voices of Bolshevism*, New Jersey.

MCNEAL, ROBERT H. (1963) *The Bolshevik Tradition*, Princeton.

MACRIDIS, ROY C., and WARD, ROBERT E. (1963) *Modern Political Systems: Europe*, Princeton, 'The Soviet Union' by Aspaturian, Vernon V., pp. 401–531.

MALENKOV, G. M. (1952) *Report to the Nineteenth Party Congress on the Work of the Central Committee of the CPSU(B.)*, Moscow.

MALENKOV, G. M. (1953) *Rech na pyatoi sessii verkhovnovo Soveta SSSR, 8 avgusta 1953g.*, Moscow.

MARCUSE, HERBERT (1961) *Soviet Marxism*, New York.

MARTIN, KINGSLEY, ed. (1958) *The Vital Letters of Russell, Khrushchev, Dulles*, London: Macgibbon & Kee.

MARTINET, GILLES (1964) *Marxism of Our Time*, London: Macgibbon & Kee.

MARX, K., and ENGELS, F. (1942) *Selected Works*, 2 vols. London: Lawrence & Wishart.

MARX K., and ENGELS, F. (1956) *Selected Correspondence*, Moscow.

MATVEEV, V. I. (1956) *Byudzhetnye prava raionnykh Sovetov deputatov trudyashchikhsya*, Moscow.

MAXWELL, B. W. (1935) *The Soviet State*, London: Selwyn & Blount.

MAYNARD, JOHN (1941) *Russia in Flux*, London: Gollancz.

MAYNARD, JOHN (1942) *The Russian Peasant and Other Studies*, London: Gollancz.

MEHNERT, KLAUS (1961) *The Anatomy of Soviet Man*, London: Weidenfeld & Nicolson.

MEYER, ALFRED G. (1957) *Leninism*, Harvard University Press.

MEYER, ALFRED G. (1960) *Communism*, New York.

MEYER, ALFRED G. (1965) *The Soviet Political System*, New York.

MEYER, ALFRED G. (1966) 'The Functions of Ideology in the Soviet Political System', *Soviet Studies*, xvii, pp. 273–85.

MIECZKOWSKI, Z. (1965) 'The 1962–1963 Reforms in Soviet Economic Regionalization', *Slavic Review*, xxiv, pp. 479–96.

MILLER, JACOB (1955) *Soviet Russia: An Introduction*, London: Hutchinson.

MILLER, J. (1957) 'The Decentralization of Industry', *Soviet Studies*, ix, pp. 165–83.

MILLER, J. D. B., and RIGBY, T. H., ed. (1965) *The Disintegrating Monolith*, Canberra.

MILLER, MARGARET (1965) *Rise of the Russian Consumer*, London: Merritt & Hatcher.

MILLS, C. WRIGHT (1959) *The Causes of World War Three*, London: Secker & Warburg.

MILLS, C. WRIGHT (1962) *The Marxists*, New York.

MITIN, M. B. (1950) *Soviet Democracy and Bourgeois Democracy*, Moscow.

MODELSKI, GEORGE (1960) *The Communist International System*, Princeton.

MOLOTOV, V. M. (1949) *Problems of Foreign Policy*, Moscow.

MOORE, BARRINGTON (1950) *Soviet Politics: The Dilemma of Power: The Role of Ideas in Social Change*, Harvard University Press.

MORGAN, GLENN G. (1959) 'The Procuracy's "General Supervision" Function', *Soviet Studies*, xi, pp. 143–72.

MORGAN, GLENN G. (1960) 'Methods Employed by the Soviet Procuracy in Exercising its "General Supervision" Functions', *Soviet Studies*, xii, pp. 168–82.

MORISON, DAVID (1964) *The USSR and Africa, 1945–1963*, London: Oxford University Press.

MOROZOV, V. M., ed. (1963) *Spravochnik agitatora*, Moscow.

MOSELY, P. E. (1961) 'Soviet Myths and Realities,' *Foreign Affairs*, xxxiv, pp. 341–54.

MOTE, MAX E. (1965) *Soviet Local and Republic Elections*, Stanford University Press.

NAIDIS, I. (1964) *Partiinoe i khozyaistvennoe rukovodstvo na predpriyatii*, Moscow.

Narodnoe khozyaistvo SSSR v 1963g. (1965) Central Statistical Administration, USSR Council of Ministers, Moscow.

NEMTSOVA, V. I. (1957) *Partia Bolshevikov v borba za mirnoe razvitie revolyutsii v Rossii (Mart-Iyul 1917 goda)*, Moscow.

NEWTH, J. A. (1963) 'The "Establishment" in Tadjikistan', *Soviet Studies*, xiv, pp. 408–20; and xv, pp. 72–81.

NEWTH, J. A. (1964) 'Nationality and Language in Turkmenia', *Soviet Studies*, xv, pp. 459–63.

NIKOLAEV, V. (1959) *Rol sovetskovo gosudarstva v period razvernutovo stroitelstva kommunizma*, Moscow.

NOVE, ALEC (1961) *The Soviet Economy*, London: Allen & Unwin.

NOVE, ALEC (1964) *Was Stalin Really Necessary?*, London: Allen & Unwin.

NOVIKOV, S. G. (1962) *Postoyannye komissii verkhovnovo Soveta SSSR*, Moscow.

ORLOV, S. D. (1965) *Novoe v rabote Sovetov*, Moscow.

OSIPOV, G. V., ed. (1966) *Industry and Labour in the USSR*, London: Tavistock Publications.

OSIPOV, G. V., ed. (1966) *Sotsiologia v SSSR*, 2 vols., Moscow.

OSNOVIN, V. S. (1957) *Pravo zaprosa deputatov mestnykh Sovetov*, Moscow.

OSNOVIN, V. S. (1963) *Normy sovetskovo gosudarstvennovo prava*, Moscow.

OSSOWSKI, STANISLAW (1963) *Class Structure in the Social Consciousness*, London: Routledge & Kegan Paul.

PAGE, STANLEY W. (1959) *Lenin and World Revolution*, New York.

PANKRATOVA, A. M., ed. (1948) *A History of the USSR*, Moscow.

PARES, BERNARD (1953) *A History of Russia*, New York.

PARKER, RALPH (1949) *Moscow Correspondent*, London: Frederick Muller.

PAVELKIN, P., ed. (1959) *Osnovy Marksistskoi Filosofii*, Moscow.

PERLO, VICTOR (1960) *USA & USSR: The Economic Race*, New York.

PETERSEN, WILLIAM, ed. (1963) *The Realities of World Communism*, Princeton.

PETHYBRIDGE, ROGER, W. (1961) *A Key to Soviet Politics*, London: Allen & Unwin.

PETHYBRIDGE, ROGER W. (1966) *A History of Postwar Russia*, London: Allen & Unwin.

PETROV, P. (1959) *Role of Soviet Trade Unions in Production*, Moscow.

PIPES, RICHARD (1954) *The Formation of the Soviet Union: Communism and Nationalism, 1917 to 1923*, Harvard University Press.

PLAMENATZ, J. (1954) *German Marxism and Russian Communism*, London: Longmans.

Plenum tsentralnovo komiteta Kommunisticheskoi Partii Sovetskovo

Soyuza, 10–18 janvarya, 1961g., Stenografichesky otchet, Moscow, 1961.

Polozhenie o postoyannykh komissiyakh mestnykh Sovetov· deputatov trudyashchikhsya, Moscow, 1956.

PONOMAREV, B. N., ed. (1958) *Politichesky slovar*, 2nd. edition, Moscow.

PONOMAREV, B. N., ed. (1960) *History of the Communist Party of the Soviet Union*, Moscow.

Programma Kommunisticheskoi Partii Sovetskovo Soyuza, Moscow, 1961.

Programme of the Communist Party of the Soviet Union, October 1961, Moscow, 1961.

RAGINSKY, M. YU., ed. (1963) *Formy uchastia obshchestvennosti v borbe s prestupnostu*, Moscow.

RAPPARD, WILLIAM E., *et al.* (1937) *Source Book on European Governments*, New York.

RAVIN, S. M. (1961) *Printsip federalizma v sovetskom gosudarstvennom prave*, Leningrad.

RAZIN V. I. (1965) *Stanovlenie kommunisticheskovo samoupravlenia*, Moscow.

REED, JOHN (1935) *Ten Days that Shook the World*, New York.

RESHETAR, JOHN S. (1960) *A Concise History of the Communist Party of the Soviet Union*, New York.

RIGBY, T. H. (1957) 'Social Orientation of Recruitment and Distribution of Membership in the CPSU', *American Slavic & East European Review*, xvi, pp. 275–90.

RIGBY, T. H., and CHURCHWARD, L. G. (1962) *Policy Making in the USSR 1953–1961: Two Views*, Melbourne.

RIGBY, T. H. (1963) 'The Extent and Limits of Authority', *Problems of Communism*, xii, pp. 36–41.

RIGBY, T. H. (1964) 'Crypto-Politics', *Survey*, No. 50, pp. 183–94.

RIGBY, T. H. (1964) 'Traditional, Market and Organizational Societies and the USSR', *World Politics*, xvi, pp. 539–57.

RIGBY, T. H. ed. (1966) *Stalin*, Princeton.

ROBERTS, HENRY L. (1956) *Russia and America:* Dangers and Prospects, New York.

ROBERTS, HENRY L., ed. (1956) *The Anti-Stalin Campaign and International Communism.* A selection of documents, New York.

RODIN, YA, F. (1958) *Deputat za rabotoi*, Moscow.

ROMASHKIN, P. S., ed. *Fundamentals of Soviet Law*, Moscow, n.d.

ROSTOW, W. W. (1954) *The Dynamics of Soviet Society*, New York.

ROTHSTEIN, ANDREW (1948) *Man and Plan in Soviet Economy*, London: Frederick Muller.

ROTHSTEIN, ANDREW (1950) *A History of the USSR*, London: Penguin.

ROTHSTEIN, ANDREW (1955) *Peaceful Coexistence*, London: Penguin Books.

ROZENTHAL, M., and YUDIN, P., ed. (1955) *Kratky filosofsky slovar*, 4th edition, Moscow.

ROZIN, L. M., and RAZDUNOV, F. S. (1964) *Komissii pri ispolkomakh raionnykh i gorodskikh Sovetov deputatov trudyashchikhsya*, Moscow.

RUBENSTEIN, ALVIN Z. (1966) *Communist Political Systems*, Princeton.

Rules of the Communist Party of the Soviet Union (1961) London: Soviet News Booklet.

RUNCIMAN, W. G. (1963) *Social Science and Political Theory*, Cambridge University Press.

RYABCHUK, G. F. (1958) *Nakazy izbiratelei*, Moscow.

SAFAROV, R. A. (1961) *Raionny Sovety deputatov trudyashchikhsya v gorodakh*, Moscow.

SAFAROV, R. A. (1962) *Territorialnye deputatskie gruppy*, Moscow.

SALISBURY, HARRISON E. (1963) *A New Russia?*, London: Secker & Warburg.

SAVENKOV, N. T. (1958) *Obyazunosti i prava sovetskovo deputata*, Moscow.

Sbornik zakonov SSSR i ukazov prezidiuma verkhovnovo Soveta SSSR 1932–1958, Moscow, 1959.

Sbornik zakonov SSSR 1932–1961, Moscow, 1961.

SCHAPIRO, L. (1960) *The Communist Party of the Soviet Union*, London: Eyre & Spottiswoode.

SCHAPIRO, L., and UTECHIN, S. V. (1961) 'Soviet Government Today', *Political Quarterly*, xxxii, pp. 124–38.

SCHAPIRO, L., ed. (1962) *The USSR and the Future*, New York. An Analysis of the New Program of the CPSU.

SCHAPIRO, LEONARD (1965) *The Government and Politics of the Soviet Union*, London: Hutchinson.

SCHLESINGER, R. (1945) *Soviet Legal Theory*, London: Kegan Paul.

SCHLESINGER, RUDOLF (1947) *The Spirit of Post-War Russia:* Soviet Ideology 1917–1946, London: Dennis Dobson.

SCHLESINGER, RUDOLF, ed. (1949) *Changing Attitudes in Soviet Russia: The Family in the USSR; Documents and Readings*, London: Routledge & Kegan Paul.

SCHLESINGER, RUDOLF (1950) *Marx: His Time and Ours*, London: Routledge & Kegan Paul.

SCHLESINGER, R. (1957) 'Problems of the Soviet Press', *Soviet Studies*, ix, pp. 223–38.

SCHLESINGER, R. (1958) 'Extension of the Rights of Trade Unions', *Soviet Studies*, x, pp. 176–80.

SCHLESINGER, R. (1959) 'The Discussion on Criminal Law and Procedure', *Soviet Studies*, x, pp. 293–306.

SCHLESINGER, R. (1961) 'The Criminal Code of the RSFSR', *Soviet Studies*, xii, pp. 456–64.

SCHLESINGER, R. (1962) 'Marxist Theory and the New Program of the Soviet Communist Party', *Science & Society*, xxvi, pp. 129–52.

SCHLESINGER, R. (1962) 'The CPSU Programme: The Conception of Communism', *Soviet Studies*, xiii, pp. 383–406.

SCHUMAN, FREDERICK L. (1961) *Government of the Soviet Union*, New York.

SCHUMPETER, JOSEPH A. (1942) *Capitalism, Socialism and Democracy*, New York.

SCOTT, DEREK J. R. (1958) *Russian Political Institutions*, London: Allen & Unwin.

SEDOV, M. G. (1959) *Revolyutsionnoe dvizhenie v Rossii 60–70 godov XIX veka*, Moscow.

SELZNICK, PHILIP (1952) *The Organizational Weapon*, New York.

SETON, F. (1960) 'Soviet Progress in Western Perspective', *Soviet Studies*, xii, pp. 126–44.

SETON-WATSON, HUGH (1960) *Neither War Nor Peace: The Struggle for Power in the Post-War World*, London: Methuen.

SHAFFER, HARRY G., ed. (1965) *The Soviet System in Theory and Practice: Selected Western and Soviet Views*, New York, 1965.

SHAKHNAZAROV, G. KH., ed. (1964) *Obshchestvovodenie* (A Textbook for the Final Year of the Secondary School), 2nd. edition, Moscow.

SHAVRIN, V. (1953) *Gosudarstvenny byudzhet SSSR*, 4th edition, Moscow.

SHEREMET, K. F., and BARABASHEV, G. V. (1965) *Stanovlenie kommunisticheskovo samoupravlenia*, Moscow.

SIMON, E. D., ed. (1937) *Moscow in the Making*, London: Longmans, Green.

SIMONOV, K. (1960) *Shtrikhi epopei*, Tashkent.

SKILLING, H. GORDON (1966) *The Government of Communist East Europe*, New York.

SKILLING, H. GORDON (1966) 'Interest Groups and Communist Politics', *World Politics*, xviii, pp. 435–51.

SLOAN, PAT (1937) *Soviet Democracy*, London: Gollancz.

SOKOLOVSKY, MARSHAL V. D. (1963) *Military Strategy: Soviet Doctrine and Concepts*, New York.

SOLOVEVA, S. V. (1963) *Postoyannye komissii mestnykh Sovetov na novom etape*, Moscow.

SOROKIN, PITIRIM A. (1944) *Russia and the United States*, New York.

Sostav deputatov verkhovnykh Sovetov soyuznykh, avtonomnykh respublik i mestnykh Sovetov deputatov trudyashchikhsya, (Statistical Handbook), Moscow, 1959.

SPULBER, NICOLAS (1957) *The Economics of Communist Eastern Europe*, New York.

SPULBER, NICOLAS (1964) *Soviet Strategy for Economic Growth*, Indiana.

SSSR administrativno-territorialnoe delenie soyuznykh respublik na 1 aprelya 1963 goda, Moscow, 1963.

STALIN, J. V. (1945) *Problems of Leninism*, Moscow.

STALIN, J. V. (1946) *Speech delivered at an Election Rally in Stalin Electoral Area*, Washington, D.C.

STALIN, J. V. (1947) *Post-War International Relations*, London: Soviet News Booklet.

STALIN, J. V. (1950) *Concerning Marxism and Linguistics*, London: Soviet News Booklet.

STALIN, J. V. (1952) *Economic Problems of Socialism in the USSR*, Moscow.

STALIN, J. V. (1952) *Works*, 13 vols., Moscow.

STAROVOITOV, N. G. (1961) *Poryadok vyborov mestny Sovety deputatov trudyashchikhsya*, Moscow.

STAROVOITOV, N. G. (1963) *Poryadok organizatsii i provedenia vyborov v Sovety*, Moscow.

STEPANOV, I. M. (1956) *Rabota raionnovo Soveta v oblasti planirovania i byudzheta*, Moscow.

STRONG, ANNA LOUISE (1957) *The Stalin Era*, New York.

SWEARER, HOWARD R. (1959) 'Khrushchev's Revolution in Industrial Management', *World Politics*, xii., pp. 45–61.

SWEARER, HOWARD R. (1962) 'Changing Roles of the CPSU under First Secretary Khrushchev', *World Politics*, xv, pp. 20–43.

SWEARER, HOWARD R. (1966) *The Politics of Succession in the USSR*, New York.

SWEEZY, PAUL M. (1942) *The Theory of Capitalist Development*, New York.

TAAFFE, R. N., and KINGSBURY, R. C. (1965) *An Atlas of Soviet Affairs*, London: Methuen.

TIKHOMIROV, YU. A. (1959) *Mestnye Sovety i sovnarkhozy*, Moscow.

TIKHOMIROV, YU. A., and STEPANOV, I. M. (1960) *Rukovodstvo vysshikh organov vlasti soyuznykh respublik mestnymi Sovetami deputatov trudyashchikhsya*, Moscow.

TIKHOMIROV, YU. A. (1963) *Sovety i razvitie gosudarstvennovo upravlenia*, Moscow.

TODORSKY, YU. V. (1955) *Postoyannye komissii mestnykh Sovetov deputatov trudyashchikhsya*, Moscow.

TOWSTER, J. (1948) *Political Power in the USSR, 1917–1947*, New York.

TROTSKY, L. D. (1933) *The History of the Russian Revolution*, 3 vols., London: Gollancz.

TROTSKY, L. D. (1937) *The Revolution Betrayed*, London: Faber & Faber.

TROTSKY, L. D. (1956) *The New Course*, London: New Park Publications.

TSAMERIAN, I. P., and RONIN, S. L. (1962) *Equality of Rights Between Races and Nationalities in the USSR*, UNESCO, Paris.

TUCKER, ROBERT C. (1959) 'Field Observations on Soviet Local Government', *American Slavic & East European Review*, xviii, pp. 526–38.

TUCKER, ROBERT C. (1961) *Philosophy and Myth in Karl Marx*, Cambridge University Press.

TUCKER, ROBERT C. (1963) *The Soviet Political Mind*, New York.

TUCKER, ROBERT C. (1965) 'The Dictator and Totalitarianism', *World Politics*, xvii, pp. 555–83.

ULAM, ADAM B. (1959) 'Soviet Ideology and Soviet Foreign Policy', *World Politics*, xi, pp. 153–72.

ULAM, ADAM B. (1960) *The Unfinished Revolution*, New York.

ULAM, ADAM B. (1963) *The New Face of Soviet Totalitarianism*, New York.

ULAM, ADAM B. (1966) *Lenin and the Bolsheviks*, London: Secker & Warburg.

ULYANOVSKY, R. A. (1965) *The Dollar and Asia*, Moscow.

UMANSKY, YA. N. (1959) *Sovetskoe gosudarstvennoe pravo*, Moscow.

U.S.S.R. Council of Ministers, Central Statistical Administration; *The USSR Economy: A Statistical Abstract*, London: Lawrence & Wishart, 1957.

UTECHIN, S. V. (1958) 'Bolsheviks and Their Allies after 1917: The Ideological Pattern', *Soviet Studies*, x, pp. 113–35.

UTECHIN, S. V. (1964) *Russian Political Thought*, London: Dent.

VAIL I. M., and KONYUKHOV, V. D., ed. (1959) *Voprosy sovetskovo gosudarstva i prava*, Moscow.

VALKOV, V. A. (1965) *SSSR i SShA*, Moscow.

VASENIN, V. K. (1965) *Deputat mestnovo Soveta*, Moscow.

VENTURI, FRANCO (1960) *Roots of Revolution*, London: Weidenfeld & Nicolson.

VERNADSKY, G. (1944) *A History of Russia*, New Revised Edition, Yale University Press.

VLADIMOV, V. (1958) *Verkhovny Sovet SSSR i mezhdunarodnye otnoshenia*, Moscow.

VLASOV, V. A. (1959) *Sovetsky gosudarstvenny apparat*, Moscow.

VODOLAGIN, V. M., IVANOV G. V. and KOSTIN, V. P. (1962) *Sputnik izbiratelya*, Moscow.

VON LAUE, T. H. (1964) *Why Lenin? Why Stalin?*, Philadelphia.

Voprosy stroitelstva kommunizma v SSSR, Akademia Nauk SSSR, Moscow, 1959.

VOZNESENSKY, N. (1948) *War Economy of the USSR in the Period of the Patriotic War*, Moscow.

VYSHINSKY, A. Y. (1948) *The Law of the Soviet State*, New York.

VYSHINSKY, A. Y. (1948) *The Teachings of Lenin and Stalin on Proletarian Revolution and the State*, London: Soviet News Booklet.

WALSH, WARREN B. (1958) *Russia and the Soviet Union*, Michigan.

WARRINER, DOREEN (1950) *Revolution in Eastern Europe*, London: Turnstile Press.

WEBB, SIDNEY and BEATRICE (1937) *Soviet Communism: A New Civilisation*, 2nd Edition, London: Longmans, Green.

WESSON, ROBERT G. (1963) *Soviet Communes*, Princeton.

WESSON, ROBERT G. (1964) 'Volunteers and Soviets', *Soviet Studies*, XV, pp. 231–49.

WETTER, G. A. (1959) 'The Soviet Concept of Coexistence', *Soviet Survey*, No. 30, pp. 19–34.

WHEARE, K. C. (1946) *Federal Government*, London: Oxford University Press.

WILLETS, H. T. (1962) 'Khrushchev and the 22nd Congress', *Soviet Survey*, No. 40, pp. 3–10.

WILLIAMS, ALBERT RHYS (1923) *Through the Russian Revolution*, London: The Labour Publishing Co.

WOLFE, B. D. (1956) *Three Who Made a Revolution: A Biographical History*, London: Thames & Hudson.

YARVICH, L. S. (1962) *Pravo i kommunizm*, Moscow.

ZAGORIA, DONALD S. (1961) *The Sino-Soviet Conflict*, Princeton.

ZHDANOV, A. A. (1939) *Amendments to the Rules of the CPSU(B.)*; Report to the Eighteenth Congress of the CPSU(B), Moscow.

ZHDANOV, A. A. (1947) *The International Situation*, Moscow.

ZILLIACUS, K. (1949) *I Choose Peace*, London: Penguin Books.

ZLATOPOLSKY, D. *State System of the USSR*, Moscow, n.d.

Supplementary Bibliography

ARUTYUNYAN, N. KH. (1970) *Partia i Sovety*, Moscow.

ASPATURIAN, V. V. (1968) 'Foreign Policy Perspectives in the Sixties', Ch. 6 of *Soviet Politics Since Khrushchev*, ed. Dallin, A., and Larson, T. B., New Jersey: Prentice-Hall.

AZRAEL, J. R. (1966) *Managerial Power and Soviet Politics*, Harvard University Press.

BARGHOORN, F. C. (1972) *Politics in the USSR*, Boston: Little, 2nd edn.

BAYANOV, B., *et al.* (1968) *Soviet Socialist Democracy*, Moscow.

BELYKH, A. K. (1972) *Upravlenie i samoupravlenie*, Leningrad.

BRINKLEY, G. A. (1973) 'Khrushchev Remembered: On the Theory of Soviet Statehood', *Soviet Studies*, xxiv, Jan., pp. 387–401.

BROWN, EMILY C. (1966) *Soviet Trade Unions and Labor Relations*, Harvard University Press.

BURLATSKY, F. M. (1970) *Lenin, gosudarstvo, politika*, Moscow.

CARR, E. H. (1969) *1917: Before and After*, London: Macmillan.

CHKHIKVADZE, V. M. (ed.) (1967) *Politicheskaya organizatsia sovetskovo obshchestva*, Moscow.

CHKHIKVADZE, V. M. (ed.) (1969) *The Soviet State and Law*, Moscow.

CHKHIKVADZE, V. M. (ed.) (1972) *The Soviet Form of Popular Government*, Moscow.

CHURCHWARD, L. G. (1973) *The Soviet Intelligentsia*, London: Routledge & Kegan Paul.

CONQUEST, ROBERT (1970) *The Nation Killers*, London: Macmillan.

CONQUEST, ROBERT (ed.) (1968a) *The Politics of Ideas in the USSR*, London: Bodley Head.

CONQUEST, ROBERT (ed.) (1968b) *Soviet Nationalities Policy in Practice*, London: Bodley Head.

CORNELL, RICHARD (ed.) (1970) *The Soviet Political System*, New Jersey: Prentice-Hall.

DALLIN, A., and LARSON, T. B. (eds.) (1968) *Soviet Politics Since Khrushchev*, New Jersey: Prentice-Hall.

DEUTSCHER, ISAAC (1966) *Ironies of History*, Oxford University Press.

DEUTSCHER, ISAAC (1967) *The Unfinished Revolution*, Oxford University Press.

FAINSOD, MERLE (1963b) 'Bureaucracy and Modernization; The Russian and Soviet case', in J. La. Polombara (ed.), *Bureaucracy and Political Development*, Princeton University Press.

FROLIC, B. M. (1971) 'Municipal Administrations, Departments, Commissions and Organizations', *Soviet Studies*, xxii, Jan., pp. 376–93.

GRIGORYAN, L. A. (1970) *Postoyannye komissii mestnykh Sovetov*, Moscow.
GRIGORYAN, L. A. (1972) *Narodnovlastie v SSSR*, Leningrad.

HANAK, H. (ed.) (1972) *Soviet Foreign Policy Since the Death of Stalin*, London: Routledge & Kegan Paul.
HAZARD, JOHN N. (1968) *The Soviet System of Government*, Chicago University Press, 4th edn.
HOUGH, JERRY F. (1969) *The Soviet Prefects*, Oxford University Press.
HUTCHINGS, RAYMOND (1971) *Soviet Economic Development*, Oxford: Blackwell.

INKELES, ALEX (1969) *Social Change in Soviet Russia*, Oxford University Press.

JUKES, GEOFFREY (1973) *The Soviet Union in Asia*, Sydney: Angus & Robertson and the AIIA.

KANET, ROGER E. (1968) 'The Rise and Fall of the "All-People's State": Recent Changes in the Soviet Theory of the State', *Soviet Studies*, xx, July, pp. 81–93.
KAPLAN, FRED I. (1969) *Bolshevik Ideology and the Ethics of Soviet Labour*, London: Peter Owen.
KASER, MICHAEL (1970) *Soviet Economics*, London: Weidenfeld & Nicolson.
KOLKOWICZ, R. (1967) *The Soviet Military and the Communist Party*, Oxford University Press.
KOZLOV, YU. M. (ed.) (1968) *Administrativnoe pravo*, Moscow.
KUTAFIN, O. E. (1971) *Postoyannye komissii palat verkhovnovo Soveta SSSR*, Moscow.

LANE, DAVID (1970) *Politics and Society in the USSR*, London: Weidenfeld & Nicolson.
LEWIN, MOSHE (1968) *Russian Peasants and Soviet Power*, London: Allen & Unwin.
LEWIN, MOSHE (1969) *Lenin's Last Struggle*, London: Faber & Faber.
LINDEN, CARL A. (1966) *Khrushchev and the Soviet Leadership 1957–1964*, Baltimore: Johns Hopkins University Press.
LITTLE, D. R. (1972) 'Soviet Parliamentary Committees after Khrushchev: Obstacles and Opportunities', *Soviet Studies*, xxi, July, pp. 41–60.

MCAULEY, MARY (1969) *Labour Disputes in Soviet Russia, 1957–1965*, Oxford: Clarendon Press.
MCNEAL, R. H. (1967) *International Relations among Communists*, New Jersey: Prentice-Hall.
MALE, D. J. (1971) *Russian Peasant Organisation Before Collectivisation*, Cambridge University Press.

SUPPLEMENTARY BIBLIOGRAPHY

MEDVEDEV, R. (1972) *Let History Judge: The Origins and Consequences of Stalinism*, London: Macmillan.

MORTON, HENRY W. (1968) 'The Leningrad District of Moscow—An Inside Look', *Soviet Studies*, xx, Oct., pp. 206–18.

MOWAT, FARLEY (1972) *The Siberians*, Baltimore: Penguin.

MUKSINOV, I. SH. (1969) *Sovet ministrov soyuznoi respubliki*, Moscow.

NOVE, ALEC and NEWTH, J. A. (1967) *The Soviet Middle East*, London: Allen & Unwin.

OSBORN, R. J. (1970) *Soviet Social Policies: Welfare, Equality and Community*, Illinois: Dorsey.

PERRIE, MAUREEN (1972) 'The Social Composition and Structure of the Socialist Revolutionary Party Before 1917', *Soviet Studies*, xxiv, Oct., pp. 223–50.

PIPES, RICHARD (1968) *The Formation of the Soviet Union*, New York: Atheneum, revised edn.

RABINOVITCH, A. (1968) *Prelude to Revolution: The Bolsheviks and the July 1917 Uprising*, Indiana University Press.

RESHETAR, JOHN S. JR. (1971) *The Soviet Polity*, New York: Dodd, Mead.

RIGBY, T. H. (1969) *Communist Party Membership in the USSR, 1917–1967*, Oxford University Press.

RIGBY, T. H. (1970) 'The Soviet Leadership: towards a self-restraining oligarchy', *Soviet Studies*, xxii, Oct., pp. 167–91.

RIGBY, T. H. (ed.) (1968) *The Stalin Dictatorship*, Sydney University Press.

RUSH, MYRON (1968) *Political Succession in the USSR*, Columbia University Press.

SAUL, N. E. (1973) 'Lenin's Decision to Seize Power: The Influence of Events in Finland', *Soviet Studies*, xxiv, April, pp. 491–505.

SCHUMAN, F. L. (1967) *Government in the Soviet Union*, New York: Crowell.

SCOTT, D. J. R. (1969) *Russian Political Institutions*, London: Allen & Unwin, 4th edn.

SHENDRIK, M. P. (1970) *Obshchenarodnoe gosudarstvo – novy etap v razvitii sotsialisticheskoi gosudarstvennosti*, Lvov.

SHEREMET, K. F. (1968) *Kompetentsia mestnykh Sovetov*, Moscow.

SKILLING, H. GORDON and GRIFFITHS, FRANKLYN (eds.) (1971) *Interest Groups and Soviet Politics*, Princeton University Press.

STEPAKOV, V. I. *et al.* (1970) *Elements of Political Knowledge*, Moscow.

TAUBMAN, WILLIAM (1973) *Governing Soviet Cities*, London: Pall Mall.

TUCKER, ROBERT C. (1969) *The Marxian Revolutionary Idea*, New York: Norton.

TUCKER, ROBERT C. (1972) *The Soviet Political Mind*, London: Allen & Unwin, 2nd edn.

ULAM, ADAM B. (1965) *Lenin and the Bolsheviks*, London: Secker & Warburg.

SUPPLEMENTARY BIBLIOGRAPHY

VASILIEV, V. I. (1967) *Sovetskoe stroitelstvo*, Moscow.

VOLKOV, M. A. (1968) *Politicheskaya organizatsia obshchestva*, Moscow.

VOLKOV, M. A. (1971) *Vysshie i tsentralnye gosudarstvennovo upravlenia SSSR i soyuznykh respublk v sovremenny period*, Kazan.

WESSON, ROBERT G. (1969) *Soviet Foreign Policy in Perspective*, Illinois: Dorsey.

WESSON, ROBERT G. (1972) *The Soviet State: An Aging Revolution*, New York: Wiley.

WETTER, GUSTAV A. (1966) *Soviet Ideology Today*, London: Heinemann.

WOLFE, B. D. (1969) *An Ideology in Power*, London: Allen & Unwin.

YAMPOLSKAYA, TS. A. (1972) *Obshchestvennye organizatsii v SSSR*, Moscow.

Index

Academy of Sciences, 92, 95
Administration, amateurs in, 3, 182, 301
  parallel, 181, 184, 225
  reorganization, 98, 301
Agriculture, collective farms, 12, 17, 60, 63, 125, 152, 162, 173, 180, 291–3, 297
  kulaks, 23, 58, 60, 63, 193
  Machine Tractor stations, 114, 125, 139, 181, 187–8, 233, 337
  NEP, 12–13, 60
  new regions, 13, 67
  Party role, 194–5, 233, 332
  production, 229, 232, 300
  reorganization, 122, 139, 142, 149, 187–8, 232
  State Committee, 233
Aid programmes, 68 and n.
Armenia, 80, 83, 163, 183, 258
Armed Forces, 125, 193, 246–7, 326, 330, 337
  Red Army, 17–18, 45–6, 49, 55–7, 79
  Party role, 234–5, 330
Ashkhabad, 113
Asia, 140
Auditing, Central Commission, 218, 319, 321–4, 325
Azerbaidjan, 79, 80, 83, 165, 183

Banking, 122, 128, 137
Belinsky, V. G., 27
Belorussia, 8, 79, 83, 110, 183, 253
Beria, L. P., 213–14, 218, 235, 279, 280–1, 284
Bessarabia, 83
Boffa, G., 30

Bolsheviks, 43 ff., 50 ff., 62, 76–9, 82, 89
Brezhnev, L. I., 13, 86, 138, 218, 230
Budget, 125, 128, 130, 180
  State, 151, 163, 164
Bukharin, 14, 58, 60
Bukovina, 83
Bulganin, N. A., 65, 137, 142, 213, 219, 279, 283, 285, 300
Bureaucracy, 14, 17, 99, 154, 232
  Party, 21, 217–18, 291–2
Burlatsky, F., 262
Byelorussia, see Belorussia

Cadet Party, 37, 40, 42, 55
Caucasus, 7
Chesnokov, D. L., 95
Chernyshevsky, N. G., 27, 28
Chicherin, B. N., 242
Churvash ASSR, 163
Class, 88, 91, 263, 267
Coexistence, peaceful, 10, 99, 245, 313
Collective farms, see Agriculture
Collectivization, 12–13, 17–18, 61 ff.
Comecon, 248
Cominform, 247
Commissars, Council of People's, 55, 65, 76, 78, 84, 143
Commissions, Standing, 126 ff., 117–8, 182 and n., 245–6
Communist International, 247
Communist Party
  accountability, 211, 216
  admission, 193, 195–6, 317–18, 319–20
  and agriculture, 194, 232–3,

361

Communist Party—*cont.*
297, 332
control of Army, 234, 330
Central Committee, 194, 212,
241–2, 244
— and Council of Ministers,
186, 224, 225–7, 229
— divisions in, 137, 283 ff., 293
— post-Stalin, 300, 304
—powers, 138, 139, 272
conservative members, 281–3,
296
Commissions, 227, 232, 234,
303, 334
delegates, election, 210, 216,
219, 321
democracy in, 208, 211, 214 ff.,
320 ff.
discipline, 195, 197
and elections, 82, 105, 183–4,
206, 228
expulsion, 58, 207, 218–20, 321
factions, 209, 218, 239, 296,
315, 322
foreign policy, 241–2, 244–6
fractions, 184, 186, 188, 225,
233–4, 331
industrial supervision, 233
Khrushchev and, 206–7, 288,
291–4, 316 ff.
legislation, 124, 139
and local government, 105,
172 ff., 187–8, 223, 228–9
membership, 193 ff., 206 ff.,
274, 316, 321 ff., 331, 333
moral code, 329
officials, 3, 210, 211, 217, 218,
291–2
opposition, 288
parallel organization, 98, 181,
184, 226
and peasants, 194, 198, 199,
204 n.
percentage of population, 196
police and, 235
Politbureau, 16, 323

— members, 220
— and state government, 133
138
— and foreign policy, 241, 243
— increased powers, 303–4
primary bodies, 194, 210
reorganization, 187, 209, 225
333, 335
rules, 206, 208, 216, 315 ff.
secretariat, 138, 141, 220, 226,
286, 303
and state organs, 226, 233,
228–30, 303, 325
structure, hierarchy, 209, 210
support for, 278
and trade unions, 199
and working class, 192 ff.
Conquest, R., 294 n.
Constitutions, 78–80, 82, 86 and n.
Control, Ministry, 3
Criticism, Party, 212–13, 222, 317,
328
press, 113, 298
public, 114
Cuba, 239–40, 246, 254, 287
Culture, Ministry of, 217
Cultural service, 14, 17, 59
relations, foreign, 243, 248

Daniel, Yu. M., 273
Davies, R. W., 146
Decembrists, 26 ff.
Decentralization, 167, 180, 301
Decisions, decrees, etc., 120, 134,
140
Defence, 11, 65 n., 138 141, 242–3
Democracy, Soviet in practice, 267,
269–70, 300
theory, 257 ff., 313
Democratic centralism, 158–9,
206–7, 211, 301, 320, 337
Denisov, A. I., 134, 142
Deputies, 78, 182, 265 and n.
functions, 109–10, 112, 116,
129–31

Dictatorship of the proletariat, 76–7, 309–11, 313
  transitional nature, 94, 223, 257, 337
District (*raion*), 5, 172–4, 179, 232
  parallel administration, 187, 225, 293
  Party and, 184–5, 212, 225, 232–3, 293
  powers, 180–1
  reorganizations, 174, 232–3, 291–3, 335
Domrachev, V. P., 233
Dudorov, L. P., 235
Duma, 25, 35 and n., 40–3

East European states, 244
Economic Commission, State, 142, 149, 150, 166
Economic Councils, 148–9, 165, 179, 187, 231, 292, 301
Economic Plan, 150–1
Education, Party Role, 17, 59, 274, 303–4
Education Act, 1958, 125, 270, 297
Egorychev, N. G., 107
Election, 104–12, 321
  direct and indirect, 79, 80, 82
  electoral commissions, 103, 105, 134, 270
  Party and, 6, 184, 186, 212, 227–8
Electrification, State Commission, 57, 148
Engels, F., 31, 88, 95, and *see* Marx
Estonia, 7–8, 83, 183

Factions, 6, 213, 218, 296
  and foreign policy, 239
  rules on, 209, 315, 321–2
Federalism, 157 ff.
Fedkin, G. I., 141
Finance, Ministry of, 138, 150, 161, 164, 180, 231

Five-Year Plans,
  1st, 61, 62 and n., 146–7
  2nd, 63, 80, 147
  3rd, 13, 65
  6th, 302
  1966, 68, 218
  7th, 147
  9th, 12
Foreign Affairs, 128, 138, 141, 168, 238
Foreign Trade, Ministry, 243, 248
Foreign Communist Parties, 241
Friendship Societies, 248
Furtseva, E. A., 217

Garbuzov, V. F., 122, 138
Georgia, 8, 25, 79–80, 83, 196, 214
Goncharov, I. A., 27
Gorki, 137
Gorky, M., 49
Gosbank, 122, 127, 137
Gosplan, 60, 98, 166–7, 180, 301
  agriculture, 122
  and Council of Ministers, 136, 141
  decision making, 230
  planning budgets, 128, 143, 148 ff., 231
Grishin, V. V., 106
Gromyko, A. A., 129, 242
Guchkov, A. L., 44

Health, 70, 93, 138
Herzen, A. I., 27, 28
Housing, 178–80, 274 and n., 299–300

Individual, cult of, 206, 322
Industrialization, 11, 12, 17, 60, 61
Industry, control of, 63, 166, 332
  and local soviets, 179, 180 and n.
  management, 198, 234
  NEP, 58
  production, 63, 67–9, 295–7, 300

Industry—*cont.*
    reorganization, 84, 165, 166, 285
Intelligentsia, 70, 71, 109, 118, 315, 317
    revolutionary role, 29, 35, 36, 192–3
Interest groups, 280
Internal Affairs, Ministry, 165, 235
Inventors, Society of, 202, 300
Investment, 128, 129
Iskra, 32
Izvestia, 113

Jews, 8 and n., 10
Justice, *see* Law

Kaganovich, L. M., 18, 142, 167, 213, 219, 281 ff.
Kalmyk ASSR, 163
Kaluga, 175
Kamenev, L. B., 45, 46, 49, 60
Kapitonov, I. V., 218
Karelo-Finnish Republic, 83, 160
Kareva, M. O., 141
Katushev, K. F., 220
Kazakhstan, 7, 8, 26, 67–8, 83
    development, 13, 162–3, 165, 173, 269
    Party in, 183, 196
Keldysh, M. V., 107
Kennedy, Pres., 239–40, 288
Kerensky, A., 42, 44, 45, 47, 50
Khrushchev, N., 64, 85–6, 93, 257, 287, 333
    and agriculture, 13, 68–9, 229, 282, 287, 300
    and Army, 125, 235, 268
    expert conferences, 215, 218, 274
    foreign policy, 239–40, 242, 244, 251, 287
    and Party, 212, 232, 285
    post-Khrushchev politics, 166–7, 176, 188, 221

    rise and fall, 18, 120–1, 137, 149, 214–15, 279 ff., 286 ff., 292
    on Stalin, 217–19
    Twentieth Congress, 99 n., 302–3, 313–14
Kirgizia, 7, 8, 83, 123, 183
Kirchenko, M., 134, 142
Kolokol, 27 and n.
Komsomol, 198, 228, 234
    and Party, 317–18, 325, 329–30
Kotok, V. F., 274
Kornechev, K. S., 233
Kornilov, Gen., 45, 47
Kosygin, A. N., 86, 138, 216, 218, 230
Kozlov, F. R., 212, 230, 282
Krasin, L. B., 62
Krasnodar, 178
Kruglov, S. N., 235
Krupskaya, N., 30
Kuusinen, V. O., 284

Labour and Defence, Council of, 143
Labour Disputes Board, 200, 202, 274
Law, Administration, 165, 235 ff., 300–1, 306, 307
    capital punishment, 300–1, 307
    Codes, 125, 130, 273, 283, 297, 300
    Comradely Courts, 93, 97, 98, 182, 300
    enforcement, 236, and *see* Police
    judges, 236
    People's Courts, 56, 182, 200, 236, 300
    Procuracy, 3, 127, 235–6, 300
    Social Courts, 182
    Supreme Court, 127, 159, 167, 273
Leadership, 53, 75, 195, 209, 296
    collective, 195, 206, 272, 287–8, 302, 322

Leadership—*cont.*
  local soviets, 183–4, 186
  Party monopoly, 95
  and sectional interests, 280, 296
Legislation, 124–6, 139–40
  Commissions, 120, 124–5, 127
    230, 270
  parallel, 139
  Party role, 158, 197 ff., 229
Lenin, V. I., 30 ff., 59, 278
  April Theses, 33, 42, 46 and n.,
    76
  Left-Wing Communism, 58, 97
  NEP, 12, 59
  State and Revolution, 88–9, 259
  theory, 25, 98–9, 192 ff., 250,
    252, 257, 336
  see Marxism–Leninism
Leningrad, 137, 161–2, 173
Leonov, L. M., 107
Liberman, E. G., 155
Lithuania, 8, 83, 183
Litvinov, M. M., 11, 242
Local government, 172 ff., 179 ff.,
    189, 270–1
  laymen in, 72, 130, 182, 265
  Party in, 105, 172 ff., 187–8,
    223–4, 228–9

Malenkov, G. M., 18, 213, 279
  fall of, 137, 219, 281, 283, 297
Malinovsky, R., 239
Management, 155, 198, 234
Mao Tse-tung, 91, 250
Mari ASSR, 7
Martov, Yu. O., 30, 34
Marx, K., 30, 50, 88, 147, 193, 250,
    258
Marxism, 95, 308, 309, 337
  adaptation in Russia, 14, 17,
    88, 96, 192, 311
Marxism–Leninism, 308–12
Maximalists, 37
Mazurov, K. T., 230
Mensheviks, 32 ff., 79
Mikoyan, A. I., 138, 142, 213, 221,
    230, 245
Milyukov, P. N., 43, 44
Ministers, Council of, 84, 124
  appointment, 119–20
  and foreign policy, 241–3
  Party parallels, 225, 229
  and Presidium, 133, 142, 164–5
  Presidium of, 141–2, 242, 285
Mirgorod, 293
Mitskevich, A. V., 98
Moldavia, 83, 183, 253
Molotov, V. M., 18, 213, 219, 279,
    281
  foreign policy, 142, 241–2, 244,
    253
Mongolia, 248
Moscow, 161–3, 196
  District, 45, 47, 161–2, 172,
    173, 181
  Soviet, 173, 175
Mukhitdinov, N. A., 128

Narodnaya Volya, 25, 30
National Areas, 7, 81, 83, 104, 129,
    159, 173, 236
Nechayev, S. G., 17
NEP, 12, 55 ff., 72 n., 145
North Ossetian ASSR, 123
Novikov, V. N., 122

Ogarev, N. P., 17
Opposition, Party, 214, 273, 303
  workers', 198–9

Pasternak, B., 298
Paukin, I. S., 233
Pavlov, S. P., 107
Peace Council, 248
Peasants, 5, 9, 109, 151, 267
  conditions, 199, 299
  Party membership, 194, 317
  and revolution, 12–13, 44, 49,
    50, 56–8
  Tsarist era, 17, 22 ff., 44, 49, 50,
    56–8

Peasants—*cont.*
    Unions, 204 n., 296
Pelshe, A. Ya., 220
Pensions, 113, 123, 270, 298
Personality cult, 206, 263, 283, 284, 322
Pervukhin, M. G., 142, 149, 167, 219, 283, 285
Petrograd, 41 ff., 76, 77
Piskotin, M. I., 92
Planning, agencies, 62
    Budget Commissions, 127 ff.
    Council of Ministers and, 149–51
    Gosplan, 62, 231
    see Five-Year Plans, Seven-Year Plans
Plekhanov, G. V., 30–1
Podgorny, N. V., 137, 230
Police, Cheka, 56, 57
    militia, 56, 93, 97–8, 182, 300
    and Party, 16, 198, 213, 235, 236
    reorganization, 14, 94, 177, 235, 300, 304
    security, 56, 57, 235
    Stalinist, 64, 213, 302–3
Polyansky, D. S., 230, 233
Ponomarev, B. N., 128
Popular Socialists, 37
Populists, 26, 28 ff.
Power conflicts, 278 ff.
Pravda, 219
Presidium, *see* Soviet, Supreme, Council of Ministers
Press, criticism in, 113, 227 ff., 302
    foreign journals, 113–14
    freedom of, 81, 211, 228, 323, 324, 326
Private enterprise, 153 and *see* NEP
Production, norms, 301
    Permanent Conference, 151, 201, 202, 231, 300
    zonal committees, 291
Propaganda and Agitation Department, 227

Province, Autonomous, 7, 8, 83, 84
    agriculture, 151, 292–3
    Party in, 184–6, 188, 225, 233, 295
    planning budgets, 129, 159–60, 162, 163
    Soviets, 173, 177, 179–80, 186–8, 225, 293
Purges, 64, 213, 295
Pushkin, A. S., 27

Radio, television, 228
Republics, Union, 83–4, 104, 123, 127–30
    Party in, 164, 216, 322 ff.
    Soviets, 160, 163–4, 179, 183, 228
Republics, Autonomous, 7, 84, 104, 123
    party in, 228–9, 326
    planning budgets, 129, 149, 160, 162, 163
Revolution, March, 41 ff.
    37 and n., 40, 45 ff., 89
    Prelude to, 22 ff.
Rokossovsky, K. R., 235
Romashkin, R. S., 92
Rostov, 175
Rothstein, A., 65
RSFSR, 78, 83, 160, 165, 183, 227

Saburov, M. Z., 142, 167, 219, 283, 285
Satyukov, 219
Schlesinger, R., 63 n.
Science, 92, 95, 149
Security, Ministry, 235
Settlements, 175, 183
Sevastopol, 173
Seven-Year Plan, 13, 69, 114, 147–8, 298–9
Shepilov, D., 219, 242, 283, 285
Shevchenko, S. F., 233
Sholokhov, M., 217
Siberia, 13, 66, 68, 173, 269

Sinyavsky, A. D., 273
Smirnov, N. G., 233
Social insurance, 200, 202
Social Sciences Conference, 92
Social Revolutionaries, 26, 36–7, 42–3, 45 ff., 55–7
Sofinsky, 181
Solomentsev, M. S., 220
Sotnikov, V. P., 233
Soviet(s), 76, 78 ff., 95, 99
    City, 46, 163–4, 173, 174, 177
    democracy in, 182
    deputies, 177, 183, 264–5, 270
    economic planning, 156, 160
    election, 104, 109
    executives, 177, 182–3, 186, 225, 293
    laymen in, 130, 182, 265
    local, role and powers, 94–6, 179 ff.
    Party and, 181, 183 ff., 223, 225, 229
    reorganizations, 174, 176
    in revolution, 25, 40 ff., 55, 58 ff., 73, 76, 81
    structure, 64, 96, 164, 173–5, 265
    theory, 223, 257 ff.
    village, 58, 161, 165, 174–8, 180–1, 183–4
    see also District, Province
Soviet of Nationalities, 7, 80–1, 84, 104–5, 118, 122–3, 126 ff.
    Economic Commission, 126, 150, 231
Soviet, Supreme, 64, 81–3, 117, 118, 122 ff.
    Autonomous Republics, 228–9
    budget procedure, 121 ff.
    Committees, 126
    Council of Elders, 5, 120, 131 n., 224
    decrees, etc., 134–5, 140
    deputies, 110, 116 n., 118, 129–30
    election, 64, 81

and foreign affairs, 245
    legislative role, 16, 124, 130
    powers, 120 ff.
    Presidium, 106, 133 ff.
    questions in, 129
    of Union Republics, 124, 160, 179, 228
Soviets, Congress of, 25, 46, 49, 55, 62, 76 ff.
Sovremennik, 27, 37 n.
Stalin, J. V., centralization, 155
    collectivization, 12, 61
    Constitution, 75, 80
    de-Stalinization, 91–2, 98–9, 206, 302
    foreign policy, 17, 90
    Foundation of Leninism, 76, 77, 195
    and nationalism, 79
    personality cult, 99
    post-Stalin politics, 117, 278, 294–5
    purges, 213, 235, 295
    in revolution, 45–6
    theory, 51 n., 63, 92, 96, 197–8, 251
Starovoitov, N. G., 108
State, agencies, 69, 230
    committees, 130, 142, 148, 149, 233, 243
    Party and, 223 ff.
    theory, 88–91, 94, 99, 164, 167, 257
    withering away of, 89–90, 93, 223, 260
Statistical Administration, 62, 150, 217, 231, 297
Strikes, 198
Strumilin, S. G., 62, 148
Suslov, M. A., 93, 128, 241
Sverdlovsk, 137

Tadjikistan, 83, 163, 183
Tartars, 7–8, 25
Tashkent, 123
Teachers, 165

Territories, 83, 84, 173, 179, 234, 236, 292, 335
Tkachev, P. N., 17
Totalitarianism, 5–6, 19 n.
Trade, foreign, 169, 243, 248
Trade Unions, 19, 97, 199 ff., 231, 297
Transcaucasia, 7
Trotsky, L. D., on collectivization, 60
    economic plans, 62
    factionalism, 213
    in revolution, 47, 49, 55, 58
    theories, 15, 33–4, 98–9, 198, 242, 250
Turgenev, I. S., 27
Turkmenia, 8, 83, 123, 162–3, 183

Ukraine, 7, 8, 25, 79, 83, 196
    agriculture, 67
    Party in, 183, 293
    and Soviet foreign policy, 253
    taxation, 162
Urals, 13, 66
Uzbekistan, 25, 83, 142, 163, 165, 173

Venturi, F., 28
Villages, budgets, 58, 161, 163
    Soviets, 5, 58, 173, 174, 178, 180

Voronezh, 162
Voronov, G. I., 233
Voroshilov, K. Y., 120, 135, 137, 213, 219, 283
Vyshinsky, A., 242

Walsh, W. B., 65
War, effects, 11 and n., 41, 64 ff.
Webb, S. and B., 15
Weber, M., 2
Women, 66, 118
Workers, opposition by, 198–9
    revolutionary, 29–34, 36, 49
Workers' and Peasants' Inspectorate, 56–7
Working class, 77, 109, 192, 198, 267, 315
Working hours, 14, 85, 299
World organizations, 248

Yugoslavs, 93

Zarobyan, Ya. N., 214–15
Zemlya i Volya, 29–30
Zemstvos, 18, 24, 29
Zhdanov, A., 91, 212, 213
Zhukov, G. E., 137, 235
Zinoviev, G. E., 49
Zorin, L., 240
Zverev, A. G., 138